Jordan's Inter-Arab Relations

Jordan's Inter-Arab Relations

The Political Economy of Alliance Making

Laurie A. Brand

COLUMBIA UNIVERSITY PRESS • NEW YORK

Columbia University Press
New York   Chichester, West Sussex
Copyright © 1994 Columbia University Press
Library of Congress Cataloging-in-Publication Data

Brand, Laurie A.
    Jordan's inter-Arab relations : the political economy of alliance
    making / Laurie A. Brand
        p.   cm.
    Includes bibliographical references and index.
        ISBN: 978-0-231-10096-0(cloth)
        ISBN: 978-0-231-10097-7(paper)

    1. Arab countries—Foreign relations—Jordan.   2. Jordan–Foreign
    relations—Arab countries.   I. Title
    DS154.16.A65B73   1995
    327.56950174927—dc20   94–22342
                                                                   CIP

⊗

Casebound editions of Columbia University Press books are
Smyth-sewn and printed on permanent and durable
acid-free paper.
Printed in the United States of America
c 10 9 8 7 6 5 4 3 2 1
p 10 9 8 7 6 5 4 3 2

For my Jordanian "family," friends, and colleagues

Contents

Acknowledgments   *ix*

Introduction   *1*

PART ONE: *Theoretical Framework and Introduction*   13

1. Economics and Alliances in the Developing World: Bridging the
   Gap Between Political Economy and Security Studies   15
2. The Economy and Economic Policy in Jordan   39

PART TWO: *The Case Studies*   85

3. Jordanian-Saudi Relations   87
4. Jordanian-Kuwaiti Relations   123
5. Jordanian-Syrian Relations   152
6. Jordanian-Iraqi Relations   196
7. Jordanian-Egyptian Relations   242

PART THREE: *Conclusions*   275

8. Budget Security and Its Broader Applicability   277

Appendix: U.S. Dollars to Jordanian Dinars Exchange Rate   *303*
Notes   *305*
Bibliography   *327*
Index   *339*

Acknowledgments

I could not have completed a detailed study of fifteen years of bilateral interaction between Jordan and five of its Arab neighbors without a great deal of assistance and support. I would like to thank the Center for the International Exchange of Scholars (CIES) for a Fulbright Islamic Civilization Grant, which enabled me to undertake research in Jordan in both the summer of 1990 and the fall of 1991. I am also most grateful to the School of International Relations at the University of Southern California for supplementary research assistance during the summers of 1990 and 1992. In addition, the Center for International Studies at USC funded a research assistant for me during the academic years 1990–91, 1991–92, and 1992–93. One of those assistants, Miles Hochstein, was critical to launching this project through his diligent perusal of literally mounds of FBIS daily reports.

In Jordan, I am indebted to numerous individuals and institutions. Dr. Fayiz Tarawineh deserves special note for his assistance with contacts in the economic and policymaking communities. Also, in alphabetical order, I would like to thank Lamis Andoni, Mustafa Hamarneh, George Hawatmeh, Hani Hawrani, Muwaffaq Mahadin, Ma`en Nsour, and Reem Qattan for their assistance, encouragement, and insights. They all gave generously of their time, although none is responsible for my approach or conclusions.

I am also indebted to members of the Hijazi, Mahadin, and Shraydeh families for serving as surrogate parents, aunts, uncles, brothers, and sisters during my stays in Jordan. In a similar vein, a special thanks on the Jordanian front goes to the center where I resided, the

American Center for Oriental Research (ACOR), its directors, Pierre and Patricia Bikai, and its wonderful staff, for their assistance and good humor in making a political scientist feel welcome among a host of archaeologists. Among those archaeologists, Gaetano Palumbo and Glen Peterman were especially supportive. Another word of thanks goes to archaeologist Cherie Lenzen who, as early as my first research trip to Jordan in 1984, challenged me to look at the kingdom in new ways. Without those challenges, this book would not have been written. I also would like to thank my husband, Jonathan, who, although he entered my life during the latter stages of this project, nonetheless provided critical encouragement and support.

Finally, on this side of the Atlantic, several friends and colleagues offered very useful comments and critiques at different stages of this project. In alphabetical order, they are: Lou Cantori, Eileen Crumm, Stephen David, Greg Gause, Jerry Green, Ray Hinnebusch, Michael Hudson, Jonathan Kirshner, Audie Klotz, Bahgat Korany, Fred Lawson, John Odell, Peter Sluglett, and Bob Springborg, as well as Kate Wittenberg and Leslie Bialler at Columbia University Press. Nevertheless, as paragraphs such as these generally note, I, alone, bear responsibility for the final product.

Laurie A. Brand
August 1994

Jordan's Inter-Arab Relations

Introduction

Economics and Security in the Third World

The end of the Cold War has called into question many of the prevailing assumptions in international relations regarding appropriate topics and region of study. One important change has been a growing acknowledgment by scholars of international politics of the importance of *domestic* politics.[1] Explanations of state behavior had long been based on a country's place and relative power (usually defined as military or technological power) in the international system; however, as a result of the momentous changes that accompanied the collapse of the Soviet Union, internal factors such as ethnic divisions, the domestic economy, and the nature of the state itself, have received greater attention. At the same time, as the threat of superpower confrontation has dissipated and conflicts elsewhere have threatened regional and international security, more attention has been devoted to another largely neglected topic, the countries outside the former East-West framework, the states of the developing world.

The combination of a growing interest in the Third World and in the role of domestic politics has also been accompanied by a reexamination of the very meaning of "security." The field of security studies was traditionally concerned overwhelmingly with external military threats to states. In recent years, however, a number of scholars have attempted to reformulate the concept to include considerations of environmental degradation, population growth, domestic insurgencies, and economic challenges, such as foreign debt, the preservation of markets, and more general questions related to obstacles to economic development. No new single definition of security has emerged from the debate that has ensued, neither from a developed world nor a developing world perspective. Clearly, however, the traditional notion of security as measured by numbers of tanks and warheads is giving way to a more comprehensive understanding of the potential sources of threat, many of which may be domestic and need not be military in nature.[2]

The study that follows explores a number of issues related to both the importance of domestic politics in explaining interstate behavior and a broadened understanding of security in the developing world. While it was launched in part as a result of dissatisfaction with previous work on the international relations of third world states, particularly those studies that dealt with the seemingly ever-shifting kaleidoscope of Middle East alignments, driving this approach is the hunch that crossing the once formidable barriers between the subfields of security studies and political economy might produce new insights into some long-standing questions regarding foreign policy and alliance politics.[3] The study was begun inductively, in an attempt to discover what patterns might emerge from weaving together the previously unwritten economic histories of several bilateral relationships with the somewhat better known (but also largely unwritten) story of the "high politics" of bilateral and Middle East regional relations. As the research progressed, it became clear that a focus on the domestic economy, in particular on domestic revenue sources, rather than on balancing military power or threat might indeed be the key to understanding and predicting alliance and alignment shifts. Gradually, the concept of financial or budget security, defined as ensuring sources of state revenue or reducing budgetary vulnerabilities, emerged as central to understanding the alignment decisions in the cases studied.

The country upon which this work focuses is the Hashemite Kingdom of Jordan—a small state, regularly described as vulnerable, largely because of its regional position and role. Since 1948 it has been a party to the Arab-Israeli conflict, the confrontation state with the longest border with Israel. Given most scholars' long-standing preoccupation with state-level factors, geostrategic location, and relative military might, it is not surprising that analysts have focused their attention almost exclusively on Jordan's role in this conflict (and its attendant security concerns), and have then derived from them explanations of the kingdom's foreign policy more generally.

The problem with relying on such a mono-causal explanation is that Jordan's regional position cannot always or, this work will argue, even in most cases, account for critical foreign policy moves; indeed, in some instances it can account for the move taken as well as its opposite. As we shall see in the case studies, Jordan's place in the regional system cannot explain the Jordanian-Syrian alliance of 1975–77, the Jordanian-Iraqi alignment beginning in 1979, Jordan's attempted rapprochement with Syria in 1983, nor its reestablishment of ties with Egypt in 1984. All of these were key, and in some cases controversial, foreign policy moves.

The explanation developed here does not deny the role of external factors (systemic or regional) in conditioning or constraining Jordan's foreign policy options; indeed, it lays them out clearly in the beginning. Nonetheless, it argues for examining another set of generally neglected factors as more specifically determinant of the kingdom's behavior. Rather than pointing to traditional notions of balancing or bandwagoning based on relative power or threat, the evidence suggests that economic variables, particularly the structure of the kingdom's revenues and the financial imperatives they imply, can often better explain an alignment or alliance shift.

Because of the country's involvement in the Arab-Israeli conflict and because of the range of factors—small size, small resource base, small population—that indicate the kingdom's vulnerability, from the point of view of those who focus on external security and system structure, Jordan constitutes a "hard case" about which to make a *domestic economic structure* argument for alliance shifts. Nonetheless, examining its regional alignment shifts against the background of bilateral and multilateral economic relations demonstrates how economic exigencies and structures, rather than military strength or power politics, can better explain foreign policy, even of a country that has officially been at war since 1948.

In the early stages of defining this project, it was clear that in order to say anything meaningful about Jordan's regional foreign policy, several bilateral relationships would have to be studied. In the first place, undertaking a single bilateral case study was unlikely to generate a sufficiently convincing generalization about the role of economics in alignment shifts: the "n" would simply be too small, and, without further cases, could be assumed to be an aberration rather than a more general tendency. Second, my years of observing and studying inter-Arab politics have demonstrated that Arab country A's relationship with Arab country B becomes fully comprehensible only in the context of A's and B's relations with other regional actors (state or non-state).[4] In other words, the dynamics of, for example, Syrian-Jordanian bilateral relations, will rarely be fully apparent if one studies solely Syrian-Jordanian interaction. One must also be aware of what is transpiring in Syrian-Saudi relations or Jordanian-Egyptian relations to comprehend the dynamic at work in the first bilateral relationship. While it is far from profound to argue that a state's relations with another state may be affected by developments in each one's relations with other states, in the Middle East, the complex and shifting nature of intraregional relations are so clearly a central part of regional leaders calculations that to overlook such considerations would be to leave out a potentially key part of the explanation.

The individual five case study countries—Saudi Arabia, Kuwait, Syria, Iraq, and Egypt—were selected for several reasons. They are all Arab countries, and they are the countries with which Jordan has had the most frequent and intense regional interaction. Moreover, they represent different economic orientations and domestic economic structures, thus providing a basis for examining and contrasting how economic factors may have played a role in bilateral relations.

For example, Egypt, Syria, and Iraq each have large public sectors, important agricultural sectors along with an emphasis on the development of basic industries, soft currencies (hence various foreign exchange restrictions), and a variety of protective tariffs or customs walls. Kuwait and Saudi Arabia, on the other hand, have traditionally operated according to free market principles, are largely dependent upon oil, and have easily convertible currencies.

In terms of Jordan's foreign aid relationships, Iraq (for a short period before it became mired in the Iran-Iraq war), Saudi Arabia, and Kuwait were major aid donors, either in the form of loans through their respective state development funds, or through their contributions to the kingdom mandated by resolutions of Arab League summits in 1967, 1974, and 1978. At the same time, Saudi Arabia and especially Kuwait imported substantial numbers of Jordanian expatriates over the years to build and staff their state bureaucracies and later, their respective private sectors as well. Thus, these countries played a key role, not only as employment safety valves, but also as sources of hard currency through the remittances sent home by expatriate Jordanians.

All of these countries were also important trading partners for Jordan during the period under examination (or at least parts thereof), but to varying degrees and for different kinds of products. From Saudi Arabia and Iraq, Jordan has been an importer of oil. To Saudi Arabia, Kuwait, and Iraq, Jordan has been a major exporter of fruits and vegetables, as well as labor. In the 1980s, the trade relationship with Iraq expanded to the point where Iraq was also a major importer of Jordanian light manufactures and pharmaceuticals. Trade relations with Egypt and Syria have also been important, if less extensive than those that developed with Iraq in the 1980s. Finally, transit trade through Jordan, especially Iraqi, but also Syrian and Saudi, has also been a key source of employment and revenue for the kingdom. Since the study was conducted inductively, it was posited at the beginning that any or all of these factors may have been significant in Jordan's bilateral relationship with each.

An examination of the political realm also reveals important bases for contrast and comparison. Egypt, Syria, and Iraq have all had or continue to have aspirations to regional hegemony, and hence, depending upon the period, have posed potential political or military threats to Jordanian sovereignty or stability. These three states have each had their own experiments with varying brands of pan-Arabism and socialism, leading them at times to seek to undermine the Jordanian monarchy. Moreover, since Jordan has been a moderate monarchy, like Saudi Arabia and Kuwait, ensuring Jordan's stability was a key Saudi and Kuwaiti concern, and Jordanian military advisers have trained, served in, or advised the military and security apparatuses of Kuwait and, to a lesser extent, Saudi Arabia.

In terms of the Arab-Israeli conflict and its role in Jordan's bilateral relations with these states, Egypt left the group of confrontation states to make peace with Israel in 1978, thus dealing itself out of the Arab mainstream for the better part of a decade, while Syria, like Jordan, continued to be a confrontation state. Jordan remained critical to all these countries because of its relationship to the Palestinians, its long border with Israel, and hence, its centrality to the peace process. Not surprisingly then, Husayn's stance on the Palestinian issue and the peace process have been key to each partner's calculations at various points.

As for extraregional alliances, Egypt, like Jordan, had a close relationship with the United States throughout most of the period under examination. So did Saudi Arabia, if less openly so until the 1990 Gulf crisis. Iraq underwent a shift from being a Soviet client to a regular U.S. customer until the invasion of Kuwait, while Kuwait maintained a fairly neutral position, at least until the oil tanker reflagging in 1987. Syria was the only state that maintained close relations with the Soviet Union during the entire period under consideration. Thus, as is the case with the economic relationships, the political relationships are also quite varied.

The five bilateral relationships are studied over an approximately fifteen-year period, beginning in the mid-1970s and continuing through the Gulf crisis. This period was delineated for several reasons. First, there was a need to cover a long enough period to monitor changes in Jordan's economic and political ties with the five case study countries through several instances of improvement or deterioration in regional political relations and in economic fortunes. For example, on the economic front, by beginning the study in the mid-1970s, the regional and domestic effects of the post-1973 oil boom may be examined, as may the effects of the recession of the early and mid-1980s attending the Iran-Iraq war and the drop in oil prices. Moreover, during this period, Egypt, Syria, and Iraq all embarked upon a process of economic liberalization, while Jordan itself in the mid-1980s tried further to liberalize its already relatively free market economy.

On the political level, this period witnessed a number of important shocks to or crises in the Arab system, all of which have affected Jordan's regional position and relations. First, the 1973 war set in motion a series of events that led in 1974 and 1975 to disengagement agreements between Egypt and Israel on the one hand, and Syria and Israel on the other. Also, not coincidentally, the Lebanese civil war, which had political and economic ramifications beyond the borders of the small state, began in 1975. By 1979, the disengagement between Egypt and Israel had developed into a full bilateral peace, the first between an Arab state and Tel Aviv. This resulted in the effective isolation, if not expulsion, of Egypt from the Arab system, thus setting in motion developments with ramifications throughout the region. A brief political flirtation between Syria and Iraq in 1979 came to naught and the two rival Ba'th parties returned to their feuding, with its implications for inter-Arab politics. Relations between Jordan and Syria, which had been on the road to increasing economic and political integration, if not union, in 1978, deteriorated to a point at which Syria massed troops on the Jordanian border in December 1980, and were not repaired until 1985. At approximately the same time, Jordanian-Iraqi relations, strained by the 1970 civil war in Jordan but now beginning to improve as a result of the closing of Arab ranks in the face of Sadat's defection, moved to a new level of cooperation, just before the outbreak of the Iran-Iraq war.

The early 1980s witnessed the Israeli invasion of Lebanon, Syrian attempts to establish an alternative Palestinian leadership, and Jordanian attempts to reassert Hashemite claims to speak for the Palestinians of the occupied territories. In the meantime, as Egypt provided increasing support to Iraq for its war effort, Jordan was working toward rehabilitating Egypt's Arab image. The period, therefore, also covers the return of Egypt to the Arab League, the establishment of the Arab Cooperation Council, the political liberalization in Jordan, and the Gulf crisis.

Thus, a careful examination of Jordan's relationship with five different Arab countries, countries with varying political and economic structures and whose relationships with Jordan have passed through periods of both political and economic flourishing and decline, should provide a sound basis for broad comparison and for generalizations regarding the role economic factors and considerations may play in alliance and other foreign policy considerations.

Constructing much of the story told in the five case studies required collecting data, not only or primarily on high politics—

Arab League decisions, mini-summit outcomes, and the like—but also on low politics, the day-to-day interaction in both the economic and political spheres. Baldwin has argued that it is a mistake not to view international economic exchange as well as other "low level" economic exchange as extremely important techniques of state-craft.[5] Moon has made a similar argument about foreign policy in general, stressing that emphasizing the headlines seriously neglects some of the most important elements in the foreign policies of small states: capital controls, exchange rate valuation, commercial policies, barriers to trade, nationalization, and foreign investment restrictions all should be seen as a part of foreign policy.[6] Thus the methodology used involved first constructing the economic and political histories of the bilateral relationships. This was done through reliance primarily on the *Foreign Broadcast Information Service* and *Middle East Economic Digest*, supplemented by various original Arabic primary sources, including interviews with a variety of former economic and foreign policymakers and advisers. After the two sets of histories were constructed they were then woven together to determine what the historical record tells about the importance of economic considerations in foreign policy, and most specifically, alignment decisions.

The conclusions that emerged, it must be noted, are based on informed analysis of a preponderance of the *available* evidence. While scholars who write on the advanced industrialized countries may rely on a variety of official publications giving economic and other data, in the developing world such statistics often are simply not available. In the case of Jordan, for example, military borrowing and spending levels, which are critical but missing pieces of my analysis, are not made public. Just as often, statistics that are available are inaccurate, incomplete, or not comparable across time for a variety of reasons. Moreover, those who study the third world are not in a position simply to wait until a 25-year rule expires for the declassification or release of documents. One works under the assumption that such documents will probably never be released, or may never have existed in the first place. Finally, having conducted research in Jordan in the mid-1980s I am well aware that had the Hashemite Kingdom of Jordan not embarked upon a process of political liberalization in 1989, I might well not have been able to gain access to many of those whom I interviewed, and the interviews I might have conducted in the absence of the liberalization would likely have produced far less in the way of valuable information.

For some, these obstacles would suggest that a study such as this should not have been attempted, or that its conclusions are suspect. As for the former contention, the idea that we should avoid the study of major areas of the world because we have less than perfect evidence is cowardly and exaggerates the accuracy of the data available on Western states. As for the latter, research on this level of politics in the developing world is often like working on a jigsaw puzzle with many missing pieces. The trick is to combine all the existing pieces in such a way as to make the most coherent picture, in the process not excluding pieces that may complicate the picture simply for the sake of parsimony. I have followed that approach in collecting my data and in trying to make sense of it all. Finally, I do not contend to have proven anything, but simply to have suggested through a careful gathering and examination of evidence from a variety of sources a novel and, I believe, better way of explaining foreign policy and alliance decisions by giving primacy to economic variables.

The study that follows is divided into three parts. The first, consisting of the first two chapters, sets the theoretical framework and the stage. Chapter 1 reviews previous work done on the impact of economics on foreign policy, on the concept of economic security and on third world alliance behavior in order to lay the basis for the development of the concept of "budget security." Chapter 2 discusses in detail the structure of the Jordanian economy and of state revenues, along with the process of economic decisionmaking in the country. Particular emphasis is placed on examining which governmental or societal forces play a role in shaping foreign policy.

The case study section follows. The first two chapters detail Jordan's relations with its two most consistent and generous foreign aid, or high-level exchange, providers over the years: Saudi Arabia and Kuwait. Familiarity with developments in these cases is critical for understanding the case studies of Jordan's relations with Syria, Iraq and Egypt, that follow. It is with these countries that lower-level exchange, such as trade and joint ventures, has been of primary importance, although Iraq serves as a kind of bridge between the two types of relationships.

The presentation in each case study chapter is divided into two or more historical periods. Each period is then subdivided into separate treatments of economic and political developments. Those more interested in the analysis and less concerned with the empirical detail used to substantiate it may want to skip to the summaries that conclude the discussions of each historical period. Moreover, while the argument builds cumulatively through the study, the case study chapters were written in such as way as to stand alone as separate analyses as well. As a result, repetition of some material was unavoidable, although every attempt was made to keep this to a minimum for the sake of those who choose to read all the cases.

The study concludes with a summary of findings, a discussion of the implications of the Gulf crisis for the analysis, and suggestions for broader application of the concept of budget security.

Final Note

It will no doubt strike some students and observers of Middle East politics as bordering on heresy to write a book on Jordanian foreign policy and say so little about the Arab-Israeli conflict. I have two explanations for such an approach. The first is that I discuss in chapter 1 the set of constraining conditions that frame Jordanian foreign policy decisions, and the kingdom's involvement in the Arab-Israeli conflict during this period is certainly prominent among them. I do not deny the role of the conflict, I simply do not focus on it.

As for the second explanation: the Arab-Israeli conflict has *always* been *the* lens through which writers have tried to explain Jordanian foreign or domestic policy. I find such explanations boring and tired and, more important for a scholarly endeavor, deficient. It has long been my contention that we should discard the conventional wisdom regarding Middle East politics, reexamine old questions (the answers to which we thought we knew) in different ways, and only if forced to, readmit former answers. In other words, I think, in general, we know far less about the Middle East than we think we do.

And, in order to learn more, we are sorely in need of more icono-
clastic forays.

What I have tried to do in this work is explore a new approach to
understanding inter-Arab relations, and in so doing, it appears to me
that the Arab-Israeli conflict itself, as well as the ever-heralded large
Palestinian presence in the kingdom, tell us far less about Jordan's
regional relations than previous works would have us believe.
Indeed, this study demonstrates that the structure of Jordan's domestic economy and the drive to secure state revenues explains far more.
This work, therefore, is not for those who are already certain they
understand the dynamics of inter-Arab relations. Rather, it is for
those who are willing, if not eager, to see conventional "wisdom"
about the Middle East challenged.

PART ONE
Theoretical Framework

1

Economics and Alliances in the Developing World: Bridging the Gap between Political Economy and Security Studies

The traditional focus of international relations on the so-called system-defining or great powers has meant that very little work, in both absolute and relative terms, has been done on the international relations of the developing world. Moreover, most of the literature that does treat these states is written in terms of their ties with the great powers, even though such relations may represent only a fraction of their foreign policy interaction. There is a clear need for studies that examine a greater percentage of developing states' foreign policy and that view such policy from the point of view of the smaller power, not merely as reactive to great power activity or demands.

This chapter makes a case for the primacy of economic factors in analyzing foreign policy in the developing world. This is certainly not the first attempt to examine the role of economics in foreign policy; however, as the literature review below demonstrates, previous works have serious limitations. To overcome some of these problems, the presentation here seeks to bridge the gap between the literature on political economy and security studies by exploring economic factors that may have national or domestic security implications. State economic structure and, in particular, the sources of state revenues, it will be argued, are basic to understanding both what economic security may mean in any given country and how attempts to ensure or reinforce it may drive foreign policy behavior, of which alliance behavior is a subset. Specifically, this work contends that issues of financial and budget security may be considered regime, if not national, security issues. As a result, alliance formation (a central topic in the traditional security literature) by a small, weak, or dependent state, may be viewed as a response, not to concerns about balancing or bandwagoning external power or threat, but rather to threats to state financial solvency.

In order to build a case for using economic variables to explain foreign policy behavior, this chapter first critiques the existing literature on the role of economic factors in developing states' foreign policy. It then examines the current debate regarding the concept of economic security, and constructs a case for including questions related to state finances and the budget as security issues. Finally, it discusses recent additions to the literature on alliances and demonstrates how a more sophisticated treatment of the domestic political economy of a given developing or small state in the context of a broadened concept of security may better explain alliance behavior than do the traditional realist or neorealist approaches.

Foreign Policy and the Domestic Economy in the Developing World

One of the problems with the limited general theoretical work on the role of economics in foreign policy is that it has often approached the topic from the point of view of the advanced industrialized states and examined issues of trade relations or financial policy. To the extent that such works have considered so-called developing countries, they have generally examined the relationship between a patron (usually a superpower) and a client state which has a key trade or foreign aid component. For example, in his classic *National Power and the Structure of Foreign Trade,* Hirschman sought to understand why and how relationships of dependency, influence, or even domination may arise out of trade relations.[1]

Other studies have examined the types of dependencies that may arise from economic or military aid relationships. As one way of trying to measure the impact of such purported dependence, some of the earliest work focused on UN voting patterns of the client to determine the responsiveness of what are then termed "dependent countries" to the political preferences of the great power patron. Richardson, for example, hypothesized that "the foreign policy behavior of a dependent country will be . . . more or less in accord with the preferences of the country that dominates its economic life."[2]

Yet, Richardson's findings indicate that, at least with regard to UN voting, economic dependence is a poor predictor of state behavior. Bruce Moon's work on the so-called "dependent state" has produced similar results, indicating the difficulties involved in measuring or predicting the effect of economic pressure on the client state. As such studies have shown, the concept a "dependent state" is itself problematic since, as Moon admits, the "precise make-up of the transactions which establish dependent relations is not entirely clear."[3]

Thus, while the attempt to classify a state as dependent may be intuitively appealing, operationalizing the concept has proven elusive: Does it imply high levels of foreign aid support from a single state and/or heavy trade concentration with a single partner? One is tempted to answer "yes." However, whatever the existing configurations, dependence by necessity implies *limited options* as well.[4] If that is the case, how limited must they be to constitute dependence? Trying to refine further the concept of dependence in this light would seem to pose more problems than it may solve. It would also appear to require such specificity as to render it useless across countries.

However, the approaches discussed above are problematic beyond the difficulties they highlight in defining and using the concept of dependence. In the first place, they usually examine only one source of dependence, usually foreign aid or trade, but not both, and certainly not both as part of the larger picture of overall state economic structure. Hence, such analyses can offer only a fragmentary explanation of state behavior. Perhaps more troubling, such approaches treat the "dependent state" as largely or solely reactive to the actions or preferences of the state on which it is dependent. Finally, only single dyads are addressed, even though, as was noted above, foreign policy relations comprise far more interactions than those between a client and its superpower or great power patron. Indeed, a developing country's relationship with a superpower may tell us very little about its relations in its regional neighborhood, the arena of most of its policy interaction.

Do previous works focusing specifically on Middle East regional politics offer any greater insights? Unfortunately, the effects of foreign aid, trade, and dependence have been downplayed or ignored in such works.[5] Paul Noble has argued that while other state systems relied heavily on military and economic capabilities, in the case of the Arab states only modest military and economic means were available, at least in the 1950s and 1960s. During this period, the radical or revolutionary states (Egypt, Syria, Iraq, Algeria) had little in the way of excess capital to use as instruments of foreign policy, and not until the OPEC revolution of the 1970s did the oil states of the Gulf begin to have the kinds of surpluses necessary to project economic power. Moreover, the level of economic development limited economic interaction and few of the bilateral relationships were of any economic consequence. Hence, he maintains, instruments of political warfare, such as propaganda, cross-frontier alliances, and subversion, were the most common form of currency.[6]

However, even if, as Noble points out, the use of political warfare among Arab states was characteristic of the 1950s and 1960s (and no systematic study has been done of Arab state economic interaction during this period to test such an assumption), this does not mean that economic factors played no role in generating or shaping the political warfare. Moreover, by Noble's own admission, and by the admission implicit in the work of those authors who have focused their studies on oil and its impact, even if economic factors are shown to have played only a minor role in foreign policy considerations and decisions prior to 1970, one should not assume that the nature or bases of Arab politics have remained constant since the 1950s. The single most important material factor to have influenced Arab politics since the early 1970s, from rising intra-regional capital and labor flows to increased economic capabilities for state consolidation, has been the oil boom.

Nonetheless, in Dessouki and Korany's recent *The Foreign Policies of Arab States*, in chapters on eight Arab countries and the PLO, economic factors are viewed as policy inputs or national attributes, but national economic structure is not discussed seriously as an independent variable capable of explaining foreign policy output, except briefly in the case of Egypt.[7] Instead, economic capability, refers to the natural resources of a country (availability) and to its ability to mobilize them at the service of its foreign policy (control). Economic capability affects both a state's objectives and its means of implementing them. Poor states, for instance, are likely to have a low level of diplomatic representation. In the case of developing countries, [they investigate] two questions . . . : to what extent is the economic infrastructure (agriculture, industry and services) capable of satisfying the economic needs of the population, thus reducing the need for foreign aid; and does economic development tend to enhance or decrease dependence on foreign sources?[8]

Economic factors appear here to be intervening variables, not really independent sources of foreign policy, although the authors do state that capabilities affect state objectives. To the degree that economic factors are considered, the question is posed in terms of dependence on foreign aid and degree of economic development. The contention here is not that these issues are unimportant; it is that the question is incomplete. Rather than seeking to understand solely how economic factors may constrain what foreign policies may be pursued, one may also legitimately ask: given a state's economic structure, what sort of foreign policy behavior may be expected? That is, to what degree are a leadership's or a regime's estimates of its economic needs and weaknesses a *source* of foreign policy—the independent variable—rather than mere measures of capabilities to carry out foreign policy constructed on the basis of or constrained by other factors? In other words, contrary or supplementary to the Korany and Dessouki formulation, what is being suggested here is that economic structure may be a source of foreign policy, specifically alignment policy, as well. A careful examination of the structure of the domestic economy, its strengths and weaknesses, state sources of revenue, and the like is basic to determining in which directions alignment shifts may take place.

Hence previous political economy approaches to understanding the foreign policy of small or developing states suffer from numerous problems that the approach which attempts to explain international behavior through domestic economic structure, especially state revenue sources, can obviate. The discussion in the next section argues for bridging the gap between political economy and security studies by broadening the concept of security to include challenges to the domestic economy.

The Concept of Economic Security

In discussions of the need to broaden the understanding of "security," no aspect is as popular or as controversial as is the economy. The range of opinion regarding the concept of "economic security" extends from those (generally students of the developing world) such as Caroline Thomas, who clearly consider such economic topics as trade, foreign aid, and debt as security issues[9], to those who concede in passing that interstate wars may be caused by domestic economic or social stress, but then go no further to try to determine whether or what kind of economic issues might, by implication, constitute a threat.[10]

Most international relations scholars writing on the topic, while admitting of an economic component to security, seem to spend considerable time trying to argue against an economic security component that extends beyond the military sector. For example, Robert Rothstein agrees that the traditional security studies' preoccupation with territorial integrity and political independence must be broadened to include a concern with domestic stability, and by extension domestic development[11]. Nonetheless, he insists that most of the attempts at broadening the concept of security have posited definitions so broad as to render virtually everything a security issue.[12] Although Rothstein does consider the difference between national and regime security (to be discussed further below), his argument about Third World poverty and security focuses on the effects that limited resources have on military spending, leading what he calls the "poverty trap" to become a "security trap" as well.

In his discussion of a "renaissance" in security studies Stephen Walt takes a similar position. He accepts an economics-security nexus when the issue concerns the relationship between military spending and economic performance, the political influence of the military-industrial complex, or the question of strategic resources and their potential to trigger international conflict[13]—all very close to traditional security concerns. However, he argues against broadening the concept of security to include poverty or recessions (as well as environmental threats or AIDS) because, in his words, "defining the field in this way would destroy its intellectual coherence and make it more difficult to devise solutions to any of these important problems." [14] Why he believes that broadening the concept would complicate finding solutions is not made clear.

Economist Giacomo Luciani's assessment of broadening the concept of security to include economic factors is also that it creates serious conceptual problems. He argues that if the concern is with the importance of economic prosperity in reinforcing domestic consensus or political stability, then a deterioration of economic conditions may be perceived as a threat to national security. However, he contends that while such an approach may be intuitively appealing, this "line of reasoning will lead to the conclusion that events such as increases in the price of oil, increases in interest rates, and indirectly, even the deficit in the federal budget in the United States are forms of aggression."[15] He does not explain why, conceptually, a threat must be understood only in terms of an identifiable and, presumably, punishable, aggressor.

Repeated objections to the concept of economic security on the grounds that the resulting definitions are messy or threaten the analytic coherence of the field sound less and less convincing with each rehearsal. Although some would no doubt argue otherwise, part of the explanation for these objections may well derive from a continuing, deep-seated bias toward understanding security threats in solely military terms. Old habits die hard, especially when maintaining them is far easier, more comfortable, and less threatening to the discipline. The concern that too broad a concept of security potentially renders the term meaningless for analytical purposes is certainly valid. Nevertheless, the traditional concept of security has been demonstrated to be inadequate to the concerns of a majority of the world's states, leaderships, and populations, which is a problem that should constitute reason for pause and serious reevaluation. Beyond that, however, while redefinition is difficult or problematic, the realm of solutions need not be circumscribed at the outset, which is what it appears these and other authors are attempting. Rather than thinking through more specific ways in which the concept may be broadened and not lose its coherence, they seem inclined to broaden it only in ways that continue to focus on the military or on issues of territorial defense.

Barry Buzan also expresses skepticism regarding the notion of economic security, but argues from different bases. He contends that capitalism as a system is by definition competitive and presumes risk-taking. In such an environment, therefore, how can any unit "ever be meaningfully secure when competition implies an ever-present danger of becoming a loser? Relative security is possible (some units do better than others), but absolute security is not."[16] (As if absolute security in the military realm *is* possible.) Moreover, he argues, the economic interdependencies that make states vulnerable can be reduced only through achieving self-reliance, which is likely to be economically inefficient and, therefore, unwise for other reasons. Nonetheless, having expressed this basic concern, if not objection, regarding the concept, he proceeds to distinguish between what economic security would mean at an individual versus a state level. At the state level, he contends, "the simplest view is to equate security with the economic conditions necessary for survival." Here he posits two constituent elements of what he terms the state equivalents of a basic human needs approach: access to the means necessary for survival, i.e., access to trade for resources not present domestically; and an ability to maintain economic "health" by "adapting towards the most advanced and successful practices elsewhere in the international system." Failure to succeed at the latter means a gradual loss in power and increased vulnerability.[17] Although this is an apparent departure from those whom one may, for want of a better word, term the militarists, it does not move us much farther toward a helpful or more easily applicable definition.

One critical element in rethinking the concept of economic security is to clarify which level(s) or unit(s) of analysis one is addressing. Although both Rothstein and Buzan take levels of analysis into consideration in one way or another, they do not do so systematically, especially when it comes to economic issues. Perhaps the most important distinction to be made because of the potential confusion it can cause, particularly regarding the question of economic security, is that between national security and regime (or leadership) security.[18] Authors writing on security in the developing world are in virtual agreement that these states face domestic security threats more often than they do aggression from abroad. European colonialism in most of these areas imposed ethnically illogical borders and established patterns of economic underdevelopment, thus laying the basis for a variety of domestic political challenges.[19] In addition, the five-hundred-year process of state formation in Europe witnessed the disappearance of the vast majority of the multitude of political entities that once dotted the map, as they were absorbed or conquered by more powerful neighbors. Today, however, the disappearance of states runs counter to international norms. (The demise of the Soviet Union and Yugoslavia should more aptly be viewed as the final stages of decolonization.) Apparent economic or political nonviability, a condition a number of developing countries have experienced or approached, has not led the community of states to accept their collapse or dissolution as political entities.[20] The case of Somalia is an excellent example. Hence, it is generally not *national* security, the security of the state as territorial entity, that is threatened. Rather, in the developing world, most threats are domestic in nature, taking the form of civil wars, domestic insurgencies, military coups, and the like. In such instances, what is in fact in jeopardy is the regime or, more narrowly, the leadership, not the very existence of the country as an entity.

Hence what one is usually talking about in developing countries is the issue of *leadership* security. It is generally these same leaderships who define or constuct what constitutes the "national interest," and therefore what constitutes a threat to it. Hence, the ease with which the two may be, and often are, conflated is readily explained. However, one can make clear analytical distinctions between the two types of security. To use several traditional examples, one might imagine a situation in which state A has irredentist claims against a small part of the territory of state B, and as a result, state A invades the territory and annexes it. Such a move would certainly by all definitions constitute not just a national security threat but aggression against state B. However, if the territory has little strategic or other importance for state B and/or the leadership of state B is capable, through whatever argument or means, of making a case to its people that reconciles them to the annexation, state A's move may well not constitute a threat to the leadership. On the other hand, a domestic insurgency in state C may well lead to a coup d'etat, but never threaten the territorial integrity of C. In such a case leadership or regime security, not national security, is threatened.

If one continues to make a careful analytical distinction between national security (defined in terms of preservation of territorial integrity and core values) and regime security (defined in terms of maintenance of power by the same leaders or ruling coalition, depending upon the complexity of the country), then a case can be made that while economic issues may prove slippery or more anomalous when confronting the former, considerations of the latter lend themselves much better to application of the concept. Price increases may lead to economic riots that force leaders to resign, failure to focus on the socioeconomic needs of particular regions or groups may lead to insurgencies that challenge the regime, or external debt may reach such levels that domestic solvency may be threatened, forcing major reforms and perhaps resulting in the ouster of a leadership.

Such an approach, which includes a concept of leadership security, also overcomes the problem of agency, which is raised in different ways by both Buzan and Luciani, although, in this writer's opinion, not convincingly. On the state level, Buzan sees the key to economic security in the position of the state within the international networks of trade, production, and finance, while on the system level he views the key as the stability of the whole network of market relations.[21] In either case, identifying a specific actor as responsible for threatening security becomes difficult. Luciani is a bit more specific in contending that in the case of many of the issues that are considered economic security threats, there is no identifiable aggressor or no clear preventative.[22] The implication is that in the absence of such an aggressor, characterizing a development as a security threat is problematic. Although neither author states clearly why agency must be identified or specified, presumably it is because defense or retribution against an unspecified actor (an unforeseen drop in world prices for a product because of a bumper crop) or an unpenalizable factor (such as the weather in the case of a flood that may cause massive loss of life) is impossible. But should the determination of whether a particular development or factor may be considered a security threat hinge on the possibility of defense or retribution against it? The rationale behind such a contention is not at all clear, is certainly not convincing, and further reinforces the suspicion that an underlying pro-militarily defined security bias is at work. In any case, the potential or real impact (which in many of these cases is ultimately at the leadership or regime level), not the specificity or coherence of agency, should be the most important factor in determining whether a development constitutes a threat to security, economic or otherwise.

Toward a Broadened Notion of Security: The Budget and Regime Security

No attempt is made here to finalize a new definition of economic security. However, from the case studies a generalization emerges regarding the exigencies of maintaining financial solvency—what I have called budget security—as a critical component of *regime* (not necessarily or even primarily national) security. This section will make the argument for including such an element as a part of the definition of economic security and, by extension, as a potentially important factor in guiding foreign policy moves.

Ayoob has suggested that security should be defined "in relation to vulnerabilities that threaten, or have the potential to bring down or significantly weaken state structures, both territorial and institutional, as well as the regimes that preside over these structures and profess to represent them internationally."[23] In a similar vein, according to Ullman, a threat to national security is "an action or sequence of events that (1) threatens drastically and over a relatively brief span of time to degrade the quality of life for the inhabitants of a state, *or* (2) threatens significantly to narrow the range of policy choices available to the government of a state or to private, nongovernmental entities (persons, groups, corporations) within the state."[24]

The understudied financial or budgetary challenges to regime or state survival fit easily into both these formulations. For, ultimately, the survival of any entity depends upon its ability to sustain or provide for itself. While the requirements of state-building and regime maintenance are many and complex, in the crudest of terms, no state, regime, or political leadership can long survive without money.

Comparative numbers of tanks are irrelevant in assessing a regional military balance if a country is threatened with economic developments that could prevent the securing of fuel or spare parts. Similarly, the sophisticated nature of a state's internal intelligence apparatus may be undermined if a budgetary crisis means that the personnel required to staff intelligence positions cannot be paid. The ruling elite or coalition must ensure that it has the requisite finances and finance flows to direct policy (military, economic, social, or otherwise) and remain in control. In some cases this means ensuring the flow of revenues so that a socioeconomic coalition can be maintained, so that a state capitalist class is pacified, so that the coercive apparatuses remain placated and sufficiently strong to manage or put down any domestic discontent, or so that benefits of various types can be distributed among the population in such a way as to buy off those who might otherwise pose a challenge. In such cases, whether specifically economic instruments are used or not, foreign policy in general and alignment decisions in particular may well constitute an integral part of the state-building or state-consolidating process. Regime security in its most basic terms may in fact be budget security, understood in terms of reproducing the conditions necessary for the ruling coalition to continue to pay the bills, preempt the development of opposition, or cultivate sufficient domestic support to make coercion against such groups possible. Determining the potential provenance of such threats is best accomplished through careful examination of domestic economic structure, particularly state revenue sources.

One of the best known examples of how state and regime security may be threatened by insolvency is that of Egypt at the end of the last century. In 1875, as a result of fiscal irresponsibility, the Khedive Isma'il (the third successor to Muhammad 'Ali) was forced to sell Egypt's shares in the Suez Canal Company to Great Britain, thus strengthening the British interest in the country. Isma'il persisted in incurring additional development debt until 1876, when he simply ran out of money and postponed his debt service payment. In response, a European Debt Commission was imposed upon the country to "safeguard foreign interests," and it gradually acquired such extensive economic and financial powers that it has been referred to as a "veiled colonial administration." These develop-ments then paved the way for a domestic revolt that ultimately led to the loss of sovereignty to British invasion forces in 1882.[25]

But one need not return to the nineteenth century to see the secu-rity threat that debt may pose to a regime. Given developments in the third world in the 1980s, perhaps no more appropriate entree to a contemporary discussion of the concept of budget security can be found than the issue of debt. Although economic policymakers often argue that debt in and of itself is not bad, when debt service reaches such a level that states can no longer afford to continue to repay what they owe their external creditors, a debt crisis of the kind that has plagued states from Latin America to Africa and Asia ensues. The reasons for the Third World debt crisis have been discussed at length widely, and will not be rehearsed here. One need only consult IMF statistics to appreciate the number of countries that as a result of var-ious combinations of factors, from mismanagement or unexpected oil price increases to primary export product price drops, have faced debt crises.[26]

Whether leaderships seek to address a debt problem themselves or are eventually forced to resort to assistance from the IMF, the poten-tial domestic impact of belt tightening constitutes the most serious security threat deriving from the budget challenge. Whatever the causes of the insolvency, government spending cutbacks of some sort, whether in the military, the bureaucracy, or various services, as well as some revenue raising measures will be needed, all of which have the potential to create domestic instability and threaten a regime or a leadership. In the case of rescheduling with the IMF, the imposed conditionality generally involves liberalization of foreign exchange and export controls, devaluation of the official exchange rate, cutting state spending (generally by eliminating such market interventions as subsidies) and raising revenues, usually through additional fees and more efficient tax collection. The latter three and particularly the last two austerity measures have the potential to trigger rioting or other forms of instability. Policies implemented to adhere to IMF conditionality have regularly been blamed for trig-gering domestic instability.[27]

Debt rescheduling also touches on another, more traditional

aspect of security, that of sovereignty. In accepting IMF conditionality, leaders in effect surrender a degree of what was sovereign economic decisionmaking power. Such a compromise may be viewed as affecting or threatening the "core values" that figure into the traditional notion of security, since such values may have included a particular form of economic organization or philosophy that would oppose various aspects of IMF conditionality. In this way, a case may be made using traditional notions of security that such economic agreements also aggress against a country's security, even though no military element or external threat is involved.

At this point, let us return to the security implications of a potential budgetary crisis. What concerns us here is the range of possible responses to challenges to financial solvency—budget security. In theory, a number of policy options are available to a leadership to address such a problem. IMF conditionality and domestic economic structure have in large part dictated the *domestic* policy instruments selected to address debt crises. However, what of the possible use of *foreign* policy to address a potential or present economic crisis? The argument made here is that foreign policy, alignment decisions in particular, may be used by a leadership to address challenges to the domestic economy. Just as in the domestic realm, clues indicating in which ways and toward which partners a state may move are to be found in the nature of the domestic economy and specifically in the structure of state revenues.

The Literature on Alliances

In order to complete the presentation of the argument, a link must now be made between financial security concerns and regime response in the form of alliance shifts, the focus of this study. In order to do so the discussion turns to a critique of the recent literature on alliances to demonstrate how adapting a version of the concept of economic security may better our understanding of how and why alignment changes may take place in the developing world.

What of work on alignment behavior by those familiar with the Middle East? In general, earlier works by Arab and Western analysts alike have been equally unsatisfying, often painting conflicts and alignments in ideological terms: between the radicals/revolutionaries and the monarchies; between the moderates and the rejectionists; between those seen as being in the Western camp, and those who relied on the former Soviet Union and its Warsaw Pact allies; between the Nasirists and the Ba'thists; or even between the Syrian Ba'thists and the Iraqi Ba'thists.[28]

In a more creative approach to the study of the international relations of the Middle East, L. Carl Brown introduced the concept of "the Eastern Question system." Drawing on precedents from the eighteenth through the early twentieth century, Brown argues that the patterns of present-day Middle Eastern politics developed through the region's interaction with an increasingly penetrative European state system. Brown terms the Middle East the most penetrated, or internationalized, regional subsystem in the world, and then uses that determination to suggest a number of principles of state interaction in the area. His first two so-called "rules of the game" concern alliances. The first is that "many different regional and extra-regional political players combine and divide in shifting patterns of alliances;" the second, that "The patterns of alliance making and breaking tend toward comprehensiveness . . . so that any diplomatic initiative in the Middle East sets in motion a realignment of all the players."[29] Brown's work remains provocative. His principles do not, however, address theoretically the driving forces behind alliance shifts.

In a more theoretical vein is Stephen Walt's *The Origins of Alliances*, a rare example of a neorealist study of a non-Western area.[30] Using Middle East cases, Walt argues for amending or modifying traditional balance of power theory to include *threats* as well as power, an important distinction. Nonetheless, in estimating power and threat, he uses the standard military, industrial, and technological measures: a country's total resources (population, industrial and military capability, and technological prowess), geographic proximity, and offensive power, although he also stresses the importance of aggressive intentions.[31] He occasionally mentions the role of domestic factors, but continues to insist that decisions regarding alliance formation and alignment are made in response to external threat.

Part of the problem with Walt's study is definitional: He states that he wants to consider both more formal "alliances" and looser "alignments," but continues implicitly to assume that the only goals of alliances and alignments would be security-related, and that the only kind of security concerns or threats about which alliances would be concluded are external and military in nature. Thus he begins by assuming intent and, based on that (often faulty) assumption, proceeds to categorize Middle Eastern alliances as constituting either balancing or bandwagoning to address external threat. As a result, he mischaracterizes Arab alliance behavior in a number of instances, such as the Baghdad Pact and the formation of the United Arab Republic, and leaves a great deal un(der)explained or misinterpreted.

None of this is to say that external threats do not play a role in alliance behavior, and Walt examines numerous cases where such factors apparently did trigger alignment decisions (although in these cases as well, domestic factors should be more thoroughly explored). Yet, what Walt has done is to try to fit all examples into the same mold, and in order to make the argument work for all his cases, he is forced to argue that the type of balancing that has taken place in inter-Arab relations differs from the military power acquiring model of traditional balancing. "In the Arab world," he contends, "the most important source of power has been the ability to manipulate one's own image and the image of one's rivals in the minds of other Arab elites. Regimes have gained power and legitimacy if they have been seen as loyal to accepted Arab goals, and they have lost these assets if they have appeared to stray outside the Arab consensus." Walt defines this second kind of balancing as conducted by political, rather than military, means and as directed at an opponent's image and legitimacy. He continues to insist, however, that common to both types of balancing is the desire to acquire support from others in response to an external threat.[32]

However, in arguing that a second kind of balancing takes place in the Arab world, one that is directed at image and legitimacy, Walt not only implicitly departs from the neorealist insistence upon the primacy of the international system and relative military power in determining state alliance behavior, but also descends into what for a neorealist is the "reductionist" realm of domestic politics. However, the conclusion would seem to be that a traditional balancing and bandwagoning approach may in fact explain very little about state alignment decisions, just as it ignores other possibilities such as neutrality.[33] Even when the logic does appear compelling, it is often so only well after the fact. Indeed, without the benefit of hindsight, an approach that relies only on balancing and bandwagoning classifications as traditionally defined may well be unable to predict the outcome(s) that obtain.

A number of recent additions to the literature on the international relations of third world states have challenged the explanatory power of traditional approaches that rely on the concept of balancing external threats and power. One example is the work of Stephen David, who has detailed a further modification of balance of power theory which he has dubbed "omnibalancing."[34] In David's formulation, omnibalancing offers three key correctives to balance of power theory. First, leaders should be understood not only to balance against threats or power, but also to appease secondary adversaries so that they can focus their resources on their main adversaries. Second, the leadership may need to appease other states in order to counter a more pressing threat from within. To do so, it may appease the international allies of its domestic opponents. Finally, David argues that in the Third World, the most frequent challenges to states are *internal* challenges to the ruler or ruling group, not threats from abroad at the state level. Since leaders may be expected to act in such a way as to keep themselves in power, they may pursue survival strategies that may not serve the larger interests of the country.[35] David's willingness to admit that domestic challenges may be just as threatening as external ones is a major step forward, as is his focus on leadership survival strategies. Both fit quite well with the distinction made above in the discussion of economic security between leadership or regime interests and state interests.

Michael Barnett and Jack Levy also argue for including domestic and social variables in foreign policy explanations.[36] Their focus is on the "impact of the domestic political economy on state trade-offs between alliances and internal mobilization as alternative means for enhancing security." They note that alliances may have an economic component, and their definition of alliance is broad, but they continue to focus on alliances as defined in the traditional military sense.[37] They do look to the domestic front for variables that may influence alliance formation, and acknowledge the value of alliances as sources of military and economic resources as well as security guarantees. However, their focus is on alternative policy instruments, including domestic ones, and their respective repercussions for dealing with *external* security threats (although they add that they do not assume a priori that external security goals are always given priority in the foreign policy calculations of states). A trade-off or substitution effect is thus created between armaments and alliances.

Barnett elaborates further on these themes in his book, which examines a traditional security concern, that of how states confront external military threats.[38] Barnett's innovation is in studying the effect of alternative war preparation strategies, (which he terms accommodational, restructural, and international) on state power, based on their impact on state-society relations. He is, therefore, very much concerned with domestic factors, although he does not seem to make a distinction between leadership and government, the distinction that underpins the difference between regime and national security in my argument above.[39]

The definition of alignment used in this work includes both formal alliances and looser alignments, the goals of which are to strengthen a state's, regime's, or leadership's economic, military, or political position against real or potential threats which may be of external or domestic provenance. What is needed then is an approach to understanding alliances and alignments that broadens the concept of security and therefore incorporates internal threats and the role of the domestic political economy along with traditional concerns.

Domestic Economic Structure and the Quest for Financial Solvency

To review what has been developed so far, this work assumes that there is often a difference between state (national) and leadership or regime security. While national security may be most easily understood in terms of external threats of a military nature, some of the most serious threats a leadership may face may be domestic in origin.

Moreover, these threats may well be of an economic, not just of a political or military nature. External aid may drop or be cut, thus forcing a state to scramble to find alternative sources of support with which to pay the army or the bureaucracy. Or, some form of internal instability may make it impossible for a traditional, key market to remain open, thus threatening the income of the private (or perhaps state) sector and directly or indirectly cutting into state revenues. While such challenges have not traditionally been discussed in the security literature, the potential they hold for creating instability is good reason to consider them threats.

Understanding the nature of many domestic threats to a regime requires an examination of the nature of the national economy. Studying domestic economic structure and, specifically, the sources of state revenue allows for a consideration of an interrelated group of the same factors that those who attempted to establish and classify dependence have tried to evaluate singly. For instance, a state may receive large amounts of foreign aid, but if that aid represents only a fraction of state revenues then its significance is far less than absolute numbers might suggest. Or, a state may have a trade relationship in which 50 percent of its exports go to a single country. However, if the total contribution of trade to the domestic economy is small, then this trade concentration is far less significant than the 50 percent standing would have indicated. Moreover, for the purposes of this study, even in a situation in which trade does contribute substantially to state revenues, the availability of substitute commodities or markets does not make the loss of a market less significant, it simply means that such a crisis is more easily addressed. Hence in this formulation, the concepts of trade and commodity concentration are important, but only when placed in the larger framework of overall domestic economic structure. Such an approach therefore requires an examination of foreign trade statistics, the nature of domestic productive forces and their contribution to the economy, the extent of foreign aid, the importance of customs duties and the like.

All of these factors are examined first in the following chapter on the Jordanian economy. However in the case studies of the bilateral relationships that follow there is separate consideration of the role that aid (grants and loans), trade, joint ventures, as well as any other particularly salient form of exchange play in the bilateral relationships. Through such an examination, the importance of economic statecraft and its role in promoting, reinforcing, or supporting domestic financial solvency are illuminated. In this way, the real economic lifelines of the state become clearer, thereby providing more fertile ground for generating hypotheses regarding state behavior. Clues emerge regarding where a state's greatest potential weaknesses are and which factors may be particularly jeopardized by domestic or international developments. Such an approach also provides insights into the nature of the dominant socioeconomic or sociopolitical coalition, and therefore enables the analyst to evaluate how the range of possible responses to crises may be narrowed based on considerations of sectoral, regional, and organizational vested interests. It also suggests what strategies or types of policy instruments— whether economic or political—a state may use to ensure the continued flow of revenue. The case studies clearly demonstrate that alignment shifts are often used to address domestic economic crises.

Hence, state or regime behavior in the Third World may often resemble not just David's political omnibalancing, but what one might characterize as economic omnibalancing: allying with a state, several states, other domestic actors or even transnational actors (like the PLO) to thwart or overcome threats to the domestic economy. According to this understanding, foreign policy in general and alliance decisions in particular may be undertaken to ensure regime stability through securing revenue sources, whether internal or external, direct or indirect. The argument here is not that such decisions are undertaken merely to increase general domestic economic welfare; rather they are made to serve a more immediate purpose of forestalling or addressing a crisis with severe budgetary implications, enhancing economic stability, or insulating against economic challenges from abroad.

Classifying Exchange Elements

The case studies that follow demonstrate that leaderships may use foreign policy, alignment policy in particular, to ensure and/or to diversify revenue sources in a quest for what will subsequently be called "budget security." However, clearly not all income sources are of equal weight or importance, and leaderships may well assign priorities to them. In examining the composition of the economic side of the bilateral relationships and the use of economic statecraft, it may be helpful to distinguish between what may be termed high-level and low-level transactions or exchange. High-level exchanges would include such forms of income as grants and concessionary loans: infusions that are usually of substantial size, are often government-to-government, and go directly into the central state coffers. Lower-level transactions would include most bilateral trade, various forms of foreign investment, customs duties assessments, and taxes and fees collected. These exchanges are generally of lesser individual magnitude, involve government at a lower level or not at all, or feature the state only as collector of individual accounts.

One would expect a leadership to place first priority on securing and ensuring (if not diversifying) the flow of the largest and/or the most fungible kinds of income. Which revenue sources represent the greatest contribution to the treasury and exhibit the greatest fungibility will vary somewhat from country to country. In some cases, general budgetary support may be given on a completely discretionary basis; in others, while it may come in the form of cash, it may well be tied to certain projects or sectors. Likewise, in some states the percentage contribution of income tax or customs duties to state revenues may be substantial, whereas in others they may represent only a small percentage.

Alternative Strategies

As a result of such diversity in economic structure and revenue sources, circumstances that precipitate a budgetary crisis in one state may pose little or no challenge to another. Moreover, a budgetary crisis may have myriad potential sources: an external shock (like the invasion of Kuwait), reduced capabilities on the part of the supplier state (as exemplified by the decline in Gulf state aid over the 1980s), or overexpenditure (mismanagement) by the recipient state. In other words, a crisis may be precipitated by either supply or demand factors.

How may a state or a leadership attempt to achieve budget security? The argument here, of course, is that a leadership may use foreign policy, particularly alignment shifts to that end. In so doing, it in effect looks outward to attempt to diversify its suppliers, to seek new kinds of support, to expand into new markets. But why such an outward-looking strategy? May a state not also look within in an attempt to bolster indigenous productive forces and gradually lessen its reliance on external sources of income?

Here Michael Barnett's classification of policy responses to the need for war mobilization is useful. Barnett details three possible strategies: accommodational, restructural, and international. An accommodational strategy involves only minor changes or adjustments in existing policy instruments; a restructural strategy involves an attempt by what he calls state managers to restructure the existing state-society compact on finance, production, and conscription; and an international strategy is one that attempts to distribute costs of war onto foreign actors.[40]

It is not difficult to imagine a modification of such a schema to apply to budget security. The definition of an accommodational strategy remains the same; restructuring would involve the state's trying to create a new mix of agriculture, commerce, and industry, or the introduction of new industries, new attempts at raising revenues and fees, or perhaps cuts in state services and allocations. This, of course, is precisely what states undertake as a part of IMF-advised and generally World Bank-funded structural adjustment programs. Finally, an international strategy would involve seeking additional or diversified sources of loans or aid, attempting to open new markets or engage new suppliers, sharing the costs of increased industrialization through joint ventures, and the like.

The selection or mix of strategies or component policy measures, however, will depend upon a number of factors. If one is discussing challenges to budget or financial security, the time has probably already passed for Barnett's accommodational strategy. Hence, we will focus on the latter two. In the first place, numerous external constraints may influence attempts to implement the international strategy: the state of the economies of the actual and potential aid providers; the type of support upon which the state relies and therefore the type of support it may then seek as a supplement or an alternative; and the configuration of political forces, domestically, regionally, and internationally, that may constrain its choices of states from which to seek aid or that determine which states are likely to respond. With such potential barriers to this strategy, the former, that of restructuring in the form of working toward a reduction in the support required through strategies of developing indigenous productive forces, might seem the better course.

This inward-looking strategy would also, at least on the surface, appear most sound in the long term, by further developing the domestic economy so that its contribution to the state budget would gradually increase or be diversified and thereby wean the state away from what many might describe as an unhealthy dependence upon revenue sources over which the country may have less control. In the shorter term, however (the time frame in which political leaderships generally think), this is a risky, if not subversive, strategy. In the first place, there may not be sufficient time to await the positive effects that such a strategy may produce. Just as important, while country specifics vary, powerful forces are likely to have a vested interest in maintaining existing political and economic relations. While weaning the state away from outside income or from a particular commodity or sectoral dependence may make sense in the context of a search for greater long-term budget security or stability, it may at the same time threaten standing class configurations, and by extension, the regime. This has certainly been the case in states where short-term stabilization or longer-term structural adjustment programs have been dictated by multilateral lending institutions. Moreover, experiences to date with structural adjustment demonstrate not only the political, but also the economic and technical problems that may impede the implementation of such an inward-looking strategy.[41] Hence, one may in fact be more likely to see attempts at domestic economic reform only as a last resort. So as not to rock the domestic boat, foreign, rather than domestic policy options may be the first choice of a regime in dealing with economic crises. Although he does not deal with economic crises, Barnett's conclusions are similar.

The argument made here as suggested by the case studies is, therefore, that a leadership may choose a policy of external alliance or realignment as its response to a real or perceived economic crisis if the realignment offers economic benefits that can delay or allay an economic threat. However, even short of a crisis situation, a leadership may still choose an alliance strategy as a means of addressing a particular pressing economic need: diversifying trading partners, securing additional or alternative financial aid sources, and the like. In either case, the alliance or alignment decision should be understood as constituting a means of ensuring or reinforcing financial solvency, which has a direct impact on the security of the leadership or the regime. Finally, as this study argues, the best means of understanding what crises may arise and what strategies may be pursued in response is through examining the structure of the domestic economy and the provenance of state revenues.

2

The Economy and Economic Policy in Jordan

While it is clear that myriad international factors may influence the foreign policy decisions of a country as economically and politically vulnerable as Jordan, this study attempts to posit a domestic political economy explanation, specifically, one based on the structure of state revenues, for Jordan's alliance or alignment shifts. However, the statistical data, to be presented below, alone do not demonstrate that budget security, as it has been defined here, has been a conscious, primary concern among policymakers. Nor do statistics indicate whether or to what extent decisionmakers have been constrained by societal or institutional forces that might push decisionmaking in another direction. To make this part of the budget security argument, the process of economic decisionmaking must be explored and several factors must be shown to be present.

In the first place, the decisionmakers must be shown to be aware of and responsive to the central role that external sources of income play in keeping the state solvent. Second, there must be substantial overlap between economic and political decisionmaking groups, or at least very close coordination and shared understandings of national priorities between them. Third, either societal forces that might lobby for their own interests must be in relative accord with the decisionmaking group (for reasons of material interests or ideology), or, the decisionmakers must enjoy relative autonomy from such societal forces so that they may proceed without significant concern for the preferences of such forces. The final necessary step in the argument is substantiated through the case studies: that as a consequence of a conscious awareness of the critical role that external sources of finance play in maintaining state security, foreign policy, particularly in the form of alliance and realignment decisions, has been used by decisionmakers precisely to reinforce or bolster the budget. At this point, however, a more thorough examination of the economic decisionmaking process in Jordan is required.

Approaches to Economic Decisionmaking

The three most common approaches to analyzing economic decisionmaking in Western industrialized states have focused on the systemic level, societal forces, and the state, respectively. The first, of course, gives primacy to a state's place and relative power position in the international system. A number of theoretical schools fit under such a classification, from the world systems theory of Wallerstein, which focuses on the processes and contradictions within international capitalism as the driving forces behind policy, to theories of economic interdependence which emphasize how increased interactions between countries may increase the sensitivity of one country to developments in another.[1]

The second, or society-centered approach looks for explanations of state policy choices in the jockeying for power and influence by domestic, civil society forces. In such a schema policy outcomes are the result of the relative power and effective interest articulation of domestic social or economic groups. Jeffry Frieden, a proponent of this approach, argues for a purely economic or materialist basis for determining such interests; however, he also admits of other factors such as ideology and bureaucratic politics, which may also play a role.[2]

Finally, there is the state-centered approach, which argues for examining the role of the state as structure and actor in determining or affecting policy choices. It examines policymakers and bureaucrats themselves, emphasizing how they respond to a variety of constraints and stimuli as they formulate and implement policy. The presumption of such an approach is that the policy preferences of such actors are at least partially separable from societal or interest group pressures and more closely approximate adherence to a "national interest"-directed conception of policy.

These three models have been used overwhelmingly in analyses of economic decisionmaking in advanced industrialized countries, with Frieden's work a notable exception. Even in Frieden's work, however, the discussion is of Latin America, and of states with long, independent histories. Can one apply the same approaches to the rest of the developing world, especially those countries in which the state apparatuses are relatively new and whose experiences with colonialism are much more recent? This chapter will examine Jordanian economic policymaking and evaluate it in the light of these three approaches. As the notes for this chapter indicate, beyond the historical and statistical information on the economy, the discussion relies heavily on personal interviews. Such an approach undoubtedly has its drawbacks, because, for reasons related at least in part to the authoritarian nature of the political system in Jordan until mid-1989, virtually no literature exists on the nature of the economic decisionmaking process in Jordan. Such is the case in most developing countries, where policymaking processes are far from transparent and where most policies are generally attributed to the personality and power of the individual leader. In the absence of other, less potentially subjective data, this chapter represents a first attempt at understanding the economic decisionmaking process in the Hashemite kingdom as part of the background necessary to make the argument about the centrality of preserving financial solvency, or budget security, to Jordan's foreign policy behavior.

External or System-Level Factors

Since its inception, the Hashemite Kingdom has relied heavily upon external revenue for its survival. This situation owes much to Jordan's strategic location, which, while it has shifted in importance over the years, has nonetheless continued to give Jordan its greatest value in the eyes of outside powers. Whether as a key land link in British imperial designs in the early period, or as a pro-Western buffer between the Arab states and Israel (which served both Western as well as certain Arab state interests), Jordan's geographic location in the Eastern Mediterranean and as a country bordering Israel,

Saudi Arabia, Iraq and (nearly) Egypt has given it an importance of which most small and natural resource underendowed states could only dream. As a result, it has managed over the years to extract financial support of various kinds from concerned states, and this form of support has set patterns of economic development and decisionmaking that have continued to the present (with some changes beginning with political liberalization in 1989).

Originally carved out of the territory that was to have become the Palestine mandate, Transjordan was established in 1921 by the British as an hereditary monarchy of the Hashemite family from the Hijaz region of the Arabian peninsula. Control of this territory was intended to bolster British strategic interests in the Eastern Mediterranean, critical in guarding access to India as well as contiguous with oil-wealthy Iraq, which had also been placed under British mandate as part of the World War I settlement.

From its political birth more than 50 percent of the Transjordanian budget was provided by the British government.[3] The need for this support derived in large part from the newness of the state as well as from the weakness of the indigenous economic base: the country had a small population, limited agricultural land (located primarily in the Jordan Valley and the north), and limited natural resources (only phosphates and potash). To preserve the state and build it as an effective and stable military base in the region required an infusion of resources from outside. The influx into the East Bank of Palestinians driven or fleeing from their homes in 1948 and the incorporation of the rump of Eastern Palestine, what became known as the West Bank, in 1950 tripled the country's population and added valuable agricultural land. This development increased the country's resources over the long term, but in the short term served only to strain further the poor state's economic and administrative capacity. British subsidies continued to sustain the economy until 1956, when the British head of the armed forces, Glubb Pasha, was dismissed by a very young King Husayn, and the Arab states briefly stepped in to replace British subsidies in a bid to wean Jordan away from its pro-Western stance.

However, in the midst of an Arab nationalist wave that was sweeping the region, a coup attempt by members of the army in 1957 led the king to dismiss his Arab nationalist-oriented prime minister. This move triggered a termination of Arab state budget support for the amirate and the United States assumed the role of primary aid provider. Again the motives are related to larger strategic concerns. The Arab states withdrew aid as punishment for a domestic policy they understood as indicative of a move away from the 1956 commitment to Arab interests that the dismissal of Glubb had represented. The U.S. was willing to step in to play the former British role because its strategic interests included maintaining regional stability to ensure the free flow of oil. Part of maintaining such stability involved supporting the security of the state of Israel, and U.S. support for a pro-Western, conservative monarchy in Jordan clearly served that goal as well. U.S. aid continued until 1967, when Jordan accused the U.S. of backing Israel in the 1967 war. Thereafter, Arab aid again took its place, and rose to unprecedented levels following the oil boom of 1973.

Over the years, Jordan's external income has taken the form of general budgetary support, various types of aid for the military and security services, assistance in the form of grants or concessionary loans for development projects, payments from the United Nations Relief and Works Agency for Palestine Refugees in the Near East (UNRWA) to provide food, education, and health care to the Palestinian refugees registered with UNRWA and living in the kingdom (one-fourth to one-third of the total population, depending upon the period), remittances from its expatriates working abroad (one-third of the total work force before 1990), royalties for oil pipeline crossage, and payments for port facilities and overland transport.

Table 1 provides a breakdown of the external revenues of the central government. While exact statistics on individual country assistance contributions are not available, Saudi Arabia and Kuwait (as well as the United States until 1980) have been the primary donors. A more detailed discussion of Arab aid is provided in the case study chapters. Table 2 lists the amounts of foreign assistance and foreign loans, while Table 3 converts these numbers into percentages of total revenue and demonstrates how they compare with domestic revenue as a percentage of total revenue. The average over the sixteen-year period was 43 percent, although the secular trend is one of gradual decline.

Table 1
External Revenues of Central Government

Thousand JD[1]

Foreign Loans
Development Loans (Part 2)

Year	Grand Total	Foreign** Assistance	Foreign Loans of (Part 1)	Total	West Germany	Kuwait	U.S.A.I.D.	Saudi Arabia	Arab Fund*	Japan	Other
1964/65	22,383	15,407	5,000	1,976	170	587	—	—	—	—	1,219
1965/66	17,859	15,272	—	2,587	206	869	—	—	—	—	1,512
1966	12,048	9,883	—	2,165	139	1,011	75	—	—	—	940
1967	44,701	40,409	—	4,292	506	628	747	1,505	—	—	906
1968	44,650	40,199	—	4,451	1,367	174	265	1,500	—	—	1,145
1969	42,960	38,377	—	4,583	26	594	1,016	1,499	—	—	1,448
1970	37,909	35,424	—	2,485	—	265	1,309	500	—	—	411
1971	43,322	35,386	3,430	4,506	541	903	772	357	—	—	1,933
1972	52,958	44,455	1,103	7,400	2,500	763	1,940	—	—	—	2,197
1973	57,054	45,608	—	11,446	6,452	1,704	1,299	—	—	—	1,991
1974	74,036	58,824	—	15,212	5,296	4,093	3,250	—	—	—	2,573
1975	116,764	100,609	—	16,155	5,185	1,079	2,556	—	1,755	—	7,335
1976	86,126	66,238	2,700	17,188	2,755	2,441	2,714	—	—	—	7,523
1977	180,713	122,202	—	58,511	11,338	7,124	13,590	4,000	5,896	1,500	15,063
1978	172,396	81,699	29,550	61,147	8,874	8,200	13,930	5,700	6,500	3,250	14,693
1979	247,926	210,302	—	37,624	3,442	10,304	2,703	2,461	1,991	775	15,948
1980	280,870	209,304	9,060	62,506	4,695	11,717	17,513	5,001	2,410	1,939	19,231

23,142	3,675	3,955	7,036	5,147	8,389	5,689	57,033	19,352	206,312	282,697	1981
25,892	5,406	1,690	2,510	6,425	3,313	2,365	47,601	17,670	199,582	264,853	1982
11,528	3,128	627	9,570	8,605	15,721	1,874	51,053	25,748	197,014	273,815	1983
10,808	7,943	4,464	9,538	1,250	11,673	222	45,898	76,298	106,108	228,304	1984
19,839	5,237	5,324	12,179	7,969	14,305	6,168	71,021	91,389	187,839	350,249	1985
20,086	14,479	5,720	6,036	12,110	4,767	4,838	68,036	91,732	143,707	303,475	1986
21,815	8,119	1,408	9,424	9,584	3,140	6,884	60,374	2,845	127,540	190,759	1987
37,649	3,900	4,989	5,894	4,412	3,962	3,320	64,126	36,995	164,000	265,121	***1988

SOURCES: Ministry of Finance, Ministry of Planning, Central Bank of Jordan.
* Arab Fund for Economic and Social Development
** Includes Economic/Technical Assistance and Expected Loans & Economic/Technical Assistance.
*** Preliminary.
1 For dollar exchange equivalents, see Appendix 1.

SOURCE: Central Bank of Jordan, *Yearly Statistical Series*, Special Issue, October 1989, Table Number 38.

TABLE 2
Summary of Central Governmet Budget

Thousand JD[1]

Deficit (-) Surplus (+)	Expenditures			Revenues and Reciepts						Year
	Capital	Recurring	Total	Internal Loans	Foreign Loans	Loans Repaid	Foreign Assistance	Domestic Revenues	Total	
2,587	9,166	34,458	43,624	0	6,976	0	15,407	23,828	46,211	1964/65
-2,397	11,178	35,810	46,988	0	2,587	0	15,272	26,732	44,591	1965/66
-3,242	10,360	28,240	38,600	0	2,165	0	9,883	23,310	35,358	*1966
2,051	23,496	44,651	68,147	0	4,292	226	40,409	25,271	70,198	1967
-9,502	23,334	57,186	80,520	0	4,451	99	40,199	26,269	71,018	1968
-3,873	23,170	65,231	88,401	8,400	4,583	648	38,377	32,520	84,528	1969
-7,906	21,678	59,028	80,706	4,200	2,485	431	35,424	30,260	72,800	1970
8,099	22,442	60,706	83,148	12,100	7,936	70	35,386	35,755	91,247	1971
-800	30,985	70,467	101,452	5,000	8,503	135	44,455	42,559	100,652	1972
-5,525	40,903	78,608	119,511	10,750	11,446	0	45,608	46,182	113,986	1973
2,318	43,019	103,603	146,622	9,000	15,212	160	58,824	65,744	148,940	1974
7,663	79,172	125,692	204,864	13,135	16,155	0	100,609	82,628	212,527	1975
-55,771	76,590	185,894	262,484	13,000	19,888	0	66,238	107,587	206,713	1976
123	142,252	195,587	337,839	15,000	58,511	0	122,202	142,249	337,962	1977
-14,626	148,619	212,891	361,510	16,000	90,697	0	81,699	158,488	346,884	1978
-47,493	194,329	321,335	515,664	32,350	37,624	0	210,302	187,895	468,171	1979
-38,128	227,092	336,053	563,145	18,000	71,566	0	209,304	226,147	525,017	1980
-29,977	255,632	391,468	647,100	18,000	76,385	7,226	206,312	309,200	617,123	1981
-38,300	250,577	442,968	693,545	28,200	65,271	0	199,582	362,192	655,245	1982

Year										
1983	210	251,599	453,675	705,274	28,825	76,801	2,268	197,014	400,576	705,484
1984	-42,374	232,713	488,092	720,805	25,500	122,196	9,620	106,108	415,007	678,431
1985	39,117	263,173	542,510	805,683	35,299	162,410	18,449	187,839	440,803	844,800
1986	-75,924	410,816	570,526	981,342	74,778	159,768	12,777	143,707	514,388	905,418
1987	-95,839	363,154	602,654	965,808	129,979	63,219	17,698	127,540	531,533	869,969
**1988	-128,118	384,595	661,085	1,045,680	88,281	101,121	23,000	164,000	541,160	917,562

SOURCE: Ministry of Finance.
*Nine months.
**Preliminary.
[1]For dollar exchange equivalents, see Appendix 1.

SOURCE: Central Bank of Jordan, *Yearly Statistical Series*, Special Issue, October 1989, Table Number 36.

TABLE 3

Percentage Comparisons of Foreign and Domestic Contributions to Total Revenue

Year	Foreign Assistance as % of Total Revenue	Foreign Loans as % of Total Revenue	Total contributions of Foreign Loans and Assistance	Domestic Revenue % of Total Revenue
1973	40.0	10.0	50.0	40.5
1974	39.5	10.2	49.7	44.1
1975	47.3	7.6	54.9	38.8
1976	32.0	9.6	41.6	52.0
1977	36.2	17.3	53.4	42.0
1978	23.5	26.1	49.6	45.6
1979	44.9	8.0	52.9	40.1
1980	39.8	13.6	53.4	43.0
1981	33.4	12.3	45.7	50.1
1982	30.4	9.9	40.3	55.2
1983	27.9	10.8	38.7	56.7
1984	15.6	18.0	33.6	61.1
1985	22.2	19.2	41.4	52.1
1986	15.8	17.6	33.4	56.8
1987	14.6	7.2	21.8	61.0
1988	17.8	11.0	28.8	58.9

SOURCE: Author's calculations from Table 2.

As a result, the Jordanian economy has developed the following defining characteristics: limited development of indigenous productive forces; a standard of living far higher than the level of indigenous productive forces would have suggested or allowed for; state services and infrastructure far more extensive than the GDP would have permitted; and a very high percentage (nearly 50%) of the work force on the state payroll. Thus, the government came to be viewed as a source of money, salaries, contracts, and security, with the treasury, in effect, a built-in system of subsidies and buying favors. The state's continuing ability to ensure its collection of these external revenues or rents was its primary insurance for the high standard of living and services the country enjoyed.

Hence there is no question that Jordan's place in the international system—geopolitically as a buffer state or base and economically as an underindustrialized primary product (phosphates and potash) exporter—has dramatically shaped many of the policy constraints (and opportunities) that Jordanian policymakers have faced. However, such a framework of constraints and opportunities does not alone determine policy choice. In a situation such as Jordan's, the leadership could either have attempted to develop its indigenous productive base further, so as to lessen its dependence on or vulnerability to outside assistance, or remained reliant upon such sources, assuming that its strategic importance would continue to enable it to court and secure new sources of aid when necessary. What is now required is an examination of the state and societal levels in order to account more specifically for the route economic policymaking has taken over the years.

State, Society and the Economy

The previous section and its tables detailed the contribution of external sources to the Jordanian economy. What, in contrast, has been the contribution of the domestic sector to the economy? As Table 4 makes clear, import duties in particular, but indirect taxes in general, have been the largest components. Income tax, on the other hand, has remained below 15 percent, and has generally hovered around 11 or 12 percent.

In order to understand this phenomenon, one must look more closely at the division between the public and private sectors in Jordan. The picture that emerges is that of a domestic economy with a public sector component that is deceptively large for a country with an avowedly free-market orientation such as Jordan. And, not surprisingly, the large size of the public sector is directly related to the state's reliance on external sources of revenue.

In the first place, employment in the bureaucracy and the perquisites that attend it have, especially since the early 1970s, been an important form of distribution and cooptation, as well as security apparatus maintenance. In other words, a gradual bloating of the bureaucracy has played an important domestic security (workforce absorption) function. In Jordan, this issue is even more salient because of the ethnic division that reinforces or underlies the public/private sector divide. Since the civil war of 1970–71, the state has

TABLE 4
Central Government Domestic Revenues

Thousand JD[1]

| Non-Tax Revenues | | | | Indirect Taxes | | | | | | Direct Taxes | | | | |
Other	Interest & Profits	Post Telgr. Telph.	Total	Add'l. Tax	Fees	Licences	Excise	Import Duties	Total	Other	Income Tax	Total	Grand Total	Year
3,206	3,484	1,246	7,936	—	2,765	1,054	3,866	6,187	13,872	614	1,406	2,020	23,828	1964/65
2,984	1,831	1,396	6,211	—	2,598	1,481	5,033	8,899	18,011	603	1,907	2,510	26,732	1965/66
2,369	1,705	1,309	5,383	—	1,752	1,259	4,598	8,356	15,965	144	1,818	1,962	23,310	1966
3,883	1,829	1,287	6,999	—	1,852	1,010	5,054	8,199	16,115	102	2,055	2,157	25,271	1967
3,289	2,883	1,004	7,176	—	1,497	1,410	5,519	8,846	17,272	44	1,777	1,821	26,269	1968
3,820	4,641	1,067	9,528	—	1,808	2,173	6,084	10,650	20,715	38	2,239	2,277	32,520	1969
2,970	4,819	1,011	8,800	1,353	1,540	1,876	5,094	9,103	18,966	23	2,471	2,494	30,260	1970
6,176	5,120	1,155	12,451	1,507	2,211	2,132	6,872	7,684	20,406	53	2,845	2,898	35,755	1971
9,875	3,832	1,102	14,809	1,920	2,693	2,552	7,780	9,543	24,488	60	3,202	3,262	42,559	1972
5,430	5,330	1,300	12,060	2,396	3,956	3,904	7,773	12,191	30,220	55	3,847	3,902	46,182	1973
12,130	8,470	1,563	22,163	2,900	4,120	4,975	8,985	16,850	37,830	364	5,387	5,751	65,744	1974
11,418	10,831	2,234	24,483	3,646	7,668	5,910	10,657	20,902	48,783	85	9,277	9,362	82,628	1975
6,143	10,099	2,275	18,517	5,286	12,664	10,605	9,097	39,985	77,637	2,094	9,339	11,433	107,587	1976
8,653	12,422	3,453	24,510	6,407	8,367	13,103	9,875	63,995	101,747	2,749	13,243	15,992	142,249	1977
13,257	14,358	7,592	35,207	6,176	13,404	13,296	6,999	61,354	101,229	3,491	18,561	22,052	158,488	1978
12,246	15,689	8,866	36,801	8,007	17,061	15,591	10,567	72,060	123,286	5,424	22,384	27,808	187,895	1979
18,331	21,173	11,978	51,482	10,118	19,541	18,902	13,210	78,031	139,802	8,084	26,779	34,863	226,147	1980
18,544	45,017	12,667	76,228	11,525	36,543	25,175	16,888	94,069	184,200	8,791	39,981	48,772	309,200	1981
25,178	53,166	20,721	99,065	12,688	37,997	24,807	24,109	109,748	209,349	10,106	43,672	53,778	362,192	1982

24,101	59,496	23,374	106,971	13,466	42,042	25,753	35,301	120,569	237,131	10,457	46,017	56,474	400,576	1983
39,888	36,348	33,333	109,569	16,550	44,512	28,719	37,192	118,047	245,020	11,717	48,701	60,418	415,007	1984
41,283	43,964	38,270	123,517	15,426	42,427	28,285	45,811	117,945	249,894	12,980	54,412	67,392	440,803	1985
119,836	39,726	45,595	205,157	14,205	41,277	29,970	51,611	112,003	249,066	12,235	47,930	60,165	514,388	1986
127,265	37,020	41,785	206,070	14,710	50,079	32,971	58,295	108,544	264,599	15,536	45,328	60,864	531,533	1987
114,400	36,000	51,000	201,400	16,300	47,000	35,560	60,300	116,700	275,860	19,100	44,800	63,900	541,160	1988

[1] For dollar exchange equivalents, see Appendix 1.

SOURCE: Central Bank of Jordan, *Yearly Statistical Series*, Special Issue, October 1989, Table Number 37.

pursued an unwritten policy of preferential recruitment of Transjordanians (native East Bankers) as opposed to Palestinians into the state administrative and security bureaucracies. This complemented the army recruitment policy: until conscription was initiated in 1976, the army was largely a Transjordanian preserve, and even thereafter remained so for career officers. The 1980s did witness the entry of more Transjordanians into the private sector, and therefore, the ethnic lines between public and private sector are no longer as clear as they once were. Nonetheless, the *perception* remains among many Jordanians that East Bankers control the bureaucracy and Palestinians control the country's wealth. Given the often problematic relationship between the Jordanian government and its Palestinian citizens, this division of labor takes on even greater political salience and sensitivity.

Attempts to estimate public versus private sector contribution to the economy are complicated in Jordan by the fact that official statistics do not differentiate between pure private sector concerns and publicly owned enterprises. For example, the Jordan Phosphate Mines Company is listed as a private sector firm because it takes the form of a shareholding company. In fact, however, the public sector has contributed 90 percent of the company's paid-up capital and holds the management and decisionmaking positions.[4] In any case, the greatest expansion in the public sector came during part of the period under consideration here (the 1970s and early 1980s), not surprisingly, with the surge in oil money and Arab aid. In mid-1986 it was estimated that the public sector employed 45 percent of the country's work force, contributed 50 percent of capital formation, and was responsible for 30 percent of exports.[5]

Table 5, which provides figures on the industrial origin of GDP as well as the various categories' percentage contributions, further elucidates why private sector income tax has contributed so little to total domestic revenues. If one tries to divide the government sector from the private sector, a rough, if perhaps somewhat low, calculation can be made by combining government services with mining and quarrying (public sector companies) and electricity (also public sector). The other categories do have some public sector contribution—for instance, in the realm of transport and communications, the national airline, Royal Jordanian, and local transport services were government-owned during this period. Using such a formula, the average of state sector GDP contributions suggested by Table 6 is between 35.6 percent and 40.9 percent, and should be viewed as a clear underestimate. Accordingly, the private sector can be credited with producing at most only 50–60 percent of GDP. Even here, caution is in order because much ostensibly private sector activity is in fact dependent upon government contracts, thus further diminishing the real private sector contribution to GDP.

After reviewing these figures both the importance of external sources of income, particularly foreign grants and loans, as well as the smaller contribution of the domestic private sector to the economy and to the budget should be clear. What reality of economic policymaking do these characteristics reflect or underpin? While the role of system-level factors has been made clear as a set or framework of conditioning constraints, which of the other two models—the society-centered or the state-centered approach—best captures the "how" of economic policymaking in Jordan?

In order to answer this question, the next sections will examine the various players or putative players in the economic policymaking process necessary to evaluate the applicability of the two approaches: the king and crown prince, the cabinet and ministers, and the private sector.

Assessing a Society-Centered Approach: The Role of the Private Sector

Support for the society-centered approach requires a demonstration that actors outside the state apparatus have played an effective role in influencing economic decisionmaking. In Jordan, in large part because of the longstanding state of martial law (to be discussed at greater length in the next section) civil society organizing of the kind generally required to articulate such interests was, until 1989, largely circumscribed by the state. However, two institutions with potential clout and interest in the economic policy arena, the chambers of commerce and industry, have been in existence throughout much of

TABLE 5
Industrial Origin of Gross Domestic Product

Million JD[1]

Net Nat'l. Product at Factor Cost(3)	GNP at Market Price(2)	GNP at Market Price(3)	GNP at Factor Cost	Other Services	Producer of Govt. Services	Financing Real Estate & Business Services	Transportation and Communication	Wholesale & Retail Trade, Restaurants and Hotels	Construction	Electricity and Water Supply	Mining and Quarrying	Agriculture, Forestry and Fishing	Year
141.2	160.6	149.0	135.5	21.4	19.7	1.5	12.0	28.0	5.5	1.0	12.3	34.1	1964
157.2	180.5	167.6	151.0	23.6	21.4	2.1	12.6	31.4	7.9	1.7	16.2	34.1	1965
157.6	185.7	170.5	149.6	25.3	22.0	2.8	14.4	28.9	9.3	2.0	17.3	27.6	1966
120.6	142.5	131.2	115.6	3.0	24.5	12.3	8.2	23.1	6.1	1.2	13.8	23.4	1967
140.9	166.4	156.1	138.2	4.7	36.4	15.0	12.9	25.6	9.7	1.5	16.2	16.2	1968
168.8	197.4	183.4	162.5	5.9	40.5	13.8	14.4	34.3	10.7	1.6	18.8	22.5	1969
159.6	187.0	174.4	154.7	6.6	42.5	18.0	14.3	32.2	7.7	1.9	15.9	15.6	1970
171.3	199.4	186.2	166.0	6.5	43.6	18.4	14.6	33.0	7.4	2.2	16.4	23.9	1971
188.5	221.0	207.2	182.8	7.5	45.9	19.6	17.3	35.7	9.2	2.5	18.5	26.6	1972
203.8	241.5	218.3	188.9	8.5	46.7	20.9	17.9	38.1	15.2	2.8	21.2	17.6	1973
265.9	279.3	247.3	242.4	9.9	54.3	22.5	22.8	42.3	16.8	3.0	40.5	30.3	1974
354.5	376.0	312.1	303.1	11.8	65.2	30.0	24.9	66.9	19.2	3.1	56.0	26.0	1975
505.0	562.4	421.6	378.4	14.7	81.7	33.8	32.5	80.1	26.6	3.9	67.8	37.3	1976
568.7	660.1	514.2	439.9	15.3	84.4	48.0	35.9	94.2	36.8	5.5	78.1	41.7	1977
678.2	781.0	632.2	551.2	16.2	95.0	67.0	59.3	102.6	51.0	7.2	94.3	58.6	1978
806.4	921.3	753.0	668.6	16.1	129.1	91.1	62.9	123.6	70.5	10.1	121.6	43.6	1979
1051.3	1190.1	984.3	893.2	19.8	170.2	105.9	79.7	166.5	97.5	17.1	167.1	69.4	1980
1293.9	1482.7	1164.2	1041.1	24.3	191.2	111.2	102.7	196.7	110.6	21.0	208.3	75.1	1981
1431.0	1673.4	1321.2	1169.6	28.2	218.5	129.2	123.5	210.9	121.9	25.3	230.3	81.8	1982

1485.3	1770.3	1422.7	1242.3	28.7	232.0	135.6	138.4	228.0	126.8	28.3	214.5	110.0	1983
1550.1	1853.6	1498.4	1315.0	37.4	238.4	144.5	143.5	241.3	127.0	33.5	250.8	98.6	1984
1526.5	1881.8	1605.9	1390.6	41.6	264.0	154.7	146.7	262.7	114.1	35.2	252.9	118.7	1985
1551.7	1919.4	1639.9	1401.1	40.5	295.9	167.3	157.2	232.0	113.0	42.0	242.1	111.1	1986
1496.0	1867.9	1686.3	1447.3	44.0	308.8	171.8	160.6	235.8	101.3	45.4	252.4	127.2	*1987
1497.2	1865.7	1702.6	1449.6	46.3	320.2	172.8	159.0	244.5	81.3	41.8	243.8	139.9	*1988

SOURCE: Department of Statistics.

NOTE: (1) = GNP at factor cost + net indirect taxes.
(2) = (1) + net factor income from abroad.
(3) = (2) − (consumption of fixed capital + net indirect taxes)
[1] For dollar exchange equivalents, see Appendix 1.
* Preliminary.

SOURCE: Central Bank of Jordan, *Yearly Statistical Series*, Special Issue, October 1989, Table Number 47.

TABLE 6
Origins of State Sector GDP (% of total GDP)

Year	Gov't Services	Mining & Quarrying	Electricity & Water	Total
1973	24.7	11.2	1.0	36.9
1974	22.4	16.7	1.0	39.1
1975	21.5	18.4	1.0	40.9
1976	21.5	17.9	1.0	40.4
1977	19.1	17.7	1.2	38.0
1978	17.2	17.1	1.3	35.6
1979	19.3	18.1	1.5	38.9
1980	19.0	18.7	1.9	39.6
1981	18.3	20.0	2.0	40.3
1982	18.6	19.6	2.1	40.3
1983	18.6	17.2	2.2	37.6
1984	18.1	19.0	2.5	39.6
1985	18.9	17.2	2.5	39.5
1986	21.1	17.2	2.9	41.2
1987	21.3	17.4	3.1	41.8
1988	22.0	16.8	2.8	41.6

SOURCE: Author's calculations from Table 5.

the kingdom's history. This section first examines their activity and input.

The Jordanian Chamber of Commerce is in fact a federation of local chambers of commerce. Prior to the incorporation of the West Bank into the Hashemite Kingdom following the 1948 Arab-Israeli war, there were a number of local chambers of commerce and industry on both banks. In 1953 the establishment of chambers in Jenin and Jericho raised the number to 11, with chambers already in existence in Amman (1923), Jerusalem (1936), Irbid, Nablus, Kerak, Ramallah, Tulkarm, Hebron, and Bethlehem (all in the 1940s). The federation was founded in December 1955, as the representative of the private sector in all economic, commercial, and service fields. By the late 1980s (following the disengagement from the West Bank) the federation counted 70,000 members belonging to branches in Amman, Zarqa, Irbid, Mafraq, Ma'an, Aqaba, Ramtha, Kerak, Tafila, Madaba, Salt, Jerash, and al-Mazar.[6]

The Amman Chamber of Industry established itself as a separate entity in 1962. Its members are public, private, and mixed sector companies, and membership totaled about 6,000 at the end of 1990. Recently, subassociations have been formed in the chamber for banking, insurance, farmers, transportation, shipping, contractors, land transport, and the like. The chamber serves as a forum for formulating and expressing the views of the industrial sector in the kingdom. Its members serve on a number of boards and committees, in some case as mandated by law and in others by invitation, as is the case with the Chamber of Commerce.[7] Members also participate in joint trade delegations and in the drafting of trade protocols.[8]

The annual reports of the Chamber of Commerce provide some insights into the influence that the institutionalized private sector has had on policymaking. Aside from a few notes regarding meetings with representatives of foreign chambers of commerce, the summaries of meetings held with ministers seem to be the best indicator of formal access by the chambers to the government. By members' own admission, the government consulted the Chamber of Industry only infrequently during the 1970s.[9] Although the record is incomplete, it would appear that the fifteen-year period witnessed less than twenty such formal meetings. Those of January 1980, May 1980, September 1985, and December 1986 were with the prime minister to discuss general problems. In March 1988 members met with the Crown Prince to discuss issues related to the role of the private sector and development. Several meetings in late 1979 and 1980 dealt with merchants' concerns over claims of price violations and with their fears that honest merchants' reputations would be hurt. Meetings in July 1979, January 1984, 1985 (month not specified), and February 1987 dealt with income tax or customs fees concerns. In a number of cases, it was decided that joint committees of various sorts should be established to address the issue or as liaisons. The fact that such committees are not mentioned subsequently indicates that they had either short or unproductive lives or both.[10]

Both merchants and industrialists claimed that they had grown increasingly vocal during the period of serious economic decline prior to the beginning of the political liberalization in mid-1989. Rather than simply waiting to read the text of a new law in the *Official Gazette,* industrialists began to initiate projects and make suggestions to the government.[11] In general, however, it seems clear that formal meetings were few and effective input quite limited, at least until the beginning of the liberalization in 1989. Although the respective chambers' members were some of the wealthiest men in the kingdom, their official lobbying organization seems not to have served them particularly well.

What of other possible sources of private sector influence, for example, that of members of the private sector who reach positions of power in the government as ministers? Here, several examples are instructive. Traditionally, Zayd al-Rifaʻi, prime minister from 1973–76 and 1985–89, was viewed as a businessman and his return to the prime ministry in 1985 was heralded roundly as a sign that the government would place priority on energizing the private sector. However, a brief examination of the record and discussions with businessmen dispel any notion that Rifaʻi was a godsend for them. In the first place, it was during Rifaʻi's first government that the bases of much government intervention were laid. For example, during this period the Ministry of Supply was created to take responsibility for providing such basic commodities as rice, sugar, and meat at subsidized prices. At the time it was argued that the security of the country required such moves. Nonetheless, while a number of wealthy merchants have been able to capitalize on the creation of this ministry, in general, members of the private sector view many of this ministry's functions as obstacles to their attempts to diversify imports.

Even during Rifaʻi's second government, however, initial promises of reforms and deregulation were left unfulfilled.[12] For example, in response to the concerns of the private sector, the cabinet decided on September 13, 1986 to form a Higher Economic Advisory Council, to which Hamdi Tabbaʻ, the President of the Chamber of Commerce, was appointed, to study economic conditions and to make proposals and recommendations aimed at: 1) coordinating economic, financial, and monetary policies at the time of their drafting and implementation; 2) developing policies to encourage savings and investment and to channel local and foreign investment; 3) organizing and developing the financial markets; and 4) deepening coordination between the public and private sectors in implementing the development plan. In short, the council was to serve as a bridge between the government and the private sector, even in the case of individual problems. The Council had its first meeting on December 4, 1986.[13] However, much to the dismay of the private sector, that was the council's only meeting during Rifa'i's prime ministership; as of the summer of 1992 it had met only twice since the change of government in April 1989.[14]

Former Industry and Trade ministers Hamdi Tabba' and Walid 'Asfur and former Finance Minister Basil Jardaneh were also cited as examples of men from the private sector who came to government and seemed to lose their will to work for the private sector. Indeed, one interviewee related a story regarding the attempt by the government to impose a production tax on industrialists, a unilateral move that caused a furor in the fall of 1991. A businessman who had occasion to dine with the finance minister raised with him the issue of consultation with the private sector before launching such a policy. Jardaneh reportedly responded, "Do I have to consult the private sector every time I make a decision?" [15] Only Industry and Trade Minister Raja'i al-Mu'ashshir, also from the private sector, seemed to continue to work for its interests, particularly for industry, while he held his portfolio.[16]

Members of the Chamber of Industry also had high praise for Mudar Badran, (a product of the intelligence apparatus, and hardly a man of the private sector), saying that he was very supportive of industry. They also mentioned former Chief of the Royal Court and former Prime Minister, the late 'Abd al-Hamid Sharaf, who reportedly spent long hours in consultation with chamber members and supported the business community during his brief time in office. However the industrialists in particular sang the praises of Crown Prince Hasan, who, in his role as advocate of economic development and increasing employment, has been, at least on a rhetorical level, very pro-industry.

In short, it would be inaccurate to conclude that, in practice, Rifa'i or any of the other private sector ministers demonstrated a pro-private sector bias in their policies or accomplishments. Why is this the case? One charge made by private sector businessmen was that the middle-level bureaucracy, suspicious of the private sector, was responsible for thwarting a number of the reforms Rifa'i had sought to implement.[17] Another was that this was an indication of the lack of

a coherent economic policy, even by the ministers most clearly identified with the private sector. Still others claimed that the overall
effect of assuming a government position was that it forced officials
in effect to "step outside" of themselves and their respective class or
other interests, an argument in keeping with a state-centered
approach.

Whatever the explanation offered, most of those interviewed
agreed that, as the records of the chambers indicate, the private sector has not been very successful in influencing policy. Owners of
large businesses have always had access to the ministries, but they
have usually approached ministers as individuals, rather than as a
group representing sectoral concerns. Former Finance Minister
'Awdah insisted that the government and the private sector were
keen to create an institutional infrastructure to formalize the consultation relationship, whereby research would be conducted that
would benefit the sector and that the government could use as well.
Nonetheless, the experience of the Higher Council established
under Rifa'i suggests that at some level in government such attempts
have been and will be resisted, or at least not acted upon.

A number of other reasons lie behind the apparent lack of influence by the private sector. First of all, and not surprising, the private
sector, although small, is not unified in its interests. For instance, the
Chamber of Commerce is likely to lobby for imports and for lower
standards or specifications on imports, while the Chamber of Industry will resist (presumably because of fear of competition). The
Chamber of Commerce might have a difference with the Banking
Association over interest rates, and the Chamber of Industry might
seek a preferential rate over the commercial sector based on the fact
that they provide employment and bring in foreign exchange.[18] A
simplistic way of understanding this problem would be to think of the
merchants in Jordan as importers and the industrialists as exporters.
In a country that has depended heavily on customs duties for its
domestic revenues and experienced pressures to protect national
industry, the contradictions should be obvious.

However, it would also be inaccurate to conclude that the two
major branches of the private sector—merchants and industrialists—
are internally unified in their interests and demands. For example,

among the industrialists there are those who concentrate on the Jordanian market while others are export-oriented. Beyond this, because of the country's paucity of resources, most of Jordan's industrialists are also importers of most of the raw materials needed for their industry. Moreover, if one takes concrete examples, family or economic interests cut across sectoral divisions. Many families first made their money in commerce and then used the profits to open industries. Thus, even within families, there have been conflicts of interest.[19]

Interviewees also mentioned that private sector members have not always been clear on where their interests lie. The implication was that their understanding of the market and the country's economic system was not sufficiently sophisticated as to allow them to determine their interests vis-à-vis a certain policy, much less formulate plans to achieve them. This also appears to be changing gradually. More and more of Jordan's businessmen are college graduates, many of them from the U.S. or Europe, and are therefore much better equipped to identify and lobby for their interests.

A related problem is that of the existing institutional structures themselves. Members of the two chambers join the same councils, sit on the same boards, and, according to interviewees, usually have a clash of interests. Even in ad hoc meetings to contest a certain government policy, representatives of the two often clash. Moreover, within the chambers themselves, while democracy may work on the board of directors, the directors view themselves as a distinct or elite group among their peers. Some believe this elite would view a fuller development of the chambers' infrastructures as a threat to its authority.[20]

A further problem is the state sector perception of the private sector. State sector employees tend to view private businessmen as selfish and unconcerned with the national interest. Moreover, as early as the 1950s, the private sector was largely a merchant sector that had already developed a dependence on the state. As one official explained, "the government would receive aid, it would spend the aid, and the traders would import. They made their calculations based on how much the government would be spending": that is, they waited to see which sectors would be targeted by government spending and then moved their activities in that direction. As a result the sector became "parasitic," heavily dependent upon implementing government-commissioned projects.[21] Finally, government bureaucrats reportedly treat the private sector as if it were a single unit (despite the obvious contradictions and divisions mentioned above), and do not want to deal with it unless it is united, which is virtually impossible.[22] Consequently, private sector influence was likely to be substantial only if there was a confluence of interests among a number of groups, so that a kind of "ganging up" process took place.

The Palestinian/East Bank division of labor has also hurt the private sector. According to interviewees, a Palestinian businessman with a problem would have been unlikely to receive sympathy or assistance from the Transjordanian bureaucrat with whom he dealt. According to interviews, at times, there was almost a perverse pleasure taken in private sector problems or losses. This began to change in the 1980s, however, as many Transjordanians joined the business community and began to feel more directly the problems with the bureaucracy.

More serious perhaps is the degree of seeming autonomy exercised by government bureaucrats, to be discussed further in the next section. Interviewees, whether public or private sector, were unanimous in their assessment that the bureaucracy was reluctant to surrender any of its authority. It therefore serves as a brake on, if not a complete obstacle to, many changes the private sector would like to see implemented. One prominent interviewee noted that some bureaucrats had openly admitted their fears that changes or reforms in procedures might jeopardize their jobs.[23] Mid-and lower-level managers rely on the gifts and bribes they derive from their role or interference in business. Hence, policies that threaten to undercut their position are likely to be opposed.[24]

Related to this problem is that ministers generally cannot force mid-to lower-levels of the bureaucracy to act. One can go to the crown prince and present a problem, and he may then raise the issue with the relevant minister. However, that will often be the end of the story because ministers can only rarely guarantee that decisions will be implemented. One interviewee said that while he did not question the sincerity of various ministers or their understanding of policies, he nevertheless doubted their political authority and their ability to bring the bureaucracy to heel.[25] Compounding this problem is the fact that although Jordan has long had a civil service system, some ministers, nonetheless have tended to appoint people from their own town or village, without regard for talent or qualifications. Hence, often there is little understanding of what needs to be accomplished in a particular job.

Another more general problem is that the government has in effect over the years "trained" Jordanians, not to challenge it, but to depend on it for a whole range of services.[26] The phenomenon of the "parasitic" private sector has already been noted. However, part of the explanation for private sector inactivity must be attributed to years of martial law (1957–1990) and political repression. In a situation in which complaints were often (mis)read, whether deliberately or not, as potential assaults upon the security of the state, few people had the courage or the power to speak out. Such an atmosphere is hardly conducive to open and effective expressions of discontent, preferences, or challenging initiatives.

Finally, and this problem is perhaps most significant for the argument of this book, the size of the private sector's contribution to the economy, as well as its dependence upon the state for a good deal of its activity, have not given it much bargaining power vis-à-vis the state. If one looks at the GDP figures, one finds that the real productive sectors of the economy—phosphate, potash, fertilizer, and cement—are public sector companies. Another major chunk of GDP is contributed by the bureaucracies.[27] Add to this the "ethnic division of labor" overlay, (Palestinians vs. Transjordanians) with its security considerations, both domestic and external, and one has yet another reason why the state might exhibit little interest in most private sector concerns.

Is one then to conclude that the private sector exercises minimal influence over government policy? A degree of caution is still in order, but all indicators point to a "yes" response, if one means influence by large numbers of people and/or through institutionalized channels. Private sector influence, however, does appear to have been irregularly exercised on an individual and ad hoc basis. This personalized style of business and politics is the norm in Jordan, a

family- and tribally-organized country where everyone knows virtually everyone else. The rather small group of decisionmakers is bound
by a network of family, school, regional, or business ties. This form of
articulation of interests does not give coherent voice to a particular
sector; however, it is not at all difficult for certain, select businessmen
to gain the ear of the relevant minister, or even the crown prince or
the king, as individuals.[28]

   That said, it would be wrong to leave the impression that private
businessmen in Jordan constitute a sector repressed and under siege,
despite the many criticisms of state financial and economic policy
they may express. Red tape and bureaucratic inertia are certainly
facts of life; nevertheless, Jordan has a substantial stratum of successful businessmen, who are aware that part of the reason for their success lies not only in the availability of contracts from the state, but
also in the relatively stable domestic climate that the state provided
during the years of authoritarian rule and martial law. Moreover, as
three of the case studies demonstrate, when the very health of the
private sector was at stake in the early 1980s, the state initiated a policy of export credits to Iraq in addition to making overtures to
expand trade ties with both Syria and Egypt. It is unlikely that the
impetus for such policies would have come from anywhere but the
private sector, even if the concerns were not articulated in formal
form through the Chambers of Commerce or Industry.

Assessing a State-Centered Approach

The previous section has argued that while individual businessmen
do have access to top economic decisionmakers, societal or economic sectors do not play a clear and consistent role in articulating
or advocating their interests as part of the economic policymaking
process. Part of the explanation for this situation was demonstrated to be the role played by certain levels of the state bureaucracy.
The next step is to examine state institutions and official policymakers to determine whether a state-centered approach provides a
better framework for understanding how economic policy is made
in Jordan. The discussion here proceeds from top to bottom of the

hierarchy, beginning with the palace and ending with the state bureaucracy.

The Palace and the Cabinet

As one former top policymaker stated unequivocally in response to a question regarding the foreign policymaking process, "over the last four decades there has been only one ruler in Jordan." In the absence of democracy, decisions have been those of the king, often in conjunction with several key advisers. On issues of foreign policy the king, the crown prince, the prime minister, and the chief of the royal court are the decisionmaking circle. The cabinet, as a body, is not involved, although its members may be consulted for their reactions or comments.[29]

Interviewees for this study indicated that the king himself is not particularly interested in economic matters, certainly not in details. He rarely has an economic briefing. However, when he does, he reportedly focuses primarily on issues related to the military budget. Former Labor Minister Jawad 'Anani contended that in foreign policy, the major goal was to secure aid for the budget and to finance the military. In addition, always present, even primary, in the king's calculations are the sociopolitical underpinnings of the regime—the Transjordanian/Palestinian divide mentioned at the beginning of the chapter. The king has periodic meetings with the leaders of the kingdom's important tribes, often in connection with state support. In the case of the budget, the king's uppermost concern has been paying the salaries of the army and the security apparatus, whose members have traditionally been largely recruited from these tribes and who have long been regarded as the bedrock of support for the monarchy. In this case, the role of societal factors has been greater than the previous section would have suggested.[30]

The "how" questions related to the economy have generally been handled by Crown Prince Hasan and, to a lesser extent, the prime minister.[31] This is clear, not only from the testimony of those involved in the process, but also from the content of public statements and the type of events in which he participates. For example, the crown prince is much more likely to be involved in a conference on development or give a speech on the importance of Jordan's regional economic role than the king. A number of interviewees credited the crown prince for taking a special interest in and encouraging industry, for example.[32] But his influence extends even further, for whenever the crown prince attends a meeting, the other relevant ministers also feel obliged to attend, which is not necessarily the case otherwise. The role of the prime minister was also described as key, but his input varies depending upon the political or economic conditions at any given time. For example, at the time of the first round of interviews for this study (fall 1991) Prime Minister Tahir al-Masri, although an economist by training, was absorbed in the Madrid peace conference and was therefore not available to deal with domestic economic issues.

Beyond these three figures—the king, the crown prince, and the prime minister—the economic decisionmaking group differs from the foreign policy group. The king has certain advisers and confidants both within and outside government whose friendship and proximity give them access, and hence, the opportunity to lobby for certain policies. The king is described as an arbiter by nature, preferring not to interfere in policy details. However, if a complaint is voiced frequently enough—either by officials or by nonofficial confidants—he will likely come to view it as a general problem. He may then draw the cabinet's attention to it and if it is not solved, may replace the relevant minister.[33] However, for *domestic* economic matters to have an influence on upper level decisionmaking they must be of real consequence—large loans, the devaluation of the dinar, and the like—so as to sweep consideration of them up to the highest levels.[34]

The Economic Security Committee

One key factor that affected the development of the economy and the process of economic decisionmaking in the kingdom was the presence of a martial law regime during most of the 1957–1990 period. While a complete analysis of the role of martial law in state economic and political development is the topic for another book, it is important to keep in mind as one considers the decisionmaking process, the participants in it, and the access and influence of those not officially a part of policymaking bodies.

Symptomatic of the conditions that existed under martial law were the establishment, development, and activities of what was called the Economic Security Committee (ESC). This body was originally founded in 1967 at the suggestion of Central Bank Governor Dr. Khalil al-Salim to address the economic problems created by the occupation of the West Bank. With martial law already in place giving the state sweeping powers, adding such a committee seemed like a natural step.[35] Composed of the Minister of Finance, the Minister of Trade and Industry, the Minister of Transport, and the Governor of the Central Bank, and standing in effect above or outside the law, the committee initially served to help solve problems faced especially by the government and some of the public companies and institutions. For example, how was one to deal with a situation in which a meeting of the board of directors of a company was to be held, but the occupation prevented the gathering of a quorum? Or, what did one do with the bank deposits on the East Bank of those living under occupation, or vice versa?

Hence, for issues about which Jordanian law was deficient, the ESC's activities were critical. Gradually, however, the committee's "mandate" broadened. It began to act as a kind of extraordinary legislative council, since the legislature itself was largely inoperative after 1967 and then suspended in 1974. The committee was permitted to make decisions that overturned existing laws, even those that had been passed *after* the occupation and that had taken the post-June 1967 reality into account. In this way, the committee came to be used to bypass existing law when it was problematic or inconvenient from the point of view of the decisionmakers or their confidants. For example, if the prime minister wanted something done quickly or something done that was officially illegal, he could refer it to the committee. The committee also made decisions about liquidating companies, borrowing to the ceiling of the Central Bank and then legalizing more borrowing, allowing the Central Bank to deposit with other banks to support the currency, issuing more currency than had been permitted, evicting people from commercial establishments, and allowing someone who would otherwise have been forbidden, to sit on the board of directors of a company.[36] In the days of increasing political repression in 1988, its decisions also dissolved the boards of a number of public shareholding companies including those of the major daily newspapers.

Many of the rulings the committee made are open to criticism, not only on legal grounds, but also on economic and financial ones. Some of its decisions were intended to benefit a particular person, company or bank, to enable them to undertake an activity that was against the law, or to avoid procedures dictated by the law.[37] Moreover, only a few of the ESC's decisions were ever published in the *Official Gazette*, the newspaper in which all legislation is supposed to appear. Most were confidential, and for specific purposes; they were usually not general edicts. Economic columnist Fahd al-Fanek noted that he had once criticized an accounting firm for its evaluation of government accounts, charging that the JD reserve level was below what it should have been by law. The company made a variety of excuses, but no action was taken. Fanek later discovered that the ESC had passed an unpublished decree allowing for a lower JD reserve level.[38]

Perhaps the most damaging step approved by the committee was that of allowing the ceiling on export credits to Iraq to be raised in the mid-1980s, an issue discussed in detail in the chapter on Jordanian-Iraqi relations.[39] The resultant problems Jordan had with Iraq over this issue were at least in part responsible for the plunge of the dinar in 1988 and the country's subsequent economic woes. Thus a number of the committee's edicts came to jeopardize the very economic security the committee was originally founded, at least in name, to uphold.

Comprising only a handful of ex officio cabinet members who were chosen by the prime minister in consultation with the king, the ESC appears to have been the institutionalized form of an inner circle for economic policy. With the king, by all reports, concerned with only the very highest level of exchange, budgetary grants and military assistance, it seems likely that most of the rest of state economic policy was left in the hands of this group of men. Their power derived from both the cabinet positions they held and their closeness to the king and the prime minister at the time, to whom they owed their appointment. It is therefore probably to this group (and their supporters or allies outside the committee) that one can trace ideas for foreign economic policy initiatives. Their involvement in lowering the JD reserves level would certainly suggest such a role, and they were probably also the impetus behind the efforts to reinvigorate trade ties with Syria and Egypt in 1983, which we will examine later in the case studies. In retrospect, this was probably the most important economic decisionmaking body during the period under study.

The Role of the Ministers

The type of regime that produces and perpetuates an institution such as the ESC is clearly one that is uninterested in or incapable of decentralizing decisionmaking. And, indeed, even for what would appear to be relatively minor matters, economic decisionmaking is highly centralized in the kingdom. Most decisions—whether important or relatively minor—are made at the cabinet level or even above, not even at the level of individual ministers. For example, in 1983 a new set of regulations regarding business and contracting was promulgated. From then on, the *prime minister's* office, not the relevant minister or undersecretary, was to make the final decision on the award of all contracts over JD 4 million.[40] Another example of this extreme centralization may be found in the content of a memorandum of complaint and a meeting held between members of the Chamber of Commerce and the prime minister on March 24, 1986. The complaint concerned difficulties faced by businessmen, including, specifically, the increase in customs on wall-to-wall carpeting, shoes, and refrigerators. As a result of that meeting the *prime minister* himself ordered the customs tariff on *rugs* to be adjusted by 50 percent.[41]

Part of the reason for the lack of ministerial involvement is that ministerial appointments in Jordan generally owe to considerations of domestic political balancing along ethnic and regional lines. All cabinets must meet certain unofficial but well-known formulae. As a result, most ministers are appointed because of ethnicity, tribal/family background, or regional provenance, not because of expertise in the field of their appointment, although there are certainly numerous notable exceptions. In such a system, where a minister's background in his/her field has generally been only a secondary consideration, a minister's power derives from a number of sources. The first is the degree of support s/he enjoys from the prime minister. The prime minister is appointed by the king and the cabinet ministers by the prime minister. They therefore have no automatic political base in the parliament or outside, as would be the case in a normal parliamentary system. Beyond his or her ties with the decision-making group, a minister's power is often determined by such factors as the degree to which s/he has developed ties in the bureaucracy (both within his or her own ministry and elsewhere), and his/her own energy and involvement. If the minister is somewhat detached, or not active at the cabinet level, then it is unlikely s/he can accomplish very much. Another source of power lies in the ministry itself. For example, the Ministry of Finance is potentially very powerful, since it includes the customs bureau, the income tax bureau, the budget, and the land and surveys bureau—all the departments responsible for domestic revenue.[42]

At least part of the problem with ensuring implementation below the cabinet level is that many individual ministers prefer not to take responsibility, opting to leave certain issues to the cabinet.[43] If that is the case at the level of minister, one can imagine what happens (or does not happen) at lower levels. As is the case for bureaucrats everywhere, there is no incentive (and in this case, also no authority) to make decisions without prior approval from above, even on very minor matters. The same holds true for the joint economic committees established between Jordan and most Arab states, discussed in detail in the case studies. With the exception of the ministers, the members are mere bureaucrats. If the relevant minister does not take an interest in solving a problem, no action will be taken. In general, then, because of the lack of authority to make decisions there is little or no follow-up.[44]

In addition to the issue of authority and responsibility is the problem of the lack of a guiding program or policy. In more general terms, however, one reason for the lack of a coherent policy is that there have not been political parties steering the government. The appointment of the prime minister has always been the king's prerogative, not a response to election results, even since the political liberalization of 1989. One can point to instances in which the economy played a role in the appointment of a prime minister, as in the dismissal of 'Ubaydat and his replacement by Rifa'i in 1985, but neither could be said to represent a coherent economic and/or political program. Ministers or prime ministers may be known for a series of actions, but there generally is not a particular philosophy in their statements or speeches.[45] As a result they often loose sight of the larger picture. Nor do ministers generally resign in protest over a particular policy.[46] More often, ministers "are resigned" for causing a problem, failing to resolve an issue, or for reasons of domestic political jockeying.

While some interviewees agreed that ministerial changes are disruptive, given the lack of a program, it is not necessarily the case that a change in minister will mean a complete change in the ministry. After all, the other mid- and lower-level bureaucrats remain in place. Instead, the change of ministers will often mean that projects in which the former minister was involved may simply be set aside as the new minister begins to establish his own priorities.[47]

The Parliament

Traditionally, Jordan's parliament was largely a rubber-stamp institution with little effective voice in policymaking. Moreover, during part of the period under study, the parliament was suspended (1974–1984), and a group of reduced size, the National Consultative Council appointed by the king, operated in lieu of a legislative body. Even when parliament was operative, the ban on political parties imposed in 1957 meant that there were no organized political groups to represent popular interests. The closest approximation to such institutions were professional associations—the unions of doctors, lawyers, engineers, and the like. They did hold their own elections and played an indirect political role.[48] However, as we have seen, the two official representatives of the private sector, the chambers of commerce and industry, appear not to have played such a role.

With the beginning of political liberalization, businessmen expressed optimism that the way would finally be open for them to voice their interests more effectively, and organizations such as the Free Liberals and the Group of 70 began to coalesce around vague business interests.[49] However, for a variety of reasons these organizations were apparently stillborn. At the time of this writing, none of the more than twenty registered political parties could be said to represent business interests, nor is there even a loose coalition or bloc in parliament associated with private sector concerns. The parliament as it now stands, and certainly as it stood in the past, reflects largely religious, tribal, or regional interests. In the 1989 elections, for example, some of the most powerful industrialists who ran for parliament did not win seats. Those who did, however, were victorious, not because of their business ties, but primarily because of their tribal or family affiliation.[50] In the 1993 elections, tribal affiliations were even more salient. Only in the wake of the 1993 elections was it announced that a new organization, the Arab Common Market Party, would soon be established specifically to articulate the interests of the business community.

The Bureaucracy

Businessmen and former ministers alike noted the obstructive role often played by members of the bureaucracy. The avoidance of responsibility by mid-and lower-level bureaucrats was mentioned earlier. In addition, bureaucrats are generally without job descriptions or instruction manuals and often have little idea what they are supposed to accomplish. However, also key to understanding the role of the bureaucracy in the policymaking and implementing process is the Transjordanian/Palestinian demographic divide discussed earlier. Transjordanian employment in the bureaucracy both symbolically and concretely embodies East Banker economic and political solidarity against the potential dominance of the Palestinians. In effect, they view themselves as protectors of the system (and the public sector in particular) against political change of most any sort. As noted in the previous section, there is a general suspicion of the private sector. Therefore, proposed economic reforms must not be seen to benefit business at the expense of the public sector, which accounts for nearly 50 percent of the country's employment (150,000 strong civil service, and 150,000-strong military) and is continually working to protect its interests. It has traditionally advocated greater state intervention and has been skeptical, if not fearful, of the idea of administrative or bureaucratic reform. Its members, most of whom are from the middle and lower classes, are dependent upon their salaries from the government and generally have no other options for employment.[51]

One example of the obstructionist role bureaucrats may play may be found in the case of the drafting of Law 219 of January 1, 1989, The Companies Law (Temporary). The private sector had been consulted on the text of the law, which contained many positive elements from its point of view. However, when the law was finally promulgated, it also included a provision that companies were not to be permitted to keep profits for reinvestment. For a state that claimed it wanted to encourage private sector investment, this was certainly a strong disincentive to the potential investor. The provision was reportedly the result of the influence of "one or two individuals" with more of a socialist than a free market orientation, who wanted to make sure that the profits were divided among the shareholders. Thus, despite the input of the private sector, bureaucratic intervention in the latter stages of the drafting of the legislation led to the inclusion of a very damaging provision.[52]

Hence, while an examination of the empirical evidence suggests that state institutions and officials below the cabinet level play little role in economic policy *making*, they nonetheless can play a key and often obstructive role in implementation or follow-up. Rather than acting in a specifically and state-leadership defined "national interest" mid-level bureaucrats seem frequently to have behaved in a very self-interested way, aimed at preserving the role and importance of their jobs. This is a key modification to the state-centered approach which views these actors as being "above politics." Indeed, their input in pursuit of their interests, seems to have had a more consistent impact on implementation than the efforts of the private sector.

Private Sector Input vs. State Direction and Control: Development Planning and Foreign Trade

Before concluding this chapter, two specific aspects of the economic policymaking process will be examined briefly to illustrate further the contrast between private sector initiative and the role of the state. Planning was chosen because of the apparently important role it plays in determining state development and investment priorities and because of the degree of institutionalized private sector input, while foreign trade is examined because of its importance to external economic relations, a critical subject of the case studies.

Planning

Planning was initiated in the kingdom in 1957 with the establishment of a Reconstruction Council attached directly to the prime ministry and composed of the prime minister and ten members, including representatives (not ministers) of economic ministries and the private sector. In 1962 the council was reconstituted to include three members of the private sector, the governor of the Central Bank and the general director of the Agricultural Loan Corporation, while the representation of the ministries was raised to the deputy minister level.[53] Economic planning began as a kind of investment plan, since the free market nature of the Jordanian economy gave the state little control over private sector activity and investment. Since it was not possible to force goals or enforce targets on the private sector, planning was therefore mostly a public sector exercise. The investment plan initially consisted of a project list and emphasized project implementation.[54]

As time went on, the process gradually developed toward more comprehensive planning in the form of an economic and social plan. In 1971, the Reconstruction Council was renamed the National Planning Council and was reorganized internally and administratively into seven sectoral departments, each of which had representatives from the ministries, as well as government and private institu-

tions. Each department was charged with studying sectoral development programs and projects, working to coordinate them in a comprehensive plan, and then monitoring and evaluating the programs
after they were selected. Particularly after the beginning of the civil
war in Lebanon, some policymakers in Jordan began to express the
belief that the country could assume Lebanon's regional role, but
that it needed a great deal of infrastructure and investment to do so.
Subsequently, planning began to include longer term goals related
to phosphates, fertilizers, and potash plants, road networks, sewage,
communications, and water networks.[55] One significant result of the
dramatic increase in state investment was a rapid expansion of the
public sector and of external debt. Consequently, as the planning
goals grew more complex, in 1984 the National Planning Council
was upgraded to the Ministry of Planning.

The various stages involved in the planning process are planning,
funding, implementation, monitoring, and evaluation. First, input
from the various concerned groups is taken at the sectoral level to
give the planners a sense of what they are working with. This input is
then passed on to the committee level, just below the level of the
prime minister. There is also input from the governorate and program level, (the next two levels below the committee level). The Ministry of Planning also conducts broad economic surveys or studies
and sends them to the prime minister for evaluation. The input and
revision process is interactive, consisting of several steps that involve
correction and re-correction. However, at this stage the very real and
critical constraints (almost always financial) become apparent, and
in the end, national priorities overcome local ones, thus dampening
the effect of local input.[56]

In addition to the participation of a few members of the private
sector on the planning council, as early as 1972–75, university pro-
fessors became involved in the process. Gradually, they participated
in what amounted to brainstorming sessions, although the actual calculations and linear programming were conducted by a local consulting firm. By the time of the 1986 plan, the outside consultations
were the most extensive to date, probably because of the regional
economic downturn and the government's belief that increasingly
hard choices required at least the semblance of involvement of the

public in decisionmaking. The general committee that formulated the plan included 400 people—representatives from the various governorates and most major economic and social constituencies—and the discussions were held at the universities: Jordan, Yarmuk, JUST (Jordan University of Science and Technology), and Mu'tah. The crown prince also made a point of visiting the governorates to look into implementation and coordination of activities for this plan.

As for the role of other ministries in the process, until the early 1980s, the role of the Ministry of Finance, for example, was secondary, as it was concerned with incoming revenues, not with soliciting funds or with determining how the revenues were to be spent. Planning was more concerned with finance and development. According to former National Planning Council head and former Finance Minister 'Awdah's account, symptomatic of the problems he and other technocrats faced upon assuming the finance portfolio was that there was the lack of a unified repository of information on the country's indebtedness: some figures were available at the Ministry of Planning and some at the Central Bank, but the Ministry of Finance itself had very little information on Jordan's indebtedness.[57]

What then of planning's accomplishments? Neither policies nor economic planning were pursued consistently: this point was stressed repeatedly and almost universally in interviews. Perhaps not surprisingly, then, even those involved in the process described planning as having had very little to do with past economic or development achievements. What accounted for the successes, primarily of the 1960s and 1970s, for better or for worse, were factors largely beyond Jordan's control: external aid, high levels of remittances, the regional oil boom, and so on. People often bragged that the economy had outperformed expectations, but as one key official noted, "in the planning process, understating is just as bad as overstating."[58]

However, as noted above, bureaucratic organization or lack thereof, as well as problems in government accounting methods, have led to unrealistic assessments of funds and costs. Here, two examples should suffice as illustrations. Officials in the Ministry of Finance used to treat foreign loans as *revenue*, not as financing to be repaid. Second, the budgets of the autonomous public institutions (among them the Ports Corporation, the Jordan Valley Authority, and the

Telecommunications Corporation) were not reflected in the central government budget: in some cases, only the subsidy or the support was included, not the full cost.[59]

Hence, while the planning process has over the years increasingly drawn on the expertise of diverse groups of people outside of government, its influence on the economic direction of the country seems quite limited. General economic policy lines, to the degree that they are set and clear—and most of those interviewed contended they were not—are formulated at the top, not in the course of the planning process. Moreover, Jordan's plans have generally been little more than statements of intent or wish lists, sometimes achieved, but often not, because of the nature of the domestic economy and because of bureaucratic inefficiencies that plagued planning as well as other ministries.

Foreign Trade

How is decisionmaking carried out in Jordan's bilateral economic relations with its Arab neighbors? In the first place, as one might suspect from the discussion above, decisionmaking is conducted at the cabinet level or above. The Ministry of Planning, for instance, does not become involved in the details of trade. General guidelines may be set to the effect that the country needs to promote exports or to diversify. (For trade statistics for the period under study, see Tables 7 and 8.) However, guidelines have never been more specific than that. The five-year plans may discuss individual commodities or the need to expand markets, and at the end of the plans there are calls for specific projects, but prescriptions for particular countries are not included.[60]

It is the Ministry of Trade and Supply (which is the heir to, with the same terms of reference as, the Ministry of the National Economy) that monitors developments in bilateral trade. As part of its efforts to implement trade policy the ministry joined with other institutions such as the Chamber of Industry to establish the Jordan Trade Centers Corporation, a government institution with some private sector backing, which promotes and oversees the workings of

TABLE 7
Jordan's Imports From . . . (in JDs)[1]

Year	Syria	Saudi Arabia	Iraq	Kuwait	Egypt	Total Imports
1973	7,799,513	3,427,263	866,919	187,002	2,753,855	108,200,000
1974	5,806,531	3,692,830	875,647	446,556	7,108,136	156,507,000
1975	6,509,033	22,905,711	698,016	578,121	6,241,839	234,013,000
1976	7,449,687	34,449,550	756,789	386,368	9,675,052	339,539,000
1977	11,096,607	37,144,194	756,415	646,295	9,589,201	454,417,000
1978	11,930,407	43,448,742	1,115,716	991,116	8,544,913	458,826,000
1979	11,427,320	69,141,410	1,892,743	723,763	9,450,090	589,523,000
1980	10,475,485	114,123,661	2,174,155	605,011	4,818,580	715,977,000
1981	12,506,305	175,783,719	762,539	517,297	3,502,013	1,047,504,000
1982	10,404,172	233,475,244	982,390	1,046,358	4,608,545	1,142,493,000
1983	16,955,768	210,963,256	4,778,831	764,684	4,609,462	1,103,310,000
1984	7,341,802	208,773,508	6,001,801	3,333,164	6,628,065	1,071,340,000
1985	5,892,969	159,058,051	72,950,931	2,893,059	4,315,380	1,074,445,000
1986	10,198,874	49,669,994	80,273,805	2,400,106	9,166,093	850,199,000
1987	8,652,203	76,761,231	99,400,613	16,956,448	9,621,725	915,545,000
1988	9,768,212	74,291,073	117,367,429	22,956,448	9,742,925	1,022,469,000
1989	19,526,000	31,983,000	212,661,000	29,782,000	18,455,000	

[1] For dollar exchange equivalents, see Appendix 1.

SOURCE: HKJ *Annual Statistical Abstract*, selected years.

TABLE 8

Jordan's Exports to . . . (in JDs)[1]

Year	Syria	Saudi Arabia	Iraq	Kuwait	Egypt	Total Exports
1973	2,585,233	2,560,000	1,007,701	1,572,716	443,857	14,010,000
1974	2,873,562	5,540,362	1,616,654	2,277,265	1,259,884	39,437,000
1975	3,674,043	4,761,035	2,450,238	2,393,816	1,034,782	40,075,000
1976	6,392,263	7,466,438	2,327,505	3,281,512	1,186,525	49,552,000
1977	7,541,718	15,090,517	4,303,586	2,795,955	1,070,047	60,253,000
1978	10,425,425	17,695,224	3,445,489	4,210,777	1,584,089	64,129,000
1979	12,264,133	19,371,780	12,719,029	4,436,540	194,144	82,556,000
1980	13,618,570	19,717,779	28,347,329	5,342,815	2,665	120,107,000
1981	10,760,016	20,881,894	63,471,888	6,812,526	16,750	169,026,000
1982	8,396,344	27,625,470	66,579,811	6,726,365	39,225	185,581,000
1983	3,566,530	35,212,476	26,010,854	10,453,555	15,165	160,085,000
1984	2,912,258	38,658,795	67,754,939	10,393,416	309,853	261,055,000
1985	3,900,976	39,083,460	65,850,384	7,734,298	3,032,916	255,346,000
1986	4,570,193	27,817,046	42,457,559	8,812,631	3,978,563	225,615,000
1987	7,201,379	26,204,464	59,865,417	8,613,109	13,447,840	248,773,000
1988	3,289,930	31,430,235	64,690,445	9,399,231	7,199,654	324,788,000
1989	7,983,000	47,712,000	123,936,000	15,503,000	10,754,000	
1990	8,415,000	46,815,000	118,544,000	11,056,000	10,622,000	

[1] For dollar exchange equivalents, see Appendix 1.

SOURCE: *HKJ Annual Statistical Abstract,* selected years.

Jordanian trade centers in other countries. The Ministry of Trade and Industry signs the bilateral trade protocols, but thereafter it is the Trade Centers Corporation that determines the commodities to be put on individual country lists, the accounts, and is then responsible for follow-up.[61]

In the case study countries examined in this work, general economic agreements and/or joint committees govern relations. While the joint committees meet regularly during periods of good political relations, final decisions have rarely been worked out at these meetings. Most often the decisions are first made at a higher level or are referred back to this level at home before new commitments are made.[62] Nevertheless, the joint economic committees have played a number of important roles. First, they have provided a framework for discussions and decisions furthering Arab economic (if not political) integration. It was for this reason that they were launched, at least from the Jordanian perspective.[63] Second, the joint committees work to ensure more or larger markets for Jordanian products. Finally, they are a means of obtaining needed inputs for the production process in Jordan.[64]

How successful have these committees been? Their workings and accomplishments are detailed in the case studies. However, a few general comments are in order here. A common refrain heard from those involved was that they had achieved very little or at least, far less than could have been the case, largely for reasons related to the state of bilateral political relations, a proposition considered in the case studies. A further argument is that there has been no follow-up to committee recommendations, which is the responsibility of the relevant ministries. It is here that implementation often breaks down.[65] The Jordanian bureaucracy has served as an obstacle or at best as a nonfacilitator on the level of implementation of the agreements of the joint committees. Obstruction as a means of preserving perceived interests has been discussed above. However, it was also suggested that individual bureaucrats may not be experienced enough to understand the importance of the relations and the proposals involved. Moreover, bilateral relations may not have developed to a point where vested sectoral or regional interests lobby for particular policies.[66] Or, as the examination of the role of the private sector indicated above, domestic sectoral interests have probably not developed sufficient coherence or organization to lobby for their interests.

Despite the efforts of the joint committees to expand markets for Jordanian goods, the private sector also has its complaints about the bilateral agreements. The primary criticism is that they eliminate competition, for they work in the following way. The committee sets levels of imports and exports in addition to specifying which will enjoy tariff reductions or be tariff-free. Any product not listed in the agreements is then difficult to trade because the merchant cannot obtain the same exemptions. As a result, through individual lobbying, merchants compete so that their product(s) will be included in the product list of the agreement. This process makes the private sector largely dependent on the government in the realm of inter-Arab trade,[67] although critics of the private sector contend that they have accepted this reliance on the government and undertake few independent initiatives to find markets.

These arguments and others will be examined in the course of the case studies. At this point the most salient point is that the state has played the leading role in the development of bilateral trade. The private sector's activity, at least until the beginning of economic and political liberalization in 1989, has been largely reactive rather than proactive. It has often waited (or been forced to wait) for agreements to be concluded by the government, and then had its input in the form of individual or small group lobbying for the inclusion of a particular product on a bilateral exchange agreement list. Again, neither the experience of planning or bilateral trade argues for the existence or operation in Jordan of coherent societal (non-state) articulators of economic interests.

Conclusions

Jordan's strategic significance to a range of actors led not only to its initial establishment as a modern state, but also to its continuing ability to draw on that range of actors for substantial support in the form of grants-in-aid for the military, the bureaucracy, and development as well as a host of concessional loans and other forms of budgetary assistance through the years. Whether as a result of inertia, lack of experience, or conscious policy choice based on evaluation of domestic political and economic trade-offs, in its early decades (outside the realm of this study) the state leadership appears to have been content to develop a heavy reliance on external sources of support rather than choosing to push more actively for expansion of the domestic productive base.

The state therefore gradually evolved as primarily a distributor or an allocator (of the rents collected from outside) rather than an extractor of resources from within.[68] Arguably, the longer this relationship between state and citizen continued, the more set people's expectations of the state's distributive role were and the more difficult breaking such a pattern or attempting to encourage new patterns became. What also appears to have developed through the emergence of the allocator-recipient relationship is a degree of state autonomy from the citizenry, both in the realm of economic and political decisionmaking. Although martial law and its many constraints was clearly a key factor in discouraging demands for popular input into decisionmaking processes, as long as the state was "providing for its own" through distribution of rents from abroad, dissatisfaction was less likely to have been expressed.

Given such a pattern of development, not only did the state enjoy relative autonomy from the input of societal forces, as the case study chapters will now demonstrate, it also made or had to make as a primary, conscious focus of its foreign policy, the collection of funds that enabled it to continue to play its allocative role, a role that underpinned the regime itself. Therefore, economic policymaking during most of the period under study, certainly when it concerned external issues, but also to a large extent when the realm was the domestic, was the preserve of a handful of decisionmakers whose primary focus was securing state revenue sources and finessing or overcoming economic constraints so that the distributive policies, particularly those that affected the critical military and security bureaucracies, could continue. The state-centered approach outlined at the beginning of the chapter emphasized the influence of state *political* structures and institutions as critical to shaping *economic* decisionmaking. The argument made here builds on this approach but is somewhat different. Here it is argued that the nature of the Jordanian *economy*, especially the structure or composition of state revenues, played a key, and frequently the decisive, role in influencing the course of Jordan's *foreign policy*.

PART TWO
The Case Studies

3

Jordanian-Saudi Relations

The early years of Jordanian-Saudi ties certainly offered no indications that the relationship would eventually develop into Amman's most important Arab source of financial support. In the "pre-state" period, the House of Sa'ud (of the Najd region) and the House of Hashem (of the Hijaz area) were bitter rivals for power within the Arabian peninsula itself. In the military conflict that ensued, the Hashemites were driven from the Hijaz as Ibn Sa'ud's men secured the territory for what became the Kingdom of Saudi Arabia. Ever since, the Saudi ruling family has suspected Jordan's Hashemites of harboring irredentist claims. Beyond that, however, they must live with the fact while they control the holy cities of Mecca and Medina, it is the Hashemites who trace their lineage to the prophet Muhammad, thus giving Jordan's ruling family a place of respect and honor in Arab and Islamic circles to which the Al Sa'ud can never aspire.

Despite the conflictual beginnings, intersections of interests eventually improved bilateral relations. Saudi Arabia's first open offer of support to Jordan accompanied similar promises from Syria and Egypt in 1955 to encourage King Husayn not to join the Western-sponsored Baghdad Pact. The Saudis also committed brigades to Jordan in 1956 (Suez), 1957 (following the coup attempt) and 1967 (the June war) as a form of moral or political support for the regime. As Saudi oil wealth increased, the financial dimension of the relationship developed even further. Following the 1967 war and again in 1974, Saudi Arabia (among other Arab states) promised budgetary assistance to Jordan. Officially, this aid was intended to help Jordan, as a confrontation state, counter the Israeli threat; however, the money was intended to buy security from Arab threats as well. Even as early as the 1950s Jordan had come to constitute a security belt for the Saudis, and it continued to serve as a buffer between the conservative peninsular states and the various revolutionary or pan-Arab political currents that swept the Arab East in successive decades. Jordan also worked to prevent arms and drugs smuggled from Lebanon, Syria, and Iran from reaching Saudi Arabia. In addition, the development of the Saudi state and economy required a skilled labor force that Riyadh lacked. In response, tens of thousands of Jordanians, most of them Palestinians, were recruited by or found work in the kingdom, whether in the public or private sector. The migration of Jordanian workers to Saudi Arabia decreased unemployment pressures at home and added substantial foreign currency remittances to the Jordanian economy.

The empirical evidence in this chapter supports the argument that a critical basis of the bilateral relationship for the Jordanians was Saudi budgetary support to help underwrite Jordanian domestic security. For its part, Riyadh provided this substantial economic assistance to Amman for both developmental and military purposes because a stable Jordan was viewed as key to Saudi security as well. "In exchange," the Jordanians provided a variety of military and intelligence services that reinforced Saudi security.

The pre-1990 period witnessed no changes in alignment between these two conservative, pro-Western monarchies. While there were instances of disagreement, given the strong Saudi predisposition not to air inter-Arab disputes in public, some, perhaps many, went without published indication or report. In any case, given the budget security argument, one would expect Jordan to be intent upon preserving its ties with its most important regional patron. The only truly serious test of the relationship came in August 1990, with the Iraqi invasion of Kuwait, after a period of decreasing and only sporadic displays of Riyadh's former generosity. This episode in the bilateral relationship is covered in the concluding chapter.

Why include coverage of Saudi Arabia, or Kuwait in the next chapter, if neither provides an example of an alignment shift? In the first place, continuity in bilateral relationships is the obverse of change. One must understand the bases of both. Second, such coverage is necessary in order to explain Jordan's response to the 1990 Gulf crisis, discussed in the conclusions. Just as important, however, as chapter 1 indicated, individual bilateral relations of small states can rarely be explained in isolation from other key relationships. As the later chapters will show, an examination of the underpinnings of Jordan's ties with Saudi Arabia, its primary external funder, is critical to understanding Amman's alliance shifts with other regional actors.

Before proceeding, a word of caution and explanation is in order. Substantiating statistics on trade exchange in these bilateral relations is not an easy task, since the figures reported in one statistical book often differ from those in another. However, even more difficult to ascertain reliably are aid contributions: what is promised is not always forwarded, and often sums are sent or assistance of various kinds is provided which is not reported or acknowledged by either side. In general, the Gulf states prefer to work behind the scenes, without fanfare. This is even more so the case in the economic realm, because they are usually dealing in direct budgetary support (often for the military) and in large amounts. Hence, what follows is an attempt to piece together the available evidence and, based on the coincidence of certain events, engage in well-founded speculation, but often speculation nonetheless, about the topics and goals of certain meetings.

The Boom Years 1975–1981

Political Developments

In early March 1975 it was revealed that Jordan was giving 21 Hawker Hunter jet fighters to the Sultanate of Oman and that a Jordanian battalion had been sent to Oman's southern Dhofar province (which borders Saudi Arabia) to help Omani, Iranian, and British troops suppress the rebellion there. While no Saudi troops appear to have been involved, the Jordanian assistance was certainly tacitly approved, if not actively encouraged, by the Saudis, who preferred to keep a low profile in regional affairs. The fact that King Husayn visited Oman in April *after* having talks with King Khalid of Saudi Arabia strongly suggested a Saudi role in the Jordanian assistance to Oman. [1]

King Husayn returned to Saudi Arabia in early June, while Prime Minister Rifa'i paid an unexpected visit on September 29 to deliver a message from Husayn to King Khalid, who himself visited Jordan in late December. On January 21, 1976 Husayn and Rifa'i flew to Saudi Arabia following a visit to Damascus, to brief Khalid on the outcome of their talks with Syrian President Asad, which must have dealt in part with the intended establishment of an Egyptian-Syrian Joint Command, as well as developments in the civil war in Lebanon, which the security-conscious Saudis were watching carefully. The Saudis had become increasingly involved in mediation efforts in the Lebanese conflict and finally succeeded in convening a mini-summit in Riyadh (to which Jordan was not a party) in October 1976, which brought an end to the first round of the fighting.

On January 9–10, 1977, the kingdom hosted a multilateral Arab meeting attended by the foreign ministers of Egypt, Syria, Kuwait, Qatar, the United Arab Emirates, and the Palestine Liberation Organization. This critical meeting, to which we shall return in subsequent chapters, dealt with the issue of financial assistance from the supporting (read oil-producing) states to the frontline states. This gathering, and perhaps the subsequent one held a few days later in Cairo, led to a reaffirmation on the part of the supporting states that the aid to the confrontation states, which had been decided upon at the 1974 Rabat summit conference, was a continuing obligation, not limited to a single year's contribution, as the recipients had feared.[2] (See *Aid* below.)

In March and April visits by Jordan's Interior Minister Sulayman 'Arar, Chief of the Royal Court 'Abd al-Hamid Sharaf, Commander-in-Chief of the armed forces Zayd bin Shakir, and Prime Minister Badran covered security issues and financial affairs. By late spring and early summer consultations were being held on the respective monarch's meetings with U.S. president Jimmy Carter. These consultations dealt at least in part with the second Geneva Middle East peace conference (the first having been held in 1973 following the war),[3] which was proposed for later in the year. Husayn himself went to Medina on July 6, accompanied by Badran, Sharaf, and bin Shakir. He stayed only one day, but the talks were described as successful.[4]

These talks may well also have dealt with finances. King Husayn had been vocal in his criticism of the Arab Gulf states for not providing the frontline states with sufficient financial assistance. The London weekly newsletter *Arabia and the Gulf* reported that the Saudis, upset by the criticism, in the summer of 1977 were reconsidering their decision to pay $500 million of the $540 million total cost of the U.S. Hawk missile system desired by the Jordanian military.[5] (See below.) Saudi defense concerns must also have been key issues as bin Shakir went on a "private" visit of several hours on July 17, during which he met with Defense and Aviation Minister Prince Sultan bin 'Abd al-'Aziz. It was subsequently reported that Saudi Arabia had agreed to allow Jordan to use its northern air bases in the event of a war with Israel; however, Saudi Arabia refused the Jordanian suggestion that a full military pact be concluded between the two.[6]

During October 1977 there were a number of visits back and forth between Jordanian and Saudi officials. Husayn received Prince 'Abdallah, commander of the Saudi National Guard, and his delegation on October 17; Prince Nayif, the interior minister, arrived nine days later for a visit of four days; and Sharaf met with King Khalid at Khubar at the end of the month. During Prince Nayif's visit a joint committee was established which was to look into border cooperation, coordination of public security organs, and communications between the two interior ministries.[7] The king himself arrived in Riyadh on November 5 as part of a series of visits to coordinate Arab positions only a few days before Egyptian president Sadat announced his willingness to visit Jerusalem.

The Saudi reaction to Sadat's visit to Jerusalem was, at least publicly, one of surprise, and Riyadh reiterated that any Arab initiative in connection with the Arab-Israeli conflict should stem from a unified Arab position.[8] In the meantime, Arab speculation had it that the Saudis and the Kuwaitis were likely to throw their weight behind efforts to mediate between Egypt and Syria (which had vehemently criticized the visit) to try to restore unity to Arab ranks, since they viewed inter-Arab feuding as a security threat.[9] Husayn was back in Riyadh with Badran, Sharaf, and Court Minister Khammash for meetings with King Khalid on December 19, which no doubt dealt with Sadat's initiative and the appropriate Arab response to it.

The diplomatic consultations continued in early 1978, with frequent exchanges of messages and a trip by Information Minister 'Adnan Abu 'Awdah to Saudi Arabia on January 10. Jordan was clearly involved in the flurry of activity, but the main arena was Saudi mediation between Egypt and Syria. Husayn arrived in Jeddah on May 20 for a two-day visit, and returned, on July 22, this time to Ta'if, the Saudi summer capital, for talks that reportedly dealt with strengthening solidarity, joint cooperation, and standing fast against aggression (a reference to the March 1978 Israeli invasion of Lebanon). A series of subsequent high-level meetings in both countries, which focused on possible cooperation between their security and civil defense establishments, led in September (the month of the Camp David talks) to the signing of a security agreement which, according to Saudi Interior Minister Prince Nayif, covered all security questions of interest, including smuggling, illegal entry, and facilities for the movement of citizens between the two.[10]

Following the signing of the Camp David Accords, Arab diplomatic contacts were stepped up again, and Husayn met with Saudi Crown Prince Fahd in Jeddah on October 1 as part of a larger Gulf tour aimed at gaining support for convening an Arab summit. Husayn's visit to the Gulf states suggests that coordination of positions among the conservative monarchies was on the agenda, since the Saudis had demonstrated a distinct lack of enthusiasm for any moves that would irrevocably ostracize Egypt. Husayn's trip had been preceded by a visit from Syrian president Hafiz al-Asad and was followed by a call by the PLO's Yasir 'Arafat, all pressing their respective points of view on the accords and urging the Saudis to support the convening of the summit.[11]

Although Riyadh opposed Sadat's move because of its impact on Arab unity, it did not want to risk the radicalization of Egypt that a boycott causing Sadat's demise might trigger. Consequently, the Saudis led a campaign at the summit to prevent Egypt's isolation.[12] As a result, the November summit resolved to establish a fund of up to $9 billion for the confrontation states, $5 billion of which would be for Egypt to persuade Sadat to remain in the fold. The balance of the funds was earmarked for annual support to Syria ($1.8 billion), Jordan ($1.2 billion), the PLO ($150 million), and the occupied West Bank and Gaza ($150 million). Saudi Arabia's contribution to the fund was set at $1 billion a year.[13]

Husayn returned to Saudi Arabia on January 22, 1979 for meetings with Khalid. Their discussions must have covered the most pressing Gulf security topics: the then recent demise of the Shah of Iran and the ongoing border crisis between North Yemen and the People's Democratic Republic of Yemen (PDRY) (again, in the Saudis' backyard) which subsequently erupted into warfare on February 23. Bin Shakir arrived in Jeddah on an official three-day visit on March 9. Sharaf followed him for a several-hour visit on March 16, the day that Jordan-, Syrian- and Iraqi-led efforts ended in a ceasefire between North Yemen and the PDRY.[14] These visits were followed by a two-day trip by Husayn to Saudi Arabia on March 21, accompanied by Badran, Sharaf, Court Minister Khammash and military secretary Lt. General Muhammad Idris. Probably as a result of these talks, a group of Jordanian military men, as part of the Arab League Military Delegation, was sent to assist in bringing about an end to the conflict between the two Yemens.[15] Again, Jordan was involved in an extraterritorial role with implications for Saudi security. More directly and openly, between 1972 and 1982, Jordan seconded 674 officers, and 1,576 military men of other ranks to the Gulf states. Of those only one officer went to Saudi Arabia. However, during the same period, 602 Saudi officers and 1,717 Saudis of other ranks were trained in Jordan. This total of 2,319 made Saudi Arabia the largest Gulf state exporter of military men for training in Jordan, followed by the UAE with 1,876 and Kuwait with 1,489.[16]

In the meantime, by early March the Saudi position on the pending peace treaty between Egypt and Israel had become clearer. On March 15 both Saudi Arabia and Jordan reacted angrily to the role the United States was playing in promoting the peace agreement, and on March 19 Saudi Arabia declared its opposition to the treaty if it retained its bilateral form and neglected guarantees for the Palestinians. Shortly thereafter, on March 27, the day following the signing, the Arab foreign and economic ministers met again in Baghdad, this time to reassert the Egyptian expulsion and boycott decisions discussed the previous November. In the meantime, Egypt had rebuffed several Saudi offers of mediation and financial support.[17] By the time of this meeting, therefore, the Saudis had been convinced to take a strong position and voted for the boycott of Egypt they had so strongly resisted the previous November.

Officials from the two kingdoms exchanged numerous visits throughout the summer and fall of 1979, a number of which were clearly related to security. The two monarchs met in Geneva on September 20, and Husayn was back in Saudi Arabia for the *hajj*18 on November 2. Prince 'Abdallah went to Amman for a two-day visit on November 10, but the Saudis were soon distracted on November 20 by the seizure of the Great Mosque in Mecca by armed militants. Husayn made a brief visit to Riyadh during this incident and congratulated Khalid on December 4 at the end of the ordeal. However, the Saudis faced further disturbances in late 1979 and early 1980 in the form of Shi'i anti-regime activity in Qatif in the kingdom's Eastern province.

Bin Shakir visited Riyadh for talks in early January and Husayn went on a two-day visit to Saudi Arabia for talks with Khalid and other senior Saudi officials on April 28. Early in the year, the Saudis had decided to raise oil prices, a move that threatened to raise Jordan's $210 million oil bill by $72 million, and the Jordanians had requested "frank and clear" oil price talks with Riyadh.[19] Otherwise, consultations continued throughout the year on security and military issues. In August there were numerous instances of Iraqi and Saudi contacts on which the Jordanians were regularly briefed, as the three states began to form a new triangular relationship. The official topic of the Saudi-Jordanian talks was generally given as "the Palestinian issue," but in retrospect it seems far more likely that the discussions concerned the increasing hostilities on the Iraqi-Iranian border and Iraqi president Saddam Husayn's possible military response.

This was certainly the case in the October 11 meeting between King Husayn and Saudi leaders, who conferred to discuss joint plans to help Iraq only a few weeks after the war began. The specifics of the discussions were not released, but subsequent events indicated that the Saudis were attempting to find means of assisting Iraq without associating themselves too closely and so as not to provoke Iran. Safran, in fact, contends that the Jordanians and the Saudis likely worked out a division of labor: Jordan, a declared ally of Iraq, would make Aqaba port available to transship weapons, while the Saudis, in the role of friendly neutral, would allow their Red Sea, not Persian Gulf, ports to be used for transshipping civilian supplies, and perhaps some nonlethal military equipment, although not heavy weaponry.[20] The consultations between Jordan and the Saudis grew increasingly frequent. Near the end of the year, when the Syrians massed troops on the Jordanian border, it was Saudi Prince 'Abdallah who mediated a troop withdrawal and the termination of the crisis before actual hostilities began.[21]

Husayn attended the Islamic summit in Saudi Arabia in January 1981 and then made another trip to the Gulf, including Saudi Arabia, in mid-May 1981. In the meantime, the Gulf Cooperation Council had been established and Husayn reportedly made a bid for associate membership, offering military assistance to "douse any future revolutionary fires in the Gulf,"[22] presumably along the lines of what Jordan had done previously in Dhofar and between the two Yemens. (It will be recalled that only a year earlier, in response to the fall of the Shah and the Soviet invasion of Afghanistan, the United States had proposed the formation and dispatch of a Rapid Deployment Force for use in the Gulf.) In early April, the king had announced a plan that included a number of points dealing with security in the Middle East, the most important of which were the principles of neutrality of the Gulf, Gulf state self-reliance for defense, and the rejection of the use of the oil weapon.[23] Nonetheless, despite his interest and his country's past contributions to Gulf security, Husayn's request for membership in the GCC was ignored.

On August 7, 1981, the Saudis inadvertently became involved in the Middle East peace proposal game, for on that day Crown Prince Fahd gave an interview to the Saudi Press Agency in which he outlined his vision of a future Middle East peace settlement. His statement, which developed a momentum of its own and became known as the Fahd plan, included a call for complete Israeli withdrawal from the territories occupied in 1967, the creation of a Palestinian state, and the right of all states in the region (including, implicitly, Israel) to live in peace. Although Sadat condemned the plan as offering nothing new, the proposal gained the support of Jordan, Morocco, the UAE and the PLO's Arafat. The Syrians, on the other hand, voiced strong opposition. The Saudis tried to garner additional support for the plan in the weeks preceding the Arab summit in Fez, Morocco and seemed confident despite Syrian opposition that the plan would be adopted more or less intact. However, the day of the summit, the Syrians announced that Foreign Minister Khaddam, not President Asad, would be attending. The same was true of the heads of the other staunchly anti-Camp David states, as well as the PLO. After four hours of sometimes acrimonious debate, Morocco's King Hasan simply adjourned the summit.[24] The Jordanian position, nonetheless, and probably not surprisingly, was one of continuing support for its primary patron's plan.

Economic Developments

AID

Saudi Arabia has been an important aid donor to Arab states since the late 1960s, when it began providing subsidies to the confrontation states in keeping with the resolutions of the 1967 Khartoum summit. Indeed, since 1974 it has been the second largest donor in the world, behind the United States. Grants have accounted for 47 percent of the assistance, while the rest has been in the form of highly concessionary loans. The grants and loans have come from a number of sources. Individual members of the royal family have always been able to dip into the massive reserves of the Saudi Arabian Monetary Agency (SAMA) to provide support. However, as the importance of project aid grew in the 1970s, the Saudi Development Fund (SDF) was established in 1975. It operates similarly to other Arab development funds, but draws on a great deal of outside expertise and administers less than 10 percent of Saudi overseas development assistance. Other agencies such as the cabinet, the Ministry of Finance, and the Ministry of Education and Higher Education have also provided assistance.[25]

By 1975, Saudi Arabia, with Kuwait, had already emerged as a major source of finance for Jordan, having provided 38 percent of all Arab budgetary support for Jordan in 1974. The first installment of (military) aid promised to Jordan by Arab states at the Rabat Arab

League summit in October 1974, $51.63 million from Saudi Arabia, arrived on January 11, 1975. It was part of the total annual contribution of $300 million promised by several Arab states to Jordan, along with contributions of $1 billion each to Egypt and Syria and $50 million to the PLO.[26] A trip to Jordan by King Faysal that same January resulted in a further Saudi grant of $57 million. According to the communique issued at the end of Faysal's visit, $47 million of this was to be for "urgent requirements" and the balance for the construction of housing for Jordanian army officers. Saudi Arabia was also providing budgetary support to the tune of $36 million in 1975.[27]

In December 1975, King Khalid (Faysal had been assassinated by a nephew on March 25, 1975) made a three-day visit to Jordan ostensibly to win support from Jordan and its then close ally Syria, for Egypt's Sinai disengagement agreement with Israel.[28] Any sympathy gained, however, appears to have been purchased, as only days after the visit, the kingdom promised to contribute $215 million to help implement Jordan's $2.3 billion 1976–1980 Development Plan. The aid, to be provided in installments over several years, was in addition to regular Saudi budgetary support payments, estimated in 1975 at $36 million.[29] To help further with development, Saudi Arabia agreed to cede to Jordan a 14-mile strip along the Red Sea coast to allow for the expansion of the port of Aqaba. Iraq had promised to help finance the expansion project, hoping to import up to 300,000 tons of transit goods per year through the port.[30]

The Saudis also played a role in financing Jordanian arms purchases. For instance, in 1975 Jordan was seeking to purchase a U.S. air-defense system, 14 batteries of U.S. Hawk anti-aircraft missiles, at a cost of $800 million. Not surprisingly, such a proposed sale to an Arab state fueled a controversy in the U.S. congress, and as a result a variety of conditions were attached to the deal.[31] In early April, Husayn canceled the deal, reportedly because Saudi Arabia had withdrawn its financial support. Reports indicated that although Saudi Arabia had been prepared to pay the original $300 estimate, it had balked at the revised $800 million price tag.[32] In May, a trip by Husayn to Moscow drove rumors that he was contemplating concluding an arms deal with the Soviets. In response, rumors circulated, but were denied, that Saudi Arabia had threatened to cut off aid to Jordan if it purchased Soviet SAM missiles.[33]

Discussions of the deal continued as Husayn and Rifaʻi began talks in Jeddah on June 5 with King Khalid, Crown Prince Fahd, and Foreign Minister Saʻud al-Faysal. Primary among the topics discussed were overall Saudi aid to Jordan, Husayn's visit to Moscow, and the reported Soviet offer to sell Jordan arms. By early August, the Saudis had reversed their decision and had agreed to finance the Hawks deal. The price of the air defense network had been reduced by the Americans to an estimated $540 million, of which the Saudis had agreed to pay all but $40 million.[34] Husayn arrived in Taʼif on August 7, as part of a Gulf tour, to discuss the arms purchase further.

According to Badran, however, despite the financing of the Hawks, the Rabat and other budgetary aid was not forthcoming from the Gulf states in the sums promised. The former Jordanian prime minister, who assumed his post in mid-July 1976, contended that by the latter part of 1976 none of the Gulf states was paying what they had promised at Rabat. Jordan was therefore forced to cut spending and Badran complained that he had struggled month to month in late 1976 to find the money to pay the salaries of the army and the bureaucracy. He, Syria's Foreign Minister ʻAbd al-Halim Khaddam, and Egypt's Foreign Minister Ismaʻil Fahmi went repeatedly together to the Gulf states to ask for the payments they had been promised. The response was never no, only the noncommittal but unchallengeable *In shaʼ ʻallah*.[35]

The year 1977 began with the conference in Riyadh mentioned earlier to discuss ways of "bolstering" (read "increasing the subsidies to") the frontline states. As a result of the meeting, the support states agreed to pay $570 million each to Egypt and Syria, $200 million to Jordan, and $27 million to the PLO for both 1977 and 1978.[36] This was about half the aid promised in Rabat, although there was still some question as to whether the Rabat commitments implied a one-time payment or a long-term pledge.[37]

On May 17 Jordanian Minister of Transportation ʻAli Suhaymat arrived in Riyadh for discussions with the Saudi communications minister on means of cooperation and for meetings with officials at the SDF concerning several development projects[38] for which Jordan was reportedly seeking $261 million in development aid.[39] SDF loans and other development-related assistance for this period are listed in Table 9. In November 1978 at the Arab League meeting in Baghdad (Baghdad I) following Sadat's conclusion of the Camp David accords with the Israelis, the oil-producing states agreed to provide annual budgetary support for ten years to the remaining confrontation states: Jordan, Syria, and the PLO. This was the formal commitment that King Husayn had been dreaming of: $1.2 billion per year, with Saudi Arabia the largest contributor. The commitment was reaffirmed at the Arab foreign ministers meeting following the signing of the Egyptian-Israeli peace treaty in March 1979.

Nevertheless, the U.S., intent upon securing the next link in the Camp David chain, continued to pursue and pressure Jordan. The second half of the Camp David Accords, that dealing with Palestinian autonomy, had not been completed, and the logical party to help move the process along was Jordan. The U.S. continued to coax and cajole Amman either to represent or to bypass the Palestinians, whose own representative, the PLO, was deemed an unacceptable negotiating partner by the Americans and the Israelis.

Arab activity in the Jordanian capital during this period was intense as rumors abounded that Jordan might be ready to follow Sadat. Could Husayn have seriously considered such a move given the commitment of Arab aid as well as a domestic population (both Palestinian and Transjordanian), not to mention Syria and Iraq, that would have fiercely opposed such a move? One would think not, but the clear courtship of Jordan by the Arab states during this period would seem to indicate that they had reason to be concerned about another defection from the ranks. Arab aid promises in the past, notably the Rabat commitments, had been demonstrated to be fragile, while U.S. aid to Egypt, effectively the "price of the peace treaty," was substantial. Certainly one would have expected the U.S. to commit itself to protect Jordan in the event of threats of Arab military retaliation for signing such a treaty. Therefore, just as easily as balancing the U.S., Israel, and Egypt by adhering to the Arab position, could Jordan not also have balanced Syria, Iraq, the PLO and his domestic constituency by joining the Camp David chorus? The problem with trying to analyze Jordanian behavior in terms of balancing

TABLE 9
Saudi Development Aid to Jordan, 1977–1981

Year	Source	Amount	Project
1977	SDF	$27.0 million	Husayn Thermal Power Station
	SDF	$25.0 million	Aqaba port piers
1978	SDF	$80.0 million	Water and electricity projects
	SDF	$73.5 million	Four development projects
1980	Grant	$10.0 million	Repair winter flood damage
	SDF	$11.6 million	Hijaz railway, housing, communication
	Grant	23 firetrucks & ambulances	
	Grant	$0.6 million	Nablus Municipality
	Grant	$5.0 million	UNRWA schools in Jordan and Syria
	Grant	$5.0 million	Jordan University
	King Khalid	$5.0 million	Queen Alia Fund for Social Development
1981	SDF	$18.0 million	Aqaba port development
	SDF	$29.4 million	Amman water project
	SDF	$30.6 million	Jordan Valley Authority projects

SOURCE: FBIS, MEED; RSS, *'Alaqat al-Mamlakah b-il-Mamlakah; EIU, Saudi Arabia: Quarterly Economic Report.*

is that it could explain either outcome, depending upon which factor(s) one concludes posed the greatest threat.

Perhaps the king truly did waver, and considered joining the Camp David process. However, if financial and budgetary concerns were high on the list of priorities, aside from the tremendous budgetary support that the Arab states were offering, the king had to bear in mind that Jordan was also heavily tied to its regional markets, more so than any other Arab state. A boycott of Jordan like that imposed on Egypt would have killed Jordan's overland transport trade, and deprived Jordan of its most important export markets, thus devastating the private as well as much of the state sector. Making a deal with Israel would also have infuriated his population. Hence in one fell swoop Jordan would have cut its economic throat *and* perhaps triggered instability at home. Here budget security alone can probably explain the king's position; a consideration that the king may have been omnibalancing (appeasing a domestic constituency) perhaps overdetermines the outcome. If the king did appear to be considering joining Sadat, chances are that it was an attempt to secure the best aid deals he could from the Arab states and to put them on notice that they could not renege on their assistance commitments.

TRADE

Overall trade figures for the period demonstrated a clear Jordanian deficit, for the various forms of aid granted by Saudi Arabia could only in part offset the increase in the cost of oil imports from the kingdom. In 1979 imports from Saudi Arabia totaled $230.8 million, 11 percent of the total import bill, making Saudi Arabia Jordan's largest supplier. Saudi Arabia had also become Jordan's largest export market, but the meat, vegetables, fruit, cigarettes, varnishes, and other goods sold to Riyadh brought in only $64.5 million, leaving Jordan with a trade deficit of $166.3 million.[40]

Minutes of the meetings of February 2, 1980 do not provide the same insight into the nature of the bilateral relationship at this level as do those of the the joint economic commission. According to the previous meeting of the committee the Saudis had complained about a .04% charge on goods which they claimed was in violation of article 9 of the economic agreement between the two. The Jordanians countered that these charges went toward road maintenance and were in keeping with an Arab League decision of March 14, 1977. In response to Saudi complaints about additional vehicle charges, the Jordanians decided to exempt Arab League country nationals of this charge. The Saudis also mentioned Amman's failure to implement article 11 of the economic agreement and its adjustment to allow Saudi cars to remain in Jordan for three months. A long discussion followed, but the two sides were unable to come to agreement and so a decision was postponed, with the issue referred to the customs authorities in each country. For their part, the Jordanians complained about a problem with Saudi license plates for Jordanian vehicles and the Saudis promised to refer the question to the relevant authorities.[41] These appear to be obscure issues and relatively unimportant in a relationship in which huge sums of military and budgetary aid and the provision of security services seem to have been easily agreed upon. Nonetheless, they recurred, indicating either tensions in the relationship that could not be expressed on other levels or perhaps the lack of coordination between lower and upper levels of the economic decisionmaking apparatus within the two countries.

TAPLINE AND OIL

As noted above, no other Saudi import had the same importance, nor was any Jordanian export to Saudi Arabia of the same strategic significance to Riyadh as was oil to Amman. The "vehicle" of oil delivery was Tapline (the Trans-Arabian Pipeline), owned by the same consortium of companies that owned ARAMCO (the Arabian-American Oil Company). Tapline had been constructed in 1950 to carry oil out of Saudi Arabia across Jordan, through Syria, and then finally on to Lebanon. In late 1960, Jordan began to obtain its crude oil needs from Tapline oil passing through its territory on the way to the Mediterranean. According to agreement, Jordan paid Tapline the Mediterranean crude oil posted price minus 22 cents (based on the distance that the oil did not have to travel since it was taken out in Jordan). In turn, Jordan received a royalty payment for each barrel that passed across its territory.[42]

Thus, officially, it was Tapline and not the Saudi government that sold the oil to Jordan. However, on a number of occasions, as an expression of its understanding of where the real power behind the agreement lay, Jordan sought Saudi intervention with Tapline on the question of prices. To the Jordanians' disappointment, the Saudi response was always that Tapline was no different than any other company operating in the kingdom: the Saudi government had no influence over its actions and insisted that the Jordanians speak with the company directly.[43]

Then, in 1970, the price of oil began to fluctuate. Expecting the price increases to be minor, the Jordanian government at first indicated that it would absorb them. However, when prices rose dramatically in 1973, the government was unable to avoid passing price increases along to consumers. A dispute then arose between Jordan and Tapline when the company sought to raise the price of the 5 million barrels a year it supplied Jordan from $2.27 to $13.64 a barrel. As a result, in late 1973 Jordan simply stopped payment, leading Tapline to suspend the $7.5 million a year in transit fees it had been paying Amman. On February 9, 1975 Tapline went a step further and suspended pumping, supposedly because it was cheaper to lift oil by tanker from the terminals in the Gulf than from the terminal at Sidon, Lebanon, where the line that passed through Jordan ended. But there is no question that the company's action was intended to pressure Jordan and Lebanon to accept the substantially higher prices demanded for the crude used in their refineries. However, in a clear and dramatic demonstration of the previously denied Saudi influence, at the end of April King Khalid ordered Tapline to resume pumping.[44]

Talks aimed at solving the dispute between the Jordanian government and Tapline were held in Saudi Arabia during the first week of June 1975.[45] However, the dispute continued, and the Jordanian Finance Minister and Central Bank Governor returned to Riyadh and Jeddah for talks on January 23, 1976. Not until March 2, 1976 was an agreement finally reached, according to which the Jordanian government acquiesced in a tripling of the price it had been paying for oil: instead of $3.67 a barrel Jordan agreed to pay the world price of $11.50. Yet, at virtually the same time, the Saudis promised $116 million in additional financial assistance to Amman.[46] Jordanian sources insisted that the Saudi aid had nothing to do with the Tapline agreement,[47] but the Saudis evidently had provided the additional financial assistance precisely for that purpose.[48] They simply preferred to work quietly behind the scenes. Arrears payments of $116 million for the oil were made by the Jordanian government by April.[49]

The potentially most serious oil-related development of 1976 for Jordan was the announcement by Tapline that it would not be able to continue operations on the same terms once the pending nationalization of ARAMCO was complete. With the reopening of the Suez Canal in June 1975 and the advent of the supertanker, Tapline had become uncompetitive. The pipeline had a capacity of 500,000 barrels a day, but since February 1975 only about 10 percent of that volume had been pumped intermittently to supply Lebanon's and Jordan's needs. Tapline's considerable losses had been borne by the Saudi government and by ARAMCO as an indirect form of budgetary subsidy that was scheduled to end with the completion of the nationalization.[50] However, in August 1979 the Saudis announced that they would continue pumping oil through the Tapline to the Zarqa refinery, located to the northeast of the Jordanian capital, despite the $40 million losses incurred.[51]

THE HIJAZ RAILWAY PROJECT

In July 1977, following discussions between Jordanian and Saudi officials, it was reported that Saudi Arabia was considering rebuilding the historic Hijaz railway, linking Medina with Amman and Damascus.[52] It promised to be an expensive as well as a politically sensitive undertaking, and the slow pace of discussions—in Amman in early October 1977, and among the Jordanian, Saudi, and Syrian ministers of transportation in June 1978—indicated that pressures were being exerted to move ahead cautiously.

Following the January 7, 1979 meeting of the tripartite committee charged with studying the project, the SDF granted a loan of US$11.7 million for the project. Although a Jordanian-Saudi delegation met only a few days later to discuss the project, the tripartite committee did not meet again until January 1980. Two months thereafter, an $11.6 million loan from the SDF was approved to strengthen a 21-km stretch of the Hijaz railway in southern *Jordan*, but not across the border.[53] The footdragging on the Saudi side seemed obvious, and probably owed to deep-seated concerns regarding reestablishing the Hashemites' ties with the Hijaz. It was not until late June 1981 that the Saudi and Jordanian governments announced that they were *beginning* to repair the Hijaz railway (and, again, only a Jordanian segment of it).[54] In the meantime, Jordanian-Syrian relations had deteriorated to the point that the Syrians were no longer involved in the discussions.

LABOR

Perhaps the most important Jordanian export to Saudi Arabia (in terms of its effect on the Jordanian economy) has been human capital in the form of expatriate labor. Such workers not only sent home remittances of critical hard currency, they also served to ease pressure on the Jordanian labor market. While Jordanians could be found throughout the Saudi economy, their contributions in the field of education were particularly notable. In May 1977 the Jordanian Minister of Education, 'Abd al-Salam al-Majali, toured the Gulf states to discuss the issue of seconding Jordanian teachers to Gulf state schools. Agreement was reached that this would be undertaken through and with the approval of the relevant ministry.[55] At this time it was reported that there were some 8,000 Jordanian teachers in Saudi Arabia. Of those, about 500 were on secondment from the Jordanian Ministry of Education to the Saudi government.[56] In September another 300 Jordanian teachers were seconded, along with six Jordanian doctors for Saudi hospitals. In October Riyadh borrowed another thirty-four Jordanian teachers.[57]

Summary

Throughout this period, Jordanian-Saudi relations were quite good, with the two governments in accord on the major regional developments: the Egyptian-Israeli peace treaty and the Iran-Iraq war. The official aid relationship, which began at Khartoum in 1967, was strengthened and virtually institutionalized during this period. Indeed, Saudi Arabia became Jordan's first, substantial aid donor, with aid including grants and development loans, assistance for military purchases, and subsidized oil supplies. As such, Saudi assistance became the cornerstone of Jordan's budget security by the early 1970s. In exchange, Jordan also played a key security role for Saudi Arabia, but a more traditional one. Jordan served as buffer between the Saudis and both the Arab-Israeli conflict and the more radical forces for change in the region. Jordan also trained Saudi officers and played a role in terminating unrest in neighboring parts of the peninsula— Oman and the Yemens.

Nonetheless, while the Saudis did provide substantial sums to the Jordanians as direct and indirect investments in their own security, they did not strike easy bargains, nor could their largess be taken for granted. The regular meetings and consultations at the highest levels between the two makes this clear. The Saudis had clear ideas about what they were "purchasing" and what they were due in return. It may be from such a stance that their toughness in the economic committee meetings derived. In the same way, they held firm on issues of border crossing as well as on any issues that appeared to touch their security, which included their balking on the efforts to rebuild the Hijaz railway.

The Years of Austerity: 1982–1990

Political Developments

It is during this period that the Iran-Iraq war began to weigh heavily, both from a financial and a security point of view, upon all the Gulf states, and by extension, upon Jordan as well. On February 5, 1982, U.S. Secretary of Defense Caspar Weinberger visited Saudi Arabia on a tour that also included Oman and Jordan. The Saudis reportedly asked for American help in establishing a Gulf arms industry and urged that Jordan be supplied with advanced weaponry.[58] Weinberger is credited with proposing the creation of a Jordanian Rapid Deployment Force, to help in circumstances in which American assistance to the kingdom would be embarrassing or difficult. The Saudis reportedly secretly approved the project, although whether they made a commitment to provide material support for it is not clear.[59] Shortly thereafter, King Husayn was asked about the likelihood of a Jordanian military role in the Gulf to protect Gulf state stability through a *Jordanian* rapid intervention force. His response was that he did not like the term "rapid intervention force," but that Jordan supported any Arab country that was or might be the target of aggression and was ready to offer all the assistance it could afford.[60]

In mid-June Husayn went to Saudi Arabia for the funeral of King Khalid, but most of the subsequent consultations between the two countries concerned the response to the June 6 Israeli invasion of Lebanon and its regional impact. These discussions and others eventually paved the way for the September 1982 Arab League summit in

Fez, Morocco, where an Arab peace plan, based on the earlier Fahd plan (1981), was agreed upon. King Husayn strongly supported the Fez plan because it was an Arab plan that fit within the general parameters of what Jordan was seeking in a settlement and, at the same time, went a long way toward meeting U.S. President Ronald Reagan's basic requirements for peace in the area.[61] Subsequently, a seven-member committee comprising Jordan, Saudi Arabia, Algeria, Morocco, Syria, Tunisia, and the PLO was established to meet with the five permanent members of the security council to explain the summit's resolutions. Husayn returned to Saudi Arabia in mid-November to review developments on the Palestine question and the results of the activities of the seven-member committee.

Most of the discussions between Jordan and Saudi Arabia during 1983 appeared to focus on the Palestine question, the May 17 agreement (the U.S.-brokered Israeli-Lebanese "peace treaty"), and the outbreak of inter-Palestinian conflict in Lebanon in late May. Regular consultations on these regional issues continued. Amman was reportedly disappointed by the lack of Saudi support during its negotiations with Arafat, which had broken down in the spring. The Saudis, who had been hesitant to encourage Husayn to join the peace process unless he could first get PLO support, did not themselves press for Arafat to come to terms with Husayn, and then reportedly used economic assistance as a means of restraining Husayn. ('Arafat, of course, at the time faced dissension in his own ranks which only weeks later escalated into full-scale inter-Palestinian combat).[62]

In 1984 the Lebanese issue and the Gulf war preoccupied Jordanian-Saudi attention. In April, Husayn, accompanied by a high-level delegation, met with Fahd. The king had telephone contacts with Fahd and Iraq's Saddam Husayn on May 24 to follow up on developments in the Gulf war and then on June 27 returned to Saudi Arabia both to perform the *'umra63* and to meet again with the Saudi monarch. Relations continued to be good until Jordan announced its decision to restore ties with Egypt. Although there had been no criticism of Jordan during 1983 as it gradually restored economic ties with Egypt and served as a conduit for Egyptian support of Iraq in the war, Saudi Arabia did criticize Jordan for taking the step of reestablishing diplomatic relations in September 1984 without seeking the counsel of other Arab states. Despite the criticism, however, there does not appear to have been any attempt at political or economic retribution.

In January 1985 Husayn met with Fahd to try to persuade the Saudi monarch to convene the long-delayed Arab summit in Riyadh and endorse his proposed formula for Jordanian-Palestinian coordination in the peace process. However, the cautious Saudis, not wanting to alienate and anger further a Syria that was already outside the Arab consensus because of its support for Iran in the Gulf war, preferred to wait.[64] In the meantime, consultations between the two continued indirectly. Husayn did not return to the kingdom until May, during which visit his discussions dealt with the political coordination between Jordan and the PLO, which had recently been formalized in the February 11 accord. During the summer and fall, the Saudis were active in working toward a Syrian-Jordanian rapprochement, which, by the end of the year, was bearing fruit.

In 1986 consultations continued on regional issues, particularly the Iran-Iraq war and attempts to mend the Syrian-Iraqi rift. Throughout 1987 there were periodic contacts and messages between the two monarchs, including meetings by Prince Nayif in Amman on security cooperation between the two.[65] As the fall approached and passed, the two were particularly concerned about preparations for the upcoming Arab summit. Husayn visited Saudi Arabia on September 29 as part of these efforts and returned only a month after the summit, on December 7. Part of the meeting no doubt concerned following up the summit's calls for a reconciliation between Egypt and Syria on the one hand, and Iraq and Syria on the other.

On February 21, 1988 Prime Minister Rifa'i arrived in Riyadh with a message for Fahd. This visit was followed by a March 16 visit by the Jordanian monarch to Saudi Arabia, among other Gulf states, for the first of four meetings between the two kings that year. The talks reportedly focused on the Palestinian uprising, which had begun early the past December, and on attempts to convene an international peace conference. However, Husayn was unhappy that the Arab summit in late spring had ignored Jordan's role in supporting the Palestinians of the occupied territories and had decided to channel all future Arab assistance to these Palestinians directly through the PLO. Husayn may well have complained about this in his July meeting. He may also have given the Saudis a preview of his intention to disengage from the West Bank, or he may simply have made an additional plea for assistance. The fourth meeting came at the end of August, with the subject again, reportedly, the uprising, the PLO, and the Palestinians, although, again, given that the dinar had begun to decline, one should not rule out the possibility that financial matters were discussed.

Husayn visited Fahd in late January 1989, accompanied by a high-level delegation. Jordan's economy was in crisis and there were reports that during the visit the king had sought to convince the Saudis to renew their annual $360 million Baghdad commitment that had expired in 1988.[66] Only a few weeks later, the Arab Cooperation Council (ACC) was established by Jordan, Egypt, Iraq and North Yemen, triggering Saudi anxiety over the potential regional role of the ACC economic/military bloc. Husayn subsequently made a visit to Riyadh to allay these fears. However, by mid-April Jordan was preoccupied with unrest at home, and there were numerous phone and other consultations between the two countries in the wake of Jordan's economic riots.

By 1990, thwarted in his attempts to have the Baghdad assistance renewed, Husayn had chosen a new fundraising theme: the threat to the West Bank and by extension, Jordan, posed by the arrival of large numbers of Jews from the collapsing Soviet Union and Jordan's consequent need of additional Arab support. In mid-February, discussions between Husayn and Fahd reportedly focused on this topic, the situation in Lebanon, and the continuing feud between Syria and Iraq.[67] However, given the political liberalization process that had begun in Jordan in the summer and led to the country's first free elections, "democratization" may well also have been on the agenda, since the Saudis made no secret of their dislike for the process.

In early May 1990, prior to the Arab League summit in Baghdad, Saudi Arabia proposed to host a mini-summit in Riyadh for Egypt, Syria, Iraq, Jordan, Saudi Arabia, and the Palestinians, designed to discuss Syrian-Iraqi reconciliation.[68] The summit, of course, never took place. On July 18, only days after the Iraqi complaints against

Kuwait and the UAE had been raised, Husayn made a trip to Saudi Arabia as part of his mediation or conciliation efforts, which also ultimately failed.

Economic Developments

AID

As the Iran-Iraq war took its toll on the Gulf states, Saudi Arabia gradually came to bear an increasing share of the dwindling Baghdad-promised aid. In January 1982 Saudi Arabia promised to cover the Baghdad financial commitments of Libya, which had stopped paying its promised support. This likely came as a result of talks Husayn held with Khalid in early January, although the press reported that the discussions had dealt with the Fahd plan and Jordanian support for it.[69] Later in January Husayn had talks with Prince Fahd, and in April returned to Saudi Arabia as part of a Gulf trip that also took him to Qatar. In 1983–84 the overall amount contributed fell from $668 million to $321 million. Riyadh then pledged to cover payments from Qatar and the United Arab Emirates if either failed to contribute the promised amount. In fact, neither of them paid in 1984, but Riyadh did not make up the shortfall.[70] Jordan was forced to seek external financing to cover the resulting deficit. Development project support did continue, and a list of projects funded is provided in Table 10.

In September 1986 the Saudi government expressed its willingness to provide funds for Jordan's announced development plan for the West Bank.[71] This plan was quite controversial when it was proposed because it was clearly a part of a Jordanian attempt to reassert Hashemite ties to the occupied territories in the face of Jordanian-PLO political feuding. However, just over a year later, in December 1987, the Saudis decided to send their $21 million contribution to the Jordanian-Palestinian joint committee (which channeled Arab state funds to the occupied territories) rather than to the controversial 1986 development plan. This move was a bitter disappointment for Amman and erased any lingering hopes that the Gulf states might reconsider their negative position on the development plan. This

TABLE 10
Sausi Development Aid to Jordan, 1982–1990

Year	Source	Amount	Project
1983	SDF	$35.0 million	Aqaba Thermal Station
	SDF	$35.1 million	Irrigation projects
	SDF	$17.1 million	Seven development projects
1984	SDF	$23.8 million	Vocational schools
	SDF	$11.4 million	Roads and railroad construction
1985	SDF	$22.4 million	Industrial Estate (Irbid)
	SDF	$56.0 million	Medical School
1986	SDF	$171.4 million	Nine development projects
	King Fahd	$0.5 million	Queen Alia Fund for Social Development
	SDF	$7.8 million	Zarqa-Ghor road
1987	SDF	$18.5 million	Medical Sciences Faculty
1988	SDF	$11.3 million	Aqaba Road projects
1989	SDF	$8.8 million	Industrial Estate (Irbid)

SOURCES: FBIS, MEED; RSS, *'Alaqat al-Mamlakah b-il Mamlakah.*

policy, in keeping with the Saudi practice of avoiding inter-Arab disputes, also appeared to be part of a strategy on the part of Riyadh to maintain leverage over both Jordan and the PLO.[72]

In another setback for the kingdom, at the Arab League summit in late May 1989 the Gulf states failed to renew their 10-year Baghdad commitment, which had expired in 1988, to provide annual support to the confrontation states. Nevertheless, Husayn arrived in Jeddah on August 1 and, certainly not coincidentally, on August 4, it was reported that Saudi Arabia had contributed $200 million in financial aid to enable Jordan to overcome the financial crisis that had triggered the domestic economic riots the previous April.[73] The support was certainly welcome, but it was ad hoc, not the kind of commitment made earlier at Khartoum, Rabat, and Baghdad.

By the end of 1989 Saudi Arabia, along with Kuwait, the UAE, Qatar, and Oman, had agreed to deposit a total of $300 million for Amman's use with the Arab Monetary Fund to support the dinar. Amman was to pay interest 2 percent below market rates.[74] In his February 1990 meetings with Husayn, Fahd reportedly offered an additional $200 million in assistance as well as spare parts for the Jordanian armed forces. Relations between the two appeared very cordial, and Prime Minister Badran stated that Fahd had "expressed full understanding of Jordan's financial and economic situation during the talks."[75] By May, however, when Husayn went to Saudi Arabia to perform the *'umra*, the promised aid was not yet forthcoming and officials in Amman were frustrated by the delay.[76]

TRADE

Just as was the case in the previous section on trade, an examination of the minutes of the meetings of the joint committees provides fascinating insights into the nature of the Saudi-Jordanian relationship below the monarch-to-monarch level. The exchanges on issues related to trade transport and vehicle entry provide the best examples among the documents studied for this project of the nature and substance of everyday politics, the role of bureaucratic implementation in bilateral relations, and the nature of the obstacles to further Arab economic integration.

In July 1985 the fifth meeting of the joint economic commission was held. Again it was decided to amend the list of tariff-free products. There was also agreement to set up temporary trade exhibitions and to exchange trade delegations. The Jordanians asked that a government-sponsored joint investment company be set up to undertake development projects in the two countries in the areas of industry, tourism, agriculture, and the like. Jordan suggested that a plan for the establishment of the company as well as bylaws be drafted and presented. The Saudi side agreed to study the proposal.[77]

For their part, the Saudis once again raised the issue of the charges on cars and trucks going into and out of Jordan. They complained again that this was against the terms of the economic agreement (discussed in 1980). When the Saudis threatened to put equivalent charges on Jordanian cars and trucks, the Jordanians agreed to lift the charge on trucks bound for Saudi Arabia, but not for Saudi trucks bound for a third country. The Jordanians asked for the same treatment for their trucks. The Saudis agreed to work on this, but asked the Jordanians to eliminate the remaining charges on Saudi trucks going to third countries.

The Jordanians also raised what was a more serious issue: the implications of the Saudi decision that Jordanian refrigerator trucks arriving at the border be required to be emptied and then have their contents carried by Saudi refrigerator trucks across the border. The result was a great deal of damaged or spoiled Jordanian produce. The Saudis countered that this policy was aimed at preventing contraband from entering the country. The Jordanians then further complained that the Saudis required drivers to have permission to enter the country of final destination and that this often caused Jordanian drivers to be delayed for a day at the border because of the early closing of customs posts on Thursdays and Fridays. The Saudis also promised to study this. These last two issues appeared to be deliberate forms of harassment cloaked in bureaucratic garb. However, since the practice continued over a long period of time, it is impossible to attribute it to a particular Jordanian policy decision or position with which the Saudis were unhappy. It may well simply have been a function of the Saudis' extreme sensitivity on issues related to their security. Or, it may have been a Saudi way of reminding the Jordanians of how dependent they were upon them.

The joint economic committee met again in December 1986. The more substantive matters concerned the disputed transport issues discussed in the 1985 meeting. The Jordanians asked again that their refrigerator trucks be exempted from the regulations that produce be transported by Saudi trucks at the border. The Saudis, however, were not to be moved, responding that these measures were taken only after a great deal of study and as a security measure. They claimed they were trying to prevent damage and that the same measures were applied to all countries. As for the Jordanian request that their drivers not be required to have the permission of the countries of destination (other Gulf states) prior to entering Saudi Arabia, the Saudis responded that the demand was based on conditions set by the other Gulf states.

In the realm of actual commodity exchange, in 1987 as in 1986, Jordan purchased subsidized wheat from Saudi Arabia. In 1987 the total was 200,000 tons[78] and by September of that year Jordan was seeking to purchase 200,000 tons of wheat annually from Saudi Arabia as a hedge against possible world shortages. In the past, Saudi wheat had been sold to Jordan for less than $90 a ton, compared with a world market price of about $175 a ton.[79] The two also signed an agreement covering the exchange of agricultural products, cooperation in animal and crop disease control, and the use of recycled water.[80]

At the end of the first week of February 1988 the joint economic commission had its seventh meeting. For the first time, the Saudis agreed to the establishment of a Jordanian trade exhibit in Saudi Arabia and expressed an interest in setting up another exhibit in Jordan in 1989.[81] Riyadh welcomed the renewed Jordanian request to buy Saudi wheat and to exchange agricultural expertise, and asked Jordan to send a technical team to the kingdom. The Jordanians also asked yet another time that their refrigerator trucks not be required to unload completely at the border, but the Saudis were unrelenting.[82]

In the October 1989 meeting of the committee, the two sides noted that trade between them was still modest, below the desired level in comparison with the possibilities. The Jordanians asked that their products not be denied entry into Saudi Arabia simply because they were similar to Saudi products before the relevant specialized authorities were consulted. The Saudis responded that no product was denied entry until a study was completed that established that the product's similarity to the Saudi product.[83]

TAPLINE AND OIL

By late September 1984 Jordan had reached yet another agreement with Tapline according to which the company committed itself to supplying Jordan with all its crude oil needs and Jordan, in return, agreed to absorb the costs of operation, estimated at $26.7 million a year. Either party could cancel the agreement, but not without two year's notice, which could not be served before October 1985. The minimum duration of the agreement was three years. In practice, the agreement did not constitute a costly undertaking for Tapline, given the glut in the oil markets at the time and the drop in the spot prices below the $29 per barrel payable by Jordan. Tapline's only concession was a 45-day grace period for payment, which meant forgone interest of 43 cents per barrel.[84] One of the reasons for the decision to keep the line open appeared to be the delays surrounding the proposed (and ultimately aborted) Iraq to Aqaba pipeline, since Jordan had intended to compensate for the termination of Tapline service through increasing its imports of Iraqi crude.[85]

INVESTMENT

Gulf investment was highly coveted by both the Jordanian public and private sectors, and had been discussed periodically in meetings of the joint economic committee. In mid-March 1986, the efforts finally bore fruit, as the Jordanian government approved a draft agreement setting up an equal equity Jordanian-Saudi company for industrial and agricultural investment. Unfortunately, only a month later the Saudis announced a freeze on all new projects, pending a clearer picture of oil prices in the international market.[86] Probably as a result, it was not until almost a year later that the Saudi-Jordanian Company for Marketing and Investment was established with capital of $500,000,[87] and not until the February 1988 meeting of the joint committee did the Saudis announce that all the necessary steps had been taken to establish the Saudi-Jordanian joint company.[88]

On March 5, 1989 the two governments signed an agreement to establish a $50 million Amman-based Jordanian-Saudi Industrial Agricultural Company, intended to invest in Jordan.[89] In the 1989 meeting of the joint committee, the two sides stressed the role that this investment company would play and the need to get business underway. What seemed to be delaying progress was the failure of each country to pay its share of the capital.[90] In the case of Jordan there was certainly a problem of liquidity. In the case of the Saudis, there may have been a liquidity problem (although that seems unlikely), a lack of political or economic will, or concern that the Jordanians would not be able to find the funds to pay their share. Again, economic cooperation on the lower bureaucratic levels or for less economically- or security-sensitive issues appeared to have far more difficulty bearing fruit.

LABOR

The attractiveness of Saudi Arabia for Jordanian labor continued, despite the regional economic downturn. Some 3761 Jordanians reportedly went to work in Saudi Arabia in 1983, including 1,240 construction workers and 995 technicians.[91] In mid-year it was reported that there were at least 140,000 Jordanian workers in Saudi Arabia, nearly half the total number of Jordanians employed overseas. It was also reported that the Saudi Ministry of Education would soon issue contracts to 2,285 more Jordanian teachers.[92]

Summary

This period witnessed a marked decline in oil state financial support for Jordan as a result of the drop in oil prices and the consequent decline in oil-state liquidity. Only Saudi Arabia continued to pay its Baghdad commitment, in addition to part of the share of the reneging states. Jordan suffered as a result of the drop in payments, but preferred to borrow abroad rather than scale back its planned expenditures. Bilateral political relations remained good, although there were a few differences over Jordan's restoration of ties with Egypt, Saudi failure to fund the 1986 development plan for the occupied territories, and the failure of the oil states to renew their Baghdad commitments in 1988.

Beyond the aid relationship, Saudi Arabia continued to provide development loans, ensure Tapline oil for Jordan, and support ongoing attempts to establish joint industrial projects, although they seem to have had little life beyond official discussions. The Saudis characteristically continued to focus in meetings of the economic committees on issues of border crossing and customs (including the refrigerator truck problems) which further demonstrated their preoccupation with internal security issues, or with making the Jordanians aware, even in more minor details, of Saudi importance to them.

Conclusions

Economic Relations

The most obvious form of economic statecraft in this case is the Saudis' use of substantial grants and loans. Of all Jordan's relations with Gulf states, indeed of all Jordan's relationships in the Arab world, that with Saudi Arabia has been most important from the standpoint of budget security, precisely because of the tremendous sums granted over the years. Whatever begging and cajoling may have been required of the Hashemites in dealing with the House of Sa'ud, even in the absence of definitive statistics there is no question that, whether budgetary, military, or developmental, Saudi aid has been Jordan's most secure and extensive form of support over the years. In exchange, of course, Jordan served Saudi security needs in a variety of ways: working as a stable buffer between the Saudis and Israel, sending troops when the Saudis preferred only indirect involvement, as in the case of Oman in 1975, providing border surveillance to thwart smuggling, and, most basic of all, succeeding in preserving itself as a conservative (as opposed to an Arab nationalist) regime on Saudi Arabia's western border. To ensure Jordan's continuation in this role, Riyadh paid well, although not as well as the Jordanians and other Arabs had often hoped or requested.

Interviews with members of the political elite in Jordan (not to mention the populace) made clear that the Jordanian view of Saudi aid differed substantially from the Saudi view. Quite simply, Jordanians considered the aid from Saudi Arabia to be their right. Arab oil money, they reasoned, belonged to the Arab nation at large and Jordan as a poorer and frontline state deserved the aid. The Saudis, on the other hand, according to Jordanians, believed that the financial aid effectively bought Jordan as a friend and ally and that that was where the story ended.[93]

Not surprisingly then, despite the "money-for-security" exchange that at base defined the relationship, the Saudis clearly saw their position in the relationship as superior, a fact that they periodically reinforced. The Gulf states have been generous, but regardless of whatever profligacy may have characterized their spending on consumer items and weaponry at home, they were not interested in underwriting wasteful spending of Gulf money by their aid-recipient Arab neighbors. There is good reason to believe, based on official testimony, that at least part of the reason for the disagreement over the funds promised at Rabat in 1974 (finally straightened out in January 1977) derived from Gulf state displeasure with Egypt's initial use of this money.

Oil and Tapline policy was another key instrument of Saudi economic statecraft. The Saudis were obviously disingenuous in their public statements regarding their influence with Tapline: they clearly were able and willing to affect Tapline policy when they so chose, as evidenced by King Khalid's order that the company resume pumping to Jordan in April 1975. However, the Saudis preferred to keep a low profile in such matters. When Jordan did finally reach agreement with Tapline over increased oil prices, the Saudis made a grant to Jordan in the same amount as the increase in the oil bill, and then denied there was any connection between the two events. Although oil supplies from Iraq eventually overwhelmed the supplies Jordan received from Saudi Arabia, for most of the period under study Saudi supply and subsidization of oil to Jordan constituted just one more key form of indirect budgetary assistance, supporting the same goals of Jordanian (and, ultimately, Saudi) security and stability as did the grants and loans policy.

In the realm of trade, given Saudi Arabia's wealth and the nature of its imports from Jordan (mostly fresh produce), the Saudi export market was far more important to Jordan than was the Jordanian market to the Saudis. Jordan exported neither the type of products nor the amounts necessary to make Saudi Arabia vulnerable to a Jordanian border closure. Much more important to the Saudis was Jordan's role as a transit country through which exports from other countries passed on their way to Saudi Arabia, or on to the lower Gulf states. This is clear from the focus on transport and transit issues in the minutes of the joint committee meetings.

Although both countries have relatively free market economies, trade and transport between the two has long been regulated by a formal protocol, unlike, for example Jordan's relationship with the also free-market Kuwait. While the customs-exempt product list is regularly revised, the protocol does not provide for individual deals nor does it set trade quotas, as is the case with the other Arab countries with which Jordan has protocols. In the Jordanian-Saudi relationship trade is the prerogative of the private sector. Having said that, the state can and has on occasion interfered in commodity exchange. There is the notable example of Saudi Arabia's forcing Jordanian trucks to empty all their goods at the border and transfer them to Saudi trucks, leaving the produce to spoil. The fact that this practice continued over a period of time—it was first noted in the minutes of the July 1985 meetings, was noted again in December 1986 meetings, but is not mentioned in the next round of talks in February 1988—makes it unlikely that it was linked to a particular Jordanian misstep, for which the Saudis sought to exact punishment. Instead, it is more likely that either a general heightened concern for security led to lower-level bureaucratic implementation of such a policy or that the Saudis, because the losses in imports to them were of no significance, simply used the policy as a way of reminding the Jordanians of their dependence and vulnerability.

The negotiations recounted in the minutes of the joint committee meetings are instructive for other reasons as well. First, they demonstrate a Saudi focus on detail and an unwillingness to bend or compromise, at least in the open. Jordanian appeals on several issues were repeatedly rebuffed and a number of what appear to be relatively minor issues related to minimal transport fees which the Saudis viewed as unfair were raised several times. Second, the discussions clearly demonstrate Saudi caution: in each case in which a new issue or proposal was raised the Saudis were very careful to make no commitment beyond "raising it with the relevant authorities" or "taking it under consideration." While the real power behind these committees generally does rest with the top decision makers, nonetheless, there is little that the Saudis agreed to in these meetings beyond revised customs lists.

Finally, there is the issue of Jordanian expatriate workers in Saudi Arabia. As will be demonstrated even more clearly in the case of Kuwait, skilled Jordanian labor, perhaps Jordan's most important export, has played a crucial role in the development of the Gulf states. Statistics are hard to come by and notoriously unreliable, but at its zenith, the Jordanian (largely Palestinian) community in Saudi Arabia may have numbered as many as 150,000. However, the size of Saudi Arabia and its more closed atmosphere prevented the emergence there of the sort of Jordanian or Palestinian community that developed in Kuwait. Like the Kuwaitis, the Saudis treated or related to the community as if it were Palestinian, the responsibility of the PLO. Thus, politically, the community's primary importance was to the PLO. However, while it did contribute to the Palestinian resistance, it also played a major economic role for Jordan: these expatriates sent back substantial remittances that shored up foreign currency reserves, just as their absence eased unemployment back home. Saudi Arabia depended upon skilled Jordanian teachers, physicians, engineers, and businessmen, while Jordan counted upon their continued absorption by the Saudi labor market and the hard currency they sent home. Jordanian skilled labor was not as easily replaced as Jordanian fruits and vegetables, so in this instance the bilateral exchange was far less lopsided.

Economics and Alliances

Unlike its relationships with Egypt, Syria, and Iraq, Jordan's relations with Saudi Arabia do not manifest clear or marked shifts, at least not until the Gulf crisis. While the Saudis were evidently displeased with Jordan's warming relations with Syria in 1976–77, and Jordan was unhappy with the decline in Saudi aid in 1976 and the failure to renew the 1979 Baghdad commitments at the 1989 Arab summit, these developments did not lead, for example, to a shift in the security arrangements between the two. Indeed, one of the striking features of Arab politics throughout the 1980s was the unformalized Saudi-Jordanian-Iraqi alliance.

Despite its size and tremendous wealth, Saudi behavior appears to be that of a state obsessed with security. The subsidies to Jordan may have been viewed by some Saudi policymakers as a form of Arab or Islamic solidarity. However, in more pragmatic terms, the grants and loans over the years served as investments in Saudi Arabia's own security: a strong Jordan could resist any political or economic pressures for radical change from within that might spill over into the peninsula; it could also constitute an effective land buffer between Saudi Arabia and the Arab East; and on occasion it meant the Saudis could count on the Jordanians to undertake military or diplomatic activity that the Saudis' preference for a low profile led them to avoid.

To be sure, the arrangement was facilitated by the fact that in the Jordanians the Saudis were not courting ideological opponents. As a conservative and generally pro-Western monarch, Husayn, too, saw a major political challenge to his regime from adherents of pan-Arab or Arab socialist ideologies, from those who were both inimical to the continuation of monarchies and sought to erase the artificial borders in the region imposed by the French and the British. Given the political division between radical and conservative and the threat the former attempted to pose to the latter, a Jordanian-Saudi coincidence of interests in security was natural, despite lingering suspicions owing to the rivalry between the two ruling families earlier in the century. The alignment or alliance equation at base was a simple and reinforcing one: Saudi Arabia paid support of various kinds to keep Jordan solvent and stable, and a consequently solvent and stable Jordan then reinforced Saudi security indirectly, and occasionally directly.

Moreover, because of Riyadh's wealth and influence in regional politics, maintaining good relations with Saudi Arabia had a multiplier effect. According to former Prime Minister Rifa'i, in relations with the Gulf states, selling a policy to the Saudis was the key to winning broader Gulf support: once the Saudis were on board, everyone else would follow.[94] A number of policymakers contended that the major difficulty in dealing with the Saudis was that they never stated directly or straightforwardly what they wanted. If one figured correctly, they showed their pleasure by increasing support; however, if one's calculations were wrong, they would decrease their support or take some other punitive action.[95]

Policymakers also contended that relations with Saudi Arabia required a kind of balancing act: if Jordan pursued too independent a course (as in the case of its relationship with Syria in the mid-1970s) the Saudis would cut support as a way of reining it in, but if it became too dependent upon them, they would in effect lose interest and might also cut their support. Optimizing support, therefore, meant determining and maintaining just the right distance.[96] Given Jordan's success over the years in obtaining Saudi support, one may surmise that in addition to the insurance the Saudis assumed they were buying, King Husayn and his advisers probably proved fairly astute in managing relations with Riyadh.

Not until the end of the 1980s did aid from Saudi Arabia seriously wane. Perhaps then it is not coincidental that by the end of the summer of 1990 Jordan had taken a position constituting the only open and serious break with the Saudis in the history of the relationship: the clear refusal to join the multinational coalition opposing Saddam Husayn. That story is covered in the final chapter.

4

Jordanian-Kuwaiti Relations

Ties between Jordan and Kuwait were characterized by cooperation during virtually the entire period under study. The stage for three decades of cooperative relations was set in the wake of Kuwaiti independence from Britain in 1961. At that point, Jordan sent 300 troops to the amirate as part of a larger Arab League force, following Iraqi President 'Abd al-Karim Qasim's threat to "restore" Kuwait to Iraq. Thereafter, Jordan trained members of the Kuwaiti military and worked closely with members of the Kuwaiti security apparatus.

As was the case in the Jordanian-Saudi relationship, the substantial Kuwaiti aid payments to Jordan were in large part aimed at reinforcing the security and military apparatus of a politically like-minded and supportive state. As a small conservative oil-producer, surrounded by far more powerful neighbors (Iraq, Iran, and Saudi Arabia) and subject to the influence of Arab nationalist and other regional forces generally inimical to monarchies, the amirate was vulnerable on a number of fronts. The Jordanian stability and cooperation the Kuwaitis bought (or "rented") with their various forms of financial support, therefore, were intended to reinforce Kuwaiti domestic security: Jordan served as a buffer between Kuwait and the Arab-Israeli battlefield; and its security forces helped the Kuwaitis keep track of a range of political activists of interest to both countries. In addition, the goodwill between the two states reportedly led King Husayn to intervene on several occasions to smooth Kuwait's often rocky relations with Saudi Arabia.[1]

In the economic realm, a large number of Jordanians (most of them Palestinians) began migrating, in search of work, to the small amirate following the dismemberment of Palestine in 1948 and eventually came to constitute the largest expatriate community in Kuwait. In addition to offering employment opportunities, after the oil boom Kuwait's development fund financed a variety of East and West Bank infrastructure projects and institutions. However, by far the most important economic link between the two countries consisted of the amirate's annual contribution of budgetary support, noted above. This financial aid relationship began as a result of resolutions of the Khartoum Arab League summit following the 1967 war, and was renewed or expanded in subsequent summits in Rabat in 1974 and Baghdad in 1979. Throughout this period, Kuwait was second only to Saudi Arabia in total aid provided. It thus assumed tremendous importance in Jordan's quest for state budgetary security. Outside this realm the primary impact of the bilateral economic relationship was on the private sector, since no government-to-government protocol regulated Kuwaiti-Jordanian bilateral trade, and the amirate gradually developed into Jordan's second most important export market (after Iraq).

The only major dispute between the two prior to the period under study followed Jordan's crackdown on the Palestinian resistance in 1970, which led Kuwait to suspend until 1973 the financial support it had promised Jordan in Khartoum. Hence, until the 1990 Gulf crisis, to be discussed in the concluding chapter, the relatively stable relations between the two countries offer no direct challenge to the economic and budget security argument developed in chapter 1. However, as with Saudi Arabia, a presentation of the development of this bilateral relationship is essential, first, to demonstrate the close nature and extent of the ties and, second, to make Jordan's relations with the other case study countries—Egypt, Iraq and Syria—more comprehensible. And, as with Saudi Arabia, substantiating statistics, particularly in the realm grants-in-aid, is not possible. Not all aid is acknowledged and not all aid promised is forwarded. Thus, the figures presented in this chapter should be viewed as suggestive of the extent of the aid relationship, but not definitive in terms of sums.

The Years of Plenty: 1975–81

Political Developments

Consultations between the two small states were fairly regular during this period. In mid-June in both 1975 and 1976 King Husayn paid brief visits to Kuwait as a part of larger Gulf tours. The press descriptions of the contents of such talks are generally not particularly revealing. However, in this case, a report of the 1976 Kuwait trip in Kuwait's *al-Siyasah* did note that Husayn intended to request $200 million in additional aid while in Kuwait.[2] Indeed, these visits as well as many subsequent ones should probably be understood as a part of a Hashemite campaign for funds. According to Mudar Badran, who was Minister of the Royal Court and then Prime Minister from mid-1976 to December 1979, Jordan faced a serious budgetary shortfall in 1976 owing to the Gulf states' failure to honor the financial commitments made to the confrontation states at the 1974 Arab League summit in Rabat.[3] As part of the fundraising campaign, Badran visited Kuwait and other Gulf states in mid-December 1976. A week later, Kuwaiti Minister of Foreign Affairs, Shaykh Sabah al-Ahmad al-Jabir al-Sabah, visited Jordan for brief talks with Husayn, reportedly dealing with the vague and traditional topics of "strengthening Arab solidarity" and "bilateral economic cooperation," again, likely code words for economic assistance, given Jordan's severe financial troubles at the time.

In mid-1977, King Husayn arrived in Kuwait, reportedly to discuss his recent trip to the U.S., and, no doubt, the proposed Geneva Middle East peace conference tentatively planned for later in the year. However, some sources indicated other possible agenda items: Kuwaiti assistance for arms purchases as well as PLO-Jordanian relations, since Kuwait was involved in mediating between Jordan and the PLO to improve what had been icy relations since 1971. The mediation efforts would presumably have been directed at achieving a unified Arab position as the Geneva conference approached.

But Geneva never came. The preemption of Geneva by Sadat's trip to Jerusalem was greeted differently in Kuwait than in most parts of the Arab world, as the amirate cautiously supported Sadat's decision.

The dissension that the trip caused in the Arab world led King Husayn, the perennial mediator, to visit Kuwait on December 19, reportedly for talks aimed at restoring unity.[4] In the spring of 1978, as the Egyptian-Israeli talks appeared stalled, both Jordan and Kuwait were involved in mediation aimed at ending inter-Arab feuding which had been precipitated or exacerbated by Sadat's trip. On October 1, following the signing of the Camp David Accords, Husayn arrived in Kuwait on a brief visit for talks with the amir, urging the convening of a summit to deal with the implications of the accords.

Of course, none of the Arab mediation between September 1978 and March 1979 aimed at preventing Egypt's defection from Arab ranks ultimately succeeded. Faced with the loss of Egypt, the Arab states viewed it to be in their interest to prevent additional defections à la Sadat. The easiest and most secure way of deterring Jordan, the obvious next target, from making a similar move was to bolster budgetary support to the kingdom. The basis for such a policy was laid through the Baghdad promises to provide financial assistance for a decade to the confrontation states. At the Baghdad Summit in November 1978, Kuwait made a key commitment to these states of $550 million annually for 10 years.

In the meantime, Sadat had assured the U.S. that he could deliver Jordan to the peace table so that he would not appear to have made a unilateral peace with Israel, and so that the second half of the Camp David Accords (dealing with Palestinian autonomy) could be completed, the presumption being that King Husayn would either deliver the Palestinians or represent them himself. Hence, throughout this period the U.S. pressured Jordan to join in the extension of the Camp David process. The king ultimately resisted these attempts. However, the extent of Arab courting of Jordan during this period indicates that the kingdom's adherence to the Arab consensus was by no means taken for granted, even after the reaffirmation of the Baghdad 1978 aid commitment in March 1979.

During the month before the Egyptian-Israeli peace treaty was finally signed, Jordanian Foreign Minister Hasan Ibrahim made a number of trips to Kuwait, reportedly to coordinate strategies for the period following "the peace." These discussions probably concerned both economic and political issues, as on April 30 Kuwait called upon the Arab states to support Jordan in the wake of the signing of the treaty. On July 10 Kuwaiti Deputy Prime Minister and Foreign Minister Sabah al-Ahmad left on the first leg of an unexpected tour which was also to include Damascus and Baghdad. The foreign minister spent two days in Jordan and delivered a message from the amir to Husayn. Upon his departure, the Kuwaiti envoy stressed that Jordanian-Kuwaiti views were identical and spoke of the dire need for Arab solidarity.[5] Only a few days later a report from Kuwait noted the recent stream of visitors—Iraqi, Libyan, and Kuwaiti—to Jordan and raised the question of whether Jordan felt it was facing a new Israeli military threat or if the kingdom was about to make a decision to join Camp David. The report, published in the respected daily *al-Qabas*, called on the Arabs not to make the same mistake with Jordan that they had with Egypt by failing to take prompt action: "If it is true that Jordan is now facing such a decision, now is the time for the Arabs to act decisively on this matter, to solve Jordan's confusion [read ensure financial support] in a manner that will secure the safety of the national ranks."[6] Kuwaiti support in the form of grants and loans increased markedly during this period. (See "Economic Developments" below.)

On January 14, 1980 the king made an official visit to Kuwait as part of a larger Gulf tour to discuss regional and international developments, and at the end of February, Crown Prince Hasan made a similar tour. While in Kuwait, Hasan met with Kuwait Crown Prince Sa'd and the two agreed to establish a joint committee on economic cooperation.[7] In May, the Crown Prince returned the visit and the list of Jordanian officials involved in the talks suggested that the meetings were concerned primarily with economic and security affairs.[8] Further confirming the security content of the discussions was the agreement announced at the end of the three-day visit in which the two jointly rejected all foreign intervention in the region. This was likely a reference to the Carter Doctrine, formulated in the wake of the Soviet invasion of Afghanistan, and its call for a Rapid Deployment Force, in which it had been rumored Jordan might participate.[9] That same month King Husayn and Crown Prince Sa'd traveled to Baghdad for further consultations on security arrangements, in part in response to Iraqi President Saddam Husayn's proposal of an Arab National Charter. The charter included suggestions for regional security cooperation and was directed at least in part against the extension of U.S. power in the Gulf implied in the Carter Doctrine. Security concerns in the region only intensified with the outbreak of full-scale war between Iraq and Iran in September 1980. On April 9, 1981, King Husayn reinforced Jordan's traditional opposition to external involvement in the region and implicitly made a bid for a Jordanian role in Gulf security by announcing his own regional security plan, which called for the Gulf states' neutrality, their taking responsibility for their own security, and their avoidance of both boycotts and the oil weapon.[10]

Whatever role the Jordanians had hoped to play in Gulf security, the Kuwaitis were looking elsewhere for reinforcement. Discussions of mutual defense and state security cooperation among the Gulf states had taken place in December 1978, on October 14–16, 1979, and on February 4 and March 8, 1981. Finally, on May 25, 1981, Kuwait joined Bahrayn, Oman, Qatar, Saudi Arabia and the United Arab Emirates in establishing the Gulf Cooperation Council (GCC). Although the council's mandate covered a variety of functional areas, regional security was clearly the primary consideration. Still seeking a role in regional security arrangements, Husayn offered military assistance as a form of associate membership for Jordan in the GCC. Unfortunately for Jordan, the Gulf states were not interested.[11]

Military Coordination

While Kuwaiti support payments to Jordan were no doubt in large part aimed at maintaining the stability of a moderate monarchy, they were also intended to reinforce and build upon a relationship of strong if often tacit security coordination. In April 1977 a Kuwaiti military delegation headed by Director of the Kuwaiti Armed Forces, Colonel Wajih al-Madani (a Palestinian), arrived in Amman. The delegation met with a number of high-ranking Jordanian officers at the General Command and acquainted itself with the laws and regulations of the recruiting and general mobilization directorate, as Kuwait was scheduled to introduce compulsory military service in 1978.[12] Perhaps not surprisingly then, in an interview with Jordan's semi-official daily *al-Ra'i*, Kuwaiti Defense Minister Sa'd 'Abdallah

Salim al-Sabah commented on the military aspect of relations: "we have and still are sending many officers of various ranks to attend military colleges, institutes, and schools in Jordan to be trained on the various types of weapons and to learn to modern methods used in the Jordanian armed forces."[13] In fact, between 1972 and 1982, Jordan seconded its own officers and trained numerous Kuwaitis in Jordanian facilities. The seconding of Jordanians to Kuwait came primarily toward the end of the period, and totaled 17 officers and 69 of other ranks. On the other hand, during the same period, Jordan trained some 595 Kuwaiti officers and 894 men of other ranks, for a total of 1,489, second only to Saudi Arabia and the UAE.[14] In the early 1980's the Jordanian Armed Forces Medical Corps also played a role in organizing the Kuwaiti Armed Forces Medical Corps.[15]

Economic Developments

AID

Kuwait was the first Arab country to use economic assistance systematically. Drawing on its tremendous oil wealth, it employed what may be called "dinar diplomacy" both to court friends and to thwart enemies.[16] The primary institutional mechanism for conducting such diplomacy was the Kuwait Fund for Arab Economic Development (KFAED), established in the wake of the first crisis with Iraq on December 31, 1961 to provide long-term, low-interest loans for development projects. Starting with capital of $140 million, the KFAED initially focused its attention on the Arab world. However, in the 1970s its capital was increased to $6.7 billion and eventually the range of countries assisted was expanded to include other Islamic and African states as well. A second institution that channeled assistance was the state reserve fund, which made political loans or grants to Arab states or for Arab causes. While many of these grants are noted in official discussions of aid, many have also been secret. Moreover, some funds promised have not been forwarded. Hence any figures on aid are mere estimates.[17] A list of KFAED loans and government grants during this period is found in Table 11.

TABLE 11
Kuwaiti Development Aid to Jordan, 1976–1981

Year	Source	Amount	Project
1976	KFAED	$8.0 million	1976–80 Jordanian Development Plan
	KFAED	$24.2 million	Raise phosphate production
1977	KFAED	$30.7 million	Phosphate mine production expansion
	KFAED	$66.0 million	Husayn Thermal Power Station
	Grant	$0.1 million	Bir Zeit University (West Bank)
	Grant	$1.5 million	West Bank municipalities
1978	KFAED	$35.0 million	Arab Potash Company
1979	KFAED	N/A	Jordan Fertilizer Company
	KFAED	$9.86 million	Aqaba phosphate fertilizer production
	KFAED	$4.08 million	Dead Sea potash production
	KFAED	$6.8 million	Development of Aqaba port
1981	KFAED	$27.2 million	Ghor al-Safi irrigation
	KFAED	$23.8 million	Amman water supply
	KFAED	$25.0 million	Jordan Valley Authority Development

SOURCES: MEED, RSS; *'Alaqat al-Mamlakah.*

Following the 1973 war, Kuwait resumed the aid it had promised Jordan at Khartoum in 1967, which had been suspended after the civil war of September 1970. In early 1975 it was reported that the Kuwaiti government had allocated $400 million to the confrontation states in response to the 1974 Rabat summit, $51 million of which was to go to Jordan.[18] This was in addition to the $55 million of regular subsidies that Kuwait provided.[19]

However, the Jordanians complained that the Gulf state promises of support made at Rabat were not being fulfilled and that as a result, by the end of 1976, Jordan was truly strapped for finances. According to then Prime Minister Badran, he was forced to cut the budget and struggled each month to find the money to pay the salaries of the bureaucracy and the army. Despite regular visits to Kuwait and the other Gulf states by confrontation state representatives, the response to requests for payment of the Rabat commitments was never a direct "no," just the famous, noncommittal *in sha' 'allah.*[20]

Then, in January 1977 the Kuwaiti government reviewed its budget—including aid commitments—for the year in light of a drastic fall in oil production.[21] Fortunately for Amman, despite the consequent drop in liquidity, the Kuwaitis decided to continue to pay the annual Khartoum-promised contribution of £16 million. Additional good news for Jordan came out of the January 1977 Riyadh meeting discussed in the previous chapter, at which Kuwait and the other support states agreed to pay at least part of their Rabat commitments.[22]

Subsequently, in addition to its 1978 agreement in Baghdad to provide a decade of budgetary assistance to the confrontation states, Kuwait also offered concrete demonstrations of support in the wake of the conclusion of the Egyptian-Israeli peace in March 1979, largely in the form of additional development assistance (see Table 11). For example, at the end of a five-day visit to Kuwait in late May 1979 Jordanian Finance Minister Dabbas announced that Kuwait had expressed a willingness to channel more of its surplus funds into development projects in Jordan and to conclude new commercial and transit agreements.[23] This promise was reinforced by the Kuwaiti Finance Minister al-'Atiqi, who was on a week-long visit at the beginning of June for meetings on Arab economic strategy and sanctions against Egypt, but who also discussed the expansion of economic cooperation and trade relations between Kuwait and Jordan.[24]

TRADE

Unlike the other states considered in this study, Jordanian-Kuwaiti economic relations were not regulated within the framework of a trade protocol, nor was a standing joint economic committee ever founded. Despite, or perhaps because of, the lack of state intervention, trade between the two countries grew markedly during this period. Throughout the period Kuwait, while increasing its imports of Jordanian products, maintained its place as the fourth largest Arab export market for the kingdom, behind Saudi Arabia, Syria, and Iraq. In 1974 Jordan had exported goods worth $8.4 million to Kuwait, up from $4.7 in 1973.[25] Jordanian exports increased to almost $10 million in 1976, $16.3 million in 1980, and $19.5 million in 1981.[26]

As for the other side of bilateral trade, Kuwaiti exports to Jordan during this period were not of great importance and exhibited minor fluctuations: in 1975 Kuwait exported $2.1 million in goods to the kingdom; in 1978, $3.3 million; in 1980, $1.86 million; and in 1981 $1.55 million. The amirate was only the fifth largest Arab supplier in 1975 and had dropped to eighth place by 1981.[27]

INVESTMENT

After the beginning of the oil boom, the idea of attracting Arab investment to Jordan became very popular, if primarily in the *minds* of Jordanians, to their continuing disappointment. Statistics on Kuwaiti investment are not available, but the consensus is that it never came close to meeting expectations. In 1975 an agreement was reached between Jordan and Kuwait according to which the Kuwait Real Estate Investment Corporation (KREIC) would invest $100 million in building and development in Jordan. As a first step, the Kuwaiti group purchased 3 million shares (at a cost of $9 million) in the Housing Bank (*Bank al-Iskan*), but they also made a commitment eventually to purchase 10 million shares. The Kuwaitis were, in turn, allowed one representative, appointed by the Kuwaiti finance minister, on the board of the bank. They were to receive no profits for two years, but were to have priority in buying any new share offerings. The agreement also specified that the Kuwaiti side was to be responsible for finding companies to undertake studies of potential projects; that the two sides would establish a number of joint companies; that the Kuwaiti side was to have up to 50 percent ownership; and that the capital for the companies was to be deposited in Jordanian banks.[28]

Jordan then permitted the KREIC to open offices throughout the kingdom, and offered it a variety of special privileges indicative of how anxious Jordan was to promote such investment. For example, its projects needed not be insured and profits were exempt from income and social service taxes for six years. The companies that would be established were not to be considered public sector, would not be subject to currency oversight, were exempted from export regulations at Aqaba, and were permitted to reinvest returns in new projects. For non-Jordanians working in the group, there were to be no restrictions on wage repatriation, and their entry and exit permits were to be facilitated.[29] In March 1976 it was reported that the KREIC had paid its $9 million contribution to the $36 million target capital for the Housing Bank, in implementation of the October 1975 agreement.[30]

On April 23, 1977 a KREIC delegation arrived in Jordan for further discussions, which included Crown Prince Hasan, of possible development investment projects.[31] In the meantime, representatives of the Housing Bank had had talks with the Kuwaitis about the possibility of increasing Kuwait's contribution. Shortly thereafter the two sides agreed to establish the Jordan-Kuwait Bank.[32] The bank was established with $15 million, of which 60 percent was Jordanian and 40 percent Kuwaiti. (The leading shareholder, with 25 percent of Kuwait's total capital, was Kuwait's Foreign Minister Shaykh Sabah al-Ahmad al-Jabir al-Sabah.) The Bank was expected to serve the large Jordanian expatriate communities in the Gulf, especially in Kuwait. Its management was interested in assisting in financing various five-year plan projects and in encouraging small industries, which sought comparatively small loans of $30,000–$40,000. The bank's management felt that this was preferable to financing commodity imports. The Jordan-Kuwait Bank was, therefore, to concentrate on lending to industry, agriculture, internal trade, and tourism. The bank was also prepared to make short-term loans to Palestinians in Gaza and the West Bank as long as they had negotiable land on the East Bank.[33]

EDUCATION AND LABOR

Other areas in which the two countries had significant cooperation were education and labor. In May 1977 Jordan's Minister of Education, 'Abd al-Salam al-Majali, stopped in Kuwait as part of a tour of the Gulf, aimed at seconding Jordanian teachers to these states. The agreement reached involved coordinating such hiring through relevant committees and with the approval of the Jordanian Ministry of Education. Majali also made clear that Jordan was willing to accept Gulf state students at its teachers colleges and the Technical Engineering Institute.[34] A few months later, a delegation from the Kuwaiti

Ministry of Education made a tour of Egypt, Jordan, and Syria to recruit new teachers.[35]

Summary

During this period Kuwait took second place only to Saudi Arabia in terms of the financial assistance it provided Jordan. While the actual grant aid was less than that forwarded by Saudi Arabia, development aid from the KFAED was far more extensive. The critical role that Kuwait thereby played in ensuring Jordan's budget security appears to have been in exchange for traditional internal and military security cooperation from Jordan, and as part of a broader Kuwaiti policy aimed at "buying friends" in the area to reduce its vulnerability. Political relations between the two were quite good, and the Kuwaitis seem to have made a point of providing additional development aid in the wake of the Egyptian-Israeli treaty to make sure that Jordan would not go the way of Sadat, a policy which appears to have been successful. Private sector economic relations also flourished, unregulated and unstimulated by special government protocols or agreements.

Gradual Economic Retreat 1982–1990

Political Developments

The Iran-Iraq war not only increased financial and commercial hardships on Kuwait, it also exacerbated longstanding, if largely latent, communal tensions between Sunnis and the minority Shi'i population. As the war continued and Kuwait's traditional, preferred position of neutrality in the Gulf region became untenable, Shi'i feelings of discrimination and dissatisfaction grew as the country tilted more and more in a pro-Iraqi direction. Internal violence and sabotage increased along with the external military threat from Iran.[36] December 1983 witnessed the worst instances of violence in the amirate, as on December 12 explosions at the International Airport, the U.S.

and French embassies and several other key installations rocked the country.

In response, Amman sought to demonstrate support for Kuwait in a number of ways. In spring 1984, Husayn sent Chief of the Royal Court Marwan al-Qasim as a special envoy to Bahrayn, Kuwait, the UAE, and Oman to call for Arab cooperation in solving regional problems. On June 3, in a meeting that he requested with Kuwait's ambassador in Jordan, Prime Minister Ahmad 'Ubaydat expressed Jordan's concern over the continuation of the conflict in the Gulf and its escalation to include attacks against Kuwaiti and Saudi tankers, which had been stepped up beginning in May. On the same day Husayn left for talks with the amir, presumably concerning Kuwaiti security.[37] Relations remained good even following Jordan's unilateral restoration of relations with the still-outcast Egypt. The Kuwaitis responded in much the same way the Saudis had: indirect chastisement of Jordan combined with reaffirmation of the need for Egypt to return to the Arab fold.[38] However, by late spring 1985 consultations between Husayn and the amir focused not only on developments in the Gulf war and developments in the peace process, but also on the threats that the Kuwaitis had made about cutting their Baghdad support because of the drop in oil prices and the marked increase in their own military expenditures. The domestic ramifications of the continuing Gulf war had finally begun to take their toll on the Kuwaiti national budget, and by extension, on the Kuwaiti-Jordanian relationship, especially in the realm of financial support.

Not quite three weeks later there was an assassination attempt against the amir, for which a number of Iraqi Shi'i residents of Kuwait were arrested. However, the major security concern continued to be the Gulf war, as in February 1986 Iran occupied Faw island, a mere 10 miles from Kuwaiti territory. This was followed by a number of veiled and not-so-veiled Iranian threats against Kuwait. In response to these developments, on April 2, 1986, King Husayn told *Jane's Defence Weekly* that Jordan was ready to support Kuwait in confronting any aggression by the Iranian regime against Kuwaiti territory, if so requested by the amirate. In the meantime, the Kuwaitis were calling upon Jordan and the PLO to return to their dialogue, which had been suspended following the effective freezing of the February 11 accord in February 1986.

The year 1987 began as an extremely important one for Kuwait, as in January it hosted the summit of the Islamic Conference Organization. The successful convening of the conference was a major coup given both the proximity of the Iran-Iraq war and the fact that Egypt was in attendance for the first time since its ejection from most Arab and Islamic organizations following its separate peace with Israel. The first half of 1987 was also critical because in January Kuwait formally requested that the U.S. reflag Kuwaiti vessels and in May the Reagan administration approved the request. On June 22, 1987, the Kuwaiti Minister of State for Foreign Affairs, Sa'ud al-Usaymi, arrived in Jordan on the first leg of a trip that was also to take him to Syria and Iraq. This trip was likely part of a concerted Kuwaiti campaign to convince Arab and other states that it had legitimate reasons for requesting the ship reflagging.[39] In September the Kuwaiti Deputy Prime Minister and Foreign Minister, Shaykh Sabah al-Ahmad, arrived in Jordan with a message for Husayn from the amir, before heading on to Moscow. In the meantime, the Iranians began launching missile attacks against Kuwait.[40] On September 30 Husayn himself made a trip to Kuwait on the fourth leg of a Gulf tour.[41] As the Iranian threats continued Husayn voiced numerous expressions of support for the amirate, and on November 22 Crown Prince Hasan announced once again that Jordan was ready to send troops to support the security of the Gulf. The offer of troops may be understood as in part a Jordanian expression of concern for the security and integrity of Kuwait, in part a gesture of political good will that also included political and moral support, but perhaps also (assuming that Jordan would be reimbursed for its military services) an offer intended to reinforce or revive the dwindling aid relationship between the two.

The November 1987 Amman Arab League summit was of great significance to both Kuwait and Jordan. Devoted almost exclusively to the Gulf war, the summit was, for the first time, able to use oil state financial pressure to move Syria to support the GCC states, to censure Iran, and send a strong signal of desire to end the war. The summit also officially gave member states the option of deciding when to renew ties with Egypt, whose weight as a "returning" member of the Arab world was viewed as a key counterbalance to Iran. Certainly to follow up on the results of the summit and perhaps to cash in for its successful sponsorship, on December 9 Jordan hosted Kuwaiti Finance Minister Jasim al-Kharafi. Al-Kharafi met with Prime Minister Zayd al-Rifa'i, Trade and Industry Minister Raja'i al-Mu'ashshir, and with the king. The following day Kharafi had discussions with Crown Prince Hasan, Foreign Minister Tahir al-Masri, Mu'ashshir, Finance Minister Hanna 'Awdah and Planning Minister Tahir Kan'an.[42] The meetings were followed immediately by a December 12 visit by Husayn to Kuwait. Discussions reportedly covered the Iran-Iraq war, Arab developments, and bilateral relations, but no other details were available. However, Rifa'i and a number of senior advisers accompanied the king[43] and one can, from the timing and from the ministers involved, assume that finances as well as security assistance were high on the agenda.

Regular contact and support continued, as the king dispatched Chief of the Royal Court Marwan al-Qasim to Kuwait in mid-January 1988 and then went himself in mid-March. These discussions likely concerned both the war and the Palestinian uprising, which had begun in December 1987. Seven months later the Kuwaitis praised King Husayn's controversial July 31 step of cutting legal and administrative ties with the West Bank. And both sides breathed deep sighs of relief when in August Iran finally accepted Security Council Resolution 598 calling for a ceasefire in the Gulf war.

However, for Jordan the direct and indirect economic costs of the war had already taken their toll and pushed the kingdom closer and closer to insolvency. First, the value of the dinar began to drop precipitously in the autumn of 1988. Husayn made a visit to the amirate on November 8 for two hours of talks. Less than a month later Kuwaiti Finance Minister Kharafi was back in Jordan for talks with Rifa'i.[44] Whatever the Jordanian arguments or pleas, they were insufficient or ineffective as the Kuwaitis did not increase their aid. But the pleas were also too late, for Jordan's problems ran far deeper than a temporary budget shortfall. In January 1989, for the first time, the kingdom was unable to make its external debt service payment. The Jordanian government–IMF agreement that followed then set the stage for the announcement of austerity measures that eventually triggered the riots of April 1989.

Kuwait was, nonetheless, vocal and forceful in its support for Jordan in the wake of the riots. A decline in Jordan's standard of living was something the Gulf states cared little about. What they did care about, however, was avoiding unrest. Crown Prince Sa'd stated that Jordan's stability was key to broader regional stability and stressed Kuwait's support for the king and the government leadership.[45] To reinforce the Kuwaiti position, Sa'd visited the kingdom on May 1 and Kuwait promised supplemental grant aid.

Given Jordan's domestic economic hardships, the kingdom turned inward to a process of political liberalization following the riots, a process that found little, if any, official sympathy among Jordan's neighbors, who no doubt feared a demonstration effect in their own states. In fact, the new freedom of expression in the kingdom led the Jordanian press to criticize roundly Kuwaiti government moves against its nascent pro-democracy movement. Nonetheless, January 1990 ended on a somewhat positive note as Kuwait lifted the ban on the Jordanian newspapers *al-Ra'i* and *al-Dustur*[46] imposed earlier in the month amid demonstrations in Kuwait for the reinstatement of the Kuwaiti National Assembly.

In February 1990 Husayn and Prime Minister Badran both received the Kuwaiti foreign minister, who conveyed a message from the amir. A few days later Husayn began an official tour of the Gulf by heading to Kuwait. This was most likely another fundraising tour. The new pitch was the threat posed to Jordanian and Arab security by the influx of Jews into Israel triggered by the opening up of the Soviet political system. Husayn argued that the influx would put further pressures on the Palestinian population under occupation and thus portended a potential expulsion of the indigenous population of the West Bank and Gaza by the Israelis. Whether a problem of content, packaging or audience, the pleas elicited no concrete financial commitments from the Gulf states.

However, suddenly, in July 1990, the focus of concern shifted from the threat of Israel and Soviet Jews to the war drums that seemed to be beating over a border and oil-pumping dispute between Iraq and Kuwait. Jordan and Kuwait were in close consultation about the nascent conflict, as both sought to avoid escalation. On July 22 a Kuwaiti envoy arrived with a message for Husayn from the amir about the Iraqi complaints and held talks with the king. Following the subsequent, failed Jeddah meeting, Husayn led a Jordanian delegation to Kuwait to discuss ways to ensure Arab solidarity in the face of the crisis. The efforts, were, of course, unsuccessful, and Saddam rolled into Kuwait early on the morning of August 2, 1990. Overnight the relationship changed dramatically and to the detriment of both sides. The full impact is discussed in the concluding chapter.

Economic Developments

AID

Grants.   The year 1982 marked the beginning of a period of reduced economic interaction between the two countries, a direct result of the impact of the Iran-Iraq war. Not only were oil revenues down, but also internal and external security threats had forced Kuwait to increase its own domestic military spending from $535 million in 1980/81 to $712 million in 1981/82 and to $833 million in 1982/83—the largest increases in thirty years.[47] In response, in September 1982 the Kuwaiti government announced that it would not be bound by the financial commitments made at Baghdad. Nonetheless, the following June the Kuwaiti National Assembly voted to *restore* to the budget $360 million in aid to the frontline states, despite the recommendation of the economic and financial affairs committee that drastic cuts be made. The assembly did, however, approve the trimming of $65 million from the aid commitment, Kuwait's share of the funds promised but not paid by Libya and Algeria. Interestingly, the debate was held in secret session and the vote on the aid measure was 28 to 23 with 6 abstentions. This exceeded the assembly's elected membership of 50 and suggested that cabinet ministers who were ex officio members had been mobilized to reverse the proposed cuts.[48] Finally, however, on May 30, 1984, the Kuwaiti parliament did vote to decrease Kuwaiti support to the confrontation states by 39 percent in order to pay the amirate's budget deficit.[49]

In 1985, as partial compensation for the reneged-upon grants, Kuwait began to provide $50 million a year in in-kind aid. Jordan decided to take the $50 million in fuel oil and in certain chemicals for the Fertilizer Company, an arrangement that lasted until the Gulf crisis.[50] However, in mid-year the Kuwaiti parliament once again called for terminating support to the frontline states in the 1985–86 budget.[51] Again, in only partial compensation, the assembly voted to increase the amount allocated for *general* foreign aid to $500 million.

These and other moves over the next few years led to subtle strains in the Kuwaiti-Jordanian relationship. Perhaps most disappointing was the Kuwaiti decision not to participate in funding the controversial 1986 Jordanian development plan for the occupied territories. Kuwaiti Minister of Finance Kharafi received Prime Minister Rifaʻi on September 10 to review relations, no doubt with a focus on economic and financial ties. Rifaʻi returned to Kuwait a month later, accompanied by Jordan's ministers of trade and supply, finance, energy and mineral wealth, as well as the governor of the central bank and several other economic advisers, reportedly to discuss the possibilities of Kuwaiti participation in the politically controversial development plan for the occupied territories announced that summer.[52] Only a few days later, Jordan's finance and planning ministers attended a seminar in Kuwait entitled "Development—Between Planning and Implementation in the Arab Homeland." The participants reviewed the Jordanian 1986–90 economic and social development plan, the development plan for the occupied territories, and Jordanian efforts to bolster steadfastness among the population under occupation. Planning Minister Kanʻan met with his Kuwaiti counterpart, the director-general of the Kuwait Development Fund, to review aspects of cooperation between Jordan and Kuwait and explore the possibility of Jordan's obtaining assistance for the implementation of the development plans.[53] On November 9 the Kuwaiti government agreed to continue its financial support for the plans.[54] Ultimately, however, Kuwaiti support for the political sensitive development plan for the occupied territories was not forthcoming, a clear blow to the kingdom and a strong message of support for the PLO over the king following the December 1987 beginning of the Palestinian uprising.

The next major disappointment came at the Arab League summit in May 1988, when the amirate voted, along with other contributors, to forward support for the occupied territories directly to the PLO, rather than through the traditional channel, the Jordanian-Palestinian joint committee. Finally, like its oil state counterparts, Kuwait ignored Jordanian pleas in 1989 for a renewal of the 1979 decade-long Baghdad aid commitment. These decisions appear to have been based on a combination of Kuwaiti economic (austerity) and political (Jordanian competition with the PLO) concerns.

Nonetheless, in August 1989, following the April riots, Jordanian Prime Minister Zayd bin Shakir traveled to Kuwait to deliver a message, presumably in part a plea for funds, from the king to the amir. Upon his return, he stated that as a result of his visit the GCC states would take measures designed to support Jordan economically.[55] Kuwait reportedly offered Jordan $80 million in aid[56] and, on September 5, the Jordanian Minister of Finance reported that Jordan expected the GCC states to deposit some $500 million into Jordanian banks to support the kingdom's economy.[57] In addition, by the end of 1989 it had been agreed that Kuwait, as well as Saudi Arabia, the UAE, Qatar, and Oman would deposit $300 million for Amman's use with the Arab Monetary Fund. According to the agreement, which was intended to shore up the still-ailing dinar, Amman was to pay interest 2 percent below the market rates and the Jordanian government would deposit an equivalent amount in local currency in blocked accounts at the central bank as collateral. The size of the contribution was to be in proportion to the country's financial capabilities, with the largest share, of course, coming from Saudi Arabia.[58]

In late June 1990, the Kuwaiti government informed Jordan of its intention to provide $75 million in aid in 1990 in three installments, in addition to further aid estimated at $60 million. This assistance was in support of the Jordanian economy and in accordance with the recommendations approved in May 1990 at the Arab League summit in Baghdad.[59] However, the Iraqi invasion of Kuwait preempted the forwarding of these funds.

Development loans.   Assistance in this area continued to be quite steady, as is clear from Table 12. Nonetheless, there were limits to Kuwait's financial good will. In July 1988 Jordan held debt repayment discussions with the KFAED, following the fund's suspension of disbursements the previous March. Amman's debt to the fund stood at around $200 million at the end of 1987, and the fund announced that disbursements would not resume until a repayment agreement had been reached.[60] Unfortunately, these discussions came just as the Jordanian dinar edged toward the precipice.

In May 1990, on the eve of the Gulf crisis, it was announced that the KFAED would lend $17 million to Jordan's Industrial Development Bank for lending to private sector industry and tourism projects. To date the fund had provided Jordan with twenty-four concessionary loans totaling KD 124 million (worth in 1990 $423.8 million) for use in agriculture, energy, irrigation, industry, mining, tourism, and road construction.[61]

TRADE

In 1982 Jordanian exports to Kuwait stood at $19.5 million, just under the 1981 figure. They reached a high in 1983 of $29 million, then dropped to $19.9 million in 1985. Kuwaiti exports to Jordan during this period stood at $2.8 million for 1982 (a 100% increase over the previous year), rose to a high of $8.5 million in 1984, and then dropped below $7.74 million in 1985 and 1986.[62] On October 20, 1986 the two reached an agreement to increase cooperation in the fields of economics and trade. Customs exemptions, investment incentives, tourism, and transport were all covered.[63] Less than a year later, in May 1987, another agreement to boost trade was signed. In September of that year the two agreed to work toward free trade in industrial projects. Phased reductions in customs duties of 20 percent were to begin in January 1988.[64] Jordanian exports to Kuwait rose to $27.6 million in 1988, making the amirate Jordan's third largest Arab export market. On the other hand, in 1987, Jordanian *imports* from Kuwait jumped dramatically to $50.5 million and again to $68 million in 1988, making Kuwait the third largest Arab source of Jordanian imports.[65]

TABLE 12
Kuwaiti Development Aid to Jordan, 1982–1990

Year	Source	Amount	Project
1982	KFAED	$21.3 million	Electricity distribution scheme
	KFAED	$8.55 million	Agricultural credit for small farmers
	KFAED	$13.6 million	Road construction
1983	KFAED	$34.1 million	Raise height of King Talal Dam
1984	Kuwait Nat'l. Bank	$50.0 million	Development projects
1986	KFAED	$24.7 million	Zarqa River Basin development
	KFAED	$4.4 million	Development of animal resources
1987	KFAED	$23.8 million	Aqaba Thermal Power Station

SOURCES: MEED, RSS; *'Alaqat al-Mamlakah.*

INVESTMENT

Despite the regional economic downturn, Jordanians continued to hope and lobby for increased Gulf state investment in the kingdom. The first productive (as opposed to service sector) joint venture between Jordan and Kuwait, the Jordanian-Kuwaiti Company for Agricultural and Food Products, was set up in February 1985. Capitalized at $10.3 million, the company had plans to establish factories to produce macaroni, dairy products, and fodder as well as to raise cattle, poultry, and fish.[66] It was subsequently announced that a Jordanian information and tourism office was also to be set up in Kuwait to promote joint ventures in this sector. About a year later, a Kuwaiti business team arrived in Jordan to study possible participation in local tourism schemes. Members of the delegation also met with Planning Minister Tahir Kan'an, who briefed them on investment opportunities in the 1986–90 plan.[67]

During April 1987, Trade and Industry Minister Mu'ashshir and Finance Minister 'Awdah visited Kuwait at the invitation of the Kuwaiti government. During their stay they attended a two-day seminar intended to interest Kuwaitis and expatriate Jordanians in investing in Jordan. Following talks with Kuwaiti investment institutions the two ministers indicated that agreement had been reached upon setting up a joint committee to follow up financing and implementation of viable schemes in Jordan. The Jordanian delegation explained the local investment climate and presented details of 25 projects valued at $600 million in the industrial, trade, agricultural, financial, and tourist sectors. They pointed out Jordan's shortages in the production of cereals, meat, and milk, and added that a number of the proposed projects were meant to ensure self-sufficiency in these areas.[68]

Shortly thereafter, it was reported that preliminary discussions were under way on a plan for Jordan and Kuwait to list their stocks on each other's share markets. Arab investors were already permitted to buy Jordanian stocks through the Amman Financial Market, although they were limited to 49 percent holding in firms in the financial, insurance, and trade sectors. The Jordanians hoped that the joint listing of stocks would give Kuwaiti investors more information on the Jordanian economy and stimulate more interest, particularly in primary issues of stocks.[69]

Several other joint agreements were concluded during this period as well. In the spring of 1988, an accord was reached between the Kuwait Public Transport Company and the Jordan Express Transport Company for a bus link between Kuwait and Amman.[70] In March 1989 a liquid fertilizer plant set up by the Jordanian-Kuwaiti Agricultural Company was opened in Aqaba. With an annual capacity of 45,000–60,000 tons, only about 10,000 tons of which was to be for the domestic market, this plant was the first of its kind in the region. It planned to target its exports at Saudi Arabia, Egypt, Turkey, North Yemen, and Sudan.[71]

EDUCATION AND LABOR

Although in June 1985 Kuwaiti Ministry of Education officials were seeking Jordanian teachers for employment in Kuwait,[72] in late spring 1986 there were rumors that some 30,000 expatriates were expected to leave Kuwait by the end of the summer. The communities most affected were the Egyptians and Jordanians. Some people had reportedly been dismissed, others were simply leaving.[73] In the event, however, a total of only 428 families returned with their possessions between January and August, numbers similar to those of returnees in previous years. According to Trade and Industry Minister Mu'ashshir, the Kuwaiti plan to reduce the number of foreign workers by 30,000 in the summer was stopped after mediation by the countries affected, and all Jordanians in public sector employment in the Gulf were assured of their jobs.[74]

Summary

Kuwait, increasingly besieged internally as the Iran-Iraq war dragged on and as oil prices fell, finally took a series of steps to reduce and ultimately terminate its Baghdad-promised support to Jordan. The loss of this income was a serious blow to the Jordanian economy: it left Saudi Arabia the sole remaining provider of Baghdad support and forced Jordan increasingly to resort to external borrowing to make up the shortfall. Although there was some strain in relations as a result of the decrease in aid (and over the amirate's apparent favoring of the PLO over Jordan in various instances of competition), political relations nonetheless apparently remained cordial, and Jordan regularly expressed its willingness to come to Kuwait's military defense if asked. The emirate did offer assistance to Jordan in the wake of the 1989 riots, and made additional promises in 1990, but aid never returned to the early Baghdad levels—a fact the Jordanian populace remembered clearly as they received the news of the Iraqi invasion of Kuwait in August 1990.

Conclusions

Economic Relations

The use of economic statecraft is quite clear in this case study, but primarily on the Kuwaiti side. The Kuwaitis used direct grants or budgetary support agreed to at Khartoum, Rabat and Baghdad for two major purposes. The first was to strengthen Jordan so that it could continue to serve militarily as a buffer against security threats coming out of the Arab East and to gain Jordan's goodwill to maintain the continuing internal security or intelligence cooperation that was such an important part of the bilateral relationship. The second, more general, purpose was to try to buy goodwill in the region, so that whenever Kuwait provided support, it was seen in *other* parts of the Arab world as an indication of Kuwaiti benevolence or commitment to a larger Arab cause.

The same was true of Kuwaiti support in the form of the KFAED's highly concessionary loans. Here, the Kuwaitis had a greater say in how the support was used, as the fund placed greatest emphasis on funding projects that contributed to the development of economic infrastructure. Again, goodwill was also purchased or "rented," as was, if more indirectly, stability through Jordan's ability to deliver more and better services to its people.

The controversial Kuwaiti decision in 1984 to cut back on its Baghdad payments and replace them in part with in-kind support in 1985 appears to have been the result of genuine economic and budgetary troubles in Kuwait, not an attempt at "screw tightening" or an indication of waning Kuwaiti interest in relations with the confrontation states (although given the internal security problems the country faced at the time it was probably also indicative of a greater need to turn inward). Nevertheless, Jordanian policymakers stressed that dealing with the Kuwaitis was not pleasant; unlike the Saudis, they were haughty and much less readily forthcoming. Jordanians recount with bitterness the fact that the king was forced to make repeated fundraising trips to the Gulf during which he often in effect had to beg for assistance. As early as 1988–89, the Kuwaitis reportedly asked the Jordanians why they had or needed the high quality educational, communications, and transportation infrastructure that they had built. In other words, they seemed to begrudge the Jordanians the standard of living and the infrastructure that their own development loans had helped to finance.[75] Whether the Jordanian charges are fair or not is not the point. What is important is that however much the Kuwaitis gave Jordan, when it came time to call in the presumed accumulated markers from over the years at the time of the Iraqi invasion of Kuwait, the Kuwaiti "investment" in Jordanian support and goodwill proved insufficient. The average Jordanian had nothing but contempt for the Kuwaitis in August 1990, the millions in aid over the years notwithstanding.

What economic instruments were available to the Jordanians in their dealings with the wealthy Kuwaitis? The Jordanians, on a number of occasions detailed above, made concerted efforts to court Kuwaiti investors. Whether in the form of interesting the Kuwaitis in projects that were part of the five-year development plans or in joint ventures such as the Jordan-Kuwait Bank or the Jordanian-Kuwaiti Agricultural Company, the Jordanians were keen on Kuwaiti investment and were willing to offer attractive incentives and exemptions to encourage the Kuwaitis to direct their dinars Jordan's way. That the Jordanians were less than successful in these efforts was in large part the result of a broader Kuwaiti policy which directed overseas investment, as opposed to loans or grants, to the much more secure and lucrative markets of Western Europe and the United States. Kuwaiti investment in other Arab states was insignificant: only 5 percent of Kuwait's funds were invested in the developing world, *including* Arab states.[76] Consequently, there does not appear to have been any deliberate discrimination against Jordan for political or other reasons, simply a desire to place investment capital in countries in which it would realize the greatest return. The Kuwaitis' meager investments in Jordan should be seen as largely positive, if really only symbolic, economic instruments with clearly *political* goals, just as their desire to invest the vast majority of available funds in the West should be seen as strategically *economic*, not political. Those Kuwaiti investments that were directed toward the kingdom were by no means central to the Jordanian economy or the state budget, although they were seen by the Jordanians as a potential engine for greater economic growth. The most critical element was always the financial assistance.

While trade was important in this relationship, its bases were somewhat different than in the other case study countries. In the first place, although a number of meetings resolved to establish some sort of joint council or committee for various economy-related purposes, none ever had the importance of the joint higher committees established between Jordan and Syria, Iraq or Egypt. Trade between Jordan and Kuwait was clearly the domain of their respective private sectors. One finds few references to official trade talks, nor is there any-thing like the setting of trade targets or quotas between these two countries. Also characteristic of the trade relationship was that Kuwait was far more important to Jordan as an export market than was Jordan for Kuwait. The majority of the Kuwaiti export totals to Jordan consisted of petroleum products of an insignificant amount for the amirate in the overall scheme of things. Given Kuwaiti finan-cial capabilities the amirate could easily have replaced Jordanian goods with those of other countries.

Although Jordanian expatriate labor in Kuwait was not discussed under the rubric of trade, in summary, it may make sense to think of it in those terms and as a form of economic statecraft. The one com-modity the Kuwaitis were keen to import from Jordan and for which they had limited alternative markets was skilled Arab labor. The vast majority of Jordanians who sought work in Kuwait left Jordan well before the period covered in this study. Indeed, the 1967 war trig-gered the last wave of migration to the Gulf and by the mid-1970s, the Kuwaitis had begun to tighten considerably the conditions for grant-ing new work permits. Nonetheless, many of those who had been in the country for decades had become an integral part of its commer-cial or governmental sectors, so that both the Kuwaiti private and public sectors had an interest and a hand in importing Jordanians. This study has pointed to the continuing Kuwaiti need for Jordanian teachers (who were overwhelmingly preferred to Egyptians). What-ever the sector and its needs, the Jordanian government viewed the presence of its expatriates in the Gulf as a key source of foreign cur-rency through the remittances they sent home.

Another set of commodities that may fit under the rubric of trade if interpreted broadly were the military and intelligence services ren-dered Kuwait by Jordan. Whether in the form of Jordanian officers seconded to Kuwait, Kuwaitis sent to train in Jordan, or cooperation in the realm of security, Jordan was exchanging its expertise for Kuwaiti payment. In this realm, too, as in the field of expatriate labor discussed above, both sides were well-served. And, in the case of security cooperation, it was the Jordanians who in fact had the upper hand because of superior experience and training. It was they who provided the expertise to the Kuwaitis and not the other way around, except perhaps in terms of some Kuwaiti monitoring of the activities of Jordanian Palestinians in Kuwait.

Economics and Alliances

While no formal alliance existed between Jordan and Kuwait, throughout the period under study there was tacit and strong cooperation in a variety of fields: upholding regional and internal security; monitoring their respective Palestinian populations; moving ahead on the Middle East peace process; and working to end the Gulf war. Both states are small in size, surrounded by economically, politically and militarily more powerful neighbors, and conservative in orientation (although Kuwait was more of a neutral in the Cold War than was Jordan).

Building on the clear coincidence of interests on these grounds, Kuwait courted Jordan with substantial grants and loans as a way of ensuring the kingdom's stability, which was seen as reinforcing order in the amirate. In the Arab world, the Kuwaitis' concern for stability was apparent in its concentration of loans to (at that time) status quo states: Jordan, Tunisia, Sudan, Morocco, Egypt, and North Yemen received more than 65.3% of the loans between 1962 and 1989. Jordan had the honor of first place, having received $401 million or 14.5% of Arab loans and 7.4% of total loans.[77] According to the official figures on cash contributed, Jordan received $2.154 billion or 7.18% of the total. (Iraq received $13.3 billion, 44.4%; Egypt—prior to 1979—$7.12 billion.)

Also relevant to the question of security and stability was the presence of the large Jordanian expatriate community in Kuwait. This community, numbering about 350,000 in its heyday (about 85–95% of which was estimated to be Palestinian)[78] had a key role in commerce and the bureaucracy and sent home substantial remittances. While the Palestinians were often referred to as a potential threat to the Kuwaiti regime, in fact they were among its most loyal supporters, as was demonstrated at numerous points during the difficult times attending the Iran-Iraq war. However, what role did they play in the bilateral political relationship? Both countries were clearly interested in monitoring any political activities by community members, but that was only one aspect of their "political significance." In interviews, Jordanian decisionmakers uniformly contended that the presence in Kuwait of these Palestinians did not give Jordan any special power in the amirate. Most had gone to Kuwait as individuals, and were not seconded by the Jordanian government. Since most had left Jordan for Kuwait in the 1950s or 1960s, their only real contact with Jordan was a passport, which was considered by most a document of convenience; hence, they felt no political loyalty or affiliation to the kingdom. Indeed, most went out of their way to avoid official Jordanian offices. For their part, the Kuwaitis treated these Jordanian citizens as Palestinians, as evidenced by the fact that after the founding of the PLO in 1964, the Kuwaiti government collected a "liberation tax" from them, which then went to the coffers of the Palestine National Fund, the PLO's treasury. Thus, if anything, this community gave the PLO or Palestinian concerns, not the Jordanian government, weight in Kuwaiti decisionmaking—a fact that on occasion worked to Jordan's disadvantage.

Indeed, despite the centrality of the "economic aid-for-security" equation to Jordanian-Kuwaiti relations, Jordanian-Gulf state diplomatic relations were often affected by developments in the Palestinian-Jordanian or the PLO-Jordanian theater. The Gulf states were clearly interested in maintaining good relations with both the PLO and Jordan, since one of the basic principles of Gulf state diplomacy has been that open inter-Arab rifts of any type are to be avoided. In the case of Kuwait, the only instances in which the amirate openly sided against Jordan in Jordanian-Palestinian disputes were in the case of the 1970 military assault against the Palestinian resistance movement, in 1987 in denying the Jordanian government assistance for its development plan for the occupied territories, and in supporting the Arab consensus at the 1988 summit to channel funds for the occupied territories directly through the PLO, deliberately bypassing Jordan.

In sum, with successes and failures, and certainly with pleading and haggling, Kuwaiti aid was a constant, if gradually declining, feature of the relationship throughout the majority of the period under study. So was political and diplomatic cooperation. Unlike in the case studies that follow, this relationship did not witness a major political shift against which to judge the role of economics until the Gulf crisis. What is clear is that Kuwaiti financial assistance was critical to the Jordanian budget; indeed, the drop in Kuwaiti aid to the kingdom helped lead the kingdom to increase its external borrowing, thereby contributing to the economic decline of the late 1980s. Efforts to maintain good relations with the Kuwaitis in order to gain needed support, as well as the continuing appeals for assistance after aid levels had dropped, should all be viewed as part of Jordanian efforts to achieve budget security.

Jordan's failure to convince the Kuwaitis to maintain the level of assistance promised in 1979, and its inability to win Kuwaiti (as well as other Gulf state) support for renewal of the ten-year-old Baghdad aid commitment certainly affected Jordanian popular response when Iraqi troops rolled into Kuwait: Jordanians displayed amazingly little sympathy for the newly occupied Kuwaitis. Nor is it coincidental that the kingdom's stance in the Gulf war (neutrality on the official level, pro-Iraq on a popular level)—the major alliance shift in this relationship—followed the years of steady decline in financial support. The drop in this assistance combined with other domestic economic and political problems in Jordan had begun to change the underpinnings of the regime in Jordan. As a result, and unfortunately for the Kuwaitis, by the time they sought to call in their cards for years of economic assistance, the king could no longer respond to foreign policy or other challenges in the same way as he might have in the past. This subject is covered in greater detail in the concluding chapter.

5

Jordanian-Syrian Relations

Of the five bilateral relationships examined in this work, Jordanian-Syrian ties have witnessed the most, and the most serious, fluctuations. The mobilization of 1970, during which Syria sent troops into Jordan to support the Palestinian resistance in its clashes with the Jordanian army came just before Hafiz al-Asad took power. But this was only the first of several turns in relations between the two. Previous work on inter-Arab relations suggests that the shifting alliances between these two countries may be explained by balancing or bandwagoning, by tensions owing to differences over ideology or superpower affiliation, or by regional political rivalries. The empirical material presented in this case study, as well as the two that follow it, suggests a different explanation for seemingly unpredictable fluctuations in ties. The weaving together of the political and economic histories demonstrates clearly that considerations of budget security, at least on the Jordanian side, account for the timing and direction of Jordanian shifts in a way that the other explanations cannot.

The Rapprochement of 1975–77

Only a few works have attempted to explore this period in inter-Arab relations and they shed very little light. In one study, Alan Taylor presents Syrian-Jordanian relations as a function only of Syrian involvement in Lebanon and explains Husayn's decision to ally himself with Asad at this time "largely because a Muslim-PLO victory in Lebanon might isolate Jordan in its immediate regional situation and also preclude the possibility of rapprochement between Amman and the PLO. In the long run, he looked to a solution to the crisis that would be imposed by the surrounding Arab states."[1] Stephen Walt, although he devotes scant attention to it, in one place attributes the improvement in Syrian-Jordanian relations to the beginning of feuding between Egypt and Syria, and in another place to a desire on the part of the two states to balance the United States and Iraq.[2] None of these three explanations is systematically arrived at, nor particularly convincing. As the empirical material presented in this section will show, a closer examination of the historical record demonstrates all of these explanations to be inaccurate.

Political Developments[3]

Syria's participation in the 1973 war with Egypt against Israel confirmed its status as an increasingly important power in the region. At the same time, ironically, the 1973 conflict marked the first step in Egypt's path toward ending its state of war with Israel. Syria, although not of Egypt's size and weight in Arab politics, was nonetheless intent upon diverting Egypt from its new path. Failing that, it was poised to assume for itself the role that Egypt would gradually relinquish.

During the same period, Jordan was recovering from successive economic recessions brought on by the 1967 war and the 1970–71 crackdown on the Palestinian resistance movement. Syria had closed its borders with, and airspace to, Jordan in 1970, while Kuwait and Libya suspended the aid they had promised the kingdom at the 1967 Arab League summit in Khartoum. In a first and tentative attempt to end the ostracism, King Husayn sent a token brigade to the Syrian front in the 1973 war. Syria was clearly militarily more powerful as well as economically stronger and more diversified than Jordan. The two also differed in superpower orientation. Nonetheless, as frontline states with large military expenditures, the two countries did share at least one key characteristic: a reliance on external (primarily Arab) budgetary assistance.

Relations between Syria and Jordan, broken in 1970, were officially resumed on October 4, 1973, shortly before Jordan sent its brigade to the Golan as symbolic assistance for the Egyptian-Syrian war effort against Israel. In early June 1974 Syrian Vice President 'Abd al-Halim Khaddam delivered a letter from President Asad to King Husayn. However, the clearest moves toward a full rapprochement (and more) came several months after the 1974 Rabat Arab League summit conference, during which the oil states had promised support for the confrontation states (Syria, Jordan, Egypt, and the PLO). In early March 1975 Asad received Jordanian prime minister Zayd al-Rifaʿi for a series of talks that touched on regional issues and bilateral relations, especially in the field of economic cooperation and commercial exchange, transport, and electricity. This series of talks resulted, at the initiative of Rifaʿi, in the establishment of a Joint Committee, the first of its kind to be set up between two Arab countries and a move that set a pattern, particularly for inter-Arab economic relations, in the years to come.[4] The committee was to be headed by the ministers of economy of the two countries and was charged with expanding cooperation between the two and with following up on the implementation of decisions. It was to alternate its meetings between Damascus and Amman, and would have several specialized branch committees: Economic and Trade Affairs; Industrial Cooperation; Electricity Concerns; Transport and Communications; and the Yarmuk (to deal with the longstanding project for joint exploitation of the Yarmuk River waters).

Shortly thereafter, on April 3, Husayn traveled to Damascus where another, more substantive, agreement on increasing trade cooperation between the two countries was signed. This agreement was followed by an accord on information (television, news broadcasts, the press, films, etc.) on May 22. Asad then made his first visit to Amman from June 10–12, 1975. As a result of this visit it was decided that the two countries should have a Joint Higher Committee, much like the committee formed a few months earlier, but charged with addressing a whole range of issues, not just economic ones. The Higher Joint Committee met for the first time July 28–30, 1975.

Rifaʿi, who had assumed the prime ministership for the first time in May 1973, contended that the rapprochement had been at Jordan's initiative. One of Jordan's primary concerns at the time was Gulf state financial assistance: despite the promises made at Rabat, assistance had not been forthcoming in the promised amounts. Top Jordanian policymakers believed that if they formed a united front with Syria, also a major recipient of Gulf state aid, they might have more success "persuading" the oil producers to forward the promised amounts.[5] This is not to say that other factors were far from Jordanian policymakers' minds: the need further to repair relations with Arab states, the desire to end Jordan's relative regional isolation, and even perhaps a hope of greater coordination to confront Israel may all have been involved at some level. The argument regarding ending regional isolation makes sense, but if that is meant (as it usually is) in a strictly political sense, then the nature of the earliest moves toward rapprochement, which were overwhelmingly economic, and which we shall see in greater detail below, do not make much sense. The evidence points to the primacy of economic factors in this period.

In the meantime, cooperation on the political level continued and broadened as well. Husayn returned to Damascus on August 18, 1975 for a four-day trip which no doubt focused in no small part on events in Lebanon (where civil war had broken out in April) as well perhaps as on the progress toward the second Egyptian-Israeli disengagement agreement (Sinai II), which was signed only two weeks later, on September 1. At this meeting the two leaders decided to establish a Joint Higher *Command*, comprising Asad and Husayn, which would in turn convene a Joint Higher *Council*, which would then issue decisions and directives relating to suggestions from the ministerial level Higher Committee. The council was also charged with working toward greater political coordination between the two, leading to the construction of a unified foreign policy including: making the necessary preparations and plans to uphold regional and national security; formulating economic policy aimed at achieving integration between the two (through coordinating economic and social development planning, establishing joint companies and economic institutions, unifying the markets of the two countries, and determining a unified customs policy); and coordinating information policy.[6]

While Jordanian-Syrian relations grew stronger, Jordan sought to mediate between Syria and Egypt, who were feuding over the Syrian role in Lebanon and over Egypt's conclusion of a second disengagement agreement with Israel.[7] Unlike Syria, Jordan's criticism of the first agreement had been restrained, as Crown Prince Hasan cautioned Egypt's Arab allies "not to judge Egypt too harshly."[8] As for Lebanon, both Syria and Jordan sought to prevent a further escalation of the civil war, just as they both, for regional and domestic reasons, sought to prevent the PLO-Lebanese National Movement alliance from overthrowing the existing regime in Lebanon.

On May 8 Husayn returned to Damascus for a meeting of the Higher Command, at which he reaffirmed his complete support for the Syrian role in preserving the unity, independence, and security of Lebanon.[9] Shortly thereafter on May 31 and June 1 Asad sent some 5,000 Syrian troops into Lebanon, plans for which he may have discussed with Husayn at this meeting. Husayn returned for a three-hour meeting on July 10 (during the siege of the Palestinian refugee camp Tall al-Za'tar), again to talk about Lebanon, as well as other matters. Indeed, Husayn was alone in the Arab world in offering "wholehearted political and propaganda support" for Syria's intervention in Lebanon.[10]

It is significant that during this period both Egypt and Saudi Arabia were attempting to pressure Syria on Lebanon and on its opposition to the second disengagement agreement between Egypt and Israel. Egyptian pressure took the form of propaganda, designed to encourage elements within Syria, including in the ruling Ba'th party, that were pressing Asad to support the regional and international policies advocated by Egypt and Saudi Arabia.[11] Saudi Arabia had stopped its *development aid* (not the Rabat-promised aid over which concern had already been expressed) to Syria in January, leading to a drastic revision of the 1976 budget. Given both Jordanian and Syrian concerns with Gulf financial aid, it is not unlikely that while not officially noted as an agenda item, Gulf state assistance was among the topics discussed in the Asad-Husayn meetings noted above.

Indeed, according to then-Prime Minister Mudar Badran, during the second half of 1976 Jordanian budgetary problems had multiplied as a result of the failure of Gulf states to provide the kingdom what it believed it had been promised at Rabat in 1974. Badran described the strain at the time as severe and contended that he was uncertain month to month how he would pay state employees' salaries. While the evidence is far from conclusive, there is reason to believe that the strong push toward unity was likely the continuation of the tactic Rifa'i noted of making common cause with Syria in order to force the Gulf states to take notice and provide the financial assistance Jordan and Syria sought.[12] Unified ranks in solicitation of funds was no doubt a more successful strategy than going it alone; in the same vein, effectively threatening the Gulf states with a political unification project between these two key confrontation states could only put additional political pressure on the prospective patrons to pay attention and pay up.

In January 1977 a number of meetings took place that appeared to preview the coming political federation between the two countries. Coincidentally or not, it was also in January that a meeting was held in Saudi Arabia to review the 1974 Rabat summit aid promises that Syria and Jordan so desperately sought. As a result, the promises were reportedly renewed. As becomes clear below, the excitement regarding political unification began to wane shortly thereafter.

A joint or federal (*ittihadi*) planning committee, with Jordanian and Syrian components,[13] met in Amman on January 5, 1977 and agreed to hold joint seminars and form joint specialized committees in the fields of planning. The joint committee held another meeting on February 21–22, 1977, in which it recommended that a development strategy including general goals be drawn up, with the year 2000 set as the most distant time frame for a joint Jordanian-Syrian development strategy. Husayn then returned to Damascus on February 6 for a one-day visit with an official delegation. He met with Asad while Badran and Syrian Prime Minister Khulayfawi also met for discussions of regional developments and of the progress being made toward integration. By early March, press reports indicated that federal unity between Syria and Jordan was expected to be announced in the next few weeks, with final touches being put on the declaration of unity.[14]

But the unity never came, and indeed, as the spring unfolded, the fervor for federal unity seemed to subside. The march of visitors between the two continued, and it was announced on March 24 that the formal declaration of unity would be issued on April 17.[15] Shortly thereafter a number of senior Jordanian Army officers, including armed forces Commander-in-Chief Zayd bin Shakir, went to Syria to attend tactical exercises. Nonetheless, despite the continued meetings of the various joint committees and a continued parade of high-level visitors, the march toward unity appeared to have stalled.

Husayn returned to Damascus on December 7, although Badran and Sharaf were back on the 27th. By this time, the primary concern was how to deal with Egyptian president Sadat's visit to Jerusalem. Asad continued to stress the need firmly to reject Sadat's policy, while the Jordanians took more of a wait and see attitude. In February Jordanian papers hailed Jordanian-Syrian cooperation and Syrian Information Minister Ahmad noted in a press conference that relations were proceeding well.[16] However, in a February 26 interview, Badran indicated that Jordanian-Syrian relations had cooled recently, although he insisted that relations were still good and that coordination and regular contact between the two leaders were continuing.[17]

Did the Jordanians or the Syrians really expect the unity attempt to succeed, especially in the light of past failures in the Arab world? Rifa'i claimed he stressed in meetings with the Syrians the need to develop complementarities, but at the *ground* level, since the lesson of the past was that starting at the top did not work. Ground-level ties, particularly economic ones, were more effective and longer lasting. Moreover, if political relations later deteriorated, the lower level relations would hold, or would not break as easily as they had in the past. Here, the Jordanians had particularly clear memories of Syria's 1970 closure of the joint border. Oral accounts also indicated federal unity was not a Jordanian priority. Badran noted that one group of Syrians involved in the discussions wanted to press for a swifter move toward unity, while the Jordanians preferred not to rush into anything. This Jordanian caution then made some Syrians skeptical of Jordanian intentions. Rifa'i insisted that although the two sides discussed some details of the unity plan in 1977, there was never a decision that it would be announced imminently, as was reported in the press.[18]

What is one to conclude from this? The timing of the initial rapprochement as well as the timing of the cooling indicate that certainly the Jordanians and possibly the Syrians as well hoped through their move toward closer cooperation and then toward unity to pressure the Gulf states, who would have found any such move threatening, to "persuade" them to make good on their Rabat promises of financial aid. Both Jordan and Syria had counted on such aid in their budget calculations, and when it was not forthcoming it appears both regarded their financial position, their budget security, as being in jeopardy.

In addition, however, as the section on economic developments argues below, much of the attention in the bilateral talks was directed toward economic matters and major steps were taken toward increasing economic cooperation between the two. No attempt is made here to second guess the intentions of the Syrian leadership. However, as chapter 2 made clear, Jordan's decisionmakers view the country's economic future and security as closely related to the good ties it has with its Arab neighbors. Having been severely hurt economically by the closure of the Syrian border in 1970, Jordan was keen to strengthen economic ties as a way of precluding the possibility of a repetition of this policy response by the Syrians. The stronger the economic ties, they reasoned, the more likely the Syrians would be to think twice about taking such a step in the future. Hence, various forms of economic statecraft took on great importance in Jordanian calculations of how to build greater economic and budget security. It is to a fuller presentation of developments in the economic realm that the discussion now turns.

Economic Developments

TRADE

As noted above, a protocol on economic cooperation was signed at the March 1975 meetings between Asad and Rifa'i. These were the first such meetings since 1967, when there had been disagreement between the two sides over the issue of the transit of Syrian goods across Jordan to Aqaba in the wake of the closure of the Suez Canal. Unlike the minutes of the 1967 meeting, the March agreement was more general and void of reference to difficulties. The two agreed to lift the barriers on exchange of products without reservation.[19] In part because of the closure of the Suez Canal, overland trade had become a key element in bilateral relations, and by 1974 Syrian ports had become significantly more important to Jordan than Beirut was.[20]

According to the April 6 agreement that followed, Syrian public sector establishments agreed to buy annually $3 million of Jordanian products whose importation had been limited. Both countries also agreed to import agricultural, animal, and natural wealth and industrial products from the other as exceptions to the standing prohibitions and as exceptions to all the administrative and currency regulations. Each agreed not to provide special assistance to its own exports to the other country when a similar product was manufactured by the other. Each side was permitted to establish a trade center in the other empowered to import goods without restrictions, with the exception of Jordanian products whose importation was limited by the relevant Syrian public sector institutions.[21]

The minutes of the August 1975 meeting of the economic council suggested that Jordan was less than satisfied with the unfolding of bilateral economic relations to date, particularly, it seems, in relation to the Syrian public sector. The Jordanians proposed that all restrictions on their products be lifted; however, if that posed a problem they suggested that, at very least, the restrictions on items produced by the Syrian private sector be dropped and that the Syrian private sector be permitted to import directly from the Jordanian private sector, without going through the public sector. In the case of other products, the Jordanians asked that the Syrian public sector be offered the first opportunity to buy and that, in the case of lack of interest or response within a one-month period, the product be offered directly to the Syrian private sector. Jordan also asked that payments be made for its exports to Syria immediately upon their receipt, and according to accepted commercial principles.[22] The failure of Syria or Syrian institutions to pay for Jordanian products was a problem throughout even this period of close economic relations.

In mid-autumn 1975 the two countries took steps to unify their customs charges. The recommendations dealt with customs fees on primary domestic products used in production in forty-four similar industries in the two countries, exempting some industries from all charges, and unifying charges on thirty-five other industries. Both sides recommended total exemption, not just from customs charges but from all charges, taxes, and other current burdens, in fulfillment of suggestions made in Amman at the August meetings.[23]

On October 19 there were also discussions of the phosphate industry. It was agreed to assemble a joint committee of phosphate specialists for greater coordination in the field of production and marketing, and to establish a program to exchange expertise. Syria also agreed to facilitate the passage of raw phosphates across Syrian territory and to work to complete all the necessary facilities to increase the capacity of the Tartus port to export larger amounts. In accordance with the Jordanian requests at the August meeting, the Syrians agreed to take steps to facilitate payment for imports from Jordan. They also agreed to the Jordanian request that Jordanian products, the importation of which was restricted to the public sector, be offered to the Syrian private sector if the public sector showed no interest.

On December 30, 1976, the joint Syrian-Jordanian customs committee concluded six days of meetings in Damascus. Perhaps encouraged by the communiqué of an August 1976 meeting of the Joint Higher Committee, which had called for greater industrial coordination, and for the completion of measures to unify customs charges on domestic primary products in industries, and on minerals, industrial equipment, and tools,[24] its recommendations also included unifying customs duties on raw materials used in similar industries in the two countries, as well as unifying duties on equipment and tools. The committee scheduled follow-up meetings in February to complete both the discussion and preparation of a comparison of the customs duties between the two in order to unify laws and legislation.[25]

INDUSTRY AND JOINT PROJECTS

The March 1975 meetings also agreed upon exchanging expertise to prepare and implement a program of industrial development that would include joint industrial projects. They further produced an agreement in principle to develop an industrial free zone, to strengthen the rail line between Damascus and Amman, to act swiftly to link the electricity networks between the two; and to revive microwave communication.[26] On August 26, 1975 a full and formal industrial cooperation agreement was signed, according to which the principle of economic integration (*takamul*) was to be the basis for industrial cooperation in all planned industrial projects in both countries in which the fixed capital exceeded $6 million. A joint Syrian-Jordanian industrial company with capital of $60 million was to be set up in Amman, just as joint land and sea transport companies were to be established.[27] The signing of the formal agreement on the land and maritime transport companies between Jordan and Syria came in Damascus on December 26.

Accord was also reached at the August 26 meeting to establish an industrial free zone, the first of its kind in the Arab world, at a cost of $15 million, on the border. There was further agreement to found a limited shareholding company to invest in the industrial free zone.[28] At this point the preliminary technical studies for the zone had been completed and the bylaws, structure, and investment, financial, accounting, storage, banking, and customs systems had all been set up. Dar'a in southern Syria was chosen for the headquarters.[29]

Meetings throughout 1976 continued to focus on the possibility of setting up joint industrial projects and of increasing the size of trade and transit between the two countries. These goals were to be accomplished by encouraging the growth of the joint companies, and through such projects as the wide-gauge railroad. It was decided that the joint industrial company should set up a white cement factory in Jordan, as well as both a ready-to-wear clothing factory and a metal frames and ball bearing plant in Syria.[30] All of these meetings were held in the framework of the projected move toward political integration.

On January 10, 1977 Jordanian Minister of Trade and Industry Najm al-Din al-Dajani arrived in Damascus to continue discussions with Syrian officials on coordination in industrial and economic sectors. The minutes of the meeting of the joint Syrian-Jordanian Committee for Industrial Integration signed January 12 called upon the two sides to prepare lists of those industries whose investments exceeded $6 million in the areas of foodstuffs, chemicals, textiles, construction materials, and mining and engineering industries. A day later it was announced that a contract was to be signed in Amman establishing a Jordanian-Syrian commercial bank, first proposed in May 1976, intended to finance development projects and assist in economic integration between the two countries.[31]

At the end of May the joint Syrian-Jordanian ministerial commit-tee met in Amman to follow up on the progress of economic inte-gration between the two countries, and in particular to review the plans of the joint companies. As a result of these meetings, the com-mittee approved the investment plan of the Jordanian-Syrian Com-pany for Land Transport, which was to cost $27 million and be insured by the two governments, and to operate the company com-mercially. It also approved the investment plan of the industrial com-pany, which included plans to participate in a ready-to-wear clothing factory, and agreed to prepare studies for the cement plant as well as for a tire and insecticide factory.[32]

In early June 1977 the Joint Higher Committee agreed on addi-tional measures to promote coordination and integration of the countries' economies, but the principles resembled much of what had been resolved or decided at previous meetings. The content of the continuing discussions of the various committees indicates both ambitious goals as well as little concrete progress on such issues as sig-nificant market integration. But again, by now, the initial fervor for political unity had already begun to fade.

THE YARMUK PROJECT

In a region that is water poor, the Yarmuk River, one of the three main streams of the Jordan River basin system, is of both economic and strategic significance. Providing 75 percent of Jordan's water supplies, the Yarmuk forms part of the boundary between Jordan and Syria, and a bit farther south, between Jordan and Israel.[33] Over the years, numerous proposals have been made to develop the Jor-dan River basin system for more efficient use, but all have ultimately foundered, largely because of the continuing state of war between Israel and its Arab neighbors.

In 1974, as Syrian-Jordanian relations gradually improved, the Jor-danian government revived planning, first initiated in the 1950s, for the Maqarayn dam on the Yarmuk. In January 1975, the Jordanians requested, and subsequently received, financing totaling $15 million from the U.S. Agency for International Development for a feasibility study and engineering design work.[34] During the March 1975 joint meetings the Jordanians agreed to commission feasibility studies on the use of the Yarmuk river waters and to follow up by setting an immediate time to implement the dam project.[35] An August 26 adjustment of a 1953 agreement between the two countries regarding the Yarmuk provided for Jordanian construction and financing of the project, as well as Jordanian compensation to those who stood to lose their lands because of the dam's construction. In return, Jordan was to have the right to use all water and electricity from the dam as long as it provided the local villages with water.[36] Jordan also agreed to provide 80 percent of the work force for the scheme, which was to be supervised by a joint Syrian-Jordanian committee. Machinery and vehicles imported for the project were to be exempted from customs duties and workers were to have freedom of passage across the border.[37]

With a live storage capacity of about 350 million cubic meters a year of water, the dam was to irrigate an additional 10,000 hectares of land in the Jordan Valley and convert 12,000 hectares to sprinkler irrigation from the existing system of surface flooding from the East Ghor Canal. In 1979, the kingdom was importing about 60 percent of its food needs. Broader economic policy was targeting a reduction of these imports.[38] But such a reduction required agricultural expansion, and, given the kingdom's limited water resources, the envisioned expansion required substantial additional water. While progress on the Maqarayn project hardly appears to have been a moving force behind the rapprochement, the prospect of gaining access to greater water resources could hardly have escaped the attention of Jordan's decisionmakers. They must certainly have seen the importance of exploiting the improvement in bilateral relations to push greater cooperation in this critical area of national economic security.

Summary

The 1974–77 period witnessed an unprecedented rapprochement between Jordan and Syria. Relations not only warmed, but approached formal unity. Regional conditions—the situation in the area following the 1973 war, Sadat's growing ties with the United States, the war in Lebanon—all certainly influenced the course of relations. However, economic concerns, which have not previously been factored into an analysis of this bilateral relationship, clearly played a key role. Both Jordan and Syria, because of the structures of their economies and the nature of their reliance on Gulf financial assistance aid, found common cause in courting the Gulf states with a united front. Indeed, both faced potentially severe budget crises at home without such aid. By working together and ostensibly moving toward greater political and economic integration, they appear to have succeeded in convincing the Gulf states to provide them the support they had already figured into annual budget calculations and which, by all accounts, they desperately needed. Moreover, it seems not to be coincidental that the moves toward unity gradually came to a halt shortly after meetings in Riyadh in which the financial aid the two states were demanding was approved. The evidence therefore strongly suggests that their alignment and the "threat" of federal unity served a purpose akin to extortion, although the funds sought had in fact already been promised.

It does not appear that Jordanian policymakers were as keen on movement toward real political integration as perhaps their Syrian counterparts were. Economic cooperation, on the other hand, was a primary Jordanian concern and a primary form of statecraft aimed at achieving greater budget and economic security. Here, Jordan was largely responding to or seeking to alter the conditions that had enabled Syria to close its border in 1970. It sought to lay the groundwork for stronger and deeper economic ties with Syria that would make Syria think twice in the future before it closed its border. Economic cooperation developed during this period to include attempts to lower barriers to trade, to increase industrial integration through participation in joint projects, and jointly to exploit the Yarmuk waters. Despite the lack of fulfillment of the most optimistic expectations, the economic statecraft of this period did lay a basis for continued cooperation through the difficult times ahead.

From Cooling to Confrontation: 1978–1983

Political Developments

The period 1978–1980 witnessed a further cooling of relations, perhaps initially because of Syrian suspicions regarding the Jordanian failure to condemn Sadat's trip to Jerusalem. However, as time went on, not only had the brotherhood of 1975–76 passed, but a new cold war had developed between the two, which almost culminated in armed clashes in late 1980. The empirical material in this section suggests again that an economic or budget security argument provides a clear explanation of what has long appeared to be a murky period in Syrian-Jordanian relations.

In the spring of 1978 Sharaf went to Damascus on several occasions. Some of the discussions no doubt dealt with the March 15 Israeli invasion of southern Lebanon, as Jordan contacted various Arab capitals to promote a call for an Arab summit.[39] Press reports also indicated that Husayn, as well as Saudi Arabia and Kuwait, was attempting to mediate between Sadat and Asad over the fallout from Sadat's Jerusalem trip the previous November. Contacts between the two on regional peace issues also continued, and by late September, Syrian sources were expressing satisfaction with the Jordanian position on the outcome of the Camp David summit.[40] Husayn had made clear he would not go the way of Sadat, although he refused to join the Steadfastness and Confrontation Front.[41] In the meantime, however, there were rumors that Jordan and Syria would meet soon to revive the concept of the Eastern Front, which dated to before the 1967 war, as a means of confronting Israel.[42] Hence, while relations were no longer as warm as they had been in 1975–76, they were nonetheless clearly cordial. Not until later in the year, at the Baghdad summit, did signs of additional stress manifest themselves.

The Arab League meetings in Baghdad in November 1978 and March 1979 were crucial to Jordan. By late 1978, Jordan, ever aid-dependent, was suffering from the fact that some Arab states had still not forwarded their Rabat-promised aid. Iraq's Saddam Husayn was the moving force behind convening the summits, and was particularly instrumental, according to reports, in convincing the Gulf states to commit to making annual aid payments to the confrontation states. Jordanian-Iraqi relations had been gradually improving in any case, and that trend was reinforced by the November summit.

The improvement in Jordan's ties with Iraq (Syria's nemesis) undoubtedly made the Syrians uneasy. However, drawn together by the threat of Camp David, the Syrians and Iraqis, who had been feuding since 1975, had begun to hold meetings aimed at reconciliation, a very positive development from Jordan's perspective. Syrian Foreign Minister Khaddam went to Amman on February 8 with a message for King Husayn shortly after meeting with Iraqi Foreign Minister Sa'dun Hammadi. On March 26 Husayn was back in Damascus for talks, this time on a trip that also took him to Iraq. However, the Jordanians were not directly included in the reconciliation process, which reached the verge of a Syrian-Iraqi unity announcement. Instead, according to policymakers, Jordan heard about developments in this critical relationship second hand, even though it had a joint command with Syria, which meant that any move toward unity between Syria and Iraq directly involved the kingdom as well.[43]

On July 21 Husayn was back in Damascus, again with an entourage. However, this meeting came about a month after an attack on military cadets in Aleppo that signaled the beginning of several years of internal violence in Syria. During this period, the Syrians began asking the Jordanians to put more effort into "internal" security to help defuse the threat to Syria from some elements operating out of Jordan. While the Jordanians were willing to assist, they argued that they could not patrol the entire border, long permeable to smugglers, to prevent the entry into Syria of all potential subversives.[44] Moreover, when it became apparent that members of the Muslim Brotherhood (Ikhwan) were involved, the Jordanians argued that the Ikhwan had not been a problem in Jordan, and that Jordan, for instance, had never asked Syria to arrest its Communists when Jordan cracked down on Communists domestically.[45] However, according to Badran, whom the Syrians later accused of sheltering and supporting the Brotherhood, given the deteriorating state of internal security, the Syrians were no longer distinguishing between reasonable and unreasonable policy demands.[46]

At about the same time, an attempted coup in Baghdad that Saddam believed had Syrian backing led to a cooling in Syrian-Iraqi relations. King Husayn actively engaged in mediation, with the blessings of both Saddam and Asad. But violence in Syria continued with clashes in Latakia in the late summer and fall. In October 1979 Jordan reportedly did hand over to Damascus some 100 Syrian members of the Ikhwan.[47] Husayn's final trip to Damascus in 1979 came on October 21 during which he sought to coordinate with Asad about the upcoming Arab summit in Tunis in November, as well, no doubt, as to discuss internal Syrian unrest and Syrian-Iraqi relations. Beyond its mediation, Jordan tried to stay out of the fray. When the charges and countercharges flew, Jordanian policymakers often did not know which side to believe, although they admitted that the Iraqis had encouraged those Syrians outside Syria who opposed the government, especially members of the Ikhwan, to engage in anti-Syrian sabotage.[48]

The internal unrest in Syria, the belief that Jordan was providing aid and comfort to Muslim Brothers hostile to Syria, Jordan's growing ties with Iraq, and the beginnings of the king's dissatisfaction with Syrian policy in Lebanon were adding further strains to a relationship that had first been tested by the spring 1977 failure of the federal unity plan to move forward and Jordan's failure to reject outright Sadat's visit to Jerusalem. Husayn himself noted problems in the relationship, but denied—most would argue, implausibly—that Jordan had played any role in the unrest in Syria. However, he stated that Jordan opposed the politics of axes and polarization (referring to the Steadfastness and Confrontation Front—which excluded Iraq), and he further stated that the Lebanese problem had not been handled properly.[49]

Rifa'i contended that, whatever was said, Lebanon was not a central issue. The king's major concern in Lebanon, at least in a Cold War framework was that "internationalization" of a conflict, which he seemed to fear in Lebanon, really meant polarization of the Arab world, and that the king did not want the East-West Cold War divisions to be fought out in the already division-riddled Arab world. For Husayn, internationalization also meant an infringement on Lebanese sovereignty (and possibly even Jordan's), which would only exacerbate standing problems.[50]

Whatever the king's concern over Lebanon, the central problem was the differing approach to the conflict on the part of Syria and Iraq, two countries whose interests Jordan has had to balance carefully over the years. Perhaps needless to say, the worse relations are between the two, the more difficult such a balancing act is for Jordan. However, the better relations are between the two, the less important Jordan is to either of them. To further complicate matters, the Saudis reportedly become suspicious whenever relations between Jordan and Syria or Iraq grow too strong.[51] The significance of these relations to the Saudis was demonstrated above by the apparently successful Syrian and Jordanian use of a "rapprochement strategy" to convince the Saudis to provide the aid promised at Rabat.

In May 1980 Prime Minister 'Abd al-Hamid Sharaf denied Syrian charges that Jordan was supporting opponents of the Syrian regime[52] as did the semi-official al-Ra'i on August 11. Information Minister 'Adnan Abu 'Awdah announced Jordan's support for the Libyan-Syrian Union on September 16[53], but relations continued to deteriorate as Jordan vocally supported Iraq's attack on Iran, launched in September 1980. In November, Damascus charged Amman with mistreating Syrian citizens heading for Jordan and threatened to take appropriate action.[54] A day later the charges of support for saboteurs were leveled again: Jordan was accused of being a haven for Muslim Brothers plotting against Syria, an arsenal for their arms, an arena for training their members, a route to enter Syria, and a bridge to funnel arms, men, and funds to the conspirators. Directly implicated were the brother of the head of the Jordanian intelligence service, the dean of Jordan University Shari'a college and Crown Prince Hasan. Jordan continued to deny all charges.[55]

At the same time, Syria was engaged in efforts to prevent the convening of a December Arab summit, which, along with Libya, Algeria, Lebanon, the People's Democratic Republic of Yemen, and the PLO, it was expected to boycott. The 1980 summit in Amman was to focus on the Arab regional economy and Syria evidently feared that it would serve further to enhance the standing that Iraq had begun to develop at the Baghdad I (November 1978) and Baghdad II (March 1979) meetings. Indeed, coming immediately after the beginning of Iraq's war with Iran, the summit threatened to catapult

Iraq to even greater regional prominence. Asad's worst fears were all materializing at one time: Egypt's withdrawal from the front, domestic instability, and the rising power of Iraq. Syria asked for a postponement of the summit and even a change of venue, but Jordan rejected the request. In response, Syria boycotted the summit and then on November 26 massed some 20,000 troops and 400 tanks on the joint border—the highest state of tensions between the two since September 1970 when Syrian troops had crossed the border in support of the Palestinian guerrillas. Jordan responded militarily to the mobilization by dispatching three of its own armored divisions to the Syrian frontier along with 35,000 reservists.[56] The Syrians were demanding not only a Jordanian disavowal of support for the Ikhwan, but also a Jordanian reaffirmation of its recognition of the PLO as the sole, legitimate representative of the Palestinians.[57] Saudi mediation began almost immediately and in a few days succeeded in brokering a Syrian withdrawal, beginning on December 9. It was rumored that Saudi Arabia had provided Syria with substantial (no figures available) aid following the mediation visit that had led to the withdrawal.[58]

Jordanian policymakers differ in their assessments—at least those they were willing to share—of the reasons behind the deterioration in relations. Rifa'i blamed the deterioration on the change in political orientation (toward Iraq) undertaken by his successor, Badran. For his part, Badran insisted that Jordan did nothing to undermine Syrian security. He insisted—although it is difficult to believe—that the training of the Ikhwan in Jordan took place without his knowledge. He also insisted that much of the responsibility for the real hostility between the two lay with Rif'at al-Asad, the president's brother. Badran argued that Asad himself did not know many of the specifics of the unfolding Cold War.[59]

Whatever the Jordanians' assessments, it seems that Asad was perhaps closest to the mark when he was quoted as saying, "Husayn will fight to the last Iraqi dinar," indicating the financial and budgetary considerations that had likely been the most influential factors in the king's decision.[60] Several top policymakers noted the strong and important role Saddam Husayn had played in convening the 1978 Baghdad summit, in pushing for Gulf state financial support for the

remaining confrontation states, and in offering to pay himself whatever promised contributions might not be made by other states. Iraq
had thus begun to demonstrate its full economic and political potential.[61] Saddam was also clearly interested in Jordan for his own strategic reasons[62], and could back up his interest with a strong economy,
a large market, and oil money. One source also indicated that Saudi
Arabia had conditioned further aid to Jordan upon a "Jordanian-Syrian political disengagement, among other things."[63] If true, this is
just one more indication that financial concerns were paramount in
Jordanian calculations. While, again, it is clear that numerous regional and domestic forces were at work, Iraq could offer both strategic
depth and economic support. Syria could offer only the former, and
at that was beset with domestic instability. When it became clear that
relations could not be maintained with both, Jordan chose Iraq, for
sound financial, budget security reasons.

Throughout 1981 Syria continued to be concerned with internal
instability. It was also preoccupied in the spring with the missile crisis
in Lebanon, with the Saudi and Kuwaiti decisions to withhold their
subsidies for the Arab (largely Syrian) Deterrent Force in Lebanon,
and with the possibility that Jordan might join in the Camp David
process. Charges and countercharges became a regular feature of
the bilateral relationship, as Syria came under increasing regional
fire for its policies in Lebanon and for its support of Iran in the Iran-
Iraq war. (Syria was then further weakened and exposed by the June
1982 Israeli invasion of Lebanon.)

In a move that was evidently coordinated with the Iranians, Syria
closed its border with Iraq on April 8, 1982 and its part of the
pipeline carrying Iraqi oil to the Mediterranean on April 10, 1983.
The intent, of course, was to increase Iraq's financial burdens; however, the move had domestic repercussions as well. Badly affected
were operations at the country's two main ports, Tartus and Latakia.
As a result, the quantities of crude oil and oil products loaded at Syrian ports fell from 162.2 million tons in 1981 to 10.8 tons in 1982.[64]

In late May 1983, secret talks took place between the Jordanians
and the Syrians to try to achieve a reconciliation. As in 1974, the
reconciliation talks came at Jordan's initiative. One of the reasons
for the attempt at reconciliation may have been a desire on

Husayn's part to strengthen his position vis-à-vis the Americans and their push for negotiations within the framework of the Reagan Plan, which had been announced on September 1, 1982. However, probably more important were several issues directly or indirectly related to Jordan's financial and budgetary health. At this point, Husayn wanted Syria to reopen the Iraq-Mediterranean pipeline. The broader economic crisis in Iraq had led to a decrease in critical Iraqi aid to Jordan. Moreover, several months earlier, Iraq had announced that it was imposing austerity measures, which meant drastic cuts in imports. This further threatened the Jordanian economy, whose private sector had rushed into the Iraqi market following the outbreak of war. Reopening the pipeline held out the hope of some economic relief for Iraq, and by extension for Jordan.[65] Beyond that, however, reconciliation with Syria would have opened up the possibility of reenergizing Syrian-Jordanian bilateral trade, which had dropped substantially since the 1980 border crisis. Unfortunately for the Jordanians, however, the Syrians were not interested at this point. The bilateral feuding continued and Jordan continued to suffer financially both directly and indirectly as a result.

Economic Developments

By late 1978 or early 1979, Jordanian policymakers appear to have made the determination that their budget security required a shift in political alignment, putting Jordan more clearly in a pro-Iraq camp. This was not a serious problem for Syrian-Jordanian relations until Syrian-Iraqi relations deteriorated in mid-summer 1979. At that point, unable to maintain peaceful coexistence with both, Jordan chose the Iraqi option, the natural consequence being a clear deterioration in its relations on all fronts with Syria. Economic developments during this period certainly serve as indicators not only of the gradual deterioration in political relations, but also of the degree to which the Jordanians and Syrians had, during the previous period, established economic institutions and ties that could have a life outside of or above politics.

TRADE

Well before the beginning of bilateral feuding, the joint ministerial committee met in early August 1978. It urged the relevant authorities to lift all administrative and financial restrictions impeding trade between the two countries, to apply the provisions of the economic cooperation agreement, and to regulate the trade agreement signed in Amman on April 6, 1975. This was likely an indication of dissatisfaction with the development of the trade relationship, although by 1979 Jordan's exports to Syria had more than tripled from their 1975 level (from $11 million to $40.7 million), while Syrian exports to Jordan had nearly doubled (from $18.9 million to $38 million.)[66]

Even as late as April 1980 Jordanian Minister of Trade and Industry 'Ali al-Nusur and his Syrian counterpart discussed joint economic relations and agreed to increase further the volume of bilateral trade.[67] However, the number, extent, and diplomatic level of involvement in the various economy-related meetings declined, and by the middle of 1980 the joint committees had ceased to function. It is therefore rather remarkable that despite the massing of troops on the border in December 1980, traffic continued to flow in both directions as the six-year old economic and trade agreement remained in full force.[68] Goods entering from both sides continued to be cleared by both countries free of customs duties. The only change was that goods transiting by land had to pass customs on both the Jordanian and Syrian sides, whereas previously they had cleared at a unified customs point.[69]

However, at this point, Syrian domestic economic problems began to have an impact on trade, quite apart from the effects of political feuding. The domestic economy was in crisis, one manifestation of which was a level of foreign currency reserves estimated as sufficient to finance only about one month of nonmilitary imports ($385 million). Two government decrees, 181 and 182 of April 22, 1981, put new restrictions on private sector access to foreign exchange. In practice, it appeared that the new law was to serve as the basis of a freeze on private sector imports.[70] Although it is difficult to distinguish between trade lost for political reasons and that lost for reasons of foreign currency shortage, Jordanian exports to Syria dropped from

$41 million in 1980 to $32.1 million in 1981 and $23.2 million in 1982.[71] Private transport faced other difficulties. Although the new regulations were not officially announced, haulers were made aware in late August 1982 that new restrictions on the transit of goods had been imposed. The most important change was a ban on goods being conveyed to destinations beyond Syria, including specifically trucks carrying cargoes to Jordan and Saudi Arabia. This, along with the ban on traffic to Iraq, substantially cut into Syria's transit income.[72] But the impact on Jordan was clear as well.

INDUSTRY AND JOINT PROJECTS

Again, at the beginning of this period the joint committees and companies continued to operate normally, if not with the same fervor of a year earlier. The general assembly of the Jordanian-Syrian Overland Transport Company met in Amman in mid-May 1978 to review a fairly successful record to date. At the beginning of 1978 it owned 300 Mercedes and 68 refrigerator trucks, and of the initial capital of $24 million, $15 million was paid up. In mid-July it was announced that the company expected a $3 million turnover in 1978. At this point the company had contracts to transport cement from Lebanon to Jordan and Saudi Arabia, and to carry imported foods from the ports of Aqaba, Latakia, and Beirut to various parts of the Middle East. In June 1978 it won a contract to haul 20,000 tons of wheat from Aleppo to Amman and began to build an operations base costing more than $2 million at Qastal, about 30 kilometers south of Amman, to be completed by the end of the year. The company was also planning to expand beyond the Middle East and was negotiating a transport agreement with Intras of East Germany to haul freight from Europe to the Gulf.[73]

Throughout the summer of 1978 there were meetings of the joint committees, all of which were aimed at continuing the process of integration. Funds were allocated for the Land Transport Company, the Maritime Transport Company, the Joint Industries Company, and the Jordanian-Syrian Commercial Bank. The proposed Jordanian-Syrian Industrial Holding Company was to have capital of $60 million and intended to seek foreign loans of $120-$180 million to finance joint manufacturing projects in both countries.[74] By the end of the year the Maritime Company had placed orders for two additional ships, one of which was to be ready in March of 1979 and the other the following November.[75]

By June 1979 the rapprochement between Syria and Iraq had reached the point that the joint Syrian-Jordanian Industrial Company was contacting foreign manufacturers as a first step toward setting up a joint venture with Iraq to assemble cars for the domestic markets of the three countries. The plan had been proposed earlier, but did not really begin to take shape until Iraq offered to join the scheme, thereby more than doubling the potential market. According to the proposed plan the Baghdad-based Arab Industrial Investments Company (set up by Iraq and Egypt in 1975 to manufacture vehicles) was to take a 50 percent share in the company and the joint Syrian-Jordanian company the other half.[76]

The Free Zone Company, on the other hand, continued to languish. The Board met in May 1979 to decide whether or not to invite tenders for the completion of the first stage of the project. A Syrian-Jordanian consortium working on the project under a $6.6 million contract had completed only 15 percent of the first stage, and completion costs were estimated at $12.6 million.[77] The commercial bank was also in trouble. In late August 1982 the Jordanian government, through the Economic Security Committee, revoked the 1979 contract with Syria establishing the Jordanian-Syrian Commercial Bank. The reason, reportedly, was Syria's refusal to open a branch in Damascus, in violation of the contract establishing the bank and its bylaws.[78]

Summary

Jordan's gradual move toward Iraq beginning in late 1978 eventually made a political break with Syria inevitable, given developments in Syrian-Iraqi relations. By early 1980 political interaction between the two had become minimal. Jordan did seek a rapprochement in 1983, but again, its goal appears to have been the reopening of the oil pipeline though Syria from Iraq in order to secure relief for both the

Jordanian and Iraqi economies. This rapprochement attempt failed and the Syrians launched a period of "coercive diplomacy," consisting of sabotage and assassinations. [79]

During the early period of the cooling of relations, 1978–1979, economic meetings and interaction continued, if not with the intensity of the previous three years. Although some of the joint ventures (the bank and the free zone) were unable to survive the deterioration in relations, others, remarkably, continued to function normally. Bilateral trade did drop, although it is unclear how much of the drop was due to the political situation and how much owed to Syrian austerity measures. Nonetheless, the border remained open, a critical fact for Jordan, a country dependent on transit trade. The bases of economic integration or cooperation that the Jordanians had viewed as critical to preventing a repetition of 1970 had at least in part succeeded in playing their economic security role. Thanks to the initiatives of the 1975–77 period, even in the most strained of days Jordan managed to avoid the economic damage that the 1970 border closure had caused.[80]

The Beginnings of a Thaw: 1984–85

Political Developments

By mid-1984, hurting from the Gulf war and eager to find a way to bring it to an end, Jordanian officials made several statements to the effect that the major difference between Amman and Damascus concerned Syria's support for Iran in the Gulf war.[81] In July Husayn and Asad exchanged cables on the occasion of 'Id al-Fitr (the feast at the end of the holy month of Ramadan), the first such message from Asad since 1980. Two weeks later, Jordan's Speaker of Parliament, 'Akif al-Fayiz, went to Damascus to attend the Arab Parliamentary Union meetings, and while in the Syrian capital met with Foreign Minister Khaddam. Thereafter additional signs of warming in relations begin to appear. The Jordanian semi-official daily *al-Dustur* urged rapprochement with Damascus on July 23[82] and in his meeting with the Jordanian parliamentary delegation, Asad stated that the chill that characterized the bilateral relations was not an inevitable result of the Iran-Iraq war. Indeed, the chill had appeared before the war.[83] Husayn subsequently confirmed this in an interview with *al-Hawadith*.[84]

This minor improvement in relations was short-lived, however, as Jordan did the unthinkable (in the Syrian view) by restoring relations with Egypt on September 24, 1984. It then continued along a path that Syria could only have found threatening by hosting the controversial seventeenth session of the Palestine National Council in Amman, while the Syrians were still trying to depose PLO chief Yasir 'Arafat. The chill was renewed as were attempts on the lives of Jordanian diplomats abroad and sabotage at home. Renewed restrictions were put on travel to Syria: permits were to be issued only in exceptional circumstances.[85] The announcement of the February 11 accord between Jordan and the PLO to coordinate activities aimed at future participation in a peace conference only made matters worse, since Asad feared the King and Arafat would soon be marching off to separate peace talks, as Sadat had done before them.

The change in prime ministers in Jordan from Ahmad 'Ubaydat to Zayd al-Rifa'i on April 5, 1985 to a large extent owed to the king's desire to improve relations with Damascus and hence constituted in effect a renewed Jordanian overture. No small matter was the Jordanian desire to put an end to Syrian-sponsored attacks on Jordanian diplomats abroad as well as sabotage at home. However, as was demonstrated above, Amman had clearly been interested in reconciliation before, as had Damascus before Jordan renewed ties with Egypt. Not until spring 1985, as Syria's problems with oil supplies from Teheran began to take a serious economic toll (see below), did it evidently feel its need for improved ties with Jordan was sufficient to enable it to set aside its outrage over the restored links with Egypt.

On August 12, 1985, Syria and Jordan agreed to receive a committee that had been formed earlier in the month at the Casablanca summit (which Syria had not attended) intended to end Syrian-Jordanian disagreements. At the invitation of Saudi Prince 'Abdallah, chair of the committee charged with trying to resolve inter-Arab disputes, Syrian prime minister Kasm and Rifa'i held talks in Jeddah on September 16–17. (Initially these reconciliation efforts were to have included Iraq as well.) As a first step toward reconciliation, Jordan and Syria agreed to stop the propaganda warfare, lift border restrictions, and increase trade.[86] Indeed, one Jordanian motive for trying to restore relations was to facilitate the exchange of produce across the border. Jordanian fruit and vegetables exported to Syria were said to be rotting at the frontier because of travel restrictions (which were not lifted until late 1985).[87]

In the meantime, however, with the exception of Saudi Arabia, the Arab states that had promised regular budgetary assistance to the confrontation states at Baghdad were not paying what they owed. Whether for reasons of budgetary constraints brought on by the regional recession, the large demands for aid by Iraq, or political discontent with confrontation state policy, the aid had largely dried up.[88] Kuwait had not only cut back, but had threatened to terminate payments to Syria entirely, reportedly because of Asad's policy in Lebanon. The amirate had also suspended aid to Jordan because of the conclusion of the February 11 accord, which it opposed. Iraq, because of its involvement in the war with Iran, had of course stopped payments much earlier. Both Jordan and Syria were clearly in need of whatever economic boost an improvement in bilateral relations could secure.

On October 20–21 Rifaʻi and Kasm met again, this time in Riyadh, as the reconciliation proceeded. One of the major issues that was solved was the presence on Jordanian soil of Syrians opposed to the Asad regime: the Jordanian government reportedly immediately asked them to leave Jordan.[89] As the reconciliation continued the most surprising development was the November 11 speech by King Husayn in which he admitted publicly that Jordan had in fact sheltered those who were plotting against Syria. The day following the speech, Rifaʻi left for Damascus, taking with him the foreign minister, the minister of trade, industry and supply, the minister of finance, the governor of the central bank, the undersecretary of trade, industry and supply, director-general of the Jordanian Agricultural Marketing Products Corporation, director of the prime minister's office and an economic adviser from the prime ministry. The list of ministers involved indicates that economic issues must have been high on the agenda. By November 13 the two sides were proclaiming that a new era had arrived. The joint communiqué from their meeting referred directly to the need to revive the joint committees. It said nothing, however, about resuming political unification efforts.[90]

Economic Developments

TRADE

By the spring of 1984 Syria was facing economic strains beyond those mentioned in the earlier period. This time, it was the Iraqi blockade of Kharg Island, which was preventing Iran from honoring its agreement to provide Syria with 160,000 b/d of crude oil. Asad sought help from Libya's Qaddafi, but Libyan light oil did not meet the needs of Syria's refineries.[91] It appears these economic strains were sufficient to lead Syria to overcome or overlook the obstacles to reconciliation that had existed for it in 1983, when King Husayn had made his first overture to Damascus.

In the context of this new move toward reconciliation, on April 25, 1984 a delegation from the Syrian Supply Company arrived in Amman, requesting the urgent shipment from Jordan of 3000 tons of citrus fruit and another shipment of 500 tons of lemons. It further requested an increase in the shipment of tomatoes from 200 to 400 tons daily. The delegation met with officials from the Jordanian Cooperative Organization and the Jordanian Agricultural Marketing Products Corporation (AMPCO) and reviewed an agreement, originally signed in 1983, aimed at facilitating the transport of agricultural products between the two. The agreement called for the exchange of produce in the amount of $9 million by each side. Up to that time $11.6 million total per year had been exchanged.[92]

On July 29, the Chamber of Commerce sent a delegation to Syria to find ways to increase trade. In a meeting with members of the Syrian Chamber of Commerce they examined bilateral trade over the previous five years (five very bad years in relations) and suggested means of increasing exchange. There was also discussion of the possibilities of Jordan's participating in the Damascus trade fair. The delegation met the Minister of Economy and Foreign Trade, Dr. Salim Yasin, to discuss the importance of implementing joint industrial and agricultural projects between the two countries and with Muhammad Shafiq Shukr, president of the Syrian Chamber of Industry, and the members of its board to discuss the possibilities of joint projects between both the public and private sectors.

While the further expansion of economic relations appears to have been stalled by Jordan's September 1984 restoration of ties with Egypt, the appointment of Rifa'i as prime minister seemed to signal full steam ahead again. On April 20, 1985 the undersecretary of Jordan's Ministry of Agriculture returned from a two-day trip to Syria, where he had held talks with officials from the Syrian General Company for Vegetables and Fruits to develop areas of cooperation.[93] Shortly thereafter, large numbers of Syrian merchants began arriving in Amman to purchase Jordanian agricultural products from farmers, following the Jordanian government's rescinding of an earlier decision that had required the marketing of Jordanian agricultural products through AMPCO.[94]

At the end of April 1985 the cabinet decided that Jordan would participate in the 1985 Damascus International Fair, in response to an official invitation received by the Ministry of Trade and Industry. In a further sign of warming relations, travel restrictions between the two began to be eased in May 1985. Jordanians arriving from Syria began reporting greater ease of passage at the border. By late September a Jordanian economic delegation led by Hamdi Tabba', chairman of the Amman Chamber of Commerce, met with Syrian Minister of Industry, 'Ali al-Tarabulsi. In response, Tabba' invited the chairman of the Damascus Chambers of Industry and Trade to visit Jordan.[95]

November meetings between Trade and Industry Minister Raja'i al-Mu'ashshir and Syrian Minister of Economy and External Trade 'Imadi led to an agreement on increasing the volume of trade (only $25 million in 1985).[96] The joint trade committees were also reactivated, cooperation rose again in transport and banking, and travel restrictions were formally lifted in November.[97] In December 1985 it was reported that Jordan had been supplying Syria with Saudi oil for the past two months, something Damascus had perhaps been seeking through the improvement in bilateral ties.[98]

INDUSTRY AND JOINT PROJECTS

In July 1984 as bilateral economic ties were being reenergized, it was announced that the Syrian-Jordanian Industrial Company's $52.6 million white cement plant near Zarqa would start production trials in September.[99] And, despite the renewed chill in official relations following Jordan's September 1984 restoration of diplomatic ties with Egypt, a delegation from the Syrian National Petroleum Company arrived in Amman on December 8 for a four-day visit to the Natural Resources Authority to exchange information with the Authority's oil exploration specialists.

Summary

Although the Jordanians attempted reconciliation with Syria in 1983 as a way of trying to ease the financial strain on Iraq, and by extension themselves, the Syrians did not respond positively until, apparently, their economic relations with Iran deteriorated and Jordan appeared to offer the prospect of economic (as well perhaps as political) relief. While this study is not intended to be a definitive statement on Syrian policy it would seem that if political considerations had been primary, Syria might well have sought reconciliation with Jordan earlier since following its humiliation in its 1982 confrontation with Israel, it was left militarily weakened and strategically vulnerable. It is true that, in 1984, after a renewed reconciliation had been set in motion, even economic problems with Iran would not allow Syria to excuse Jordan's rapprochement with Egypt and its warming relations with the PLO. This was simply too great a threat to Syrian political security. However, after sufficient fury was demonstrated, the return of Rifaʿi to the Jordanian prime ministership seemed to open the way for the improvement in ties that Jordan sought in order to lay the basis for an end to inter-Arab feuding and to reenergize trade. As a result, the two sides held serious discussions aimed at reviving bilateral trade and revitalizing the joint companies, although the unity discussions of the mid-seventies were not resurrected.

The New Reconciliation?: 1986–1990

Political Developments

The events of this period indicate that although relations had been restored, Jordan would not in the near future move fully into a Syrian camp. The kingdom's political and economic relationship with Iraq had grown too strong and important to jeopardize. In the face of the domestic economic difficulties that Jordan confronted as direct or indirect results of the Gulf war, it made sound economic sense to repair ties with Syria, for the reasons outlined in the previous section. It also made political and economic sense to work toward an Arab consensus to try to end the war. Jordan's reconciliation with Syria certainly helped ease Syria's regional isolation (based on its support for Iran). It also lay the groundwork for moving toward a unified Arab approach to the Gulf war, with an eye to bringing the conflict to an end, something from which all parties stood to benefit by that time. Clearly, all the while Jordan was striving for good relations with the Syrians and engaging in mediation to repair strained inter-Arab ties, the primary state in its calculations was Iraq, at least when Syria and Iraq were the two countries in the balance.

The 1986–1990 period witnessed a number of fluctuations in Jordanian-Syrian ties, but nothing that dramatically changed the course of the relationship. Diplomatic representation between the two was restored in early April 1986 and Asad made his first visit to Jordan in nine years on May 5. This followed the collapse of a planned Arab summit and the demise of the February 11, 1985 Jordanian-Palestinian Accord (thus putting Jordan and Syria both in the anti-'Arafat camp). The exact substance of the talks was not officially reported, but Kuwait's *al-Qabas* reported that military issues were at the heart of the talks: at the time there were rumors that a Syrian-Israeli confrontation was imminent.[100]

As part of the larger aim of improving inter-Arab ties and ending the Gulf war, Jordan embarked on another round of mediation between Syria and Iraq in the spring of 1986. Accompanied by Rifa'i, Minister of the Royal Court 'Adnan Abu 'Awdah, and Foreign Minister Tahir al-Masri, Husayn, who had been in Baghdad only nine days earlier, made a surprise visit to Damascus the evening of May 24. On July 27 Husayn was back in Syria; however, the composition of the delegation that accompanied him indicated that economic topics were prominent on the agenda of this fourth Syrian-Jordanian summit of 1986.

Husayn made four visits to Syria in the spring of 1987: one in early February, two in April, and one in May. These discussions were no doubt also a part of the king's mediation efforts. He was back in Damascus on June 24 and September 1 for one-day meetings, while Rifa'i traveled to Damascus in early July and in mid-August. Rifa'i also made two secret visits to Damascus as part of the mediation efforts between Iraq and Syria.[101]

By the time of Husayn's September visits to Syria at least one topic of conversation was the proposed November Amman Arab League summit conference, which had been postponed for several years and which aimed at forging a unified Arab position on the Gulf war. Syria had two major reservations about attending such a meeting: that the Gulf war would be the single agenda item and that its long-standing position of supporting Iran would leave it isolated in the inter-Arab gathering; and that the summit would readmit Syria's nemesis Egypt to the Arab League, an eventuality that Syria hoped to postpone as long as possible. In the event, the Gulf war was the major focus of discussion, but Egypt was not readmitted, one of the quid pro quos for Syrian attendance. Husayn made one more visit to Syria, in late November, to discuss the summit resolutions and ways of speeding up the Syrian-Iraqi reconciliation.[102]

In early 1988, there were numerous consultations between the Jordanians and Syrians regarding the Palestinian uprising, which had begun in December 1987, and regarding the subsequent visit by U.S. Secretary of State George Shultz to the region. In mid-summer Asad, who had his own interests in seeing the Palestinians pried away from the Jordanians, praised the king's controversial July 31, 1988 decision to disengage legally and administratively from the West Bank.[103] However, in the Syrian view at that time, more pressing were the developments in Lebanon, where the deteriorating security situation made scheduled elections increasingly unlikely. Asad and Husayn met on November 22, 1988 to discuss Iraq's support of Michel 'Awn, the anti-Syrian renegade Lebanese army general who had claimed the Lebanese presidency, and to discuss the implications of the PLO's then-recent declaration of a state.[104] The two continued to differ on Lebanon: the king stated on numerous occasions the need for *all* foreign troops (including Syrian) to leave Lebanon. Not surprisingly, this position was in line with the Iraqi stance, and Jordan was rumored to be permitting the movement of weapons across its territory bound for 'Awn's forces.

On another front, at this stage Jordan and Saudi Arabia were reportedly mediating between Syria and Egypt. Periodic contacts had taken place since the Islamic Conference Organization meeting in Kuwait in January 1987, but because of the end of the Iran-Iraq war and the subsequent signs that Iraq intended to play a more active role in the politics of the Arab East, a Syrian rapprochement with Egypt became more pressing for Asad. This was especially the case since, although not formally readmitted to the Arab League, Egypt formed part of the Jordanian-Iraqi-Egyptian axis that had evolved since the early 1980s. Since the 1987 Amman summit had given the green light to Arab states to reestablish ties with Cairo, Egypt was clearly on its way to returning to the Arab fold. Syria was the only obstacle to Egypt's formal return, but it had to find a face-saving way of restoring ties.

Whatever political currency Jordan may have gained with Syria for its mediation efforts with Egypt was probably lost with the announcement of the formation of the Arab Cooperation Council, a regional grouping including Jordan, Iraq, North Yemen, and Egypt, in February 1989. Syrian relations with Egypt had not yet been restored and now the region's two most powerful states, Egypt and Iraq, had formally joined forces. It is unlikely that any of Husayn's reassurances to Asad could have eased the Syrian president's concerns over these developments.[105] At the same time, the respective countries' views on Lebanon continued to differ, and relations grew strained as Jordan insisted that a negotiated, Arab solution was the answer for Lebanon and that a military solution should be ruled out, despite Jordan's role in enabling Iraqi arms to reach 'Awn.

But Husayn was soon distracted from regional developments as economic riots in April 1989 forced him to direct his attention more fully to the domestic scene. Relations with Syria had certainly not reached the breaking point, nor were they expected to, but the king's support for the Arab consensus on Lebanon at the May Casablanca summit (a position that refused to give the Syrians carte blanche in Lebanon) angered Asad, and the appointment of Mudar Badran as Chief of the Royal Court, and, subsequent to the November 1989 elections, his selection as prime minister, was a sign that improving relations with Syria was not a priority. (It will be remembered that the Syrians had accused Badran of having allowed the training of Syrian Muslim fundamentalists in Jordan in the late 1970s and early 1980s.) Husayn did, however, continue to serve as a mediator between Asad and Egyptian President Mubarak in an attempt to achieve a Syrian-Egyptian rapprochement, efforts that finally bore fruit in late December 1989.

Economic Developments

TRADE

Despite some important differences in regional policies noted above, economic relations during this period continued without major setbacks or interruptions. The joint economic committee met in March 1986 to discuss means of facilitating the flow of national products into the markets of both countries. The minutes of the meetings set the trade target for each country at $58.2 million per year (after an average of about $14.6 million in the past few years).[106] In the third week of June Trade and Industry Minister Mu'ashshir and Undersecretary of Agriculture al-Lawzi made visits to Damascus to discuss trade cooperation. A payments agreement, a standing problem for Jordan in its relations with Syria, was then reached by Jordan with the Syrian Central Bank covering bilateral trade of $40 million in 1986. However, the Jordanian Ministry of Supply, Trade, and Industry stated on June 18 that goods imported from Syria would be cleared through customs only if they had import licenses and payment documents from commercial banks cleared by the Central Bank of Jordan.[107]

Syria also arranged a barter agreement with some of its Jordanian creditors. The deal covered Syrian trade debts to the public and private sectors in the amount of $40 million, accumulated between 1983 and 1986. Syria was to supply glass, cotton thread, fruit, barley, and chick peas. The deal also reportedly involved reexports to Jordan of Syrian phosphates to cover $7 million of the debt owed to the Jordanian government, Royal Jordanian Airlines, and private pharmaceutical and agricultural industries. Two-way trade in 1988 was also expected to be covered primarily by barter arrangements.[108] In a February 1989 meeting the Joint Higher Committee set a trade target of $65 million each in 1989; bilateral trade in 1988 had reached about $39 million.[109]

In early December 1989 the Federation of Jordanian Chambers of Commerce hosted its Syrian counterpart, the Syrian Federation of Chambers of Commerce, for discussions of developing trade and establishing joint projects. The Syrians also met with the ministers of trade and industry, planning, and the president of the Chamber of Industry. At the end of the visit the two sides signed a cooperation protocol designed to boost trade and promote investment in the joint free zone.[110]

INDUSTRY AND JOINT PROJECTS

The two countries began 1986 by announcing the opening of the joint industrial zone on the common border, and by resuming Alia's and Syrian Air's daily flights between the two capitals. In a series of meetings on transportation-related issues the two governments agreed to set aside a sum of $8.73 million to be shared equally by the two, to overhaul the fleet and update the work of the Land Transport Company. They also renewed the customs exemptions for the land and maritime transport companies, which had continued to flourish, for another ten years.[111] The Joint Land Transport Company had made its first profit in 1986 ($780,000) after four years of losses,[112] while the Maritime Transport Company reported profits of $6.5 million in 1987.[113]

THE YARMUK PROJECT

When relations were normalized in the fall of 1985 there was renewed talk of reviving the Maqarayn dam project, which had lain dormant during the period of political feuding. The Syrians had recently constructed dams and artificial lakes to divert water from the tributaries of the Yarmuk and to develop agriculture along the southern border with Jordan and Israel. On various occasions the Jordanians had had lengthy discussions with the Syrians on this issue,[114] but the Syrians continued to have objections to the dam project because of its strategic location on the shared border with Jordan so close to Israel.[115]

In mid-August 1987, Rifa'i went to Damascus to renew the discussions and by September 3 the two sides had reached an agreement according to which Jordan would build a dam and a reservoir near the Maqarayn station on the Yarmuk. The water behind the dam in the reservoir was to be used to irrigate Jordanian lands and for other Jordanian projects. It was also to be used to irrigate Syrian lands and to generate power.[116] However, some analysts argued that the agreement had been reached at the expense of Jordan's riparian rights, since the project, originally planned for Syria, was to be built in Jordan. Their view was that Jordan had accepted the terms of the agreement because of its desperate need for water and because Syria had finally accepted an American-brokered arrangement according to which Israel would have a share in utilizing the Yarmuk water.[117] Moreover, Jordan was slated to fund the dam project, although sources of financing had not yet been settled.

An October 1988 report noted that international financing of up to $260 million was expected for the $440 million dam. Syria was to receive 75 percent of the power generated, but would not contribute to construction costs. The dam was to have a storage capacity of 225 million cubic meters of water and was to be used to irrigate 3,500 hectares in the Jordan valley and 500 hectares in the highlands; 50 million cubic meters of water annually were also be supplied to greater Amman.[118]

As Syrian-Jordanian relations took a negative turn during the spring of 1989, work on the dam was completely suspended and Jordan removed all the facilities it had established in Syria for the project. Syria had allegedly increased its pumping of water in violation of the agreement between the two. In addition it had established eighteen barricades on the river before the water reached the Jordanian side.[119] As of July 1990, Jordan had decided to turn to Arab and Islamic organizations for funding for the project. The World Bank and USAID had refused to commit funds because of Israeli objections regarding the issue of riparian rights.[120]

Summary

The period following the reconciliation was somewhat rocky for the political bilateral relationship. Jordan and Syria continued to differ over policy in Lebanon, and Jordan allowed Syria's archenemy, Iraq, to ship arms to its erstwhile ally in Lebanon, Michel 'Awn. Economic relations seemed to recover, particularly in the realm of trade, although by the end of the period Jordan's own austerity measures made clear the need to cut imports. Moreover, even though trade volume and value increased, Jordan continued to suffer from Syria's need to arrange barter agreements to pay for bilateral exchange.

The joint companies continued to function, but there were no discussions of additional joint ventures. The key joint project at this stage that was again put on hold was the Maqarayn dam. This was both politically and strategically more sensitive than any of the joint industrial projects. Even when political relations have been good, progress has been, probably deliberately, slow. In periods of less than full cooperation, as relations developed between the two by 1988–89, work on the dam has been suspended.

Conclusions

This chapter has covered several critical changes in the Jordanian-Syrian bilateral relationship: the rapprochement of 1975–77, the deterioration of 1979–80, a failed attempted rapprochement in

1983, a second rapprochement of 1985–86, and somewhat rocky relations in 1988–89. The role of economics, specifically budget security, in driving alliance decisions has been shown in several instances and will be summarized below. First, however, some conclusions or generalizations regarding the use of economic statecraft as a means of reinforcing or building economic security will be reviewed.

Economic Relations

One of the lessons that emerges from the examination of economic relations between the two countries is the diversity and effectiveness of economic tools of statecraft used. What economic instruments of foreign policy may a relatively resource poor country such as Jordan use with another aid dependent (if militarily stronger and economically more diversified) country? Jordan was the first Arab state to suggest and actively use as part of its inter-Arab foreign policy the practice of encouraging the establishment of joint economic committees. This has both an ideological and a pragmatic base, probably closely linked. Jordanian policymakers stress the importance of developing greater integration among Arab states as a natural fulfillment of their belief that the Arab world is at base a single unit. Most also stress, however, that Jordan is weak relative to its neighbors and that only through developing strong economic and political ties with them that can it ensure its survival. In the case of the joint committees, the ideological and pragmatic goals merged.

Such committees later served as a model, not only for Jordan in its other Arab bilateral relations, but for other Arab states as well. Jordanian economic policymakers repeatedly stated that, having witnessed the failed attempts at political unity undertaken by various Arab states in the 1950s and 1960s, they decided a better strategy was to begin with more modest projects, and on a bilateral, rather than a multilateral, basis. In this way, the Jordanians argued, they were building the basis for more extensive unity in the future. At very least the benefits from the expanded economic relationship as well as the sunk costs would force Syria (or any other state for that matter) to think twice before attempting to cut all relations, as Syria had done in 1970.

The very first committee formed following Husayn's visit to Damascus in 1975 was a joint economic committee—not a committee to draft a joint constitution, form a joint military command, or discuss unification of security measures, although those measures came later. Economic discussions were prominent among the early attempts at restoration of relations in 1984 as well. Moreover, despite the very real obstacles to greater economic cooperation—the differing role and restrictions on the private sector, currency controls, the competitiveness rather than complementarity of the products produced, exchange rates, problems in financing trade (leading to barter or countertrade agreements), hard currency shortages, differences in the political systems, lack of hard currency, various kinds of bureaucratic red tape, and so on—the two began work almost immediately on another economic instrument, a series of joint ventures, cutting across economic sectors.

The record makes clear that the joint ventures were far from overwhelming successes. The Free Zone Company and the joint Commercial Bank failed to become operational at all. Nonetheless, policymakers take pride in the relative success of the two transport companies, the white cement factory, and the carpet factory. Moreover, one official who had been very closely involved in the joint companies from the beginning said that one of the reasons for the failure of certain joint ventures had to do with the enthusiasm of the moment leading the planners to move too quickly, and not think through all the potential problems.[121] The companies were established on the basis of slogans derived from ideological enthusiasm, without the prior completion of careful feasibility studies. The Free Zone Company was noted as an example: it was placed on the border for no reason other than it seemed appropriate. In fact, it would have made more sense to locate it in an area where the necessary support services were already in place. Another example was the Syrian-Jordanian Commercial Bank. Advance studies had indicated that the Syrian banking system had serious problems, but the Syrians reportedly thought they could benefit from the Jordanians' experience. Unfortunately, the banking systems were incompatible, and Syrian Foreign Minister Khaddam was reportedly opposed to the project.[122] The cement company, although it became fully operational, nevertheless was not a complete success story because Syria never contributed its full share of the capital; it took cement but often failed to repay its debts.[123] However, one official involved in the joint companies also stressed that the success of such companies required a real commitment to the idea of the company and to integration, implying that some managers or administrators simply did not have sufficient interest in or devotion to the projects.[124]

In addition to joint companies and committees, in the Syrian-Jordanian relationship we have encountered attempts at development planning coordination, increasing trade, lowering or abolishing certain tariffs and taxes, linking electricity grids and communications networks, exchanges of visits by members of the private sector, and so on. The success of these other tools of economic statecraft, aside from contributing to the general atmosphere of cooperation, is less clear. As was the case with joint ventures, Jordan's main purpose was to build functional economic ties that would make a complete cut in relations more difficult in the future. It also, of course, sought to expand the market for Jordanian products.

Jordan had long been concerned with the size of inter-Arab trade, only about 7 percent of total Arab trade (although Jordan's percentage of trade with the Arab world is much higher). Syrian-Jordanian trade certainly increased during periods when relations were good, but suffered (although it was not cut off completely) when relations deteriorated. Part of the problem with trade was related to continuing differences over customs duties, exchange rates, foreign currency reserves, and competitive, rather than complementary, products. However, a major obstacle to increased exchange also resulted from the strong, if gradually decreasing, role of the Syrian state in trade. On the Syrian side political decisions from above could much more easily shut off markets to Syrian importers or exporters than was the case with largely free-market Jordan.

Another obstacle to effective cooperation with the Syrians, according to those interviewed, was that the Syrians stressed development of self-reliance over importing. More problematic, several former policymakers generalized about the Syrians saying that they were very easy to deal with, but no sooner had one concluded an agreement than the Syrians embarked on ways of getting around it. Their payment record was particularly poor. What generally happened was that at some point, when Jordan needed something, it would obtain it on barter terms from Syria, in order to settle the debt. However, even then, the Syrians usually artificially raised the price and altered the exchange rate so that Jordan lost in the end.[125]

In closing it is important to keep in mind that aside from the attempt to carve out a larger share of the Syrian market in 1984, the uses of economic statecraft were primarily aimed at building a stronger general base of relations with Syria. The memory and pain of the border closing with Syria in 1970 was still fresh in many policymakers' minds. Constructing more extensive economic ties, whether in the form of trade, joint companies, or a shared dam, was, in addition to whatever economic and developmental needs they fulfilled for Jordan, also intended to serve the political/ economic goal of making the cutting of ties a much less likely step in the future.

Economics and Alignment

What of the larger question, the importance of economics and specifically, sources of budget revenue, for driving or influencing foreign policy decisions? This chapter has detailed a number of cases that support the argument, as well as few others that are not so clear.

In the case of the rapprochement of 1975, Rifa'i contended that the idea to make common cause with Syria was primarily motivated by the desire to constitute a common front to elicit funds from the Gulf states. Mudar Badran confirmed that the Gulf states had not forwarded their promised contributions following the Rabat summit in 1974 and that the Egyptians, Syrians, and Jordanians literally went begging together. These countries' annual budgets were drawn up with the assumption that such substantial aid would be forthcoming. Hence, Gulf state balking at forwarding the promised contributions threatened them with potentially serious financial shortfalls.

Rifa'i played down the importance of traditional explanations for the Syrian-Jordanian alignment, such as the need to form a common front against Israel; yet it would be hard to believe that the policy-

makers' calculations ignored Jordan's desire to end its political out-
cast status or Syria's perceived need to strengthen its regional position as Sadat appeared to be pulling away from the Arab consensus.[126] Nonetheless, the timing of the rapprochement and the leading role of economic committees in its early days strongly suggest
that the economic factors were the primary considerations.

At this stage one might ask why Jordan sought to coordinate with
Syria as opposed to Egypt, since all three evidently sought to convince the Gulf states to forward the promised Rabat aid, and since
Husayn's political orientation was more in line with Sadat's pro-Western tilt. The economic explanation, that of the need to build economic ties with Syria to prevent a repeat of 1970, makes most sense.
Egypt clearly represented a large potential market, but it was not a
key to Jordan's overland trade, as Syria was, nor had Jordan had a
1970-like experience with Egypt. Syrian receptivity to Jordanian overtures in the face of its post-1973 war feuding with Egypt may also have
played a role. In any case, a balanced relationship would have been
almost impossible: the Cairo-Damascus rivalry forced Jordan to
choose between the two.

In the matter of the 1979–80 deterioration, the case is much clearer. Iraq simply had much more to offer than did Syria, and it was
courting Jordan economically and politically. Given the near impos-
sibility of Jordan's maintaining close relations with both states
(except during the rare periods when Iraq and Syria are not feuding), it sacrificed the Syrian connection. Other factors, such as the
cooling of relations between the two because of Jordan's initial failure categorically to condemn Sadat, or the deterioration in the
domestic front in Syria, certainly played exacerbating roles. However, the timing of the shift is best explained by Jordan's drive for more,
and more secure, economic backing.

In the case of the 1985–86 rapprochement, the usual explanation
is that Jordan wanted to end attacks against its diplomats and establishments abroad, and to try and expand influence with Syria in the
Arab world so that Syria would work to convince the Iranians to end
the Gulf war. However, timing is critical, and the *Jordanian* rapprochement initiative came in early 1983, at about the same time that
the Jordanians were trying to expand ties with Egypt. Although the

Egyptian market is far larger, there is every reason to suspect, especially given that the first overtures were economic ones, that the Jordanians, burned by the continuation of the Iran-Iraq war and Iraq's inability to continue its aid payments or many of the contracts it had awarded earlier, were seeking relief by expanding their activity in other regional markets. Here, because of proximity, relative wealth (or lack thereof), and market size, Egypt and Syria made the most sense. The Jordanians were also hoping, of course, that Syria might reopen the oil pipeline from Iraq, thus providing Iraq and, by extension Jordan, some needed economic relief.

Of course, the other side of the equation is Syrian concerns, the role that economic factors played in driving Syrian foreign policy. This chapter was not intended to be a study of the Syrian economy or Syrian foreign policy, so only tentative conclusions can be drawn. The argument about constituting a united front to present the Gulf states with demands for more financial assistance may well have been an important Syrian motive in 1975 for joining forces with Jordan. However, it would be seem unwise to overlook some obviously political or strategic factors that must also have figured into Asad's calculations: the fears over a defection by Sadat, the beginning of the civil war in Lebanon, concern for stability in the Levant, and keeping the PLO in tow.

In 1979–80, again it appears that domestic stability and concern over Iraq's regional position played a major role in the deterioration of relations, although from the account of the deterioration pieced together from oral sources it seems that it was ultimately Jordan's choice of Iraq that sealed the fate of the relationship with Syria, not a Syrian "expulsion" of Jordan from the relationship. The rapprochement of 1985 is a better candidate for the economic argument from the Syrian side. Recall that in 1983, Jordan made initial overtures, but was rebuffed. Then in 1984, as there appeared to be progress, again with economic delegations in the lead, Husayn's restoration of ties with Egypt alienated the Syrians. However, by 1985, the Syrians were again interested. Is it coincidental then that by the spring of 1985 the Syrians were having trouble with their oil supplies from Iran and were in need of improved ties with the other Arab states? Or, was the state of the war such that the Syrians were hoping for an end and hence wanted to terminate their relative isolation? Could it also have been that Syrian policy in Lebanon, which by spring 1985 was sponsoring an Amal-led proxy attack against the Palestinian camps in Lebanon, was also in need of whatever additional support it could secure? All of these factors may have played a role. Only a thorough study of Syria's economic relations with these states is likely to provide more definitive answers regarding to what extent budgetary considerations may have driven Damascus' foreign policy.

What does seem clear is that in the Syrian-Jordanian relationship the traditional maxim about politics always winning over economics does not hold. Economics have been shown to play a central role both in lower-level (daily exchange) and in state-level (external aid-related) action and decisions. However, the key to understanding the role of economics in this case lies in focusing not only on what the bilateral economic relationship is, but also—because of the absence of aid in the bilateral equation—on what it is *not*. In the case of Syrian-Jordanian ties, the aid dependence of the two on third party states, not on each other, best explains or accounts for the role of economic factors. When the oil states failed to provide the expected assistance, there was a clear Jordanian drive for stronger ties with Syria. In other cases, cordial ties with Damascus were certainly desirable, but only so long as they did not impinge upon the primary aid relationships. Hence, Jordan's relations with Syria were largely financially driven, but are comprehensible only in the context of the two countries' respective relations with the Gulf states and Iraq, the "Arab financial assistance club."

6

Jordanian-Iraqi Relations

It was the British who, in installing monarchs from the Hashemite family on the thrones of both Transjordan and Mesopotamia in 1921, established a strong base for modern political ties between Baghdad and Amman. Not until July 1958, when the Hashemites of Iraq were overthrown and replaced by a revolutionary nationalist regime, did bilateral ties deteriorate. Relations were cool if not strained throughout the 1960s as Iraq, preoccupied with domestic problems and state consolidation, remained a generally marginal force in inter-Arab politics. Baghdad did attempt to mediate between Jordan and the Palestinian resistance in 1970, but its 25,000-man strong expeditionary force stationed in Jordan remained aloof from the fighting when mediation efforts failed.[1]

The history of the period under study involves only one major alliance shift: Jordan's move away from Syria and into a closer and closer economic, military, and political relationship with Iraq. As the empirical material in the case study below demonstrates, this major change was undertaken in large part for reasons related to the financial and budgetary support Iraq was willing and able to provide the kingdom at a time of economic crisis. The beginning of the Iran-Iraq war in 1980 served further to strengthen ties. Denied access to the Persian Gulf, Iraq was eager for imports from and through Jordan, and the Jordanian private sector, with state encouragement, responded with enthusiasm. Moreover, given the kingdom's traditional involvement in transit trade, Jordan was more than willing to expand its highway and port system (thanks to Iraqi grants and loans) to accommodate Iraqi needs.

That the war would drag on for years, leading to a drop in oil prices and a regional recession that ultimately led, not only to the suspension of Iraqi aid but also to a significant reneging on promised support from the other Gulf states, was something Jordanian policymakers could not have foreseen. However, in order to address its evolving economic crisis, the king sought to form an even closer, if expanded, alliance with his Iraqi partner after the war in the form of the quadripartite Arab Cooperation Council. Again, as the case study that follows will show, in this alliance decision as in Jordan's first move toward Iraq in 1979, considerations of economic security were paramount.

The Lean Years: 1975–1978

Political Developments

At the beginning of this period, although on the sidelines of power, Iraq was involved in a number of inter-Arab disputes. For example, press reports indicated that there were Iraqi incursions into Kuwait in early 1975.[2] On another front, in spring 1975, when settlement of the Iraqi-Iranian-Kurdish problem seemed to be at hand, Iraqi-Syrian tensions surfaced, as Baghdad complained about the low rate of water discharge from the Syrian Euphrates dam. Arab League mediation by Egypt and Saudi Arabia led Syria in June unilaterally to offer to supply Iraq with river water from the Euphrates; however, by spring 1976 a new dispute had arisen between the two over oil transit royalties and over Iraq's opposition to Syria's role in Lebanon. Iraq then responded by suspending oil pumping through Syria.[3] On November 2, Iraq closed the joint border and increased patrolling by heavily armed units. This move, reportedly an expression of its rejection of the decisions reached at the Cairo summit on the future of Lebanon,[4] marked a new stage in the deterioration of relations between the two. In response, as if the Kurds had not already suffered from sufficient cynical outside manipulation, the Syrians apparently became involved in supporting a new round of Kurdish anti-Iraqi guerrilla activity.[5]

Iraqi-PLO ties were no better. With the exception of the strain in relations between Syria and the PLO in 1976 and 1977, PLO-Syrian relations were good during this period. Perhaps as a result, as the PLO tried to rein in some of its smaller or more radical factions, such as Abu Nidal's breakaway organization, Iraq gave them sanctuary. When the PLO, particularly Fateh, countered with more open and vocal criticism of the Ba'th for fostering schisms in its ranks,[6] the Iraqis responded by assassinating a number of Fateh or PLO moderates. For its part, Jordan accused Iraq of complicity in the November 1976 Palestinian guerrilla attack on the Amman Intercontinental Hotel, although this did not develop into an open clash.[7]

Despite political and ideological differences between the two, by 1975 the security and economic rationale for cooperation with Jordan had become compelling (although Jordan's growing relationship with Syria, in part obstructed Iraqi overtures). For Iraq, with only limited access to the sea, Jordan represented an alternative to Syria as an overland route for the transshipment of imports and exports. In the post-1975 period, as Iraq began to emerge from relative isolation, it may have regarded Jordan as a useful "moderate" Arab partner. For its part, as the decade progressed, Jordan saw in Iraq not only a country that could offer strategic depth, but also a wealthy and economically diversified state that could provide the various kinds of support the aid-dependent kingdom needed.[8] By the mid-1970s, Iraqi development loans had not only begun to help indirectly to ease pressures on the budget; they also enabled Jordan to modernize some of its physical infrastructure, enhancing its ability to serve as a transport and transit center. Iraq also offered a huge potential market for Jordanian goods. These factors all work rather *indirectly* to enhance budget security. The advantage in the case of Iraq was that, particularly after the increase in oil prices in 1973, it also had the resources to provide direct financial assistance, the most central element in Jordanian budget security considerations.

Baghdad's major Arab concern in the mid-1970s was apparently to undermine Syrian influence in the Levant. Intimidation, however, was clearly not the formula for success. Perhaps as an alternative strategy, in early October 1977, the Iraqi delegation to the Arab Gulf countries' Conference of Trade Ministers presented a case for inter-Arab cooperation. It offered a number of agreements to promote joint action and to establish joint economic institutions, among them, an Arab market zone. Such a zone would have doubled the market size served by Iraqi exporters. It would also have reduced competition, especially in petrochemicals, from its Arab neighbors, and preferential tariffs would have appreciably reduced the economic penetration of the area by the Iranians, who had been far more active and successful than the Iraqis in regional trade.[9] Unfortunately for the Iraqis, the proposal was not acted upon.

In the meantime, despite a gradual increase in development loans (see below), diplomatic interaction between Jordan and Iraq in 1977 appears to have been limited to a visit to Iraq by Jordan's Youth and Culture Minister Fawwaz Sharaf in mid-July and a letter from King Husayn to Iraqi president Hasan al-Bakr in early October. While the August signing of a pact permitting Iraq to rent a section of the Aqaba port seemed to signal a warming of relations, in September, the execution by the Iraqis of a Jordanian student charged with working for Jordanian intelligence led to a full-scale propaganda war between the two. Amman responded by issuing an order forbidding its students to study in Iraq in the future. [10]

The cautious Jordanian position on Egyptian President Sadat's November 1977 trip to Jerusalem and the subsequent Jordanian-PLO rapprochement also drew Iraqi fire. But in this as in other matters, Baghdad seemed more concerned about the effect of such developments on Syria and on its own standing in the Arab world than about the actual content of the policy. Of course, inter-Arab differences were largely, if temporarily, set aside as the September 1978 meetings at Camp David produced accords that ultimately served as the basis of an Egyptian-Israeli peace treaty. And, following Camp David, the number of visits between Jordanian and Iraqi officials increased markedly. On October 1, Iraq issued a call for an Arab League summit in Baghdad. Jordan's Interior Minister Sulayman 'Arar met with then second-in-command, Saddam Husayn, on October 4; Iraqi Foreign Minister Sa'dun Hammadi met with Jordanian Minister of State Hasan Ibrahim at the UN on October 5; and on the same day Iraqi Revolutionary Command Council (RCC) member

Hikmat Ibrahim arrived in Amman with a message from Iraqi President al-Bakr for the king. [11]

Only a few days earlier the RCC, the Iraqi ruling body, had issued a response to Camp David which had included a proposal that the Arab states set up a fund to provide for Egypt's financial needs (presumably to prevent it from going ahead with its peace treaty) and to insure the needs of the western, northern, and eastern fronts as well as those of the PLO and the people in the occupied territories. The Iraqi proposal suggested that the appropriations be no less than $9 billion a year, subject to the needs of the battle, for a period of ten years.[12] Not coincidentally, then, the Arab summit held in Baghdad on November 2–5 called for a $9 billion fund of support for the confrontation states: Jordan, Syria, and the PLO. According to Jordanian policymakers, Saddam was the primary mover behind the convening of the 1978 meeting and in convincing the Gulf countries to give money to the remaining confrontation states.[13] Saddam also reportedly offered to pay any amounts reneged upon by the other contributing states in addition to promising an Iraqi contribution of $520 million a year for ten years.[14]

As noted in previous chapters, Jordan was in particularly dire financial straits at the time. The Gulf states had not forwarded all the assistance they had promised in 1974 at Rabat, despite a meeting held in Saudi Arabia in January 1977 in which the issue had supposedly been settled. Former Chief of the Royal Court and Prime Minister Mudar Badran described how, in 1976, for example, he had been forced to take serious measures to cut spending and to find money to pay the salaries of bureaucrats and the members of the armed forces.[15] Thus, in pushing for the 1978 summit and in focusing on aid to the confrontation states, Saddam had performed a very valuable service for the Jordanians. (In addition to the monetary incentive, however, it seems the king also formed a close personal relationship with Saddam as a result of their 1978 meeting.) Thus the king was made to feel the financial power of Iraq at a time when the Jordanian budget desperately needed funds. The fall of the shah only a few months later and the threat of Khomeini served as additional stimuli for Jordan's moving closer to Iraq, but the primary stimulus appears to have been related to budgetary considerations.

Economic Developments

AID (SEE ALSO AQABA PORT, BELOW)

Iraqi aid to Jordan during this period was irregular. The Iraqi Development Fund, like a number of its Gulf counterparts, was established in 1974 in the wake of the dramatic rise in oil prices. Talks held in June 1975 between the two sides reviewed a Jordanian request for a loan for electric power projects, which would have brought Iraq's financial commitment to Jordan to around $60 million.[16] Subsequently, Iraq agreed to make the electric power loan interest-free.[17] In early 1976 Iraq expressed a willingness to provide additional development financing for Jordan, and had begun studying a proposal requesting funds to help finance the $2.3 billion 1976–1980 five-year development plan.[18] On March 24 Iraq approved a $63 million loan to Jordan for various road construction projects,[19] all of which, of course, would directly benefit Iraq.

In August 1977 it was reported that Iraq was contributing $386,563 toward the establishment of agricultural cooperatives for fertilizer and fodder storage in Jordan.[20] About a year later, on October 5, 1978 Iraq granted Jordan $30 million in aid because of Husayn's stance on Camp David.[21] And following December 1978 trade talks, it was announced that the Iraqi government would extend a 15 million dinar [22] loan to the Arab Potash Company and another 5 million dinar loan to the chemical fertilizer company.[23]

TRADE

Bilateral trade figures in 1974 showed Jordanian exports to Iraq of $4.8 million and imports from Iraq of $2.55 million.[24] Just over a year later, the two countries signed an agreement calling for an increase of bilateral trade to $19 million for 1975.[25] In meetings in June 1975, both sides expressed a desire to raise the level of exchange to $12 million each.[26] Jordan's exports in fact did rise in 1975 to $7.5 million, although imports from Iraq dropped slightly to $1.52 million.[27] In March 1976 the bilateral foreign trade targets were further increased to $13.7 million, although the trade levels remained about the same in 1976 as they had been in 1975.[28] Similar trends continued, as bilateral trade for 1977 reached only about $15 million.[29]

INDUSTRY AND JOINT PROJECTS

In June 1975, Iraqi Minister of Industry and Minerals, Taha al-Jazrawi (later better known as Taha Yasin Ramadan), led an Iraqi team to Jordan to discuss Iraqi investment in Jordanian development projects, joint ventures, and other forms of bilateral economic cooperation.[30] The minutes of the joint committee meeting called for the establishment of a tomato juice factory[31] and exploration of the possibility of Iraqi participation of 10–20 percent in the capital in the Jordan Fertilizer Company. The two sides were also looking into raising the level of Iraqi participation in the Arab Mining Company, which was to give priority to Jordanian potash products.[32] In the joint committee meeting in May 1977 there were more discussions of the tomato juice factory; however, at the time of the joint committee meeting in April 1978, it was still in the discussion stage. A free zone project was also mentioned for which the Iraqis were to be compensated for the land used in the amount of 150,000 dinars.[33]

AQABA PORT AND TRANSIT TRADE

On March 31, 1975, the two countries signed an accord whereby Iraq was permitted to use the Aqaba port for importing goods at a rate of 300,000 tons per year.[34] To supervise the Iraqi imports, the Iraqi State Overland Transport Company opened an office in Aqaba during the first week in June 1975.[35] According to an agreement several months later, Jordan was to increase the tonnage of Iraqi imports and exports allowed through Aqaba port to 350,000 tons annually for 1976 and was working to increase this to 400,000 tons for 1977, eventually to reach at least 600,000 tons at the time of the completion of a new pier.[36]

Jordan had also agreed to build four new jetties with supplementary equipment according to the following conditions which clearly indicate the extent of Iraqi interest and participation in Jordanian infrastructure development: the Iraqi government would give Jordan an interest free loan to cover 50 percent of the costs, as long as the size of the loan did not exceed $25.9 million; the work would be completed during the last quarter of 1977; there would be regular consultations between the two about the progress of the project; the payback of the loan would take place through paying 50 percent yearly of the returns on the Iraqi goods, beginning one year after the completion of the jetties; Iraqi imports and exports would have priority in using the new jetties; the Jordanian government would build a 50-kilometer road between Azraq and H-5[37] and widen and improve the road between H-5 and the Iraqi border (180 kilometers); the Jordanian government would build a Ma'an—Ras al-Naqab—Mafraq road of 74 kilometers; and the Iraqi government would give Jordan a $13.8 million loan at 2.5 percent to cover the costs of the road. Iraq subsequently agreed to forego the interest on about $46 million of these loans for port and highway construction.[38] Following talks with Jordan's Minister of Finance in August, the Iraqis agreed to rent a 50,000 meter-square area at the Aqaba port as a free zone for storing imports and exports.[39]

In mid-November 1977 Syria ceased issuing transit passes, thus closing the border to goods bound for Iraq. Combined with the earlier disruption of the Iraqi-Turkish railway, this move rendered Aqaba of even greater importance to the Iraqis. In mid-February 1978 Iraqi Transport Minister Dr. Mukarram Jamal Talabani left for Amman to discuss means of facilitating the transport of merchandise to and from Iraq through Jordan.[40] In the April trade talks that followed, the joint committee stressed the importance of encouraging the use of Aqaba port for the transit of agricultural and industrial goods to and from Iraq.[41]

Summary

The record of political relations during this period is quite mixed as Iraq, preoccupied with a domestic Kurdish insurgency, seemed to involve itself in regional affairs in largely disruptive or subversive ways. However, the economic record is quite different. Beginning in 1975, as its feuding with Syria heated up, Iraq began to show interest in increasing its access to the port of Aqaba. To that end, it began to provide support for various forms of infrastructural development that both increased the port's capacity and facilitated moving goods through it. By the time bilateral political relations began to improve in 1978, a basis of trade and infrastructural links had already been established between Jordan and Iraq. The most significant development from the point of view of Jordan's concern with budget security, however, was the Iraqi push for greater Arab economic support of the confrontation states at the November 1978 summit. At a critical time of decline in expected Arab aid, Iraq stepped in to offer and promote support. Iraqi actual and potential largess served as the foundation for Jordan's gradual alignment shift away from Syria in the next two years.

From Egypt's Peace to Iraq's War: 1979–1980

Political Developments

The visit of Iraqi Foreign Minister Hammadi to Amman in November 1978 signaled the beginning of a real improvement in political relations, and Baghdad's success in pushing for and convening the November summit catapulted it to a new and central place in Arab politics. For example, Jordan's Minister of State for Foreign Affairs, Hasan Ibrahim, consulted with (then still second-in-command) Saddam in early March 1979 on problems between the two Yemens. This meeting was followed by King Husayn's visit to Baghdad on the heels of a trip to Syria. Syrian-Iraqi relations, generally characterized by feuding and acrimony, had warmed dramatically in the shadow of Camp David. In the meantime, of course, the other major regional development, the overthrow of the Shah of Iran, had raised the anxiety level in Iraq, as it pondered what the ramifications of the transformation in Iran might be.

On June 30, 1979 Saddam himself arrived in Amman for two days of talks with Husayn, the first time a top Iraqi leader had visited the Jordanian capital since before the 1958 revolution. Only two weeks later Saddam assumed the Iraqi presidency and wasted little time in making a bid for greater regional influence in the vacuum left by the Shah's departure. In a speech on February 8, 1980, marking the anniversary of the 1963 revolution, Saddam proposed a charter governing inter-Arab relations. According to the Iraqi president, the charter's purpose was to bolster, not replace, Arab commitments such as the joint defense pact. The pact included such principles as mutual understanding, settling inter-Arab disputes through dialogue, and renouncing the use of force. It also rejected foreign military alliances and the presence of foreign troops on Arab soil, at a time when the U.S. had proposed a Rapid Deployment Force to protect the flow of oil. Saddam dispatched envoys to various Arab capitals in mid-February to discuss the charter's implementation, and the proposals found sympathetic ears in both Amman and Riyadh.[42] King Husayn and Crown Prince Sa'd of Kuwait subsequently went to Baghdad for security consultations related to the charter.

In the meantime, it was becoming increasingly clear that Iraq was determined to cement links with Jordan. In mid-May, King Husayn visited Baghdad and "unprecedented cordiality was shown" between the two leaders. Border skirmishes with Iran had erupted periodically since the spring, and the two reportedly had reached agreement on Jordanian-Iraqi military cooperation in the event of an external attack on either. For Iraq, cementing the link with Amman was a critical development, ensuring that it would not be isolated politically or economically in its struggles with Iran and Syria.[43]

In the summer the two leaders had several personal meetings in addition to numerous contacts by telephone and letter. Saddam had also consolidated his ties with Saudi Arabia through an August 5–6 visit with a group of senior advisers, the first time an Iraqi leader had been in the Saudi capital since the 1958 Iraqi revolution.[44] At the end of the talks, which purported to deal with the Israeli annexation of Jerusalem, the Saudis reportedly committed themselves to support Iraq in the increasingly likely event of a war with Iran.[45] King Husayn, hoping for and presumably confident of, a swift Iraqi victory, was one of the few important Arab leaders to support Saddam's adventure openly once the war officially began in September. The king consulted regularly with the Iraqi leader regarding the situation on the front, put Jordan's medical facilities at Iraq's disposal on October 1, and visited Saddam several times in the fall. In November Jordan hosted an Arab League summit on the regional economy which, in further showcasing Iraqi power, led to a Syrian boycott and a massing of Syrian troops on the Jordanian border. This was the final stage in the deterioration of Syrian-Jordanian relations. Jordan was now clearly in the Iraqi camp.

Economic Developments

AID

During this period, Iraqi financial assistance exhibited a marked increase. On March 2, 1979, the Iraqi government donated $16,700 to build mosques and in mid-August it provided a loan of 2 million dinars to Jordanian cooperative societies.[46] Only a few days later Iraq awarded $2.7 million to finance a housing project for journalists in Amman, as Saddam personally handed the sum to the president of the Jordanian Press Association, Rakan al-Majali.[47] Other loans were made to finance the construction of an alternative road from Amman to Zarqa ($8.4 million), additional housing projects ($5 million), a technical college offering degrees in engineering and related subjects at Mu'ta ($50 million) near Kerak, and $3.34 million each for the Royal Scientific Society and several philanthropic societies.[48]

The trend continued and touched numerous economic and social sectors in Jordan. For example, in May the Iraqi government gave $167,000 to a home for the elderly; on July 28 it was announced that the Iraqi Women's Union had given a sum of $16,700 to the Queen Alia Fund; and on August 11 an Iraqi government contribution of $500,000 to the Ibrahimiyyah College on the West Bank was confirmed.[49] In early September it was announced that $100 million of additional financial assistance would be given to economic projects, above and beyond the substantial grants made earlier in the year for transport and port improvement schemes.[50] On September 8 it was reported that the Iraqis had contributed $227,000 to build a mosque in the northern town of al-Husn, just south of Irbid.[51] Only a week later, Iraq provided scholarships for 80 Jordanian students for vocational education in Iraq, agreed to finance the construction of a microwave link between the two raising the number of direct telephone lines from six to 6,000, and on September 23 contributed $500,000 to the civil aviation center.[52] In mid-September two loans from Iraq were approved, both from the Iraqi Fund for External Development. The first, $13.36 million, was for setting up a free zone at Aqaba and the second, $5 million, for financing a housing program in Irbid.[53]

TRADE

In March 1979 the Iraqi-Jordanian joint economic committee agreed to increase trade to $33.4 million per year.[54] The two sides agreed to simplify the process of clearing goods through customs, to encourage tourism, and to give Jordanian agricultural products priority in local marketing.[55] Just over a year later, in late April 1980 a series of bilateral talks was held covering the fields of economy, culture, technology, transport, water, education, industry, and trade cooperation. As a result, on May 1 a new agreement for economic and technical cooperation between the two governments was signed, according to which, trade between the two was to be increased to $41.6 million per year in each direction.[56] By the time of the outbreak of war with Iran, Iraq had become the largest market for Jordanian exports, with an increase between 1979 and 1980 of some 269%. Jordan's most important exports to Iraq included washing powders and pharmaceuticals, as well as building materials, plastic goods, woven fabrics, and fruit and vegetables.[57]

INDUSTRY AND JOINT PROJECTS

A number of joint ventures were discussed in early 1979. In February Iraq and Jordan concluded talks about establishing a joint food canning industry. In March the issue of the tomato paste factory project was again raised and the Iraqis promised to make a final decision on the matter as soon as possible.[58] Agreement on a tourist bus route between Amman and Baghdad was signed on July 21 for four trips a week from each capital. However, there appear to have been delays, and in the end, not until November 13, 1980 was it announced that a twice-daily coach service between Amman and Baghdad, operated by Jordan's JETT bus company and Iraq's General Establishment for Passenger Transport, using existing bus fleets, was to start operations on December 1, 1980.[59]

In September 1980, at a meeting of the joint industrial committee, in response to an Iraqi request, the Jordanians provided a list of domestic industries and projects they wanted to develop. The Iraqis were interested in projects the Jordanians sought to undertake jointly, especially in mining, food, building, textiles (weaving), engineering, and chemicals. The two sides agreed to set up a joint industrial holding company that would conduct technical and economic studies, and implement projects in the form of specialized branch companies.[60]

AQABA PORT AND TRANSIT TRADE

The growing economic and security importance of Aqaba to Iraq and the Jordanian enthusiasm for taking advantage of Iraqi interest in developing the port as an economic boon to the kingdom became increasingly clear during this period. By early February 1980 companies from both Kuwait and Jordan had signed haulage contracts with the Iraqi State Establishment for Specialized Transport to allow imports to be transited through Mina Shuwaykh (Kuwait) and Aqaba because of congestion at Iraq's ports.[61] In late February it was announced that Iraq intended to hire Jordanian vehicles (and provide fuel) to transport half the goods it imported through the Gulf of Aqaba, some 1 million tons a year.[62] Even the U.S. Department of Commerce was reportedly stressing to businessmen the advantages of Aqaba as a transit and warehouse base for exports going to other Middle Eastern countries, like Iraq.[63] Meanwhile, in mid-February the Iraqi government had approved in principle a grant of $13.2 million to Jordan to raise the standard of services and bolster the projects of the Free Zone Company in the Aqaba Free Zone.[64]

On May 1 several Aqaba-related loans and grants were announced. First were loans of $50 million for a road linking Aqaba with Azraq, (to be used by trucks taking goods to Iraq), $13.3 million for expansion of the Free Zone, and $10 million for port development. At the time Iraq was transshipping 2 million tons of imports a year through Aqaba, one-half of which were carried by Jordanian trucks and two local companies on behalf of Iraqi ministries.[65] Only a few weeks later, a joint company dubbed the Iraqi-Jordanian Land Transport Company (IJLTC) was officially founded, with its primary mandate to buy and operate vehicles to transship Iraqi imports arriving at the port of Aqaba.[66] Iraq expected to use the port for about 10 percent of its imports by 1980 because of congestion at Basra.[67]

Aqaba's importance further increased with the outbreak of war. Iraq's own ports of Basra, Umm al-Qasr and Faw were very close to the border with Iran and hence were subject to Iranian bombing. The Jordanian port, on the other hand, was more than 300 miles from the Iraqi border, and 800 miles from the areas where the fiercest fighting was taking place. The swift development of even greater Iraqi dependence upon Aqaba as a transit center and on Jordan as an economic partner after the beginning of the war was clearly facilitated by the pre-1980 highway and port infrastructural expansion projects detailed above.[68]

EUPHRATES RIVER WATER

Talks were held with Iraq in July 1979 regarding the feasibility of channeling drinking and irrigation water from the Euphrates to water-poor Jordan. Projections of water supplies likely to reach Jordan from a completed Maqarayn dam on the Syrian-Jordanian border indicated that less water than originally planned was likely to be drawn.[69] Moreover, that project remained in the planning stages, with an uncertain but seemingly gloomy future. Hence the interest in an alternative water source.

Summary

Forced to choose between relations with Iraq and Syria, Jordan chose gradually to move into the Iraqi camp for sound financial reasons. The Baghdad summits and Saddam's role in them in mobilizing Arab financial support for the confrontation states, along with his own promises of support, must have seemed a budgetary dream come true for the Jordanians. Political relations continued to warm and King Husayn was an early and strong supporter of the Iraqi war effort in the fall of 1980. Developments on the economic front had laid the foundations for such a trend. Trade levels increased and a series of joint economic projects were initiated to further reinforce ties. Just as, if not more, important, unrequited aid from a variety of official and non-official Iraqi sources poured into Jordan, with Iraqi state development aid largely targeting the further expansion of Aqaba port and access to it. The Aqaba link only increased in importance with the outbreak of war with Iran and Iraq's effective loss of the Gulf as an import and export lane. Jordan could only have been expected to take further economic advantage of Iraqi interest.

Iraq at War: 1981–1984

Political Developments

Husayn visited Iraq in March, May, and August 1981 for talks and briefings on the situation at the front. In late January 1982, after discussions with Saddam, King Husayn announced that he had opened the door to volunteers from the Jordanian Army to fight with Iraq. On February 1 the cabinet ordered the establishment of a committee under the prime minister to follow up on the volunteer initiative and to make the necessary financial and administrative arrangements. The cabinet also decided to open a special account in the central bank to receive donations from various organizations and individuals for what were called the Yarmuk Forces. Jordan reportedly opened sixteen training centers and volunteers began heading for Iraq in February.[70] In total, about 3,000 men went to fight alongside the Iraqis. Nevertheless, the king's seemingly enthusiastic support for Saddam's war effort did not lead him to commit regular Jordanian army troops to the front, and shortly after the June 1982 Israeli invasion of Lebanon, Husayn reportedly flew to Iraq to suggest that Saddam use the Lebanon war an excuse for calling for a ceasefire in the Gulf.[71]

Meanwhile, in April 1982 Syria had closed its borders with Iraq and at the end of the month Iran had mounted a major offensive in southern Khuzistan against the remaining lands held by Iraqi troops in the Ahwaz salient, including the town of Khorramshahr. On May 23 the Iranians broke through the defenses of the town and on May 25 the Iraqis admitted that they were withdrawing all their troops from the town. Following this success the Iranians proceeded to push into *Iraqi* territory. The combination of falling oil income and the increasing costs of war had begun to take their toll on the Iraqi economy. The fall of Khorramshahr and the subsequent Iranian invasion of Iraq in July 1982 made clear that all available resources had to be devoted to the war effort.[72] By early 1983 it was reported that payments for foreign contracts had fallen behind schedule and that no major new development projects were being undertaken. By late 1983, inflation was running between 30% and 50%.[73] The implications of these developments for bilateral economic relations will be discussed below.

In the meantime, Husayn made brief visits to Baghdad on February 10 and June 4, 1983, and on November 23 for talks that reportedly focused primarily on the fighting in the Palestinian refugee camps in northern Lebanon between Yasir 'Arafat's men and Syrian-sponsored troops.[74] In early 1984 there were several visits back and forth, between Iraqi Foreign Minister Tariq 'Aziz and Jordan's Foreign Minister Tahir al-Masri and Chief of the Royal Court Marwan al-Qasim. In March, in the wake of a new Iranian offensive, Jordan's Minister of the Interior Sulayman 'Arar and Minister of Trade and Industry Jawad 'Anani went to Baghdad, not only for economy-related meetings, but also in order to sign a border demarcation agreement, according to which Iraq ceded 50 square kilometers to Jordan to settle a dispute that dated back to the mandate period.[75]

The king made several visits in 1984, the final one on October 16, only a few weeks following Jordan's September 25 reestablishment of diplomatic ties with Egypt. Iraq had also been discussing the need for Egypt to return to the Arab fold, and there was speculation at the time that Iraq, too, might resume ties at any moment.[76] In seeming confirmation, in the first week of October Iraq lifted the ban on the entry of Egyptian newspapers.[77] Ultimately, however, the restoration of ties did not materialize until after the 1987 Amman summit gave the official green light. Nonetheless, Iraq continued to strengthen its other links with Egypt, including receiving and buying military supplies (a relationship that had begun even before Sadat was assassinated in 1981), not to mention receiving personnel.

Economic Developments

AID

A Jordanian delegation arrived in Baghdad on January 2, 1981 for talks on bilateral cooperation in trade, transport, education, and scientific research. Minutes were signed on January 6 which included a working plan for the establishment of Mu'tah University near Kerak. In May 1980 Iraq had provided an $50 million loan for the expenses associated with establishing this military/technical university.[78] In a slightly new twist, in early February 1981 Saddam gave a $100 million grant to the Jordanian Ministry of Information. This was one of the first, but certainly not the last, of such moves by the Iraqi president. It became a pattern in the 1980s as he carefully sought to cultivate journalists throughout the region. Stories of gifts of cars and money to journalists visiting Iraq were not uncommon.

In late February Jordan's Minister of Labor Jawad 'Anani went to Baghdad for three days of talks aimed at expanding cooperation in the spheres of labor and social security. During his stay he signed an agreement according to which Iraq offered a loan of $3.3 million to the Jordanian Social Security Corporation to meet the basic requirements of social security in Jordan.[79] Iraqi money continued to flow during the spring of 1981: on March 16 Baghdad contributed 200,000 dinars to the Federation of Charitable Societies; on March 25 the Iraqi Awqaf Ministry contributed 55,000 dinars to a number of Islamic centers; and on April 4 it gave 1 million dinars to the Queen Alia Fund.[80]

To help fund the Jordanian five-year plan, the Iraqis agreed to provide $10 million for the thermal power station at Aqaba and $5 million for the Amman sewage and waste system project, through a loan from the Iraqi Development Fund.[81] In November it was reported that Iraq, which had been urging Jordan to diversify its arms suppliers, would help to pay for a $200 million SAM-6 anti-aircraft missile system that the kingdom planned to buy from the Soviet Union.[82] However, these were among the last exhibitions of Iraqi generosity.

TRADE

At the beginning of this period Jordanian suppliers were quick to seize upon the export and market opportunities offered by an Iraq at war. Jordanian firms reportedly received preferential treatment from the Iraqi government, with tenders of 15 percent more than the lowest bid accepted.[83] Jordan's Trocon (TransOrient Engineering and Contracting Company) was appointed the main contractor for stages eight and nine of the Baghdad University expansion scheme.[84] In early summer 1981 a $13.3 million contract to build irrigation and drainage networks for the Kamaliyyah project also went to an unidentified Jordanian company,[85] and in September, Jordan's International Contracting and Investment Company (ICICO) won a $7.5 million contract to build an agricultural museum in Baghdad. ICICO was already working on a $25.4 million contract to build high-rise apartment buildings for the Baghdad municipality.[86] Trade statistics showed Jordanian exports to Iraq up from $86.7 million in 1980 to $184.8 million in 1981. At the same time, imports remained low: $6.8 million in 1980, dropping to $2.2 million in 1981.[87]

Despite Arab assistance, which was itself declining, the war was beginning to take its toll on Baghdad. In mid-1982, Iraq suddenly closed its markets to Jordanian products and canceled all contracts with Jordanian merchants, transport companies, and contractors as part of an austerity program aimed at cutting imports in half. By 1983 "only those projects capable of aiding the war effort or expanding Iraq's potential for increased oil production and export were receiving funds."[88] Jordanian exports to Iraq suffered considerably. While Jordanian exports to Iraq in 1982 remained close to their 1981 level at $193.8 million, in 1983 they dropped to only $72.8 million. During the same period, Iraqi exports to Jordan, which stood at only $2.7 million in 1982, jumped to $13 million in 1983.[89] In an attempt to preserve markets and protect Jordanian suppliers from potentially disastrous results, in late March 1983 (about the time of the drop in Arab aid to Iraq)[90] the Jordanian government made $65 million in short-term credit available to finance Iraqi imports of Jordanian goods: $45 million of the Jordanian credit was to be used to pay for Iraqi imports of Jordanian-made goods; the remainder was to support the service sector and joint ventures.

In August 1983, probably in response to the import credit agreement, Iraq's State Organization for Consumer Goods signed purchase agreements with 102 Jordanian companies for goods valued at $13.5 million.[91] About a month later, the Jordanian Ministry of Trade and Industry proposed that to reduce the Iraqi trade deficit, Jordanian companies buy $35 worth of goods from Iraq for every $100 of Jordanian goods bought by Iraq. Iraq would finance its purchases through confirmed letters of credit. The proposal promised not only to help correct the trade imbalance, but also to enable Iraq to dispose of surplus goods while also reducing the cash Iraq needed to finance its imports from Jordan.[92]

In late December, in response to Iraq's continuing budget problems, Amman agreed to provide Baghdad with another $125 million in credit for 1984, again, to be used to buy Jordanian goods or to pay debts owed Jordanian companies working in Iraq. This credit was offered on terms similar to those of the previous year: half of the amount was to be at repaid at 6 percent interest, while the remainder was interest free.[93] Probably as a direct result, shortly thereafter, clothing export contracts valued at a total of $5.5 million were won by representatives of Jordanian firms in Iraq.[94] As a further measure to facilitate trade with a financially strapped Iraq, in May 1984 Jordan's Arab Potash Company proposed a commodity agreement according to which the Iraqis would pay in sulfur.[95]

INDUSTRY AND JOINT PROJECTS

Plans for joint ventures continued in the early part of this period, before the severe economic problems set in. For example, the joint ministerial meetings in April 1981 again discussed establishing a Joint Iraqi-Jordanian Company for Industry as well as possible Iraqi participation in Jordanian projects in yarn and weaving and in a cement factory in the south. The Jordanians presented a draft of bylaws for the joint industrial company and the yarn and weaving company, the capital for which was to reach 4 million dinars: Jordan was to provide 2.1 million and the Iraqis 1.9 million. As for the Southern Cement Company, the Jordanian side suggested that the Iraqis contribute 15–20 percent of the capital. The Iraqis welcomed in principle the establishment of the Iraqi-Jordanian Company for Industry and participation in both projects. They then further suggested establishing a joint food canning plant to support trade and help lead to greater economic integration.[96] An agreement on the industrial company was finally signed in September 1982.[97]

AQABA PORT AND TRANSIT TRADE

By early 1981 Jordan had already become the main supply route for war materiel and civilian goods imported by Iraq, and appeared to be holding up well under the strain of massive expansion.[98] Pressure on the Aqaba port following the closure of Iraq's Gulf ports in late 1980 was substantial, as an average of 80 vessels with Iraq-bound cargo were waiting to unload at any given time. The resulting delays reached up to three months. In late December, therefore, the Iraqi government dispatched a special committee to Aqaba to organize the unloading of perishable and vital cargoes.[99] To facilitate transit and trade further, in March 1981 a delegation from the Iraqi Development Fund met with officials from the Jordanian Ministry of Public Works to discuss financing both the $62.3 million 140-kilometer desert highway from Suwaqa (south of the capital) to Ma'an and the $30 million 90-kilometer road from Juwaydah to Muwaqqar and Azraq.[100]

In October 1981 Jordan reported agreement on $4.5 million of a May 13, 1980 $10 million loan from the Iraqi Development Fund for a project to increase the absorptive capacity of the Aqaba port. There was also an agreement to increase the volume of Iraqi goods received at Aqaba port to 3 million tons.[101] A further indication of the importance of the overland routes and the desire for expansion came in May 1982 when a team of Iraqi experts visited Jordan to discuss building a railway between Aqaba and Baghdad, primarily to transport goods between the port and the capital.[102]

In August 1982 it was announced that the IJLTC had postponed plans to double its fleet to 1,500 vehicles. Negotiations with several firms had been underway; however, the company decided to concentrate instead on increasing the efficiency of the existing fleet.[103] This may well have been in response to Iraq's new austerity measures. However, the company did announce profits of $36.7 million for 1982. It had carried 940,000 tons of goods in 1982 and planned to increase this to 1.5 million tons in 1983.[104]

OIL

While Jordan had long received its petroleum needs from Tapline from Saudi Arabia, the war's disruption of Iraqi refining capabilities as well as Baghdad's increasing budgetary difficulties, which rendered making payments for imports in foreign currency increasingly difficult, ultimately led to the introduction of oil as a critical commodity in the bilateral relationship. By late fall 1980, damage to Iraqi oil installations from Iranian bombing was already extensive. The 140,000 b/d Basra refinery and the 100,000 b/d Dura refinery were reported to be nonfunctioning. Other early victims of Iranian air attacks included the Khor al-Zubayr petrochemical complex, the Faw oil terminal, the 30,000 b/d Kirkuk refinery, pumping stations on the trans-Syrian pipeline, oil stations at Khor al-Amaya and al-Bakr, the 10,500 b/d Khanaqin refinery, and a sulfur plant in al-Dura.[105] Domestic shortages of refined products were being met by imports from neighboring countries, including Turkey.

As a result, in the Iraqi-Jordanian joint committee meeting of October 1981, the two sides examined the issue of cooperation in oil exporting and refining. Jordan expressed its willingness to refine an additional 2,000 tons daily of crude oil at the Jordan Petroleum Refinery Company's (JPRC) Zarqa plant for the Iraqi Oil Marketing Establishment if the oil was ensured by Saudi Arabia through Tapline. Only two months earlier, Jordan had offered to help build a terminal a few kilometers south of Aqaba for the proposed Iraqi 1,400-kilometer oil pipeline, but at that point, the Iraqis had called the proposal unfeasible.[106] However, in February 1983 Jordan's Minister of Trade and Industry Walid 'Asfur announced that Iraq had agreed in principle to export Iraqi crude oil through Jordan via a special pipeline to be constructed for that purpose. Two other pipelines were also under discussion at the time: an expansion of the pipeline through Turkey and a new line through Saudi Arabia to the Red Sea.[107] The Jordanian pipeline was to be laid from the Iraqi oilfields across the northern part of the kingdom to its terminal in Aqaba.[108] Details of this proposed pipeline were further discussed during meetings in January 1984.[109] At the time, Jordan was still receiving its petroleum needs from Saudi Arabia through Tapline. However, this supply was scheduled to end in 1985 and Jordan's oil bill was expected to reach $700 million.[110] Hence, in addition to seeking additional realms for lucrative expanded cooperation with Iraq, the Jordanians may well have been testing the waters regarding future (subsidized) oil deliveries from Iraq after the Tapline agreement ended.

Bechtel was the prospective contractor for the project, but there were concerns about the political strings that might be attached to the financing. Jordan was to bear two-thirds of the estimated $1 billion cost of the project and collect transit fees on the oil pumped through the pipeline. However, a potential sticking point in obtaining financing arose when Jordan and Iraq insisted that they would refuse to repay loans if the pipeline was destroyed by sabotage. Both countries believed that if the U.S. undertook the financing, it was much less likely that Israel, which they saw as the primary threat, would strike the pipeline.[111]

Further evidence of the reality and the potential for cooperation based on oil came at the end of March 1984 when Jordan's Trocon was reportedly about to sign an oil barter agreement with Iraq for payment due on a $110 million contract. Rumors had circulated during the previous two years about Jordanian contractors' receiving payment in oil for Iraqi debt, but the Trocon deal was the first confirmed instance of JPRC using oil from a source other than Saudi Arabia (Tapline). Conclusion of the deal was dependent upon JPRC's agreeing to a price for the oil.[112] In April 1984 a formal and broader oil barter agreement was signed with Iraq and was expected to relax some pressure on Jordan's foreign currency reserves. Jordan was to receive 10,000 barrels of Iraqi crude oil per day in exchange for providing commodities and services. The Iraqi deal was estimated to be worth $110 million and was to last for one year.[113] By June the first quantities of crude had arrived in Jordan.

Discussions of financing for the proposed Iraqi-Jordanian oil pipeline continued in the spring and summer of 1984. The contractor, Bechtel, had requested that the Export-Import Bank consider financing Iraq's one-third share in the project as well as Jordan's two-thirds share. The bank initially appeared more likely to provide funding for only the Jordanian share, although the U.S. Department of State was known to be pushing for a favorable outcome on the financing of the Iraqi portion.[114] At the end of June 1984 it appeared that final negotiations on a full contract award would begin in early July.[115] Ex-Im ultimately committed itself to finance $500 million; the other half of the financing was expected to be raised from other Western sources.

In August 1984 a joint Jordanian-Iraqi team went to London to discuss with American, British, and French financial institutions possible Western loans to build the pipeline. Following the London talks, however, Western press reports focused on the differences between the Arabs on the one side and the Western financiers on the other regarding security for the project. The Americans were evidently not forthcoming on the issue of providing the guarantees sought by the Jordanians and Iraqis.[116] The project was unraveling. The combination of Israeli threats and insufficient security guarantees from the U.S. led Iraq to announce the postponement of the project.[117] Perhaps not surprisingly, then, on September 27 Iraq and two foreign companies signed a contract to implement the first stage of laying an Iraqi pipeline to export crude oil across *Saudi* territory to the Red Sea port of Yanbu'.[118] Jordan had lost out on the oil pipeline, but the principle and practice of Iraqi payment in oil for services and imports had been established and served to tie the two economies even more closely together.

EUPHRATES RIVER WATER

In the summer of 1981, several possible areas of cooperation with Iraq were being discussed, the largest of which was the proposed scheme for supplying Euphrates water to Jordan.[119] The following March, Iraq reiterated its willingness to provide Jordan (as well as Kuwait and other Gulf states) with water. The cost of the 650 kilometers of pipe, pumping stations, water purification plants, storage tanks, and power supply was estimated at $1 billion for the first stage; a second pipe was projected to be needed ten years thereafter.[120] Jordan's other option for increasing its meager water supplies, the Maqarayn or al-Wahdah dam, had not progressed, most recently, because of tensions in the political relationship with Syria. The proposed pipeline was eventually to carry about five cubic meters of water a second from the Euphrates, although there were concerns in Baghdad that the river's future levels would be affected by dams planned in Syria and Turkey.[121]

Summary

Political relations continued to be close during this period. Husayn remained a staunch supporter of Iraq's war effort, going so far as to assemble a volunteer force to fight with the Iraqis. Nonetheless, the king was not alone in the region in his anxiety over the continuation of a war the Arabs had assumed would be of short duration. As the battle dragged on and the political ramifications and the negative economic impact of the war became clearer, the king undertook what mediation he could to encourage the Iraqis to take steps to end the fighting.

On the economic front, 1981 began as a good year with aid, loans, and joint projects high on the bilateral agenda. However as the war continued, and Iraq grew harder pressed economically, particularly after Arab aid to Baghdad dropped, Iraqi aid to Jordan also dwindled, and Jordanian private sector activity, which had boomed after the initial outbreak of war, faced the impact of serious Iraqi austerity measures by mid-1982. To support its exporters, Jordan introduced an export credit program for 1983; and by 1984 it had reached an oil barter agreement with the Iraqis to address further the issue of payments for Jordanian products. Had the war ended shortly thereafter these stopgap measures might have worked. But as the next section demonstrates, Jordan had unwittingly allowed itself to be drawn into a deeper but transformed economic relationship that ultimately severely threatened the very national economic security the relationship had initially been strengthened to serve.

Iraq at War: 1985 to the 1988 Ceasefire

Political Developments

Husayn visited Baghdad at the end of January 1985 for consultations on what became known as the Palestinian-Jordanian February 11 Accord, which provided the bases for a joint approach to future Middle East peace talks. Mid-March witnessed the most spectacular meeting in recent regional history as, only three hours after Egyptian President Husni Mubarak's arrival in Amman for talks, he and the king headed for Iraq. The timing of the visit was significant—the war had recently heated up with the shelling of Basra and other Iraqi cities— as was the fact that it was the first visit by an Egyptian president to Iraq since Camp David, to which Iraq, at least rhetorically, had led the opposition.[122] In response, during the following week, there were attacks on Royal Jordanian offices in three European capitals, apparently by Syrian agents.

In late December 1985, Prime Minister Zayd al-Rifa'i and RCC member Taha Yasin Ramadan signed an agreement whereby a higher committee was to be formed by the two countries along the lines of what had been set up between Syria and Jordan ten years earlier. A number of subcommittees were also established to deal with economic and trade issues as well as with industrial cooperation, energy, transportation, communications, and educational and technical cooperation.[123]

Husayn's primary quest during this period continued to be to find a way to end the Iran-Iraq war: the political, economic, commercial, and human toll on the Arab world at large and on Jordan in particular had already reached unacceptable levels. State security threats by Iran, internal instability, drops in expatriate remittances, the decline in Gulf state liquidity and commerce—all had adversely affected the region. The swift defeat of Iran that the king, the Saudis, and the Iraqis had envisioned in the early autumn of 1980 had developed instead into a bloody and costly stalemate.

Husayn briefly visited Baghdad on May 2, accompanied by top political and economic ministers. Bilateral consultations at the foreign minister level took place throughout the summer and Husayn returned to Baghdad at the end of July for a brief meeting, in preparation for the extraordinary Arab summit (to be held in Casablanca in August), and then again in late October. At the time, Syrian-Jordanian reconciliation was underway and Husayn was no doubt eager to reassure the Iraqis about those developments. Husayn was also reportedly involved in trying once again to bring about an Iraqi-Syrian reconciliation. An Arab League team was formed at Casablanca for that purpose; however, according to Ramadan, by the end of December, no progress had been made.[124]

The king made official visits to Baghdad on May 13 and 26, ostensibly for a round of talks on the war, but it is just as likely that the talks were part of his efforts to achieve a Syrian-Iraqi rapprochement. He returned to Baghdad for the same purpose on July 19. The two communicated indirectly through envoys and directly by telephone until the king returned on November 28. By this time, however, the attempts at Syrian-Iraqi mediation had again come to naught. Nonetheless, in the spring of 1987 there were rumors, naturally denied, of a meeting between the Syrian and Iraqi leaders on the Jordanian border. Asad and Saddam reportedly did meet in early May at a desert post close to the triangular frontiers of Jordan, Saudi Arabia, and Iraq. But reconciliation continued to prove elusive.

By late summer contacts were underway to convene a summit to discuss the Iran-Iraq war and to try to forge a unified Arab position. Up to that point, Syria had been the major obstacle to convening such a summit because of its support for Iran. In a major triumph for King Husayn, the summit was finally held in early November in Amman. Agreement on the question of the Gulf war was reached as was the position that each Arab state was free to restore relations with Egypt as it saw fit. In the wake of the summit, which Syria did attend, Iraq restored diplomatic relations with Egypt on November 13.

The most important development of the period was that on July

18, 1988, Iran unconditionally accepted Security Council Resolution 598, and immediate steps were taken to implement a cease-fire in the Gulf war. In mid-August Husayn, accompanied by other Hashemite princes as well as other members of the political elite, went to Baghdad not only for talks, but also to congratulate Saddam on his "great victory" in the war. Following these bilateral talks Saddam reportedly presented Husayn with 169 Iranian tanks out of appreciation for his support during the war.[125]

Economic Developments

At the beginning of this period, in 1985, Iraq faced the prospect of rescheduling $1.952 billion in principal of previously rescheduled debt to its main creditors: France, Japan, and West Germany. To make matters worse, it was estimated that it was likely to run a record $3.9 billion balance of payments deficit without taking into account any foreign debt repayments. The country had virtually no reserves and budget cutting was not considered a viable option. Budgetary appropriations were directed primarily at completing ongoing schemes already labeled as strategic. The prospect of increased revenues from crude oil through the planned pipelines to Saudi Arabia and Turkey was the only economic bright spot.[126]

TRADE

Up to this point, Jordan had benefited in three major ways from the Iran-Iraq war. The first was through the expansion of Aqaba port into a major import-export facility, serving primarily, but by no means exclusively, Iraq. The second was in the form of the expansion of its transport sector as a result of trucking goods to and from the port. Third was the opening up of the Iraqi market to Jordanian products, to the point where by late 1985 Iraq was absorbing one-third of Amman's exports. (Although if phosphates were excluded the figure was closer to 50 percent.) A quarter of the crude oil handled by the Zarqa refinery was from Iraq, and it was this oil that enabled the government through the central bank to repay Jordanian companies that had provided goods or services to Baghdad.[127]

A January 23, 1985 protocol provided for an increase in the trade quota to $41.3 million each for Amman and Baghdad, and for an Iraqi promise to import Jordanian tomato paste, no less than 100 million eggs, and 22,000 tons of phosphates.[128] Beginning May 1, Jordan put at Iraq's disposal another $80 million—$10 million per month—in what amounted to export credits: 50 percent was to be for goods of Jordanian origin and 50 percent for services. By May 31, 1985, Jordan's financing of Iraqi imports through the Central Bank had reached $429 million.[129] The sixth session of the Jordanian-Iraqi joint ministerial committee, held at the end of 1985, called for trade exchange to increase to $750 million in 1986 (a seven-fold increase over the 1984 level), although trade statistics for 1985 showed only $170 million in exports to, and (because of the oil) $188 million in imports from, Iraq.[130]

Meetings a year later called for an increase and diversification of trade so that the volume would reach $800 million in 1987,[131] and $900 million for 1988.[132] In the event, exports jumped from $123.7 million in 1986 to $192 million in 1988; imports, on the other hand, skyrocketed from $233.4 million in 1986 to $348 million in 1988.[133] Nonetheless, these figures were still well below the targets set by the joint committee.

The Export Credits Scandal. Trade was certainly booming but trouble was brewing. The problem was first publicly acknowledged in early 1988. A special committee from the Jordan Chamber of Industry's Board of Directors had been formed to study the results of the classification of the products exported to Iraq and those products for which letters of credit had been opened. According to the trade protocols, Iraq was permitted to import Jordanian manufactures of up to a ceiling of $185 million using the Jordanian export credits. However, it was found that a large percentage of these exports were in fact not Jordanian products.[134] Only goods with at least 40 percent of their value added *in Jordan* were eligible for Central Bank financing. The non-Jordanian products were simply being relabeled as Jordanian to take advantage of the government financing provisions. The Iraqi demand for consumer goods in the mid-1980s after several years of war was tremendous, and the Jordanian private sector's desire to make money was evidently too intense to abide by the law. While no one officially admitted this in interviews, it seems likely, given the relationship between the government and the private sector in Jordan, that Jordanian monitoring of deals had been insufficient, and that powerful individual businessmen probably enjoyed either the tacit support or the willful ignorance of the powers that should have been overseeing such matters.

This problem brought into stark relief Jordan's dependence on its leading trade partner and had a clear and negative impact on the business environment and the economy.[135] It was estimated that Iraq's private sector had opened letters of credit of $240 million in excess of the figure allowed under the protocol after Baghdad lifted the restrictions on private traders as part of a general liberalization of the Iraqi economy. Jordanian officials blamed the Iraqis for inadequate supervision by their government, but the Jordanian private sector was hardly blameless. In talks in April, Iraqi officials suggested that Jordan increase its imports from Iraq or cancel the exports orders, but this solution was viewed as unsatisfactory.[136]

The Central Bank of Jordan was supposed to reimburse local exporters for goods going to Iraq worth $185 million. About $130 million had been paid when the licenses were frozen at the beginning of May after it was revealed that letters of credit totaling $450–500 million had been taken out in the first three months of the year. This freeze naturally caused financing problems for Jordanian manufacturers who had stockpiled large amounts of raw materials on the strength of Iraqi orders. Many businessmen were dependent upon the Iraqi market and, in the fashion of a private sector that has long relied upon the state for contracts and support, they urged the Jordanian government to step in. However, an all-time low level of foreign currency reserves at the time made the government reluctant to intervene. Conversely, because of the Iraqi war effort, and the desire to provide both "butter" and "guns," Baghdad preferred to remain aloof.[137]

The Central Bank then moved to crack down on Jordanian exporters unwilling or unable to await the findings of the government committee examining the validity of letters of credit (LCs), who had tried to sidestep the export finance problem by arranging barter deals with their Iraqi counterparts. The customs department was instructed not to clear any imports from Iraq not specified in a January 1988 exchange agreement between the two central banks. The agreement specified three categories of imports: oil; barley and dates; and transformers, electrical equipment, and veterinary drugs. No other imports were to be cleared without express authorization from the Central Bank.[138]

Jordanian teams went to Iraq for further discussions of the problem in June and July. By August 28, following the Gulf war cease-fire, an agreement was reached to finance the Jordanian exports in excess of the 1988 trade agreement. However, the problem was not officially solved until late October. Iraq agreed to settle letters of credit worth $75 million in excess of the 1988 trade quota agreement of $185 million. Sulfur exports were to cover $15.5 million worth of state-sector purchases. Three stages were agreed upon for covering $50 million in private sector imports: 45 percent of the value of each LC was to be paid from the 1988 protocol; 30 percent of the LC's value was to be forwarded to the 1989 protocol; and the rest was to be paid by the importer after two years.[139] On September 21 the government announced that exports to Iraq would be resumed in early October.[140] But, as we shall see below, the damage was already done, the combined pressures on the Jordanian economy were simply too great, and in the fall of 1988, the Jordanian dinar's value dropped precipitously, constituting the greatest challenge to the country's economic security to date, and ultimately ushering in a new economic and political era.

INDUSTRY AND JOINT PROJECTS

In late August 1985 the two countries' ministers of industry met to discuss increased industrial cooperation. The meetings included the founding session of the Iraq-Jordanian Industrial Company (IJIC). The IJIC was officially established in January 1986 with capital of $20 million, shared equally. Plans were made for the company to begin producing tomato paste in the Jordan Valley and pickled vegetables in Numaniyyah, Iraq by the end of 1986.[141] In January 1987 the IJIC announced its intention to buy a tomato paste factory in Jordan (for about $3.2 million) and a vegetable pickling plant in Iraq for about the same amount. On February 21, 1988, the IJIC decided to establish a Baghdad-based company, to be capitalized at $25.8 million.[142]

AQABA PORT AND TRANSIT TRADE

In January 1985 contacts were underway to organize and coordinate further the process of transporting, unloading, and storing goods destined for Iraq through the port of Aqaba. Re-exports of wheat, barley, and corn were expected to rise to 3.5 million tons in 1985, as compared with 2.6 million in 1984, and several Jordanian companies succeeded in winning contracts to ship, handle, and transport grain in 1985.[143] Despite the already strong relationship, Jordan's Ministry of Transportation continued to promote Aqaba to the Iraqis. Adding to Aqaba's appeal were the facts that transportation costs had been held steady and a free trade zone had recently come into operation.

In addition to the Jordanian-Iraqi connection, Aqaba had also become a key transit point for war materiel going from Egypt to Iraq and for Egyptian workers going to and from Jordan and Iraq. Jordan's restoration of relations with Egypt in September 1984 had provided the necessary political underpinnings to develop further the infrastructural requirements for increased Egyptian-Jordanian-Iraqi cooperation, in the short term to support the Iraqi war effort but in the longer term to increase regional economic cooperation and integration. Indeed, in early November Jordan's Transportation Minister Farhi 'Ubayd announced that Jordan and Iraq had agreed to establish a land-sea route linking the three countries. The line, which was to connect Baghdad and Aqaba by land and Aqaba and Sinai by sea, was to improve communications and transport, as well as boost Arab trade and contribute to Arab economic integration.

As a natural consequence, in February 1986 Jordanian officials discussed the possibility of setting up a joint transport company with Egypt and Iraq. In April the relevant Egyptian committee approved the contract establishing the Arab Bridge Company for Maritime Navigation, the proposed Egyptian-Iraqi-Jordanian joint venture. The company was to engage in all aspects of shipping and maritime transport, including the purchase, sale, operation, and ownership of all types of vessels and means of maritime transportation and sea equipment. The headquarters were to be in Amman and the $6 million capital was to be shared equally among the three.[144]

By the end of the war, the number of ships that docked annually at Aqaba port had risen from 1,500 to 2,500, and the Jordanians were concerned about protecting their investments and ensuring continued revenues once the Persian Gulf was no longer threatened. Indeed, the port had already begun to develop its infrastructure to accommodate such new Iraqi exports as sulfur and super triphosphate. To allay Jordanian concerns following the cease-fire in the Iran-Iraq war, the Iraqi government confirmed at the highest levels that the port of Aqaba would remain a principal port for Iraqi imports and exports in the coming years. In return, Amman committed itself to continue to build jetties to process Iraqi commodities and to maintain its practice of exempting these commodities from fines owing to delays, just as had been the case during the war. Iraqi commodities were also to continue to receive import and export priority, and be exempted from storage fees. At that point the number of trucks operating on the Aqaba-Baghdad line totaled 12,500, meaning that Aqaba received 800–1,000 trucks daily, carrying 25,000–35,000 tons of cargo.[145]

OIL

Oil cooperation further increased during this period, as Iraq became a major supplier to Jordan. On January 23, 1985 the two countries concluded a protocol on bilateral cooperation in prospecting for, extracting, refining, and distributing oil.[146] In August it was announced that a new berth for exports of Iraqi oil would come into operation at Aqaba by the end of the year, although it was not actually ready until mid-April 1986. About 10,000 tons a day of crude and fuel oil, transported overland from Iraq, were to be exported through the berth, built at a cost of $8 million.[147]

Jordan also began to receive limited quantities of finished oil products from Iraq in 1985, first LPG and fuel oil, and then eventually crude oil. As part of the trade protocol, the JPRC was encouraged to import as much as possible from Iraq.[148] By the end of 1985 oil imports from Iraq had reached about 25,000 b/d, meeting 1/3 of Jordan's needs (up from 1/6 of its needs at the beginning of the arrangement).[149] Saudi Arabia and Kuwait stepped in to supply oil to Iraq's other customers. It was confirmed in May 1986 that Kuwait and Saudi Arabia were in effect giving Iraq oil for its customers. In exchange, Iraq agreed to "return" the oil eventually.[150]

Summary

Political relations remained close and expanded during this period with the crystallization of a Jordanian-Iraqi-*Egyptian* axis, which had evolved out of a personnel, material, and materiel transport and supply relationship begun even before the assassination of Anwar al-Sadat. Very early in the war effort, Egypt had begun supplying Iraq with weaponry and personnel, and Jordan had served as the transit country. The establishment of the sea-land transport line among the three was further evidence of the importance and raison d'etre of the relationship.

On the economic front, however, the news was less positive. A cease-fire in the Gulf war was not reached until August 1988, and in the meantime, the Jordanian export credits program had been so abused by both the Iraqis and the Jordanian private sector that the ceiling was violated by several hundred million dollars. Before the end of the war, Iraq was uninterested in dealing with the problem. Yet, after the war, its own financial distress put it in no position to help reverse the damage done to the Jordanian economy by the resultant drawing down of Jordan's foreign exchange reserves. By the late summer of 1988, Jordan was again in need of an external financial bailout.

Given the pending economic crisis, why did Jordan not turn to its familiar pattern of alliance shifting to address the problem? To a certain extent it did, as we shall see, by working to establish a more formal alliance with its Iraqi and Egyptian (as well as Yemeni) partners: the Arab Cooperation Council, which was to help address Jordan's growing economic problems through creating a larger market for both labor and goods, greater cooperation and integration. But part of the answer lies in the options Jordan had. Amman was not in the position it had been in 1978, when it was being actively courted by another Arab state with wealth and power. In 1988 there was no alternative alliance partner who could or was willing to offer a better deal. Jordan could only hope to build on the economic basis it had laid in the early and mid-1980s, no doubt assuming that Iraq's extrication of itself from the war with Iran would eventually enable it to return to its pre-war position of prominence and economic power in the region. Unfortunately for the Jordanian regime, the problems were too serious and time was running out.

From the ACC to the Gulf Crisis: 1989–1990

Political Developments

Shortly after the ceasefire had been officially announced on August 20, it was reported that Jordan was preparing a draft plan on unity to be proposed to Egypt, Syria, Iraq, Lebanon and the Palestinians. Its first stage was intended to develop a system of economic cooperation which would lead to economic integration.[151] Even as early as the disengagement speech (July 31, 1988), the king had alluded to the EC as an example Arabs should follow. The emphasis was on economic integration—an indication of what kind of problems the king knew had to be addressed to maintain the kingdom's economic health and security at the time.

Saddam and the king held two rounds of talks in Baghdad in the fall of 1988, on October 2 and again on November 24. Moreover, during this period Egyptian-Jordanian-Iraqi interaction increased markedly: in early fall, Mubarak made two trips to Iraq in less than 45 days. Husayn undertook numerous trips as well, some of which were part of his mediation between Syria and Egypt but others of which were clearly aimed at creating a regional grouping working toward greater integration. While some commentaries stressed that this grouping was to revive the military concept of an Eastern Front against Israel, the king's and his ministers' statements all focused on the economic benefits that such a grouping would bring.[152] Again, given the increasingly serious economic straits in which the kingdom found itself (by January the IMF had had to be called in to arrange a rescheduling agreement for Jordan's external debts) the economic rationale given for the grouping makes sense.

Husayn returned to Baghdad on February 4, 1989 for a two-day working visit dealing with Arab issues, bilateral ties, and the negotiations between Iraq and Iran. However, the most important development in bilateral and regional relations came in mid-February at a quadripartite summit in Baghdad among Saddam, Husayn, Mubarak, and 'Ali 'Abdallah Salih of North Yemen at which the new regional grouping the king had spearheaded, the Arab Cooperation Council (ACC), was established. The founding of this organization formalized the Egyptian-Iraqi-Jordanian "axis" that had been evolving during the 1980s. From the outset Jordan stressed the economic potential of the ACC: the four states had a combined population of 80 million, total GNP of more than $100 billion, total exports of $15 billion and imports of $30 billion. In its efforts toward greater economic integration, the ACC (in Jordan's calculations) could expand the markets for Jordan's products, increase job opportunities for its skilled unemployed, and open up business opportunities for its private sector.[153]

It is also possible that the ACC strategy was akin to the "joint begging" strategy used by Jordan and Syria in the mid-1970s. As we have already seen, the Gulf states are very sensitive about Arab integration or cooperation schemes of which they are not a part, and the Saudis were reportedly extremely unhappy with the founding of the ACC. Perhaps the attempt was also in part intended to coerce the Gulf states into paying to prevent the organization from becoming a vibrant reality. This argument becomes more compelling if one keeps in mind that, in the short term at least (the term in which most decisionmakers think) the members of the ACC were more partners in debt than in anything else, each saddled with staggering obligations to external creditors.[154] If Husayn genuinely thought the ACC could offer short-term economic relief he was either misinformed, desperate, or both.

Whatever the calculations, economic conditions in Jordan only worsened, triggering economic riots in April 1989. Following the riots, Husayn was back in Baghdad on May 11 and 12 to discuss coordination among ACC members. The visit was of particular importance because it preceded both the ACC and the Arab League summits. However, despite pleading for Gulf state support to counter the threat posed by the Likud-headed government of Israel and the growing influx of Soviet Jews into Israel, the king was ultimately disappointed by the summit's failure to extend or renew the support for confrontation states that had been decided more than a decade earlier in Baghdad. The king used the same campaign tactic with Saddam, following the summit, but was promised only that Iraq would give full military support to Jordan if it was attacked.[155]

In January 1990, Saddam made a surprise visit to Amman, where his talks with Husayn resulted in the formulation of a joint Jordanian-Iraqi position on the Middle East peace process and on the Palestinian question. The two also reportedly discussed the Egyptian-Syrian rapprochement (ties had been officially restored on December 27, 1989), and Egypt's planned mediation between Syria and the PLO, who had been feuding, sometimes bloodily, since 1983.[156]

A few days thereafter, Iraq and Jordan announced that they had decided to form joint military battalions to serve as emergency forces to confront any foreign challenge or threat to either country. The new military organization was based on the formation of special combat units from both the Jordanian and Iraqi armies.[157] A similar report was carried by Radio Monte Carlo in February, regarding a joint air squadron, which was to enable Jordanian pilots to avoid reducing the number of their training hours, a problem triggered by the country's economic crisis.[158] A Jordanian commentary in the semi-official *al-Dustur* indicated that this was the first step toward establishing a unified Arab military force, in keeping with the calls for a revival of the Eastern Front to confront Israel.[159]

Husayn returned to Iraq on February 8 for a working visit, and was back again on March 3 and May 5 for talks. The second round of talks was certainly in part to prepare for the upcoming summit in Baghdad, of which the king had been an avid proponent, again hoping to drum up interest in providing Jordan financial support. However, it was also in the spring that the Iraqi decision to execute the Iranian journalist Bazoft, the alleged Iraqi attempt to smuggle nuclear triggering devices, and Saddam's speech on April 2 regarding burning half of Israel, created an anti-Iraq hysteria in some parts of the West. Analysts' and policymakers' concerns focused on what they saw as the increasing likelihood of an Israeli-Iraqi confrontation.

Of course, ultimately the confrontation that developed was inter-Arab, not Arab-Israeli. As the crisis between Iraq and Kuwait unfolded in July 1990, King Husayn, in his traditional role of mediator, took a very active part in trying to find an Arab solution before tensions escalated further. While clearly sincere and extensive, Jordanian mediation efforts were to no avail. And if Jordan thought it had paid the economic price for a close relationship with Iraq during the Iran-Iraq war, it had seen nothing yet.

Economic Developments

AID

Following the emergency Arab summit in Baghdad, May 28–30, 1990, Iraq was the only Arab state to make a formal commitment in response to King Husayn's plea for aid. Iraq was also reportedly planning to speed up repayment of its debt to Jordan, which at the end of 1989 stood at about $600 million.[160] On June 1, 1990 it was reported that Iraq had decided to give $50 million in financial aid to Jordan for 1990, and would consider additional support in 1991, in response to the May Baghdad summit and its resolutions.[161] Based on these commitments, the king may well have thought he had good reason to bank on Iraqi help in restoring Jordan's economic health, although at this point Jordan had already been involved for more than a year in implementing austerity measures dictated by IMF conditionality to address Jordan's external debt and chronic budget deficits.

TRADE

Developments in this sector were largely related to the economic crisis in which Jordan found itself and to the existing debt owed Jordan by Iraq from the export credits scandal. On December 17, 1988 the joint committee agreed to raise the level of trade exchange to $900 million during 1989, to diversify the commodities exchanged, and to increase the number of trade centers in each country, allowing the centers to sell directly to the citizens.[162] However, when the committee met a year later, it decided to *reduce* the level of commercial exchange by $100 million to $800 in 1990. (Iraq was facing a huge foreign debt and Jordan's agreement with the IMF required a reduction of imports.) The agreement also envisaged Amman's importing about $350 million worth of Iraqi crude in exchange for goods and services, up from $300 million in 1989. No mention was made of changing the system of repayment of Iraq's debts to Jordan, but repayment was proceeding at a rate of about $15 million a month.[163]

OIL

The year 1988 ended with bad news in this sector, as Iraq announced on December 24 its intention to stop exporting crude oil through Aqaba when the agreement expired on April 30, 1989. By the first of the new year, Iraq had stopped exporting 65,000 barrels of crude oil a day across Jordan and 25,000 across Turkey. The decision was forced by Iraq's commitment to the production quota approved by OPEC, which amounted to 2.64 million barrels a day.[164] However, in mid-January the Iraqis indicated that priority would be given to exporting other Iraqi oil products through Aqaba.[165]

In April Jordan reached agreement in principle with Iraq and Saudi Arabia to receive Iraqi oil through linking an Iraqi pipeline running through Saudi Arabia with another pipeline which was then pumping Saudi oil to Jordan. It was estimated that the project would save Jordan $40–50 million a year in transportation costs. At that point, Jordan was receiving about 80 percent of its oil needs (18 million barrels per year) from Iraq. Jordanian estimates placed the cost of the project at about $2 million, although the Saudi estimate was reportedly $6 million. The exact specifications of the project were not released.[166] Further discussions about this oil connection were held in July 1990, but were interrupted by the Iraqi-Kuwaiti crisis.

AQABA PORT AND TRANSIT TRADE

On June 18, 1989 a joint technical committee dealing with transport issues approved a project to construct a 1,130-kilometer railway between al-Haditha in Iraq and Aqaba at a total cost of $1.887 billion. It was expected that it would transport 2.5 million travelers and 10 million tons of goods a year. In Jordan the project was viewed as a major step toward economic integration among the ACC countries.[167] In August, Iraq, Jordan, and Egypt signed an agreement to establish a closed land transport line for passengers between Baghdad and Cairo, using one coach with an average of one trip daily, through Aqaba and Nuwaybi'. The line was to be operated by the Arab Bridge Company for Maritime Navigation, jointly owned by the three countries.[168]

It was also reported in August that 90 percent of the platforms and port resources at Aqaba were still being used for transporting various commodities to and from Iraq, just as they had been during the war. Imports via Aqaba had dropped 8 percent in 1989; however, the Jordanians were still hoping that Iraq would reconsider its decision to stop exporting oil byproducts via Aqaba, given that a special platform costing $55 million had been built to export these products.[169] At this stage, of course, no one could have foreseen that trade and transit through the Aqaba port would be one of the major casualties of the coming Iraqi invasion of Kuwait and the imposition of UN sanctions on Baghdad.

Summary

Even before the end of the Iran-Iraq war, King Husayn had evidently been contemplating the need for a subregional grouping that would promote economic cooperation and integration. With the end of the war, he set out to sell his ideas abroad. Not surprisingly, Iraq and Egypt, Jordan's erstwhile political partners, were key states the king courted: both because of their large market size, but Iraq in particular because of the standing relationship between the two countries, and the hopes (encouraged by Iraq during the war) that those who had stood by Baghdad would benefit from postwar reconstruction contracts. The result, of course, was the ACC. Military cooperation between the two countries was strengthened in its wake, and Iraq did offer financial assistance to Jordan in May 1990, after the 1989 Arab summit had failed to renew Baghdad summit commitments. However, with a war-ravaged economy Iraq was in no financial position to provide the support it had offered in 1979. While Iraq did continue to pay off (in oil) the debt accumulated in the export credits scandal, it nevertheless announced that it planned to cut back on its use of Aqaba facilities, thus threatening to wound further the ailing Jordanian economy.

Given the damage to its own economy caused by the Gulf war Iraq was simply not in a position to provide the economic support the king had hoped for, nor could the ACC, at least in the short term (and, of course, ultimately, there was no long term). Moreover, if a major purpose behind the formation of the ACC was to frighten the Gulf states into providing aid, this strategy also failed. And, despite the king's apparently close relationship with Saddam, he was as surprised as outsiders were by Saddam's next destructive adventure, this time into Kuwait.

Conclusions

Economic Relations

In its attempt to counter Syrian influence in the region by gradually courting Jordan, Iraq's primary economic instruments were grants and loans. It made its first major attempt at winning influence with Jordan (and others in the Arab world) by campaigning for the convening of an Arab summit in the wake of the signing of the Camp David Accords, and by proposing annual oil state support for the confrontation states. Iraq even went a step further by promising to pay the shares of any state that might renege on its commitment. Iraq then proceeded to shower Jordan with smaller grants (some governmental, others officially nongovernmental) and development loans.

Perhaps just as important, and an element that distinguishes the

Jordanian-Iraqi relationship, is what may be called the focus on infrastructure development as foreign policy, both economic and political. Both Jordan and Iraq had an interest in the further development and expansion of the Aqaba port and the Jordanian highway system. Since imperial quills had left Iraq with only minimal access to the Persian Gulf, most trade had to enter the country over land from Turkey, Syria, or Jordan. Given Baghdad's standing feud with Damascus, the transit lanes through both Syria and Turkey were subject to closure. Hence, Aqaba and overland routes from Iraq to it, took on greater and greater significance. For its part, Jordan was eager to enhance any infrastructure that raised income, in this case in the form of locational rent, transit, and storage fees, not to mention the increase in employment through the growth of the trucking and hauling sector.

Aqaba's significance grew exponentially following the outbreak of war in the Persian Gulf. Overland transit trade through Jordan became not just a matter of greater convenience: after the war started, Iraqi ports were too close to the frontlines with Iran to be used at all. Aqaba, distant and safe, became Baghdad's main port, and further developing its capacity directly affected Iraqi economic and political security. Again, the Jordanians were only too happy to have such external financial support for facilities which further strengthened their internal economic infrastructure, provided increased revenues and employment, and solidified economic ties with an Arab neighbor.

Two other major infrastructural projects were proposed during this period: an oil and a water pipeline. The proposed water pipeline was intended both to demonstrate and increase Iraqi influence in the area. Clearly an Iraqi initiative, this project appears not to have been seriously considered by Jordanian policymakers, who contended that the kingdom would have been foolish to allow itself to be put in such a dependent position for a commodity as vital as water. The oil pipeline was a somewhat different story, as it appears to have been a project in which both sides were keenly interested. It promised not only to cut Jordan's oil costs, but also to raise further revenues in the form of transit royalties. For the Iraqis, of course, the primary concern was to have an additional, safer facility and exit point through which to export oil. In the case of this project, while both countries wanted Western security guarantees against Israeli attack, it seems the Iraqis, with clear memories of the 1981 bombing of the Osirak nuclear reactor, were by far the more concerned with a possible security threat. Ultimately, in the absence of sufficient assurances, the Iraqis instead struck a deal with the Saudis for a pipeline farther from the Arab-Israeli front.

The war and the significance (and convenience) of Aqaba also opened further opportunities for Jordan to increase its exports to Iraq. While Jordanian businessmen were initially anxious about the negative effect the war might have on commerce, they wasted little time in taking advantage of the besieged Iraqi market. Trade boomed, thanks in large part as well to the supportive policies of the respective governments. Jordan had a desire to expand its markets, both to increase revenues and to further the process of Arab integration it had long pushed, while Iraq, particularly after the outbreak of the war and the closing of its ports, had need of virtually everything. This mutual need and enthusiasm, combined with the continuation of the war and increasing Iraqi financial woes, ultimately, however, did serious damage to the Jordanian economy.

When the Iraqi austerity measures were first announced in 1982, Jordanian exports were hard hit. As a result, Amman instituted a program of extending export credits to Baghdad. This program should be understood as a political or economic tool used with the domestic Jordanian audience in mind: there was little chance of Iraq's abandoning its relationship with Jordan, or even of relations souring, had Jordan cut back on its exports. (Although it is possible that providing continuing access to exports was viewed by policymakers as a way of helping to ensure the steadfastness of the Iraqi populace in the face of war and to ensure a place for Jordanian products in the country after the peace.) More important, the export credits were intended as a form of support for *Jordanian* businessmen, to help them continue making money by enabling their Iraqi purchasers to continue buying. Since one of Jordan's most important state revenues has been from customs tariffs of various sorts, the state may also have been looking for a temporary way of supporting its own long-term trade (and revenue) relationship with Iraq.

Even before the export credits issue became a scandal, Iraq was forced to begin concluding deals on the basis of bartering, the most important deal being the provision of Iraqi oil in exchange for Jordanian goods and services. It was an exchange that, while clumsy, served both countries' interests. Unfortunately, the war dragged on, and the ceiling on export credits was violated by an import-hungry Iraq and an export-greedy Jordanian private sector. Eventually, Jordan's foreign currency reserves were drained to so low a level that the stage was set for the precipitous decline in the value of the dinar in the fall of 1988. Hence, the economic statecraft, faultily pursued in an effort to shore up Iraq's ability to purchase Jordanian products, ultimately jeopardized Jordan's economic security.

Another tool of economic statecraft was the establishment of joint ventures. Here, as in attempts at trade expansion, Jordan was pursuing its longstanding policy of increasing its own economic security through closer ties and greater economic integration with its neighbors. On an ideological level this was based on implementing the principles of Arab nationalism. On a more practical level, the reasoning was that the development of economic ties would make much less likely the complete severing of ties in the event bilateral relations grew strained. As we shall also see in the case of Egypt, the joint ventures that were most successful were the transport-related ones: the IJLTC and the Arab Maritime Bridge Company. In both cases, the companies served not only an economic need, but, certainly from Iraq's standpoint, a security need as well, since the companies further facilitated the transport of goods and people to and from Baghdad during the war. The other joint ventures appear to have been far less successful.[170]

In the case of some of these projects, the Iraqis may well have believed that by binding the Jordanians closer and closer to themselves, they were making less and less likely any meaningful political alliance between Jordan and Syria in the future. However, certainly after the beginning of Iran-Iraq war, it seems most likely that the primary Iraqi concern was to implement policies that directly or indirectly supported the war effort.

Economics and Alliances

The key periods for changing alliances in this relationship were the 1979–80 period and the conclusion of the ACC agreement in 1989.

As we saw in the case of Syrian-Jordanian relations, the Jordanian shift from its close, if by 1980 somewhat troubled, relationship with the Syrians, is best explained by the economic benefits the Iraqis had to offer. Iraq, with a large and relatively well-educated population (estimated at 14 million in 1982)[171], substantial oil reserves, abundant water supplies, and extensive agricultural land, more than any other Arab state, was blessed with the combination of resources necessary for the development of a strong and diversified economy. Iraq was also clear and forthcoming in its promises of aid at a crucial time for Jordan, following a period in which Rabat-promised aid was not forwarded and the number of years' commitment involved in the Rabat pledges was in question. At this point, Saddam, anxious to play a more central role in Arab politics, pushed for the convening of the Arab summit in November 1978 to address the consequences of Sadat's trip to Jerusalem, and made financial support for the remaining confrontation states a major element in its proposals.

As Syria and Iraq repaired ties in the wake of the Sadat trip, Jordan was not forced to choose between the two. However, as that relationship gradually unraveled in late 1979, and as Syria increasingly faced violence and sabotage at home, Jordan could not remain neutral. With its own relations with Syria already suffering over charges that it was harboring anti-Syrian Muslim Brothers, Amman's desire to build stronger ties with Iraq was incompatible with preserving good relations with Damascus. Given the choice between a Syria that offered military depth, a reasonably large market, but that was plagued with domestic instability, and a clearly economically ascendant and militarily powerful Iraq with tremendous oil reserves, Jordan appears to have made a choice based largely on economics: Iraq over Syria. This is a quite different explanation than that offered by Walt: that a Jordanian-Saudi-Iraqi axis emerged in 1979 to balance Syria and the growing threat from Khomeini's Iran.[172]

The relationship with Iraq then blossomed quickly. Grant and loan money flowed freely. The infrastructure relationship discussed above, which had begun well before the official political or economic rapprochement, served as a solid foundation for more sustained infrastructural growth and interdependence. The outbreak of war also contributed to the trend, boosting commercial relations and increasing Jordan's role as Iraq's sole, secure (re)supply route. The ties continued to develop, even in the face of the Iraqi austerity measures of 1982. Moreover, despite the financial woes that the 1988 export credits scandal brought Jordan, and the apparent inflexibility of the Iraqi government in dealing with the problem until the war had ended, relations did not sour. By that time, the commercial, infrastructural, and transit (not to mention military) links were so well developed that shifting economic orientation, had there been an alternative, would have involved major domestic economic dislocations.

Hence, following the war, Amman continued to bank on Iraq-in-reconstruction as a major market for Jordanian goods and services. The establishment of the ACC only further solidified ties, although in a largely symbolic way since even after its first year the grouping constituted little more than proposals for cooperation on paper. One of its major obstacles, beyond the traditional bureaucratic problems, was the growing distance between Iraq and Egypt, each of whom had intended to use the ACC as a vehicle to promote further its own regional influence. In the nascent and, in spring 1990, largely unspoken competition between the two, Jordan continued to lean toward Iraq: despite its considerable debts, Baghdad still had oil and was willing to offer financial support to Jordan at a time when the kingdom was suffering and the other oil states showed little interest. Egypt, of course, could offer no aid. And if security against Israel was truly high on the king's mind, Egypt's peace treaty with the Jewish state precluded its playing a role on that front as well.

By the time the Gulf crisis began, Jordan had been closely tied to Iraq for a decade. Trade relations, military cooperation, grants and loans on both a governmental and societal level made Iraq and its strong man Saddam enormously popular in Jordan. Iraq's role in the export credits scandal was not widely discussed, although Jordanians were well aware that the Gulf states had reneged on their financial obligations to the kingdom. Given such a background, it is not surprising that pro-Iraq sentiments were held and voiced strongly by broad sectors of the Jordanian population as the crisis unfolded. What was more surprising to many was that greater awareness of the tremendous threat to budget security that the failure to join the anti-Iraq coalition posed was apparently not manifested at the decisionmaker level. That episode is discussed in the final chapter.

7

Jordanian-Egyptian Relations

Rivalry for regional influence was the key characteristic of relations between these two British client states until the early 1950s. However, following Egypt's 1952 revolution and Gamal 'Abd al-Nasir's "victory" in the 1956 Suez Crisis, the regional balance shifted markedly in Egypt's favor. Subsequent Egyptian policy toward its Arab neighbors, including Jordan, involved instruments that ranged from propaganda to more activist subversion to influence domestic and regional policies. Jordan's King Husayn was a particularly common target because of his geographic proximity and his continuing pro-Western orientation in the face of the Arab nationalist states' preference for nonalignment or the Soviet bloc.

The two leaders did not manage to repair relations until war appeared on the horizon in late spring 1967, just in time to lose huge pieces of their respective territories—the Sinai Peninsula, Gaza Strip, and the West Bank—to Israeli occupation as a result of the June war. Thereafter the gap between the two narrowed further. In September 1970, Nasir succeeded in brokering a cease-fire between the Palestinian resistance and Jordan's Husayn, only to die the following day. Hence, it was not really until Anwar al-Sadat's presidency that Jordanian-Egyptian relations begin to show signs of marked expansion and improvement.

By the beginning of the period under study, Egypt had severed most of its ties with its former Soviet sponsor and had begun to cooperate with the U.S. in a regional peace process so that, on this level, the barriers to greater cooperation between Egypt and Jordan had disappeared. (Although, on a regional level, Jordan's warming relations with Syria prevented a fuller development of ties owing to Syrian-Egyptian tensions.) But the countries shared another characteristic critical to this analysis: both were developing an aid dependence on the Gulf states. In this light, and in terms of the budget security argument, Egypt's value in Jordanian foreign policy considerations derived, not from an ability to offer direct financial assistance, but rather from the more indirect contribution relations could make to Jordanian economic (and other) security through increasing the kingdom's access to the huge Egyptian domestic market. On the one hand, expanded trading and industrial ties with Cairo offered Amman the opportunity to overcome some of the diseconomies of scale that had hindered Jordanian attempts at domestic commercial and industrial expansion. On the other, as was the case in Jordan's relations with Syria, Amman sought to deepen economic ties with Cairo as part of a broader strategy of building economic and political security through developing closer ties with its neighbors. The more extensive the economic links, Jordanian policymakers reasoned, the less likely Egypt might be to sever them at some future date.

The period under study witnessed two major shifts in Jordanian-Egyptian relations, and in both cases this chapter will demonstrate that economic factors played at least a key role, and perhaps the determining one. In 1979, Jordan followed the Arab consensus and broke relations with Egypt. The decision would perhaps seem to have been a foregone conclusion, given the aid promised by the confrontation states and given the negative reception Sadat's peace with Israel had encountered on a popular level throughout the Arab world but especially among Palestinians, many of whom were Jordanian citizens. Nonetheless, whether because the Americans were exerting opposing pressure or because the king simply wanted to temporize a bit in order to make sure that the Baghdad aid did not meet the same fate as had the Rabat aid promised five years earlier, concerns about whether Jordan would go the way of Sadat continued to be expressed through 1980. Ultimately, of course, the consensus held.

Or at least it held for a while. By 1983 the Iraqi market for Jordanian exports appeared to be shrinking, and the restoration of relations with Egypt offered the possibility of some economic relief for the Jordanian private sector. In addition, of course, Egypt had developed into an important source of manpower and war materiel for the Iraqis, using Jordan as overland conduit. Amman was certainly in a position and willing to support the Iraqi war effort, with the clear goal of seeing the war brought to an end. Hence, despite the absence of an official Arab League resolution permitting the restoration of relations with Egypt, Jordan moved ahead in 1984 and formally restored ties with Cairo, the second major shift during this period. The only significant economic and political fallout from this move was a temporary freezing of a then ongoing rapprochement with Syria, a matter that was overcome a few months later. Hence, while the role of political factors should not be ignored, the oft-neglected economic factors can be demonstrated to have had just as significant, if not more significant, a role in decisions regarding alliances shifts.

From Disengagement to Camp David: 1975–1979

Political Developments

The 1973 War, viewed as a victory in the Arab world, gave Egypt's President Sadat a credibility both domestically and regionally he had not previously known. His subsequent move toward disengagement agreements with Israel in January 1974 and September 1975 and his concomitant opening up of Egypt's heavily state-sector oriented economy beginning in 1974 further distanced him from the political and economic legacy of his predecessor, the charismatic 'Abd al-Nasir. What has been termed a "politics of pragmatism" emerged in the region with the 1973 war; however, what was increasingly in question was whether Sadat intended to be a team player or preferred to move ahead on his own. [1]

On January 3–4 1975, the foreign ministers of Egypt, Syria, Jordan, and the PLO met in an attempt to coordinate policies, but reportedly achieved little.[2] Syria, already feeling betrayed by Sadat's 1973 war performance, was concerned at this point that Egypt's path toward a second stage of disengagement from Israeli forces in the Sinai portended a break with the Arab consensus. As Jordanian-Syrian relations warmed, Sadat visited Jordan in late May, the first Egyptian president ever to visit the kingdom. Crown Prince Hasan returned the visit in July and Prime Minister Zayd al-Rifa'i met with the Egyptian president on October 19 to discuss the Arab-Israeli conflict. Nonetheless, the state of Syrian-Egyptian relations against the background of growing Syrian-Jordanian ties prevented any real improvement in Egyptian-Jordanian ties at this stage, although Jordan did not join Syria in condemning the second Sinai disengagement agreement between Egypt and Israel, in September 1975.

Beginning in mid-1975, regional attention was focused on the unfolding civil war in Lebanon. Both Egypt and Syria sought to prevent an escalation of the conflict that might invite Israeli intervention or lead to the installation of a new government run by the coalition of Palestine Liberation Organization-Lebanese National Movement forces. However, the two former 1973 war allies differed over the issue of Syrian hegemony in Lebanon, which Egypt naturally opposed. A reconciliation between Syria and Egypt finally came at a mini-summit in Riyadh in October 1976, and then opened the way for an improvement in Egyptian-Jordanian ties.

In November 1976 the two sides agreed to upgrade diplomatic relations from chargé d'affaires to ambassador, but the first major step toward strengthening political ties began with official talks between Sadat and Husayn from January 13–15, 1977. The year was billed as a decisive one, since it had been planned that Middle East peace talks would be convened in Geneva at some point near the end of the year. Commenting on the talks between the two leaders on January 17, Egypt's Foreign Minister Isma'il Fahmi announced that there were no differences in views between the two on an Arab strategy or on the need to establish a Palestinian state. Moreover, in Egypt's view, the relationship to be established between Jordan and the Palestinians (a relationship that was still quite rocky at the time and an issue of some contention) was a matter to be left to the Jordanians and Palestinians to determine.[3]

Consultations on issues related to Geneva continued throughout the spring. Discussions focused on developing a joint strategy, although the two sides differed on the proper role for the Palestini-

ans and on the nature of a Jordanian link with the PLO, with whom
the king was still feuding. The lack of agreement on key issues was
indicated by the fact that no joint statement was issued following the
meetings.[4]

Shortly before Sadat's surprise visit to Jerusalem, his vice-presi-
dent, Husni Mubarak, made a trip to Amman, and both 'Arafat and
Husayn were in Cairo for several hours of talks with Sadat on November 6. When on November 11 Sadat announced his willingness to
visit the holy city, Jordan responded cautiously. As was typical of Jordanian policy, Amman's focus was on the potentially divisive impact
the move would have on Arab ranks. Husayn offered an official position on the Jerusalem visit on November 28 in an address to the
nation:

> Our position was and still is that solidarity among the Arab frontline
> countries and unified positions are the only means to achieve any
> sound and just settlement. . . . Although we have our reservations
> about the substance and form of the Egyptian initiative, we still under-
> stand what prompted Sadat to make this decision—a decision that
> required extreme courage and a break with several traditions, norms,
> and psychological barriers on which we had built our stance toward
> Israel and our way of handling the Palestinian cause."[5]

Shortly thereafter, Husayn, accompanied by Prime Minister Mudar
Badran and Chief of the Royal Court 'Abd al-Hamid Sharaf, went to
Cairo. The king expressed his admiration for Sadat's courageous initiative aimed at establishing a just peace in the area, but he again
stressed the need for Arab unity and solidarity.[6] This was clearly a
response to concerns on the regional level. Jordan's Gulf state financial patrons were among those most likely to support a wait-and-see
approach. Had Husayn been reacting to the Jordanian street, he likely would have behaved quite differently, for on a popular level, particularly among Palestinians, there was outrage at Sadat's move. Perhaps in deference to "the street" Husayn declined Sadat's invitation
to visit Cairo shortly after the Jerusalem trip, saying that while he
always welcomed the opportunity to visit Egypt, nothing new had
transpired in Egyptian-Israeli contacts, and hence a meeting was not
really necessary.[7] In hopes of selling the initiative, Mubarak visited
Amman on January 31 as part of a tour of Arab capitals. However, by

late February the Egyptian-Israeli talks were stalled and Husayn began to express pessimism about Sadat's initiative.

In the meantime, in typical consensus-seeking style, Jordan called for the convening of an Arab summit to discuss the new situation created by Sadat's initiative. In practice this meant trying to restore solidarity in the face of inter-Arab divisions over Egypt's discussions with the Israelis. Consultations continued through the summer, although not at the highest level. By then, however, Sadat had made his decision to go to Camp David for discussions with Israeli Prime Minister Menachem Begin, under U.S. auspices. He reportedly called Husayn on September 11 regarding what was transpiring in the talks and had hoped to meet with him afterward in Morocco for briefings on the process. Exercising caution, the king reportedly declined to meet with Sadat until he had learned exactly what had been agreed to at Camp David.[8]

What he eventually did learn did not please him, and the king set out on several rounds of diplomacy in October to win support for the Iraqi call for an Arab summit to address the ramifications of Sadat's move. At the Baghdad summit conference on November 2–5, agreement was reached (despite strong Saudi pressures to the contrary) to expel Egypt from the Arab League and impose a boycott if Cairo did sign a separate peace agreement with Israel. At Baghdad II, the meeting of Arab foreign and economic ministers on March 27–31 immediately following the signing of the peace treaty, the Arab states voted to implement the expulsion and boycott decisions.

In keeping with the resolutions of the meeting, Jordan subsequently announced the withdrawal of its ambassador from Cairo and its support for the economic and political boycott of Egypt. The Arab demand was that all economic, financial, and technical aid to Egypt be stopped; that all official and private deposits be withdrawn from Egyptian banks; that all agreements be frozen; and that the Arab League headquarters be moved. This included freezing or terminating Egypt's membership in a wide range of other inter-Arab organizations, companies, and regional funds. In many cases, however, deals already arranged or projects already funded were excluded from the boycott. This was the most serious inter-Arab use of economic statecraft since the imposition of the boycott on Israel in the 1950s.

Economic Developments

TRADE

Trade between the two countries remained fairly steady during the early 1970s. Jordanian exports to Egypt hovered around the $1.5 million level and imports fluctuated between $7.5 and $10.5 million. The first sizable jump occurred between 1973 and 1974 as exports jumped to $3.75 million and imports soared to $21.3 million.[9] A trade protocol signed in November 1975 raised the trade share for 1976 from 4.5 million sterling pounds (to which the Jordanian dinar was pegged—$7.7 million) each to £6 million each ($10.2 million), with £400,000 ($680,000) for each country's trade center.[10] The next discussions came more than a year later in February 1977 and a trade protocol was signed increasing bilateral trade by 25 percent over the previous year.[11] At this point, Jordan was one of the few countries with which Egypt continued to have barter relations.

A new trade protocol, concluded in March 1978, was ratified on September 25, in the midst of the Camp David negotiations. The new instrument provided for an increase in the volume of trade between the two to $50 million per year (the currency in which the amounts were expressed had officially been changed to dollars since the last protocol), $25 million for each side. According to the protocol, commodities exchanged between the two were to be exempt from customs duties, fees, and other taxes. Hard currency was also to be used in the exchange.[12] Bilateral trade in 1977 had totaled $35 million. In 1978 it dropped slightly, although Jordanian exports to Egypt increased by 50 percent. However, as a result of the boycott, in 1979 Jordan's exports dropped to just under $668,000, only 12 percent of their 1978 level, while imports dropped by 50 percent.[13]

INDUSTRY AND JOINT VENTURES

In the 1975 protocol, both countries had agreed in principle to the establishment of a joint Egyptian-Jordanian Maritime shipping company with the goal of increasing trade between the then recently opened Suez Canal and Aqaba.[14] Syrian-Jordanian relations also had an emphasis on joint ventures during this same period, no doubt reflecting similar concerns: access to a larger market, greater economic security through integration with regional partners, and greater national political security through extended economic ties that would presumably make the cutting of ties so painful as to discourage such a move. However, probably for reasons related to excessive Egyptian bureaucracy or to inadequate capital, it appears no real progress was made on this company before the imposition of the boycott in March 1979.

Summary

The tensions in the Egyptian-*Syrian* relationship triggered by the 1973 war and Egypt's subsequent behavior made a full resumption of Egyptian-*Jordanian* relations impossible in the early to mid-1970s. The Jordanians were interested, but they had clearly given priority to the Syrian relationship, at least initially because of their desire to rebuild ties in order to prevent a repetition of the costly border closure of 1970. However, the Egyptian-Syrian rapprochement of October 1976 and the subsequent discussions of a 1977 Geneva Conference made a warming of Egyptian-Jordanian ties both possible and necessary. Economic relations during this period were gradually growing, particularly in the sector of bilateral trade. This was a natural development given Jordan's desire to expand economic ties for both economic and political security reasons.

Unfortunately, Geneva was preempted by Sadat's unilateral courting of Israel, to which Jordan initially reacted cautiously. It was not until the general Arab opposition to Sadat's separate peace included the wealthy oil states (who had at first been hesitant) that Jordan's opposition also solidified. The financial incentives from these states (and Iraq) served as a reward of sorts for breaking ties with Egypt. As a result Jordan remained a confrontation state, and the joint economic projects that had been proposed were tabled as Jordan adhered to the Arab League-imposed economic sanctions.

Adherence to Sanctions: 1979–1984

Political Developments

Although the U.S. pressed hard to convince Jordan to join the Camp David process in 1980, Husayn was not convinced. The king repeated numerous times that Camp David contradicted true peace for the region and that there was no future for the treaty. Jordan even forbade Egyptian novelist Nagib Mahfuz and writer Anis Mansur entry into the country because of their support for Camp David.[15] Nevertheless, Jordanian policymakers insist that because of Egypt's economic and political weight in the region, the king never completely closed the door on Cairo. Contacts continued in the hopes of eventually finding a formula to reintegrate Egypt into Arab ranks.[16]

The first part of the formula in fact came with Sadat's assassination in Cairo on October 6, 1981. Although his successor, Husni Mubarak, was committed to the peace treaty with Israel, he was not among its authors or signatories. Hence, dealing with him had a much different symbolic connotation than did dealing with Sadat. In early January 1982 it was reported that Husayn had sent a message to Mubarak indicating that he was interested in improving relations. Jordanian officials reportedly conveyed that they had no objection to direct contacts between the two countries and that Jordan understood the Egyptian position and the limitations on it.[17] In mid-January there was even praise in the Jordanian press for Egypt's steadfastness in the face of Israeli demands for compromise on the issue of Palestinian autonomy, the second part of the peace treaty and the part on which no progress had been made.[18] On April 24, 1982 Egyptian newspapers and magazines reappeared in Jordan after a three-year absence. A few days later, in a speech before the National Consultative Council (NCC) as the Israelis were completing their withdrawal from Sinai, Husayn called for the return of Egypt to the Arab fold.[19] However, soon thereafter, Arab attention turned to Lebanon, which Israel invaded on June 6.

In the wake of the Israeli invasion and the announcement by U.S. President Reagan of his peace plan on September 1, Egypt's Minister of State for Foreign Affairs Butrus Butrus-Ghali argued that the Reagan Plan superseded former agreements, including Camp David, and that Egypt would not participate in tripartite talks with the U.S. and Israel unless they were held within a new framework. This statement followed that by Egyptian Minister of Defense, Field Marshall Abu Ghazalah, which called on the Arabs to comply with a unified strategy to confront the Israeli threat. The Jordanian understanding of the statement was that the Egyptians viewed Camp David as outdated and that Cairo still considered Israel to be the main threat to *all* the Arabs, including Egypt.[20] Both countries were clearly interested in restoring ties, although each had different priorities: Jordan, the economy (see below); Egypt, expanding the peace process, and returning to the Arab fold.

Shortly thereafter, Butrus-Ghali arrived in Jordan on a short visit as part of Egyptian-Jordanian consultations on a common vision of the future of the occupied territories before King Husayn's visit to Washington on December 2. Mubarak's adviser Usama al-Baz and Butrus-Ghali visited Amman in February 1983 for consultations and on March 7 Mubarak and Husayn met in New Delhi at the nonaligned summit. In mid-October there was a call in the Jordanian press for Egypt's return to the Arab fold.[21] Shortly thereafter, Egypt's Middle East News Agency (MENA) announced that it had decided to open an office in Amman as of November 1, 1983.[22]

Nonetheless, Jordan did not appear willing to break with the Arab consensus and officially reestablish political ties with Egypt. In November, in response to a question on Egypt's possible return to the Arab fold, Minister of Foreign Affairs Marwan al-Qasim indicated that any position reached collectively by the Arab League could be changed only by a similar Arab decision at the same level.[23] The fact that PLO Chairman Yasir 'Arafat stopped in Egypt on December 22, 1983 after his evacuation from Tripoli, Lebanon may well have made expanding ties a bit easier by giving Mubarak a certain legitimacy in (some) Palestinian eyes. On January 2, 1984, Husayn again received Usama al-Baz, who delivered a message from Mubarak on efforts to reinvigorate the peace process and on the results of talks the Egyptian president had had with 'Arafat during his then recent visit to Cairo. Later in the month Minister of the Royal Court 'Adnan Abu

'Awdah visited Egypt for discussions with Mubarak. About this time it was reported that Egypt had played a critical role in developing an approach in which Jordan and the PLO, with Arab and Islamic support, would try to persuade Western Europe to act as an intermediary and call for an international conference in which all parties to the conflict, including the U.S., Israel, the USSR, and the PLO, would participate.[24]

Jordan's position had been to adhere to the Arab consensus regarding Egypt, but not to close all doors. Given its manpower, as well as its military, economic, and cultural importance, Cairo could not be ignored forever, and Jordan wanted a clear, unified Arab policy for its future return. Even before Sadat's assassination Egypt had been serving as a supplier of war materiel to Iraq, and Jordan clearly saw both Egypt's role and strengthening these growing ties as critical to overcoming the weaknesses in Arab ranks caused by the war. Although the warming of Jordanian-Egyptian relations helped the Iraqis, the Iraqis themselves were unwilling to take formal steps to improve ties at that point. Saudi policy at the time was less clear, but as always was opposed to further exacerbating Arab divisions, this time by possibly upsetting the Syrians. Therefore, Jordan had to balance its desire for expanding ties with Egypt with concerns regarding how negative the Syrian response would be.[25]

A flurry of diplomatic activity between the two served as a prelude to the September 25, 1984 Jordanian restoration of ties with Egypt. The official announcement stated that Jordan, "out of its appreciation for the cohesion of Arab Egypt—leadership and people—with the struggle of the Arab people of Palestine, Iraq, and Lebanon and so that the transient alienation will not turn into a permanent fact to be exploited solely by our enemy, has decided to restore political and diplomatic relations with the Arab Republic of Egypt. . . . "[26] Although Jordan had clearly been moving in this direction, testimony indicates that apparently the king made a unilateral decision which took his advisers by surprise. Most members of the Jordanian government had supported the reestablishment of political relations with Egypt, but had felt the issue needed more study.[27]

Jordan was quick to stress that the restoration of ties did not mean that the country's position on the Egyptian-Israeli peace treaty had changed. Nonetheless, Amman still had some explaining to do to justify its position to other Arab states. A *Jordan Times* article argued that the

> resumption of diplomatic relations with Egypt lays to rest to some extent the fiction of the Arab boycott of Egypt. If the boycott has shown anything, it has been that the Arabs need Egypt, more than Egypt needs the Arabs. It is noteworthy that the break in diplomatic relations meant very little in practical terms, as bilateral trade, labor, education, tourism, and military relations were maintained between Egypt and most of the other Arab states.[28]

This was confirmed by Jordanian policymakers. Trade ties had never been completely severed and Husayn felt more harm than good would have been done by keeping Egypt completely out of the Arab picture. The assessment was certainly self-serving, as the economic discussion below makes clear, but it also contained a certain degree of truth. While states such as Saudi Arabia voiced their displeasure at the reestablishment of ties, the displeasure was largely superficial and again resulted from the Saudis' unhappiness with any step that caused open friction in Arab ranks. Other Arab states had been reestablishing ties tacitly, which is more the Saudi style. The Jordanians were simply the first to do so officially.[29]

Economic Developments

Although some private-sector money continued to flow into Cairo,[30] from 1979 through 1981 Jordanian-Egyptian economic interaction markedly declined. Jordan's central bank instructed commercial banks and moneychangers that they were to observe a "complete ban" on trade with Egypt.[31] The only exemptions from this ruling were for imports from Egypt already in transit or for which letters of credit or import licenses had already been issued, or for personal effects and gifts with no commercial value.[32] In 1980 Jordan exported a mere $8,182 worth of goods and imported only $14.7 million, 50 percent of the 1979 level.[33]

Despite Jordan's official adherence to the economic sanctions, in early April 1979 it was announced that EgyptAir would resume services to Amman, with ten flights a week. The flights had been suspended on March 27 when Jordan withdrew its ambassador from Cairo. Moreover, Jordan continued to grant work permits to Egyptians: in September 1979 the Ministry of Labor announced that it had issued 15,000 work permits to Egyptians,[34] who tended to fill agricultural, construction and domestic service jobs that Jordanians refused. In January 1982 it was reported that, in response to an Egyptian move allowing Jordanian citizens to enter the country without prior visas, Jordan had decided to exempt Egyptian labor in Jordan from residence laws.[35] At the end of 1982 the Minister of Labor issued a decision calling for exempting Egyptian workers from obtaining work permits for Jordan.[36]

Egyptian willingness to cooperate during this period is easily understood, as any exception to the general boycott must have been seen as a source of legitimacy and as a potential building block for the future reestablishment of full ties. For Jordan's part, the role of Egyptian labor in its (and the Iraqi) labor markets was already too important to take measures against it. Boycotting Egyptian labor would have badly hurt the Jordanian agricultural sector, and forced price increases in such industries as bread baking, which have food security implications. The dismissal of Egyptian labor would also have increased prices in the construction industry, for example, and led more families to bring domestic labor from South Asia. Hence, the importance of Egyptian labor to both Jordan and Iraq continued to grow, even during the early years of the boycott.

REVIVAL OF TRADE

On April 9, 1983 a Jordanian delegation from the Ministry of Trade and Industry arrived in Cairo for talks. This was viewed as a Jordanian-Egyptian attempt to resume trade exchange.[37] At this point, the Jordanian government determined that the Arab League boycott applied only to the *public* sector, thereby freeing the private sector to trade with Cairo. Only those Egyptian companies violating the anti-Israel boycott remained off-limits to the Jordanian private sector.[38] On April 15, trade relations were reestablished between the two countries through the conclusion of an agreement that reactivated the March 1978 protocol. At these meetings Jordan extended an invitation to an Egyptian economic delegation to visit Amman in the near future to discuss means of boosting bilateral trade ties. The two sides agreed that a joint committee would meet in the autumn to review economic ties and introduce the necessary amendments to the 1978 trade protocol.

One major change in the original protocol, which also exempted goods from customs duty, was the suspension of the payments agreement. In the 1970s, Egypt had used this facility effectively to gain large chunks of free credit from Jordan. The new arrangement meant that Egypt would be obliged to settle its bills immediately in hard currency, a clear advantage for the Jordanians. The few quota restrictions on consumer goods that existed in 1978 were also lifted, again to Jordan's benefit, since these were to be its main exports to the Egyptian market.[39]

Economically, the restoration of ties was quite significant for both sides. For Jordan, the contraction of the Iraqi market after the initial boom raised the specter of economic decline, particularly for the private sector. The reopening to the private sector of the Egyptian market, the largest in the Arab world, offered the prospects of badly needed relief. For Egypt, the boycott had closed off traditional Arab markets for fresh vegetables and processed foods. To compensate, it had been forced to find other outlets, primarily in the EC. However, the recession and the inclusion of Greece, Portugal and Spain into the EC had made that grouping less likely to take Egyptian products.[40] Hence the reopening of Jordan was a first step for Cairo toward reentering its traditional Arab markets.

Trade protocol talks, scheduled to begin in November 1983, in fact began on December 21, with both sides expressing eagerness to develop ties. The delay was widely believed to have been caused by a dispute about customs tariffs: the previous April, the two had agreed to abolish regular tariffs, yet Cairo continued to exact customs duties on imported Jordanian goods.[41] The protocol signed at the meetings stated that the national products, including foodstuffs, exchanged between the two countries would be exempted from customs and other taxes.[42] In addition to trade, the discussions covered financial affairs, the banking sector in both countries, the conditions of Egyptian workers and investments, and strengthening bilateral communications, especially transportation through the cities of Suez, Nuwaybi' and 'Aqaba. Talks focused on setting up joint projects between Egyptian and Jordanian businessmen, and on establishing a joint transport company to link Egypt with the countries of the Arab East.[43]

Despite the hopes of many Jordanian financiers and politicians that moving in the direction of Egypt would trigger a rebound in exports following the virtual closure of the Iraqi market, in the event, Egypt was slow to respond. By August 1984 only two significant letters of credit worth $10 million had been opened for Jordan in Egypt.[44] Of course, at this point, diplomatic relations had yet to be restored. Jordanian exports for 1984, while up to $800,000 from the meager $41,400 the previous year, were still well below the levels of the late 1970s. Imports, on the other hand, rose by more than 30 percent to $17 million.[45]

On September 24, a day before political relations were restored, an Egyptian delegation arrived in Amman to discuss the development of trade between the two, to contact Jordanian industrialists about potential deals, and to sign contracts concerning the remaining part of the trade protocol signed by the two countries in December 1983, valued at $10 million.[46] It was later reported that one of the topics discussed by the two sides was the question of building a dock on the Egyptian side of the Gulf of Aqaba to be linked to the Jordanian port.[47] Two weeks later it was decided to establish a Jordanian-Egyptian bank for development to be equally shared by Jordan and Egypt and to have branches in both Cairo and Amman.[48]

Summary

Although diplomatic relations were broken in 1979, King Husayn reportedly never completely closed the door on ties with Cairo. The revival of relations, even before the official reestablishment of ties, was possible in part because of the role Egypt played in supporting the Iraqi war effort, in part because of the shrinking of the Iraqi market for Jordanian exports and its impact on the Jordanian private sector, and in no small part by the 1981 assassination of Anwar Sadat. Jordan felt the Arab world needed Egypt, particularly as it was facing a threat from the east, and with Sadat, the author of the peace treaty, gone, it was easier politically to work with his successor. The restoration of political ties in September 1984 was strongly criticized by Syria, and at least rhetorically by the Gulf states, but aside from Syrian subversion against Jordan, no state moved to reprimand or punish Husayn.

On the economic front, Jordan adhered to the letter but not the spirit of the anti-Egypt boycott. It quickly restored flights between the two capitals and Egyptian labor, which served a number of key sectors and played a significant role in several others, continued to be recruited into Jordan. By mid-April 1983, Jordan took what should have appeared to be a bold step in restoring private sector trade relations with Egypt at the same time that it attempted a similar initiative with the Syrians. While the Syrians balked, the success of the new policy toward Egypt went almost unnoticed, a lucky development for the Jordanian private sector, which was in desperate need of alternatives to the war-plagued Iraqi market. Indeed, the security and prosperity of the Jordanian private sector appears to have been a major concern in both of these rapprochement initiatives.

A New Era: 1985 to the Gulf Crisis

Political Developments

The official restoration of ties between Egypt and Jordan was followed on October 9–11 by an official visit to Jordan by Mubarak, accompanied by a delegation including the ministers of foreign affairs, agriculture, information, planning, and the economy. Shortly thereafter, a joint higher committee was formed to draft the Jordanian-Egyptian action strategy and implement the program of bilateral cooperation.[49] Political consultations also continued throughout the fall, including discussions by phone of the controversial 17th Palestine National Council meetings held in Amman in November.

On January 21 Egyptian Foreign Minister 'Ismat 'Abd al-Majid made a one-day trip to Jordan to deliver a message to Husayn and on January 30 *al-Majallah* reported that Jordan and Egypt had signed a "strategic cooperation agreement" whereby each would provide military assistance to the other in case of a threat.[50] Exchanges of visits by military delegations followed. In an interview, Egyptian Defense Minister Abu Ghazalah stated that the following weeks would witness joint maneuvers of Jordanian and Egyptian special forces, and that Jordanian officers had observed the Egyptian Army's maneuvers between April 7 and 11.[51] The unprecedented joint maneuvers actually took place at the end of June in Egypt's Western desert.

On May 20 Mubarak received Husayn in Cairo on a one-day visit to discuss recent developments, including U.S. Secretary of State Shultz's recent visit to the area. By the fall, however, PLO-Jordanian coordination on the peace process was running into trouble. Egypt continued to stress the importance of Palestinian-Jordanian solidarity, just as it announced its support for the Syrian-Jordanian rapprochement.[52] Jordanian-Egyptian coordination continued at the highest levels, but Egypt did not side openly with Jordan in its feuding with the PLO.[53] Egypt did, however, engage in numerous attempts to reconcile King Husayn and 'Arafat.

Regular contacts and consultations between the two leaders and other high-level officials continued in 1987 on the Iran-Iraq war, Lebanon, bilateral relations, and the proposed but elusive international peace conference. Although Mubarak did not attend the summit held in Amman on November 7, 1987, he nonetheless visited Amman shortly thereafter to discuss the outcome, one important element of which was the decision to allow Arab League states to determine when they would restore relations with Egypt. In early 1988, there were consultations regarding the Palestinian intifada and the Egyptian president outlined a controversial peace initiative to solve the Palestinian problem.

Consultations continued over the latest developments in the Gulf war and over the visit of U.S. Secretary of State Shultz to the region as part of an attempt to deal with the Palestinian uprising. During the summer, Mubarak was reportedly again mediating between 'Arafat and Husayn, and the Egyptian press hailed the July 31 Jordanian disengagement from the West Bank, saying that it would pave the way for the establishment of an independent Palestinian state.[54] By the end of October, the PLO-Jordanian reconciliation had reached the point that the three leaders—Husayn, Mubarak, and 'Arafat—gathered for a summit in Aqaba to discuss the peace process and the options open to the Palestinians.

In early 1989 the bilateral relationship was overshadowed to a certain extent by the establishment of the Arab Cooperation Council (ACC) on February 16 and its subsequent quadrilateral arrangements. Husayn had been working tirelessly since the Gulf war ceasefire for the establishment of a sub-regional grouping that would work to promote greater integration, particularly economic integration, along the lines of the EC. During the previous fall he had shuttled back and forth among a number of states trying to sell the plan. In the end, the Arab Cooperation Council joined Iraq, Egypt, Jordan and North Yemen, states in which Jordan saw the opportunity to expand markets both for its products and its labor.[55]

Nonetheless, only two months later, Jordan experienced economic riots and much of the king's attention was by necessity drawn to domestic affairs. The rest of his regionally directed energies during this period concentrated on campaigning for greater Arab attention to the increasing numbers of Jews who were emigrating from the Soviet Union to Israel. Egypt and Jordan continued coordination in the framework of further developing the ACC, but progress there was very slow, with little of substance to show by February 1990, a year and four summits later. Indeed, problems were already beginning to develop. Saddam Husayn was flexing his rhetorical muscle and in effect making a bid for leadership of the Arab world. This constituted a direct challenge to Egypt, which had assumed for itself the leadership mantle after its return to the Arab League in May 1989. Jordan had to attempt to maintain good relations with both, but it was clear from Amman's statements and actions that the tilt was in the Iraqi, not the Egyptian, direction. Jordan's economic ties with Egypt continued to pale in comparison with Jordanian-Iraqi economic relations. Hence, with the war over and with the Iraqi market again open for business, Jordan focused on those potentially far more lucrative ties.

The Egyptian-Jordanian bilateral contacts that took place in the time remaining before the Iraqi invasion of Kuwait were aimed at trying to mediate the Iraqi-Kuwaiti dispute before it deteriorated further. As a result, there was a great deal of ultimately unproductive shuttling back and forth during the final weeks of July 1990. The third major alliance shift in the relationship then came as Egypt lined up with the international coalition, and Jordan opted for neutrality (with a pro-Iraqi tilt) during the Gulf crisis and war.

Economic Developments

TRADE

Only a week after Mubarak's October 1984 visit to Jordan, Crown Prince Hasan arrived in Cairo for a visit which included participation in a seminar on Egyptian-Jordanian cooperation in agriculture and in the exchange of technical expertise. The prince later indicated that the first meetings on the scope of cooperation between Egypt and Jordan had in fact been held *about six months earlier*, in the absence of official political ties.[56] Subsequently, the joint higher committee began its deliberations on the prospects for cooperation in the economic, trade, tourism, maritime transport, and air transport fields. The meetings discussed means of exchanging technical expertise in extracting and processing potassium, in operating a ferry line between Nuwaybi' and Aqaba, and in the auto and clothing industries.[57]

Egypt's desire to reenter Arab markets and Jordan's need to expand its own markets to offset setbacks in its relationship with Iraq were clear in the October 1984 meetings. The agreements reached exempted national products from customs and other taxes and fees normally imposed on imports and exports, and set trade targets at $75 million each, with the goal of eventually reaching an ambitious $500 million. This represented a major, quantitative shift in the history of bilateral economic and trade relations between the two countries, for in 1978, before relations were severed, trade had totaled only about $30 million.[58] The accord also included a shipping agreement to regulate the size of commercial exchange[59] and a call for free commercial exchange in hard currency for both the public and private sectors (according to the laws of each country). The lowest proposed amount was set at $50 million for each side, of which the private sector's share was to be at least $10 million.[60] Despite this apparent encouragement of the private sector by both governments, the fact remained that it was primarily state-sponsored contracts that composed bilateral trade. Private sector-initiated and -directed interaction represented only a small fraction of the exchange.

In early December an agreement on the first consignment of goods to be sold to Egypt as part of the trade protocol was signed: Cairo was to buy $10 million worth of textiles, home appliances, and clothing. However, not much success could be reported on a pending cement deal, as talks broke down over a price dispute characteristic of problems inherent in this and other bilateral trade deals. Egypt's Cement Supply Bureau, which was purchasing from Jordan's Southern Cement Company (SCC), was insisting that *Egyptian* trucks be used to transport the cement to Aqaba.[61] By April, however, a deal had been struck, as a $110 million barter agreement was signed which included a one million ton purchase from the SCC, to be exported in June 1985. Jordanian prices were reportedly 10 percent higher than international prices, but the quality was reportedly sufficient to make up for the difference.[62]

The April 1985 meetings also revised upward the trade targets from 1985's already ambitious $150 million to $250 million for 1986. (The final trade statistics for 1985 in fact showed Jordanian exports of only $7.7 million, which was itself a tenfold increase over the previous year; imports, on the other hand dropped to their 1983 level of $12 million.)[63] The decisions also included a provision allowing the Egyptian private sector to import from Jordan, with the free transfer of money, beyond the share determined in 1984. In addition to contracts with the SCC noted above, and the Jordan Fertilizer Industries Company, the two sides agreed upon the following: putting Jordanian contractors bidding for work in Egypt on an equal footing with their local counterparts; exchanging $5.4 million worth of agricultural goods in the next two months; and encouraging joint ventures.[64] In May 1988 a new agreement was signed raising trade exchange to $350 million[65], more than twice the 1987 level. It had a $110 million barter component and a $110 million private sector trade target.[66]

On January 28, 1989 the joint committee agreed that the size of trade between the two countries would be $350 million annually.[67] However, in the meantime, Jordan was rocked by economic riots, and IMF austerity measures required a cutback in imports. Hence, when the committee next met, on July 15, 1990, the new protocol called for only $250 million of exchange, out of which $80 million was allocated for barter deals. A unique aspect of the 1990 protocol was that it laid down the principle of free trade between the two outside the framework of the protocol: that is, both sides could increase the trade volume between them, although this meant the payment of customs duties on commodities exchanged outside the protocol's framework.[68] The actual trade figures showed a great deal of fluctuation: Jordanian exports to Egypt were $11.4 million in 1986; $40 million in 1987; and $21.4 million in 1988. The level of imports was much more stable: $26.5 million in 1986, $28.7 million in 1987, and $28.8 million in 1988.[69]

INDUSTRY AND JOINT PROJECTS

Shortly after the restoration of ties in September 1984, discussions began on a range of joint projects. On February 24, 1985, talks were held regarding the establishment of a joint bank with Egypt by Central Bank of Jordan Governor Muhammad Sa'id al-Nabulsi and a visiting Egyptian team. Agreement was reached and the bank was to be capitalized at $10 million.[70] Two months later, the joint higher committee agreed in principle to establish a holding company, with capital (equally shared) of $50 million. The company was to specialize in establishing joint agricultural, trade, and tourism projects.[71]

The next meetings of the joint higher committee dealt with some of the joint ventures in greater detail. On November 26, 1985, it was agreed (again) to establish an Egyptian-Jordanian holding company with $50 million in capital. In January 1986 the two countries formally laid the groundwork for the company, which was to undertake joint investment projects, issue bonds to be marketed in Egypt and Jordan, and market its products in both countries. The new company was slated first to set up a $10 million fishing company, based in Alexandria, Egypt, to help both countries attain self-sufficiency in salt water fish.[72] The following April, meetings of the joint higher committee led to an agreement to establish a joint fodder and meat company and, two months later, the establishment of the joint Egyptian-Jordanian meat production company, with capital of $30 million, was announced.[73] Talks were held in the fall regarding a joint contracting company, using capital from the joint holding company, to win some of the contracts that were then going to foreign contractors. However, the Joint Holding Company was itself just getting started, and its first meeting was not held until the end of August 1987.[74]

Clearly, the apparent flurry of joint company discussions did not mean that all was proceeding smoothly. According to July 1988 decisions of the Higher Committee, Jordan had yet to pay its share of the capital of the Egyptian-Jordanian Company for Investment and Development. A year later, a meeting of the Egyptian-Jordanian Holding Company, discussed the (evidently few) steps taken to date to set up a company producing red meat and fodder in Egypt.[75] According to testimony and the written record, most of the joint ventures discussed above had little or no life beyond the founding resolutions. While Jordanians argued that the Egyptian bureaucracy obstructed a great deal, it is also clear that capitalizing these projects was a problem for both sides.

One important exception was in the realm of maritime transport. The Egypt-Jordan link had become important in the early days of the Iran-Iraq war, when Egypt began supplying Iraq with labor and war materiel. As the war dragged on and as Jordanian-Egyptian ties grew, the significance of the transport connection between the two countries increased. In January 1985 the Jordanian and Egyptian ministers of transportation had held talks to discuss how to organize sea transportation between the two. Included in the talks was discussion of a proposed shipping line to link the Aqaba port with Nuwaybi' in the Sinai. The line was to reduce costs for haulers and halve the travel time from Aqaba to Cairo to only nine hours. The line was slated to be operated by a joint venture between the Jordan National Shipping Lines and the state-owned Egyptian Shipping Company. The link was also intended to minimize border procedures and increase tourism and *hajj* traffic.[76] The final agreement on the line was signed on March 28. On April 25 a trilateral meeting among Husayn,

Mubarak and Oman's Sultan Qabus served to inaugurate the new ferry line.

Despite its seemingly auspicious beginnings, the joint venture got off to a rocky start. The company lost $6,500 a day on the line during its first month. Prices were too high and passengers complained about the requirement that they change the equivalent of $150 into local currency upon their arrival in Egypt.[77] In an effort to attract commercial customers and cut losses, the Jordan National Shipping Lines subsequently reduced charges for trucks and refrigerator vans on the ferry by up to 75 percent. Egypt then also agreed to further reductions in charges.[78] Nonetheless, performance was still judged suboptimal. Therefore, in the May 1987 meetings of the higher committee it was recommended that representatives from Egypt, Jordan, and Iraq meet to look into the steps necessary to establish a company run by all three countries to take over the ferry line. The formal establishment of the new company, the Arab Bridge Company, headquartered in Amman and with capital of $6 million shared equally by the three governments, came on December 1, 1987.[79] The new company reported a profit of $1 million in its first six months of operation, and a $2.1 million profit for 1988, with passenger travel up 38.7 percent from 1987.[80]

LABOR

On January 30, 1985 Egypt and Jordan signed an agreement for cooperation in the field of labor and manpower. The agreement provided for equal rights and responsibilities for workers from both countries, as well as exchange of information and expertise in the fields of occupational training, social insurance, industrial security, manpower planning, and social development.[81] However, the labor market in Jordan was quite different from what it had been in the late 1970s. A high birth rate, increased educational facilities, and reduced demand for Jordanian labor in the Gulf had gradually led to increasing unemployment in the kingdom. On January 1, 1987 a new ruling came into force according to which Egyptian workers could no longer be employed in Jordan without prior approval from the Egyptian and Jordanian ministries of labor. At the time, Egyptians, numbering about 250,000, constituted the largest expatriate labor force in the country.[82] While the majority of Egyptians in Jordan worked in jobs Jordanians refused to take—as domestic servants or as unskilled laborers in agriculture or construction—this did not seem to figure into what were largely political calculations.

In an apparent about-face, in early summer 1989, the Jordanian Ministry of Labor recommended the abolition of labor permits for nationals of the ACC. But this was more political rhetoric than a serious initiative. Whatever the ministry might say, large numbers of foreign workers remained a politically sensitive topic, particularly as unemployment among Jordanians continued to rise. Moreover, given the economic crisis through which the kingdom was passing and the need to raise revenue wherever possible, the state was unlikely to implement a major revenue reduction policy, which exempting such laborers from permits would have constituted. At the time such permits cost Arab workers $53 per year if they worked in agriculture and $175 for other sectors. Other foreign nationals were paying $530 for such permits.[83]

Summary

Political relations during this period expanded to include coordination on the Iran-Iraq war, PLO-Jordanian relations, and the peace process. Egypt's involvement in the war effort eventually led to a crystallization of a trilateral, Jordanian-Egyptian-Iraqi axis, despite Iraq's failure to restore official ties with Cairo at this time. The axis was, however, formalized in February 1989, in the ACC, the organization Husayn hoped (in vain) would further Arab economic integration and alleviate some of Jordan's domestic economic ills.

Bilateral economic ties also developed during this period, and indeed, had preceded the official reestablishment of formal diplomatic relations. Developments in the field of bilateral trade were of particular importance as projections for trade levels were raised dramatically and a new, if still minor role was given to the two countries' respective private sectors. Joint ventures were another matter, however, as the numerous proposals and the semblance of movement really masked minimal progress. Lack of political will and economic crisis certainly played a major role. Only the most economically and politically critical of the ventures, the sea-land transport company, managed, after initial difficulties, to remain active and realize a profit.

Conclusions

Economic Relations

With the largest population in the Arab world (about 45 million in 1977) and increasing at a rate of 1 million every nine to ten months, Egypt constituted the largest market in the region. For Jordanian business, in bad times captive to and in good times constrained by its small domestic market, Egypt offered significant possibilities. Cairo's proximity was an additional, key advantage. In addition, of course, the state and nature of the Egyptian economy meant that while Cairo could serve as a partner in trade and joint ventures, it would never serve as an aid provider. As a result of all these factors, the Jordanians used several types of economic statecraft with Egypt, primarily trade and joint ventures, with the goal of expanding and diversifying Jordan's markets.

The development and expansion of economic links was probably also desirable as insurance against economic or political attacks from a future regime that might be less sympathetic. The imperative here seems to have been somewhat less than in the case of Syria, although that may have been simply because the Jordanians had not previously had the opportunity to develop extensive economic ties with Egypt. Under Nasir, ties had generally been strained, as King Husayn had been a prime target of Egyptian propaganda. Sadat's arrival on the scene and his abandonment of much of his predecessor's program made improved ties possible.

Not surprisingly, then, trade was the first area on which the joint committee focused. Both sides had an interest in principle in expanding trade and to do so required little in the way of additional work or infrastructure. Yet interest and enthusiasm alone were not sufficient to overcome several substantial problems. One was the issue of payment, a result of each country's perennial hard currency shortages. The trade agreement addressed this issue in the following way. An Egyptian who imported goods from Jordan was to deposit payment for the goods into an account in an Egyptian bank; likewise, a Jordanian who imported from Egypt paid into an account in a Jordanian bank. Then, a Jordanian who exported to Egypt was paid from the Jordanian account, just as his or her Egyptian counterpart would be paid by an Egyptian bank. This was one reason why setting and adhering to the quota established by the protocol was so important: if one exceeded the target one was not likely to be paid because no currency was being exchanged between countries.[84]

One of the most serious problems plaguing Egyptian-Jordanian trade relations (as well as other inter-Arab trade relations) has been that of the competitive, rather than complementary nature of domestic products. For example, one of the items Jordan was to export to Egypt as part of the $10 million protocol was stoves. By unfortunate coincidence, the Egyptian Ministry of War Production was manufacturing a similar stove, but (according to the Jordanians) of poorer quality. When it became clear that Egyptians preferred to buy the higher quality Jordanian stoves an angry Minister of War Field Marshall Abu Ghazalah reportedly torpedoed the entire protocol.[85]

The second economic instrument by which Jordan attempted to promote greater economic integration between the two countries was joint ventures. Here the experience was a bit different than that with Syria. In the case of Egypt, a joint *holding* company, not several joint government companies, was established. Muhammad Saqqaf, who had been in charge of joint companies, said this was because by the time Jordan began to restore ties with Egypt, the ideological tide had shifted from support for the public to a concentration on the private sector. In addition, waning state financial capabilities in the mid-1980s meant that some projects were threatened from the beginning because of insufficient capital. This was the case with the red meat and fisheries projects. The projects were never launched because neither country was willing or able to pay its share of the start-up capital.[86]

The Aqaba-Nuwaybi' line was the one big success story, although not until it was reorganized and run by the Egyptian-Jordanian-Iraqi Arab Maritime Bridge Company. Again, as is clear in the cases of

Syria and Iraq, transport companies seem to have a better chance of success than many other ventures. The company required little if any additional infrastructure and served a standing (and, broadly construed, security) need: the transport of passengers and supplies among the three countries.

One element that appears to have been key to the success or failure of economic statecraft in this bilateral relationship was the role of the bureaucracies in both countries. According to participants, if negotiators have been instructed to make things work, they will; if not, they will find myriad problems to block progress. This situation was noted with greatest frequency in discussions of Jordanian deals with Egyptian government officials. One classic example of Egyptian stonewalling concerned the joint husbandry project. The two sides had agreed that a feasibility study was to be undertaken. However, in subsequent discussions of the project, an Egyptian representative contended that the text of the original agreement stated that not the project itself, but the feasibility of *studying the project* was to be studied first. Although the Jordanians countered that this did not make sense, the Egyptians said that that was the way the requirement read.[87] This and similar incidents transpired during a period when political relations were quite good: high-level bilateral political relations had nothing to do with the problem.

Jordanian sources also noted that the Egyptians often went to negotiations poorly prepared, frequently unaware, for example, of what commodities were already on customs lists. The Jordanians also argued that when a Jordanian team would go to negotiate with the Egyptians, they would be four or five, whereas the Egyptians would arrive with a team of 20 or more, each of whom had his or her own ideas and could veto something, but none of whom had the authority to approve anything. These factors led some Jordanians to wonder how seriously the Egyptian representatives in economic talks or their superiors took such matters.[88] On the other hand, there was plenty of testimony regarding bureaucratic obstruction of implementation or of general lack of concern for follow up on the Jordanian side as well.

What about the most "spectacular" economic statecraft initiative during this period, the Arab boycott of Egypt? The boycott, as well as a decade of substantial financial support for the confrontation states, was first discussed at the Arab League summit in Baghdad in November 1978. However, the sanctions were not immediately implemented, primarily because of pressure from Saudi Arabia. In their concern not to trigger unrest in Egypt, the Saudis convinced the Arab states, led by Iraq, to postpone imposing a boycott unless or until a peace treaty was finally signed, an outcome which was not completely certain at that point. While King Husayn had given Sadat the benefit of the doubt when he first made his trip to Jerusalem, after the signing of the Camp David accords and after the call by the Iraqis for a summit to discuss this issue as well as the issue of increased financial support to the confrontation states, the Jordanians moved closer to the hard-line rather than the Saudi position on this issue. Once the treaty was signed, there was little question about implementing the resolutions of the 1978 summit calling for a boycott: it was a position that stood to win Jordan substantial financial support and it was very popular in the Jordanian street. This issue is further discussed below.

That Jordan was the first state officially to reestablish ties with Egypt is less a reflection of the failure of the boycott than an indication of a general Arab wearying of the Iran-Iraq war and of Jordan's desperation: on the economic front, the Iraqi option had not realized its full potential because of the war; on the political front from a Jordanian perspective, the absence of Egypt from active involvement in Arab politics rendered the Arab world weaker in its battle with revolutionary Iran. Although the Jordanian press claimed that economic ties and political channels had remained open during the early years of the boycott, the boycott actually had hurt both countries. It did not force Egypt to abrogate its treaty with Israel, but, as Baldwin has argued, there are various ways of measuring the success of instruments of economic statecraft like boycotts and sanctions.[89] The boycott did force Egypt to find alternative markets and, just as important, it deprived Egypt of a voice in the politics of the region during a critical decade.

Before concluding this section, a word on labor is in order. Over the years, Jordan developed not only as a major exporter of largely skilled labor to the Gulf; it also became a major importer of unskilled labor, largely from Egypt (and to a lesser extent from Sri Lanka and the Philippines). Jordan's importation of Egyptian labor is an economic policy, but is not really a tool of economic statecraft (although periodic statements from various ministries regarding changing the conditions or cost of obtaining or renewing employment permits may be). Jordan's treatment of its Egyptian guestworkers was of more symbolic than substantive economic import in the bilateral relationship. In some ways, the presence of this labor is more important in Jordanian domestic politics: on the one hand, it is a constant reminder to unemployed Jordanians that large numbers of foreigners work in the country, even if they hold jobs that Jordanians value less than unemployment; on the other hand, the role of this labor in such key sectors as agriculture helps keep domestic food prices low. Employers do not want to be deprived of their cheap labor and Jordanian citizens would not look kindly upon having to pay more for certain basic products if these people were replaced by Jordanians earning Jordanian-level wages.

Economics and Alliances

This survey of fifteen years has covered a warming of relations between Egypt and Jordan in 1976–77; a deterioration leading to the breaking of relations and economic boycott in 1979; a reestablishment of ties in 1983–84, and the formation of a regional grouping, the ACC.

In the case of the developments in 1976–77, the major obstacle to an earlier improvement of relations was the strength of Jordanian-Syrian ties in the context of strained Egyptian-Syrian relations. Why Jordan gave priority to developing relations with Syria rather than Egypt at this particular time has been discussed at greater length in chapter 5. Here, suffice it to say that the economic impact of Syria's 1970 border and air-space closure was still quite fresh in Jordanian policymakers' minds and had done sufficient damage as to make the avoidance of a possible repetition a central focus of policy. In any case, the close ties with the Syrians constrained Jordan only for a while: both testimony and secondary evidence indicate that the Syrians, Jordanians, and Egyptians had made common cause by late 1976 in lobbying the Gulf states for payment of the 1974 Rabat commitments. Thereafter Jordan was freer to expand its own ties with Egypt without jeopardizing its relations with Syria.

As for the deterioration in relations in 1978–79 and the ultimate imposition of the boycott, Jordan has always stressed the importance of Arab consensus, of maintaining unity of ranks. Therefore, aside from considerations of domestic Palestinian discontent or of regional retribution, which may have influenced Jordanian considerations, Egypt's unilateral peace with Israel violated one of the basic principles of Jordan's regional interaction: the need for unity. Of course, one of the primary reasons for such a policy, beyond the king and his advisers' Arab nationalist (of a conservative bent) inclinations is precisely the kingdom's economic and political vulnerability, and the consequent presumption that Jordan's best hopes for survival lie in avoiding what the king calls the "politics of axes" and in building broad coalitions: the safety in numbers theory.

In the case of the boycott, there was not only safety, but also booty, in numbers. Supporting the boycott, and remaining aloof from the Camp David process not only pleased key domestic constituencies for political reasons, it also brought the kingdom the largest promise of Arab aid in its history: at least $1.2 billion a year for ten years. It also was a key element in cementing the still nascent political and economic relationship with Iraq, which had been a prime mover behind the Baghdad summit's call for such support for the confrontation states. The question then arises, would Jordan, in the absence of the promise of such Arab aid, have gone the way of Sadat? Was the promise of aid sufficient to keep the king from contemplating his own separate deal? These questions have been addressed in detail in the chapters on Kuwait and Saudi Arabia, where the outpouring of aid offers in the wake of the treaty and as the Americans tried to pressure Jordan to join the peace process, was discussed. The short answer is that the aid was probably necessary, but not sufficient. To have refused to break ties would have meant forfeiting the promised Arab budgetary support and angering much of the population. To have gone a step further and joined Camp David, as the Americans and the Egyptians wanted, would likely have meant increased American financial support (although one can only speculate whether it would have matched the levels promised by the Arab states), but would also probably have led to an extension of the Arab political and economic boycott to Jordan, which, given the nature of Jordan's inter-Arab economic ties, could well have brought financial ruin. It is unlikely any amount of American aid could have offset the havoc that a comprehensive Arab economic boycott of Jordan would have wreaked. Hence the economic security rationale for remaining outside Camp David in and of itself is quite compelling. Add to that the more commonly noted political rationale for Jordanian policy—the fact that most of the Jordanian population, both Palestinians and East Bankers, would have objected vehemently to going the way of Sadat—and the outcome is in fact overdetermined. Nonetheless, the centrality of the economic factors should not be ignored or downplayed.

What of the restoration of relations, which began with the resumption of trade in early 1983? While it is clear that neither economic nor political ties were completely severed, the timing of the real warming of relations indicates that economic factors played a major role. The primary trigger was Iraq's failure to fulfill its potential as market and aid supplier to Jordan. Not only did the costs of the war turn Iraq from an aid provider into an aid recipient, they also forced Baghdad to implement unforeseen austerity measures. As a result, instead of witnessing a boom in its trade and contracts with Iraq, Jordan and its business sector bore part of the brunt of the shrinkage in Iraqi markets. Jordan then had to scramble for additional markets. The most likely targets were close to home: Syria and Egypt. While the economic results of the move were disappointing, this does not undermine the economic argument regarding why and when the restoration of ties was sought.

Certain political factors did intervene to render the reestablishment of relations more palatable regionally and domestically. First, Sadat had passed from the scene, which meant that the author of the treason was gone. Moreover, Mubarak had been one of the few Arab leaders to provide support to PLO chief Yasir 'Arafat and his people as they fought Syrian and Palestinian opponents in Tripoli, Lebanon in November 1983, which made the Egyptian leader more acceptable to some, both domestically and regionally. 'Arafat's surprise stop in

Egypt after his evacuation from Tripoli only reinforced the growing positive impression of Mubarak. Perhaps most important regionally, however, was the increasing support that Egypt had been providing Iraq in its war effort against Iran. This made a reintegration of Egypt more critical and more acceptable to the wealthy Gulf states, who saw in Egypt's contributions to Iraq indirect contributions to their own security.

Hence the political ground was set for Jordan to make such a move if it so chose. Other Arab states were gradually restoring economic and other ties. The timing of the reinvigoration strongly argues for an economic impetus, although the formal reestablishment of political ties a year and a half later, a move Jordanian policymakers felt needed more careful study, was evidently taken by the king unilaterally, and without forewarning.

The final alliance move discussed here, the formation of the ACC should be seen in the context of Jordanian-Egyptian ties as an expression of the kingdom's desire to exploit more fully the potential of the Egyptian market to absorb Jordanian exports. Given Egypt's peace with Israel, Jordan could not have been looking to it for potential military support in the event of armed confrontation with the Jewish state; nor, given Egypt's overwhelming poverty and indebtedness, could the kingdom have been looking to Mubarak for any kind of economic support in the form of aid. Thus, what Egypt had to offer was potentially important for Jordanian producers, but in terms of economic security, it was not as easily parleyed into direct support for the state or the regime as grants and loans were. As a result, as Saddam and Mubarak gradually drifted apart politically in 1990, Jordan continued to stay the Iraqi course.

In conclusion, Egypt has been viewed as and continues to be a large, still underexploited market. Substantial potential for expansion remains, despite the problems with currency regulations and state bureaucratic inertia. Although Jordan was clearly constrained by domestic and regional political forces, there was a strong economic motive in several important Jordanian foreign policy moves toward Cairo. However, in the case of Egypt, the policy has generally been based on the *weakness*, rather than the *strength*, of bilateral economic ties. This is similar to the role of economics discussed in the case study of Jordanian-Syrian relations. The low level of economic exchange between the two, combined with the fact that Egypt was not an aid provider meant that Amman's relations with Egypt were influenced first and foremost by its relations with states possessing superior economic resources, resources that could make a more substantial difference to Jordan's budget security. Again, however, this is a quite different conclusion from the standard refrain that economics plays little or no role in inter-Arab politics. The evidence here has again shown economics to be key and often decisive in determining or triggering critical alliance shifts.

PART THREE

Conclusions

8

Budget Security and its Broader Applicability

Throughout the preceding chapters the concept "budget security" has been used to refer to a state or leadership's drive to ensure the financial flows necessary for its survival. The case for adopting the notion of budget security can be made quite clearly and succinctly. Territorial sovereignty cannot be defended against an external threat if there are insufficient funds to pay the troops or buy spare parts. In the same vein, a leadership may be unable to survive a domestic challenge that results from economic disarray or mismanagement.

An understanding of the structure of the domestic economy and, in particular, the sources of state revenue are the clear starting points for determining the potential bases of budget (in)security. Such an approach permits examination, not just of aid or trade, but of all revenue sources together. Trade or external assistance figures may tell very little about dependence or vulnerabilities if not examined in conjunction with other sources of state revenue, so that their *relative* importance can be determined and the points of sensitivity ascertained.

Jordan, the focus of this study, has been characterized by a heavy reliance on grants and loans from abroad and upon income, such as expatriate remittances, that has little relation to domestic productive forces. Hence, Jordan's drive for budget security has focused first and foremost on securing and diversifying suppliers of assistance, and only secondarily on the protection and expansion of markets. Given the importance of external aid suppliers to Jordan over the years, it should not be surprising that significant developments in its foreign policy, particularly alignment shifts, have in fact had domestic budgetary goals. Demonstrating that link between domestic economic structure and foreign policy has been the primary task of this study.

The case studies have pointed to several important examples of shifts in alignment attributable primarily to the state's or the leadership's desire to protect its revenue sources. It is useful at this point to reexamine the major alignment shifts that have been discussed to review the explanatory power of budget security versus the traditional balancing and bandwagoning approach.

Syria-Jordan, 1975–76

To the extent that this rapprochement is discussed in the literature, it is generally attributed to a number of traditional political motives. One argument holds that Syria was seeking regional reinforcement at a time when Egypt appeared to be moving toward a separate deal with Israel. However, such a conclusion is more easily reached with hindsight: although U.S. Secretary of State Henry Kissinger was clearly working toward further disengagement agreements and was focusing on Egypt, it was not clear at this time that Sadat would move toward a separate peace. (Moreover, the second disengagement agreement was not signed until September 1975.) Indeed, the only opprobrium Sadat encountered at this stage was from Syria, not from the chorus of Arab states that assailed him following Camp David. Another traditional political explanation is that, given the then recent (November 1974) Arab League recognition of the PLO as the sole, legitimate representative of the Palestinians, King Husayn was seeking to counter what had been a blow to his prestige by reviving ties with Syria. Moving out of relative regional isolation (which had resulted from the conflict with the Palestinian resistance in 1970–71) through an alliance with Syria certainly promised to enhance Jordan's regional position, although at the time the Syrians were still openly supportive of the PLO.

But if Jordan was simply seeking to move out of regional isolation or to strengthen its hand regionally, why choose Syria as opposed to another country, such as Egypt, which had to that point been a central force in Arab politics? It is possible that the history of the disastrous 1967 military alliance with Egypt and the resultant loss of the West Bank was still fresh in decisionmakers' minds, making them wary of Egypt. It may also be that the Syrians showed greater receptivity, feeling that they had been betrayed by the Egyptians in the 1973 war. However, none of these political explanations can account for the content or form of the rapprochement, which, in the earliest of the bilateral meetings and agreements, put *economic* concerns at the top of the agenda.

As the case study demonstrated, Jordanian policymakers insisted that the move toward a closer alignment with Syria was driven by their desire to present a united front to the Arab Gulf states in appealing for assistance: begging in unison made more sense that begging alone. Hence, economic interests were primary. But Jordan's need for reinforcement in facing the Gulf states does not explain its choice of Syria over Egypt, for Cairo was also interested in pressing the Gulf states to pay their Rabat commitments. The other element that was salient from the point of view of Jordanian policymakers was that because of the importance of transit trade (through Syria) to Jordan, a receptivity on the part of the Syrians to Jordan's overtures to improve relations offered Amman the opportunity to develop ties in such a way as to secure an open border and hence the critical trade route. Jordan had no such relationship with Egypt. And, since improving ties with both at the time was impossible because of Egyptian-Syrian tensions, Jordan opted for Syria, which was more crucial to its budget security.

Jordan-Arab States, 1979

Jordan's refusal to join in the Camp David process has received little study, since it has been taken for granted as part of a unified Arab position. Ostensibly for ideological reasons, but certainly also for practical ones, Jordan has always stressed the need for Arab unity and been loathe to act outside the "Arab consensus." In one instance of such a departure, its reestablishment of diplomatic relations with Egypt in September 1984, the king must have been certain of largely rhetorical retribution from other Arab states. However, in the wake of the August 1990 Iraqi invasion of Kuwait (on which, more below), there was another, far more important, "consensus" to which Jordan did not adhere. Therefore, it is worth reexamining Jordan's position on the 1979 boycott and U.S. and Egyptian attempts to enlist Jordan in the Camp David process.

Leaving aside ideological explanations based on Arab solidarity, was Jordan balancing the power and threat of Israel and the United States (and perhaps Egypt) by joining with the other Arab states? That would seem a plausible explanation from the point of view of international relations theory. Or, to offer an alternative explanation, was Jordan bandwagoning because of the threat of Arab sanctions or possible sabotage (both internal and external) had Amman failed to adhere to the sanctions or, worse, joined with Sadat? Since such an explanation also makes sense, it highlights the difficulty involved in trying to make balancing or bandwagoning determinations: the conclusion is determined by one's assessment of the source of the greatest threat and such an assessment may not coincide with that of the relevant policymakers. Rather than asking whence the greater threat, the better question may be, whence the greater incentive?

Jordan eagerly supported Iraq's calls for an Arab summit to address the results of Camp David and, not surprisingly, embraced the Iraqi proposal for increased support for the confrontation states. Whether the king would actually have joined what was begun at Camp David or not remains an open question; however, as the case studies showed, other Arab states did have questions regarding the king's intentions and, in response, forwarded additional aid and loans, presumably to ensure his steadfastness. Ultimately, of course, the king rejected the U.S. approach and lost U.S. financial assistance; however, "in exchange" he had gained a commitment of a decade of far greater support than the U.S. had been offering. In so doing, he also avoided triggering what would certainly have been substantial discontent among both his East and West Bank constituencies.

In the final analysis, Jordan's adherence to the sanctions and avoidance of the Camp David process may have been overdetermined. Nonetheless, an explanation that considers budgetary threats and incentives goes much farther toward explaining the

essence of the Jordanian decision than do explanations based on calculations of external threat.

Jordan-Iraq, 1979–80

This rapprochement poses perhaps the greatest challenge to balancing and bandwagoning for, examined closely, Jordanian behavior
simply cannot be characterized as either. By 1976–77, Iraq was clearly demonstrating its power and its desire to play an active role in
inter-Arab politics. However, it was not in any sense threatening Jordan, and hence Jordanian behavior cannot be characterized as bandwagoning. Nor, despite the cooling of relations with Syria, was Damascus threatening Jordan until well after Amman threw in its lot with
Iraq. Therefore, neither can Jordanian behavior be accurately
described as balancing Syrian power (which was clearly on the wane
because of domestic instability) by moving toward Iraq.

Indeed, rather than seeking what one may call negative explanations—explanations based on fear and threat—this, again, appears
to be a case of positive incentives that fit nicely into Jordan's heavy
reliance on external aid. Iraq simply had more to offer Jordan than
did Syria. Syria was also aid-reliant and was increasingly mired in a
domestic battle with its Islamists. Iraq's inter-Arab efforts as well as its
own willingness to provide support (buttressed by a strong economy
and substantial oil wealth) provided powerful incentives to move the
kingdom away from Syria and in the direction of Iraq.

Jordan-Syria, 1983–85

Unlike the three cases discussed above, this period witnessed a rapprochement, but not a move toward a more formal alliance as had
been concluded in the 1970s. However, again, neither balancing nor
bandwagoning captures what was at work here. By early 1983, Iraqi
austerity measures began to have an impact on Jordan. The Jordanian private sector had become quickly and intensively involved in the
Iraqi market, and the slowdown threatened to hurt Jordanian busi-

ness severely. In the spring of 1983 Amman extended initial feelers to Damascus, reportedly in connection with a Jordanian desire to convince the Syrians to reopen their part of the oil pipeline that had carried Iraqi crude to the Mediterranean, presumably to ease some of the economic pressure on Baghdad. Recall that this attempt met with little Syrian enthusiasm. Attempts were made again in 1984, during a period when Syria was suffering from a cutback in Iranian oil deliveries, and there was greater responsiveness, although the Syrians drew back after Jordan reestablished ties with Egypt. The final rapprochement did not finally come until late 1985. Again, timing is important: the traditional explanation that Jordan wanted to try to improve relations with Syria because of attacks on its diplomats and to counter the weight of the PLO does not apply to the early period, when the Jordanians first sought the improvement. Only economic factors explain the timing both of Jordan's attempts at rapprochement and Syrian receptivity to them.

Jordan-Egypt, 1983–84

Jordan's reestablishment of ties with Egypt also does not fit balancing or bandwagoning. It is true that Jordan sought the reintegration of Egypt into the Arab world as a way of countering the Iranian threat to the area. But to say that Jordan reestablished ties with Egypt to balance Iran again misses the mark. Jordan was the first Arab state to reestablish official ties with Egypt, and in so doing angered the Gulf states (more because of lack of consultation and for the move's potential for creating further divisions in the Arab world than because of their opposition to Egypt's return to the fold) and Syria. Moreover, the resumption of economic ties preceded the reestablishment of diplomatic ties by about eighteen months. Again, as in the case of Syria, by late 1982-early 1983 the Jordanians were scrambling to make up for losses in their Iraqi export market. Egypt, from which Jordan had been largely cut off since the imposition of the Arab League sanctions in late March 1979, offered a huge potential market that had been of considerable economic significance prior to Camp David. Its size and proximity made it a natural target for expansion.

It is true that King Husayn, recognizing Egypt's importance to Arab politics, tried to maintain some ties with Cairo even after the March 1979 peace treaty. It is also true that Egypt had begun to supply Iraq with war materiel even before Sadat's October 1981 assassination. Again, however, timing and content are important, and the initiation of an *economic* rapprochement in the spring of 1983 strongly suggests that it was concern for reinvigorating bilateral exchange to make up for the apparent loss of the Iraqi market that underlay the decision.

The ACC, 1989

To a large extent, the announcement of the ACC served merely to formalize the trilateral relationship among Egypt, Iraq, and Jordan (with North Yemen for good measure) that had been evolving since the early part of the decade. Military, political, and economic cooperation were already quite extensive, as the case studies have documented. Can one detect balancing or bandwagoning here? Certainly not as a group, although individual state motivations differ. North Yemen may have been balancing Saudi Arabia, but that appears to be the extent of balancing and bandwagoning. Iraq and Egypt both seem to have intended to use the organization for increased regional power projection. Jordan, on the other hand, may have had some concerns about Israel in mind, but this project was proposed immediately following the Iran-Iraq war, which suggests another set of considerations.

From his first suggestion of what eventually became the ACC, the king called for the establishment of an EC-like model, and argued that regional subgroups should be the first step. He placed primary emphasis on economic integration, and with good reason. In the first place, Saddam Husayn had promised to reward those who had stood by Iraq during the war. Since Amman had been one of Baghdad's staunchest supporters, the Jordanian leadership had every reason to believe that Jordan would be among the first in line for a substantial share of reconstruction contracts. Thus, through the ACC Amman no doubt wanted to ensure and increase Jordanian access to the Iraqi market, not only for the kingdom's goods, which had flooded the republic during the war, but also for its labor, which found fewer and fewer openings in the Gulf states during the 1980s. While closer integration with Cairo did not offer the prospect of employment for Jordanians, nonetheless, Egypt did constitute the largest market in the Arab world; increased efforts toward lowering trade barriers and increasing exchange as the ACC promised could only work to Jordan's advantage. These considerations must all then be placed against the backdrop of increasing unemployment in Jordan and, in the period of the king's campaign for the organization, the precipitous drop in the value of the Jordanian dinar and the rescheduling of the kingdom's external debt with the IMF in January 1989. The ACC's ultimate failure to meet the king's economic expectations in no way vitiates the initial role of these factors in Husayn's calculations.

The Gulf Crisis: The Hard Case?

Any reader familiar with the 1990–91 Gulf crisis and war must have wondered by now how an argument based on budget security can be applied to Jordan's alliance behavior during this period. Indeed, the reader may well be tempted to conclude that Jordanian decision-making during this crisis completely undermines the argument. Before explaining why the budget security argument made in chapter 1 is not weakened by Jordan's Gulf crisis foreign policy, a brief description of the crisis and its impact on the kingdom is in order.

The Gulf crisis marked perhaps the greatest challenge for Jordanian leaders in the kingdom's history. On only two prior occasions had decisionmakers faced somewhat comparable situations. The first was in 1956, when the kingdom initially indicated its interest in joining the Baghdad Pact, then being promoted by the United States and Great Britain. At that point, both domestic forces and powerful regional forces (Egypt, Saudi Arabia, and Syria) combined to convince the king not to join. The second came in September 1970, when the decision was made to crush the Palestinian resistance movement. In this case, however, the Jordanian population was badly divided, as was the Arab world. While Jordan incurred widespread opprobrium—Syria closed its borders, while Libya and Kuwait cut their Khartoum-promised support—Saudi Arabia did not end its critical aid. In the case of the 1990–91 Gulf crisis, however, the Jordanian population was united on one end of the political spectrum, while the wealthy and powerful Arab states were all on the other.

Thus, each of these cases embodied a different combination of forces. In 1956, internal and Arab regional pressures united against the king's expected decision to join the Pact to produce the opposite decision. In 1970 Husayn had support among key sectors of his subjects, criticism from a divided Arab world, but strong U.S. and tacit Israeli support in the background. In the case of the Gulf war, however, Husayn had only the vociferous support of his people, since the other noncoalition Arab states had very little weight in regional politics. Jordan's position incurred the wrath of its powerful and wealthy Arab neighbors as well as virtually the entire international community, most notably, Jordan's long-time supporter, the United States.

It is important to stress here that while the Jordanian people were clearly and unabashedly pro-Iraqi in their demonstrations and discourse, the official government line was not so until after the air war began in mid-January 1991. Jordan refused to recognize Iraq's annexation of Kuwait as its nineteenth province, repeatedly stating that it continued to view the Sabah monarchy as the legitimate government of Kuwait. At the same time, however, while proclaiming its adherence to the principle of the inadmissibility of the acquisition of territory by force, neither Husayn nor any of his advisers condemned Iraq by name for its aggression against Kuwait. The king was clearly trying to withstand countervailing pressures from within and without. He insisted, more or less convincingly depending upon one's point of view, that condemnation or recognition of Saddam's moves would have compromised the possibility of a diplomatic solution. In this respect he was simply following a traditional Jordanian policy of seeking to settle inter-Arab disputes in an inter-Arab framework, and to that end made numerous attempts to avoid the internationalization and escalation of the conflict. What was different about this conflict, however, was that the international community had defined away neutrality: any state that was not with the coalition, as constructed by the United States, was depicted as being pro-Iraqi. Unlike past conflicts, in this case there was no middle ground.

What about the influence of economic factors on Jordan's position? There were clearly strong economic considerations at work that militated against Jordan's cutting ties with Iraq through adhering to the UN-imposed sanctions, regardless of other political considerations. Chapter 6 has already detailed the gradual development and expansion of the Jordanian-Iraqi economic and political relationship. During the first three quarters of 1989, Jordan relied on Iraq for 82.5 percent of its petroleum, importing a total of 2.1 million tons of Iraqi crude oil and other oil products.[1] Jordanian farmers had standing contracts with Iraq for a reported $200 million.[2] And, as Tables 7 and 8 show (chapter 2), Iraq was also Jordan's number one trading partner. Thus, implementing sanctions threatened not just future Iraqi good will, but also a very real and important market for Jordan's exports.

However, the equation is not quite so simple, for, as we have seen in the discussions of Kuwait and Saudi Arabia, Jordan's reliance on these countries for aid and markets was also substantial. During the first three quarters of 1989, Jordan had imported 133,626 tons of Saudi Arabian crude, and 307,609 tons of Kuwaiti crude.[3] The issue of Kuwait for the short term was somewhat moot, since the occupation of the country meant that, at least temporarily, it was lost as a market to Jordan no matter what position the kingdom took on the larger issues. Jordan also faced a disruption in the flow of remittances from its large expatriate community in Kuwait, a factor that might have argued for a more circumspect, long-term-oriented policy in order to ensure the economic and employment future of this community.

In terms of financial support, while Gulf state largess had clearly been on the wane during the 1980s, nonetheless, Saudi Arabia and Kuwait remained the most likely potential Arab sources of aid and concessionary loans. And both states in the wake of the Iraqi invasion indicated their willingness to reward support for the anti-Iraq coalition. For example, Saudi Arabia agreed to provide half Jordan's crude oil needs in order to encourage Jordan to line up with the coalition.[4] Conversely, when that policy of "encouragement" did not work, on September 20 Saudi Arabia announced that it was ending its oil shipments to Jordan; it closed its border to Jordanian traffic and expelled Jordanian diplomats.

Thus, as the crisis unfolded, Jordan had several options, all unappealing. To join the coalition would have meant the loss of Iraqi markets and oil, although after the sanctions were imposed Iraqi markets were largely closed (despite the leakage) no matter what position the kingdom took. The sanctions also meant that Kuwait was temporarily lost as a market: the future of its relations with Jordan would be determined by the outcome of the crisis. Here there were two possible positive and two possible negative outcomes. If Jordan joined the coalition and it was victorious or if Jordan sided with Iraq and it was able to hold out then Jordan stood to win. If, on the other hand, Jordan chose to side with the future loser (whether Iraq or the coalition), at very least access to Kuwait would have been lost, which is of course, what happened.

Joining the coalition would have offered Jordan the possibility of increased Arab and Western aid to offset losses incurred during the crisis, whereas failure to join the coalition both ruled out any such assistance and offered no other options. Acquiescing in coalition policy would also likely have meant swift and more substantial financial assistance for Jordan to address the (largely South Asian) refugee problem Jordan faced as those fleeing Kuwait poured across its borders. In the event, as the crisis unfolded, and Amman remained outside the coalition, the international community was quite slow to assist Jordan in its efforts to provide relief to the incoming refugees.

Any attempt at precise accounting of these trade-offs would be foolhardy since statistics and projections are at best imprecise. Nonetheless, from the standpoint of short-term budget security, the pro-coalition option would appear, at least on the surface, to have been the wiser strategy. Why then did the king act otherwise?

It may be argued, with some plausibility, that the king's sense of Arabism, which by all accounts is quite strong, motivated him to seek an inter-Arab solution and ultimately refuse to abandon Iraq. However, then one would have to be able to argue why such a sense of Arabism did not prevent him from undertaking the assault against the Palestinians in 1970, or even more important, why his Arabism led him to stand more firmly by Arab Iraq than by Arab Kuwait. One could also argue that the king simply miscalculated, although his survival for some four decades as monarch of a small and vulnerable country in the Middle East certainly suggests that it would be the uncommon exception. More plausible is that the traditional bases or factors used to assess options had changed, and the king was reacting to the new environment.

One of the key components of the new environment was popular opinion, the "Jordanian street." However, the argument has long been made that Husayn must take into account his domestic constituency. The reference is to the Palestinian component of the population, with the implication being that the king could not take certain steps if they were likely to upset the kingdom's Palestinians. There are two problems with this contention. The first is not directly relevant to our discussion, but will be mentioned in any case: whatever differences may have existed between Jordan's Palestinian and Transjordanian communities, at least in the past, the issue of conciliation with Israel was not a point of contention, as both sides opposed such a move. The second and more important consideration is that, while the Palestinian community in Jordan is large, its size and importance have not stopped the regime from taking a number of steps over the years to which the community was opposed, most notably, but by no means exclusively, the military assaults against the Palestinian resistance in 1970–71. Hence, if one wants to argue that . ιe king has always been sensitive to "the street," one must also be able to explain the many occasions on which he was apparently able to ignore it. It would seem prudent to reexamine those past crises in which popular opinion has been deemed to have played an influential role to determine if in fact its role was as central as it has been described. In any case, it remains to make the case for why the pressures from below had special significance in the Gulf crisis, and for how they relate to the concept of budget security.

The basis of the argument made here is that developments in the 1980s, in particular the evolution of a serious economic crisis, gradually undermined the traditional bases of budget and regime support. When the crisis finally exploded in economic riots following the announcement of IMF-requested austerity measures, the regime reacted by launching a process of political liberalization, a survival strategy that aimed at defusing discontent while setting the stage for significant changes in the political and economic system. As a result of the relaxation of political repression that accompanied the liberalization, by the time of the Gulf crisis, Jordanians were better positioned to express publicly and vocally their position on the Iraqi invasion of Kuwait.[5]

A close examination of the background to these developments reveals the following. On the political front, the Jordanian parliament had been suspended in 1974, and replaced in 1977 by what was called a National Consultative Council (NCC), whose members were appointed by the king. The parliament had hardly been a lively or contentious body, but the NCC had even less clout, much less popular legitimacy. Hence the recalling of parliament in early 1984 seemed to bode well for institutionalized political development in the country. However, by early 1985 internal political repression was on the rise again. A new election law was drafted in 1986 and new general parliamentary elections were promised, but were subsequently postponed.

In the meantime, the political atmosphere in the kingdom grew increasingly tense, particularly when, in early 1986, political coordination between the PLO and Jordan broke down, and the kingdom closed all the offices of Fateh, the largest constituent faction of the PLO. But PLO-Jordanian difficulties were only a part of the problem, and the regime was simply not disposed at the time to allow for the expression of criticism. In June 1987, the Jordanian Writers' Association, one of the last remaining fora for political and cultural expression, was closed. Tensions continued to mount after the beginning of the Palestinian uprising in December 1987 led the Jordanian government to take increased security measures against Palestinians on the East Bank. The king's decision to disengage from the West Bank on July 31, 1988 simply underscored the friction in Palestinian-Jordanian relations.

However, the political difficulties and the regime's security response might have been less severe had Jordan not at the same time begun to experience economic problems as well. As we saw in the case study chapters, after a number of years of continuous (if not consistent) Arab aid, by 1983, the Iran-Iraq war had begun to take its toll on oil-state financial contributions. Government policy at the time of the declining aid aimed at compensating for the shortfall, not through serious measures intended to cut expenditures or invigorate the domestic economy, but rather through borrowing from abroad. In this way, the government avoided adjustments that would have undermined part of its governing formula: underwriting employment (primarily for the Transjordanian core) and a variety of other subsidies from which a majority of the population benefited.

To its credit the Jordanian leadership also sought to revive economic ties with Egypt and Syria, in addition to its policy of extending export credits to Iraq. In each of these cases the policy was clearly aimed at promoting the health of the domestic export sector, both public and private. However, by mid-1988, the Iraqi export credits fiasco combined with burgeoning external debt began to drive down the value of the dinar. By January 1989, Jordan was unable to meet its debt service payment and was forced to negotiate with the IMF to reschedule its external debt. This was a clear signal that the economic structure that had underpinned the governing formula of the past was crumbling. Jordan could no longer count on massive infusions of external aid to support its "beyond its means" distributional lifestyle. While the Arab states made offers of support in the wake of the April 1989 economic riots, they also made clear in the 1989 Arab summit that their Baghdad commitments would not be renewed. Jordan was simply going to have to cut its budget and raise revenues domestically. Both of these targets were in keeping with IMF requirements. As we saw above, while budget cutting threatened one part of the governing formula—the support of the Transjordanian bureaucracy and army—revenue raising threatened the other—the state's demand for political acquiescence from the important and largely Palestinian bourgeoisie in exchange for few extractive (taxation) demands.

In sum, the economic crisis of the late 1980s meant that the government's distributional capabilities severely declined. With no new financial savior available, the state was no longer capable of fully providing its traditional part of the economic and political bargain to either the largely Transjordanian public sector or the largely Palestinian bourgeoisie. The budget could no longer bear the regime's part of the political acquiescence bargain. Therefore, as the kingdom continued along the path of debt rescheduling and budget reduction, the king initiated a process of political liberalization in the summer of 1989, which led to Jordan's first free elections in thirty-five years.

The key point is that even before the Gulf crisis two trends were clear: the financial capabilities of the Jordanian state were contracting, leading to a decrease in its distributional capabilities; and, the extractive role of the state was increasing, with a growing contribution to state coffers of taxes and fees of various sorts. These two trends then pointed to a third: with the bases of regime economic support shifting (and with the political liberalization well under way and very popular), the state would have been very hard-pressed financially (even with a massive infusion of Kuwaiti or Saudi assistance) to call up and sustain the repression needed to silence its pro-Iraqi population into acceptance of a pro-coalition stance. Moreover, given that the traditional institutions of coercion, the army and the intelligence apparatus, are overwhelmingly staffed with Transjordanians, who were just as enamored of Saddam as were the Palestinians, the cost to the regime both in material and legitimacy terms would have been tremendous. It seems highly unlikely that it would ever have crossed the king's mind to "fight" his population in the way he likely would have had to had he chosen a clear pro-coalition position. Moreover, short of a massive transfer of assistance directed specifically at the army and internal intelligence, it probably would have been extremely difficult to prevent massive defections.

Hence the economic decline and its impact on the traditional bases of regime support, combined with the Jordanian popular position on the Gulf crisis, left the king with few options. (Indeed, the fact that he was able to sustain his version of neutrality was a testament to his skill in reading and understanding his subjects.) By 1990, budget security for Jordan had a much more important domestic component than it had had at any other time during the period under consideration in this study. With the revenues and aid from the oil states dwindling and unlikely to be restored on a long-term basis, the economic crisis of 1988–89 further increased the importance of domestic extraction. Add to this the unparalleled and unified Jordanian popular mobilization that accompanied the invasion of Kuwait and the resources (both material and moral) that would have been needed to check or repress this outpouring of emotion and one has the most important components in explaining Jordanian policy toward the coalition and Iraq.

Indeed, the king's official stance was a masterful modification of an extremely pro-Iraq, anti-U.S. and anti-Gulf state position. Some might argue therefore that the king really did have complete control of the policy agenda and that, contrary to the argument being made here, the "Jordanian street" was not a serious consideration. However, that the king felt the need to be sensitive to public pressures was borne out, for example, in his handling of the issue of adherence to the sanctions: the decision to comply was announced through a secret memorandum sent to government offices and was downplayed in the country. Moreover, throughout the period the king and the crown prince stressed that Jordan was being made to suffer economically for its political stance.[6] Such statements shored up morale both to help soften the economic blow and to increase the chances that Jordanians would view their monarch's stand as a principled one, for which they were being punished by the less principled.

The argument here is not just that pressures from below have a greater potential impact on Jordanian foreign policy in the wake of the liberalization than they did before. There is a budget security aspect to the argument as well. As we saw in chapter 1, a state can deal with an economic crisis in two major ways: it can seek a short-term fix, which involves securing additional revenues rather quickly and avoiding painful domestic economic restructuring; or it may attempt to address the crisis through a series of policies that amount to restructuring. The second strategy, while perhaps sounder for the national economy in the long run, is, nonetheless, potentially subversive in the short run, both because it probably cannot address the crisis quickly enough and because diversifying may require upsetting existing sociopolitical coalitions.

There are numerous examples of Jordanian policymakers' crafting policies intended to protect the economic status quo rather than attempting to diversify or restructure. One early example was the Jordanian government's policy beginning in 1979 to allow Jordanian labor freer mobility to go to the Gulf for work. This was in effect the path of least resistance, for the other alternatives—preventing such workers from taking their talent outside the kingdom in search of better-paying jobs elsewhere, providing incentives to the domestic labor market to offer more opportunities to such skilled labor, or attempting to channel Jordanians into jobs that they traditionally had avoided—would likely have met with substantial resistance from various quarters. Instead, the state allowed Jordanians to work abroad and then encouraged the importation of expatriate Arab and Asian labor willing to work for less in the jobs that Jordanians eschewed. In other words, rather than seeking substantially to expand white collar employment or in effect to force those trained for white collar work into jobs they did not want, the policy allowed the surplus to leave. In this way, not only was the balance maintained, but remittances from abroad were thereby increased. Moreover, by additionally forbidding foreign labor to join unions, the state also severely undercut the potential for the development of a labor movement of any consequence.

Another example is from the mid-1970s, when many were touting the possibility of Jordan's taking Lebanon's place as *the* banking and service center of the Arab world. One high-ranking Jordanian official admitted off the record that he was present at meetings at which opposition to this notion was expressed at the highest levels. It was not that Jordan was incapable of taking on the role; rather, there was real concern about what Jordan's becoming a service-oriented economy would mean for domestic politics. Top policymakers were certainly interested in foreign investment, at least on a theoretical level; however, they did not want to open up the country to large numbers of foreigners, and put a strain on the housing market and on services. They also felt that opening up a conservative country like Jordan might eventually lead to the same instability that Lebanon was encountering.[7] As a result, Jordan in effect passed up the opportunity to assume Lebanon's regional role.

A third example of avoidance of structural change came during Zayd al-Rifaʿi's second prime ministership. Although he was given a mandate for energizing the private sector by the crown, economic liberalization in fact made only marginal headway under his leader-ship. One may lay the blame at the feet of the bureaucracy, but one must also find an explanation for why greater emphasis was not placed on pushing for reform if it was indeed so critical to the gov-ernment's program. Here again, the desire not to undertake changes that might have caused a restructuring of domestic economic or social relations (particularly, in this case, affecting the crucial East Bank bureaucracy), must have played a significant role.

In each of these cases, the preferred response was to seek external solutions, and avoid remedies that might trigger internal dissent or instability, even though in the long run the domestic changes might well have resulted in a more diversified and self-sufficient economy. The difference between each of these cases and the economic crisis faced by the kingdom in 1989 was that none was as severe, and in each case short-term safety-valve solutions were available. By 1989, Jordan had exhausted the financial good will of its traditional donors and no other quick-fix solutions remained. As a result, it had no option short of, first, IMF stabilization measures, and then, more thoroughgoing policies aimed at restructuring. It was left to the polit-ical liberalization process to defuse whatever politically subversive effect the economic measures would have. Only in such a context is Jordan's Gulf crisis behavior fully comprehensible.

Traditional balance of power theory as modified by Walt to include balance of threat would not have been able to predict Jor-dan's behavior in the Gulf crisis. In the first place, identification of provenance of greatest threat would have been problematic. It seems likely that traditional security studies scholars would have character-ized Jordan's behavior as bandwagoning, indicating that Iraq was the threatening power. But that was not the way Jordanian decisionmak-ers understood the conflict. To the contrary, they saw the U.S. and the broader coalition of forces as the primary threat, because of the potential their intervention had to trigger a wider conflagration into which Jordan might have been drawn against its will. Should one then conclude that Jordan was "balancing" against the international coalition? Such an assessment makes little sense either. In fact, Husayn appears to have tried to steer a course of neutrality, for which there is no provision in a balancing and bandwagoning framework.

If balancing considerations did figure into the king's analysis they most likely concerned the requisites for internal economic and political stability versus external political demands and economic threats and incentives. Indeed, a convincing explanation of the king's position requires that the changing nature of the country's political system (from authoritarianism to free elections and freer speech) and economic structure (away from the distributive and toward the extractive state) be factored into the analysis. While it would be an oversimplification to state that budgetary concerns tell the whole tale, an explanation that treats domestic revenue sources as a key to understanding state behavior does provide the part of the analysis that transforms the explanation from one based on irrationality, miscalculation or cowardice, to one based on a rational weighing of a range of security considerations.

Budget Security and Arab-Israeli Peace

With the destruction of Iraq and the curtailment of its regional power during the second Gulf war, there was little question that Jordan would make its way to the U.S.-Russian sponsored Middle East peace talks that began in Madrid in October 1991. Again, there were simply no other options. However, little progress was made until the so-called Oslo agreement of August 1993 was announced (during the final stages of completing this work), thereby reenergizing the Arab-Israeli negotiations. An examination of the Jordanian response to the unfolding of events since the signing of the Palestinian-Israeli accord further reinforces the salience of the budget security argument.

In the first place, it is clear that old habits die hard. The promises by various members of the international community to provide development aid and other assistance to help support and institutionalize the peace have struck a resonant cord with Jordanian decisionmakers. Several years of austerity have not erased the sweet memories of the kingdom's former aid addiction. New infusions of money in the quick-fix tradition could well help ease the country's current struggle with austerity, which has left increasing numbers of Jordanian below the poverty line and has seen a concomitant increase in the appeal of Islamist trends in the country.

Selling the peace process in Jordan raises numerous sensitive and potentially stability-threatening issues, many of which could be calmed or soothed (or so decisionmakers appear to believe) if new aid commitments are made. The first issue simply concerns easing the country's way through the continuing period of austerity. A population that feels itself to be less under siege economically, and understands that the peace process is responsible for bringing the relief, is less likely to take an openly oppositional stance. While the king has, to date, skillfully handled the major channel of organized opposition to the peace process, the Islamists, the receipt of additional aid could certainly strengthen his hand.

As the peace process unfolded, King Husayn's trip to Washington, D.C., in July 1994 for a meeting with Israeli Prime Minister Yitzhak Rabin produced another clear example of the impact of the drive for economic assistance and solvency on the kingdom's foreign policy. At this stage, the critical question was whether Jordan would end the state of war, or simply the state of belligerency, with Israel. The Jordanians were concerned both with securing a deal for up to $1 billion in debt relief and with obtaining new weaponry for the armed forces. According to a July 27 *Jordan Times* article, "When it became apparent to His Majesty that the difference between the two states [belligerency and war] paled in comparison to the political and economic advantages of doing the latter [ending the state of *war*] he did not hesitate to declare the end of the state of war with Israel."

In all discussions of aid that may come into the region, Jordanian policymakers are very concerned that Jordan not be shortchanged or bypassed. Hence, the Jordanian demand, for example, that the kingdom be compensated for the years that it has hosted its large Palestinian refugee population. To be sure, the demand in part reflects a desire for recognition of Amman's contributions, but it also reaffirms that many of these refugees are eligible to return to a Palestinian entity, and hence, reduce to some extent the Palestinian population in the kingdom, an outcome many Transjordanians dream of. However, even if there is substantial Palestinian repatriation from Jordan, the larger issue that concerns some Transjordanians is the possibility that, because most of Jordan's wealth is held by Palestinians, without external assistance, their state will eventually either become a kind of economic colony of the Palestinian entity, or a wealthy and ascendant Palestinian bourgeoisie, whether it returns to Palestine or continues to reside in Jordan, will in fact come to control the country, thus further changing the sociopolitical coalition that underpins the regime.

Thus, for a number of reasons, Jordanian policymakers are as keen as ever to secure external development and budgetary assistance. Receipt of such funds could certainly help smooth the kingdom's passage through the rough waters of austerity. Some may even believe that it could postpone or obviate additional adjustment or austerity measures. However, the most central concern of the Transjordanian sector of the population, whether decisionmaker or average citizen, is that without such assistance, Jordan will eventually lose not only its economic, but also its cultural and political sovereignty to a Palestinian counterpart. It was this concern over possible loss of sovereignty that led Jordanian decisionmakers to take a special interest in who controls the bridges between Jordan and the new entity (lest instability on the Palestinian side lead to a new population exodus to Jordan) and it was this concern that led many in the fall of 1993 following the PLO-Israel accord to call for the postponement of Jordan's elections lest Palestinians who might soon be "going home" be allowed to vote in East Bank elections.

The shape of the future peace, therefore, is an extremely sensitive issue, one that goes to the "core values" of the Jordanian state, and one in which budget security is closely tied to the prospects for the continuation or loss of effective economic and political sovereignty.

Broader Applicability

This study began as an inductive project to attempt to determine the role of economics in inter-Arab relations. In the course of the research, I was surprised to find policymakers who would in one breath insist that politics always won out, and then proceed to relate accounts of policy decisions in which they themselves (not my interpretation of their words) demonstrated that economics had been if not the determining consideration, at very least an extremely important one. I find this significant and recount it here, because some will no doubt contend that Jordan was the fatal "easy case" and that to demonstrate the viability of my approach, a "hard case," one in which the importance of budgetary considerations would not automatically suggest themselves should have been selected. To such a critique, two responses are in order.

The first response is to remind the reader that this project was aimed at hypothesis generation, not at hypothesis testing. The notion of budget security and its importance were generated through the long process of research and interviewing. It suggested itself as a result of close work with a great deal of empirical material that was not originally screened to confirm or disconfirm a preselected hypothesis. Hence, the "easy case" contention by no means vitiates the importance or conclusions of the study.

The second response is that because the conclusions are so counterintuitive for most students and scholars of the Middle East, the study has made a contribution as it stands. Part of the problem in dealing with Arab politics is that everyone is sure s/he understands decisionmakers motivations because of the more obvious and often articulated political reasons behind policy choices. This project, while not discounting such explanations, nonetheless, has argued that other variables need to be examined, and that the real motivations behind "obviously" political decisions may not be strictly or even largely political after all. This should not be interpreted as constituting a crude form of economic determinism. The argument here is not that *all* foreign policy choices and moves are based solely or primarily on economic considerations: regional and domestic political forces, as well as the ideology and personality of decisionmakers certainly play a role in many decisions. However, the conclusions should lead analysts to reexamine the still unfortunately widely prevailing notions that high politics in the Middle East is based on the political whim of a few men.

Nonetheless, neither of these responses obviates the need to question the potential broader applicability of the concept of budget security. Here I would like briefly to discuss two other cases that appear to be potentially fruitful for further study and then offer some reasons for testing the broader applicability of the concept.

While the primary focus of this research was Jordan, in the course of gathering data, several cases of alignment shifts by other countries appeared to have been related to the same budget security considerations. They demand further, careful examination along the lines followed in the case studies in this work. I note them briefly here, not to "prove" my case, but rather to argue that Jordan should not be viewed as a hopelessly unique and, therefore, uninteresting case from a theoretical point of view.

The first is the case of Syria. Considerations of Syrian foreign policy demonstrate a marked tension between those who regard Asad and his foreign policy as pragmatic, and those who see nothing but a policy driven by Syrian Ba'thist ideology. For the record, with the possible exception of some of the developments in the Iraqi-Syrian relationship, Syrian foreign policy has generally seemed eminently pragmatic, not ideological, to me. In any case, in the course of the research three developments were particularly striking.

First, it seems clear that at least part of the reason for the Syrian-Jordanian rapprochement in 1975–76 was the joint "begging strategy" noted in the case study. While larger regional considerations may have been more important to the Syrians than budgetary ones, that needs to be demonstrated, not simply assumed. The second instance has to do with Syrian-Iraqi relations in the wake of the signing of the Camp David Accords. At this stage, relations between Baghdad and Damascus warmed considerably, a development usually attributed to the need to close Arab ranks in the shadow of the impending peace treaty between Egypt and Israel. However, there is also reason to believe that, like Jordan, Syria saw the wealth and potential of Iraq and, also heavily dependent upon external aid, sought to repair relations for its own economic advantage.[8] The final example concerns Syria's ultimate willingness to restore ties with Jordan in 1985. Recall that Jordan had been making overtures since 1983. Syria, however, did not respond until 1984, after it had problems receiving and paying for Iranian oil. Recall as well that it was reported well after the fact that Jordan had begun supplying Syria with Saudi oil during this period. Again, an explanation based on budgetary concerns appears a reasonable possibility.

The second case is that of Egypt. Egyptian political scientist Ali E. Dessouki has entitled a chapter on the foreign policy of Egypt "The

Primacy of Economics." Although the primacy of economics is not really thoroughly developed in his presentation, he does make economic arguments about a number of Egypt most significant alignment changes. For example, he argues that in the mid-1970s, the Cairo-Riyadh alliance was predicated on expected economic gains from Saudi Arabia and other Gulf states. He also notes that Sadat's trip to Jerusalem in 1977 was largely motivated by the need to reduce defense expenditures, to encourage foreign private capital to enter the country, and to win more U.S. aid. All of this, of course, is placed against the background of Egypt's attempts to mobilize external resources to ease the growing deficit, what Dessouki calls the "population-resources gap."[9] In the case of Egypt, of course, the need to attract or mobilize external resources also required a move away from its close relationship with the Soviets and toward the West. In Dessouki's words, "When a ruling elite decides to pursue a development strategy based on foreign aid and capital, it follows that all necessary steps will be taken to attract and reassure its creditors."[10] Egypt's alliance shifts in the 1970s should then be seen as largely dictated by these requirements.

Hence we have two other states, both of which are and have been major regional players, and neither of which is remotely the "artificial" entity Jordan has often been described as, whose foreign policy or alignment decisions also suggest that budget security may well be high among decisionmakers' priorities. All three of these states are reliant (moderately to heavily, depending upon period and criteria) on external sources of income, particularly external aid, thus suggesting that the concept of budget security in explaining foreign policy behavior may be most significant in countries that are major recipients of external aid, a type of state that can be found beyond the Middle East. Again, however, only a very narrow understanding of budget security would limit its applicability to securing external aid.

It is for this reason that the idea of focusing on the structure or composition of state revenues was proposed at the outset. One can image a situation in which state A, heavily dependent upon the marketing of a particular product, finds itself, for whatever reason, unable to sell to its major market, state B. The potential threat to the economy and by extension, the state budget of A, may be so severe that A is forced to improve ties with state C, which may serve as an alternative market. In the same way, assume state A has long depended upon shipping its products overland through state B. Then, for reasons of domestic political turmoil, state A can no longer safely send its produce through B. As a result, in order to forestall economic disaster it is forced to improve relations with state C, which offers an alternative overland route. What state C may demand in return in either of these two cases will help shape the nature of the new relationship, whether it will involve an upgrading in relations, a warming in relations, or a stronger commitment. But in each case, budget security could be said to have been threatened, leading to a foreign policy initiative specifically designed to address or prevent a potential shortfall. These cases are intended only to be illustrative; one could certainly imagine others.

Moreover, although the focus in this study has been on its impact on a specific aspect of foreign or security policy—alignment shifts— budget security is useful as a general concept whether its impact is on foreign or domestic policy. It is certainly a relevant concept in examining the domestic instability and loss of relative economic sovereignty to external lending agencies caused by the debt crisis of the 1980s. In such cases, leaderships faced default or potential economic deterioration or collapse. Unable to mobilize sufficient resources, whether domestic or external, to address the shortfall under the pre-existing conditions, they had little choice but to go to the IMF. Agreements with the IMF permit states some financial repayment breathing room and may make them eligible for additional external loans, both of which forestall collapse. However, the IMF agreements generally require that greater domestic resources be mobilized and/or that fewer state resources be spent on populist policies such as subsidized food and services. The implementation of such policies may well trigger unrest itself (e.g. Egypt 1977 and Jordan 1989), but without such agreements these states would have found it virtually impossible to find additional resources to enable them to address their debt crises. More recently, budget insecurity is perhaps nowhere more evident than in the numerous moves to liberalize political/and or economic systems across the developing world, as well as in Eastern Europe and the Soviet Union. Many of these moves derived largely, or at least in part, from imminent economic collapse.

What these theoretical and more specific examples indicate is that in the developing world, states that enjoy only limited resources, capital, and development are the norm. Their heavy reliance upon external aid, one or a few commodities, limited markets, a particular trade route, and the like, renders the concept of budget security extremely relevant. As David pointed out in his presentation of omnibalancing, regimes or leaderships may be expected to act, or at least attempt to act, in such a way as to ensure that they remain in power. While external threats do challenge some of these states, economic solvency and survival seem more real and pressing challenges to many others. In such conditions, states unwilling to upset existing socioeconomic or political coalitions, or unable (for whatever reason) to mobilize resources domestically to address their basic financial distress may be expected to turn outward to do so and, in their attempt, may seek to conclude new alliances.

Trying to explain such behavior in terms of balancing or bandwagoning state-level power or threats misses much of what most threatens developing countries. Threats to regime stability must be understood to be broader than the traditional domestic political or external military formulations. No state or leadership can long survive without income. Securing that income, whatever its present or potential sources, should therefore be viewed as just as integral to state security as defending borders against foreign military assault. For, when all is said and done, empty treasuries fund no soldiers.

Appendix

U.S. Dollars to Jordanian Dinars Exchange Rate
1964–1991

Year	Official Rate, End of Period	Official Rate Period Average	Year	Official Rate, End of Period	Official Rate Period Average
1962	2.8000	2.8000	1977	3.1746	3.0375
1963	2.8000	2.8000	1978	3.4130	3.2733
1964	2.8000	2.8000	1979	3.3898	3.3299
1965	2.8000	2.8000	1980	3.2415	3.3543
1966	2.8000	2.8000	1981	2.9498	3.0293
1967	2.8000	2.8000	1982	2.8450	2.8384
1968	2.8000	2.8000	1983	2.6918	2.7550
1969	2.8000	2.8000	1984	2.4691	2.6036
1970	2.8000	2.8000	1985	2.7192	2.5379
1971	2.8000	2.8000	1986	2.9061	2.8583
1972	2.8000	2.8000	1987	3.0395	2.9522
1973	3.0390	3.0462	1988	2.0964	2.6916
1974	3.1746	3.1113	1989	1.5432	1.7532
1975	3.0303	3.1393	1990	1.5038	1.5069
1976	3.0211	3.0122	1991	1.4815	1.4689

SOURCE: International Monetary Fund, *International Financial Statistics Yearbook*, Vol. XLV (Washington, DC: IMF, 1992), pp. 440–41.

Notes

Introduction

1. For recent examples see Jack Snyder, *Myths of Empire: Domestic Politics and International Ambition* (Ithaca: Cornell University Press, 1991) and Helen Milner, "International Theories of Cooperation among Nations: Strengths and Weaknesses," *World Politics* 44 (3): 466–496. Of course the important work of such scholars as Peter Katzenstein and Peter Gourevitch has long been in this tradition.

2. See for example, Jessica Tuchman Mathews, "Redefining Security," *Foreign Affairs* (Spring 1989): 162–177; Richard H. Ullman, "Redefining Security," *International Security* (Summer 1983): 129–153; and Joseph S. Nye, Jr. and Sean M. Lynn-Jones, "International Security Studies: A Report of a Conference on the State of the Field," *International Security* (Spring 1988): 5–27.

3. Nye and Lynn-Jones, ibid., p. 25.

4. This is also clear in a number of classic works on the "Arab system": Malcolm Kerr, *The Arab Cold War* (New York: Oxford University Press, 1971); Patrick Seale, *The Struggle for Syria* (New Haven: Yale University Press, 1987); and Alan Taylor, *The Arab Balance of Power* (Syracuse: Syracuse University Press, 1981); among others.

5. David Baldwin, *Economic Statecraft*, (Princeton: Princeton University Press, 1985), chapter 3, especially pp. 40–50.

6. Bruce Moon, "Political Economy Approches to the Study of Foreign Policy," in Charles F. Hermann, Charles W. Kegley, Jr., and James N. Rosenau, *New Directions in the Study of Foreign Policy* (Boston: Allen & Unwin, 1987) p. 41.

1. Economics and Alliances in the Developing World

1. Albert Hirschman, *National Power and the Structure of Foreign Trade* (Berkeley: University of California Press, 1980).

2. Neil Richardson, *Foreign Policy and Economic Dependence* (Austin: University of Texas Press, 1978), pp. 69–70.

3. Bruce Moon, "The Foreign Policy of the Dependent State," *International Studies Quarterly*, 37 (3): 322.

4. Adrienne Armstrong, "The Political Consequences of Economic Dependence," *Journal of Conflict Resolution*, 25 (3): 409–411.

5. See for example, Malcolm Kerr, *The Arab Cold War* (London: Oxford University Press, 1971) and Alan Taylor, *The Arab Balance of Power* (Syracuse: Syracuse University Press, 1983).

6. Paul Noble, "The Arab System: Pressures, Constraints, and Opportunities," in Bahgat Korany and Ali E. Hillal Dessouki, *The Foreign Policies of Arab States*, 2nd ed. (Boulder: Westview, 1991), 60–61.

7. Ali E. Hillal Dessouki, "The Primacy of Economics: The Foreign Policy of Egypt." In Korany and Dessouki eds., pp. 156–187.

8. Korany and Dessouki, "A Literature Survey and a Framework for Analysis," in Korany and Dessouki eds., pp. 19–20.

9. See, for example, her *In Search of Security: The Third World in International Relations* (Boulder: Lynne Reinner, 1987) and her volume coedited with Paikiasothy Saravanamuttu, *Conflict and Consensus in South/North Security* (New York: Cambridge University Press, 1989).

10. See, for example, Janet Gross Stein, "The Security Dilemma in the Middle East: A Prognosis for the Decade Ahead," in Bahgat Korany, Paul Noble, and Rex Brynen eds. *The Many Faces of National Security in the Arab World* (New York: St. Martin's, 1993.

11. Robert L. Rothstein, "The 'Security Dilemma' and the 'Poverty Trap' in the Third World," *The Jerusalem Journal of International Relations*, 8 (4) (December 1986): 9.

12. Ibid., pp. 11–12.

13. Stephen Walt, "A Renaissance in Security Studies?" *International Studies Quarterly* 35 (1991): 227.

14. Ibid., p. 213.

15. Giacomo Luciani, "The Economic Content of Security," *Journal of Public Policy*, 8, 2, p. 155.

16. Barry Buzan, *People States & Fear: An Agenda for International Security Studies in the post-Cold War Era* (2nd ed.) (Boulder: Lynne Reinner, 1991),p. 235.

17. Ibid., pp. 241–42.

18. It is understood that there is a difference between leadership and regime security. Leadership security involves ensuring that those particular personalities who are in power remain so. Regime security is a bit broader, for leaders may be overthrown, but if the dominant coalition and system of rule remain the same, the regime remains in tact. However, for the purposes of this argument, the distinction between national and leadership security is the most salient.

19. This is a point made by virtually all authors writing about Third World security. See Mohammed Ayoob, "Unravelling the Concept of National Security in the Third World," in Korany, Noble and Brynen eds., pp. 33–36; Brian L. Job, "The Insecurity Dilemma: National, Regime, and State Securities in the Third World," in Brian L. Job ed., *The Insecurity Dilemma: National Security of Third World States* (Boulder: Lynne Reinner, 1992); and Buzan, Buzan, *People States & Fear*, chapter 2.

20. Job, "Insecurity Dilemma," p. 13.

21. See Buzan, Buzan, *People States & Fear*, pp. 248–250.

22. See Luciani, "Economic Content," p. 155.

23. Mohammed Ayoob, "The Security Problematic of the Third World," *World Politics* 43 (2): 259.

24. Richard H. Ullman, "Redefining Security," *International Security*, 8 (1): 133

25. Derek Hopwood *Egypt: Politics and Society 1945–1981* (London: Allen & Unwin, 1982), pp. 10–12.

26. See Henry S. Bienen and Mark Gersovitz, "Economic Stabilization, Conditionality and Political Stability," *International Organization* 39 (4) (Autumn 1985): 731.

27. Ibid, pp. 29–30. Of course, as Bienen and Gersovitz point out, absent the option of turning to the IMF for assistance, instability may well have been even greater in some countries or have touched a greater number of countries.

28. See note 5, above.

29. L. Carl Brown, *International Politics and the Middle East* (Princeton: Princeton University Press, 1984), p. 16.

30. Stephen M. Walt, *The Origins of Alliances* (Ithaca: Cornell University Press, 1987).

31. Ibid., pp. 21–26.

32. Ibid., p. 149.

33. See Glen Snyder, "Alliances, Balance, and Stability," *International Organization*, 45 (1) (Winter 1991): 128.

34. Stephen R. David, "Explaining Third World Alliances," *World Politics* 43 (2): 233–256.

35. Ibid., pp. 235–36.

36. Michael N. Barnett and Jack S. Levy, "Domestic Sources of Alliances and Alignments: The Case of Egypt, 1962–1973," *International Organization*, 45 (3): 369–395.

37. Ibid., p. 370.

38. Michael N. Barnett, *Confronting the Costs of War: Military Power, State and Society in Egypt and Israel* (Princeton: Princeton University Press: 1992).

39. Ibid., chapter 2.

40. Ibid., pp. 31–33.

41. See, for example, Joan M. Nelson, ed. *Economic Crisis and Policy Choice: The Politics of Adjustment in the Third World* (Princeton: Princeton University Press, 1990).

2. The Economy and Economic Policy in Jordan

1. G. John Ikenberry, David A. Lake, and Michael Mastanduno, "Introduction: Approaches to Explaining American Foreign Economic Policy," *International Organization* 42 (1): 4.

2. Jeffry A. Frieden, *Debt, Development, and Democracy: Modern Political Economy*

and Latin America, 1965–1985 (Princeton: Princeton University Press, 1991), chapter 1.

3. A. Konikoff, *Transjordan: An Economic Survey* (Jerusalem: Economic Research Institute for the Jewish Agency for Palestine, 1946) p. 94.

4. Fahd al-Fanek, "Is Jordan Ready for Privatization?" *Jordan Times*, August 31, 1986.

5. *Ibid.*

6. Amman Chamber of Commerce, *Accomplishments and Activities of the Amman Chamber of Commerce During the Period 1983–85* (in Arabic) (Amman, 1986), p. 6.

7. Amman Chamber of Industry, *Amman Chamber of Industry: Organization and Functions* (Amman, 1991) p. 1.

8. Interview with Khaldun Abu Hassan, president of the Amman Chamber of Industry, November 2, 1991.

9. Interview with 'Ali al-Dajani, long-time official of the Amman Chamber of Industry, November 2, 1991.

10. Federation of Jordanian Chambers of Commerce, *Annual Reports*, selected years, 1978–1990.

11. Dajani interview.

12. Interview with former Minister of Labor, former Minister of Supply, and former Minister of Industry and Trade, Jawad 'Anani, July 20, 1992; and interview with Dr. Safwan Bataynah, former economic adviser to Prime Minister Zayd Rifa'i, October 3, 1991.

13. Federation of Jordanian Chambers of Commerce, *Annual Report for the Year 1986* (Amman, 1987), p. 77.

14. Interview with Tawfiq Qa'war, prominent businessman, July 17, 1992.

15. Interview, July 1992.

16. Abu Hassan interview; Dajani interview.

17. Qa'war interview.

18. Qa'war interview.

19. 'Anani interview. This is gradually changing, however, as more businessmen concentrate on a single sector. Moreover, the market is growing and therefore the division of labor between trade and industry is becoming clearer.

20. 'Anani interview.

21. Interview with Dr. Safwan Tuqan, Deputy Minister of Planning, November 19, 1991.

22. Interview with Wasif 'Azir, former director of the Jordan Phosphates Company and General Manager of the Business Bank, Amman June 22, 1992.

23. Interview, summer 1992.

24. Interview with Zaki Ayyubi, prominent businessman, June 23, 1992.

25. Ayyubi interview.

26. Interview with Muhammad 'Asfur, President of the Federation of Jordanian Chambers of commerce, July 15, 1992.

27. Interview with economist Fahd al-Fanek, July 21, 1992.

28. Qa'war interview.

29. Interview with former Foreign Minister and former Prime Minister Tahir

al-Masri, July 14, 1992; interview with Tahir Kan'an, former Minister of Planning and Minister of Occupied Territories Affairs, June 22, 1992.

30. 'Anani interview.

31. Al-Masri interview.

32. One interviewee used the phrase *al-quwa al-muharrikah*, the "driving force" to describe the crown prince's involvement in economic affairs. Another refered to him as *amir al-tanmiyah*, literally, the prince of development.

33. 'Anani interview.

34. Kan'an interview.

35. Al-Fanek interview.

36. Al-Fanek interview.

37. Unpublished opinion piece written by Fahd al-Fanek that was rejected by the Jordanian censor. Photocopy provided the author by Fanek.

38. Al-Fanek interview.

39. For a full discussion, see chapter 6.

40. Economist Intelligence Unit, *Syria and Jordan: Quarterly Economic Report*, no. 4, 1983, p. 24.

41. Federation of Jordanian Chambers of Commerce, *Annual Report for the Year 1986* (in Arabic) (Amman, 1987), p. 35.

42. Tuqan interview; al-Fanek interview.

43. Tuqan interview.

44. Bataynah interview.

45. Al-Masri interview.

46. 'Azir interview.

47. 'Azir interview.

48. Laurie Brand, *Palestinians in the Arab World: Institution Building and the Search for State* (New York: Columbia University Press, 1988), pp. 177–179.

49. 'Azir interview.

50. Interview with Ma'an al-Nusur, Ministry of Planning, November 10, 1991.

51. Al-Masri interview.

52. 'Azir interview.

53. Several unpublished, undated papers provided the background material for this section: "A Pamphlet on the Historical Development of the Planning Apparatus," and "The Experience with Planning in Jordan," both from the Ministry of Planning.

54. Interview with Musa Abu Mayzar, long-time employee of the Ministry of Planning, November 24, 1991.

55. Abu Mayzar interview.

56. Abu Mayzar interview.

57. Interview with the former Head of the National Planning Council and former Minister of Finance Hanna 'Awdah, December 2, 1991.

58. Tuqan interview.

59. Tuqan interview.

60. Interview with Rima Khalaf, Director of the Jordan Trade Centers Corporation, October 26, 1991.

61. Khalaf interview.
62. Tuqan interview.
63. Interview with former Prime Minister Zayd al-Rifa'i, July 11, 1992.
64. Interview with Samir 'Umaysh, Ministry of Industry and Trade, October 5, 1991.
65. Bataynah interview.
66. Interview with Munir Hamarneh, economist at the Council for Arab Economic Unity, Amman, October 7, 1991.
67. 'Asfur interview.
68. See Giacomo Luciani, "Allocation vs. Production States," in Giacomo Luciani ed., *The Arab State* (Los Angeles: University of California Press, 1990), pp. 65–84.

3. Jordanian-Saudi Relations

1. Economist Intelligence Unit, *Saudi Arabia and Jordan: Quarterly Economic Report* (hereafter QER: Saudi Arabia and Jordan), no. 2 (1975): 11.
2. *Middle East Contemporary Survey* (Hereafter *MECS*) 1976–77, p. 59.
3. Foreign Broadcast Information Service/NEA (Hereafter FBIS), June 7, 1977.
4. FBIS, July 7, 1977.
5. QER: Saudi Arabia and Jordan, no. 3 (1977): 14.
6. *Middle East Economics Digest*, hereafter MEED, September 2, 1977.
7. FBIS, October 31, 1977.
8. FBIS, November 21, 1977.
9. FBIS, December 7, 1977.
10. FBIS, September 18, 1978.
11. Nadav Safran, *Saudi Arabia: The Ceaseless Quest for Security* (Cambridge: Harvard University Press, 1985), p. 262.
12. Alan Taylor, *The Arab Balance of Power* (Syracuse: Syracuse University Press, 1982), p. 76.
13. Safran, *Saudi Arabia*, p. 263.
14. Ibid, p. 278.
15. Anthony Cordesman, *Jordanian Arms and the Middle East Balance* (Washington, D.C.: Middle East Institute, 1983), p. 193.
16. Ibid., Table 3, p. 22.
17. Taylor, pp. 76–77.
18. The *hajj* is the pilgrimage to Mecca, the holiest city in Islam.
19. MEED, January 4, and February 8, 1980.
20. Safran, *Saudi Arabia*, p. 369.
21. See chapter 5.
22. *Middle East Contemporary Survey*, 1981–82, pp. 688–89.
23. Royal Scientific Society, *'Alaqat al-Mamlakah al-Urdunniyyah al-Hashimiyyah b-il-Mamlakah al-'Arabiyyah al-Sa'udiyyah, 1978–88* (Amman, 1990), p. 15. (Hereafter, *'Alaqat al-Mamlakah b-il-Mamlakah*).

24. Safran, *Saudi Arabia*, pp. 332–38. The Steadfastness Front comprised Libya, Algeria, Syria, the PLO and the PDRY. Its representatives gathered in Damascus on September 20, 1978, in the wake of the Camp David meetings, to determine ways of confronting its results and to explore the possiblity of setting up a unified military command.

25. Gerd Nonneman, *Administration, Development and Aid in the Middle East*, (New York: Routledge, 1988), pp. 152–55.

26. MEED, January 17, 1975.

27. Economist Intelligence Unit, *Saudi Arabia and Jordan: Quarterly Economic Report*, no.1, 1975, p. 14.

28. MEED, January 2, 1976.

29. MEED, January 16, 1976.

30. MEED, August 1, 1975. See chapter 6.

31. MEED, January 16, 1976.

32. MEED, April 9, 1976.

33. MEED, May 21, 1976.

34. MEED, August 6, 1976.

35. The phrase literally means "If God Wills," but is often used in the Middle East as a way of avoiding committing directly to do something. Interview with former Chief of Jordanian Intelligence and former Prime Minister Mudar Badran. Also FBIS, January 13, 1977.

36. FBIS, January 13, 1977.

37. MEED, January 13, 1977.

38. FBIS, May 17, 1977.

39. MEED, May 20, 1977.

40. MEED, October 3, 1980.

41. "Minutes of the Meeting of the Jordan-Saudi Joint Committee, February 2, 1980," pp. 80–85 in *Majmu'at*.

42. Interview with Sa'd al-Tall, Director-General of the Jordan Petroleum Refineries Company, July 13, 1992.

43. Al-Tall interview.

44. QER: Saudi Arabia and Jordan no. 2 (1975): 17.

45. MEED, June 6, 1975.

46. MEED, March 12, 1976.

47. MEED, March 26, 1976.

48. Al-Tall interview.

49. QER: Saudi Arabia and Jordan no. 2 (1976): 16.

50. MEED, August 12, 1977.

51. *MECS* 1979–80, p. 643.

52. MEED, July 15, 1977.

53. MEED, March 21, 1980.

54. Royal Scientific Society, *'Alaqat al-Mamlakah b-il-Mamlakah*, p. 9.

55. MEED, May 6, 1977.

56. MEED, May 4, 1979.

57. Royal Scientific Society, *'Alaqat al-Mamlakah b-il-Mamlakah*, p. 5.

58. Safran, *Saudi Arabia*, p. 418.

59. *Ibid.*, p. 433.

60. FBIS, April 1, 1982.

61. *Middle East International*, May 17, 1985.

62. *MECS*, 1982–83, pp. 645–46.

63. The *'umra* is pilgrimage made to Mecca at a time other than the formal dates for the pilgrimage in the Islamic calendar.

64. *Middle East International*, January 11, 1985.

65. FBIS, September 9, 1987.

66. MEED, February 3, 1989.

67. FBIS, February 15, 1990.

68. FBIS, May 7, 1990.

69. FBIS, January 7, 1982.

70. MEED, July 13, 1985.

71. FBIS, September 16, 1986.

72. *Middle East International*, December 19, 1987.

73. FBIS, August 4, 1989.

74. MEED, December 19, 1989.

75. MEED, March 2, 1990.

76. MEED, May 18, 1990.

77. The following discussion is taken from "Minutes of the Meeting, July 13, 1975," in *Majmu'at*, pp. 86–95.

78. MEED, May 9, 1987.

79. MEED, September 16, 1987.

80. MEED, July 13, 1987.

81. "The Seventh Round of the Jordanian-Saudi Joint Economic Committee, February 7–8, 1988," photocopy from the Ministry of Industry and Trade.

82. Ibid.

83. "The Eighth Round of the Jordanian-Saudi Joint Economic Committee, October 8–9, 1989," photocopy from the Ministry of Industry and Trade.

84. FBIS, September 24, 1984.

85. MEED, September 7, 1984.

86. MEED, April 5, 1986.

87. Royal Scientific Society, *'Alaqat al-Mamlakah b-il-Mamlakah*, p. 11.

88. "The Seventh Round of the Jordanian-Saudi Joint Economic Committee, February 7–8, 1988."

89. MEED, March 12, 1988.

90. "The Eighth Round of the Joint Jordanian-Saudi Economic Committee, October 8–9, 1989," photocopy from the Ministry of Industry and Trade.

91. MEED, February 3, 1984.

92. MEED, June 15, 1984.

93. Interview with the late Khalil al-Salim, former head of the Senate Finance Committee and former Governor of the Central Bank, October 15, 1991.

94. Interview with former Prime Minister Zayd al-Rifa'i, July 11, 1992.

95. Rifa'i interview; interview with former Foreign Minister and former Prime Minister Tahir al-Masri, July 11, 1992.

96. Rifa'i interview.

4. Jordanian-Kuwaiti Relations

1. Interview with former Prime Minister Zayd al-Rifa'i, July 11, 1992; interview with Bassam al-Sakit, former economic advisor to the crown prince, October 8, 1991.

2. MEED, August 13, 1976.

3. Interview with former Chief of Jordanian Intelligence and former Prime Minister Mudar Badran, July 19, 1992.

4. FBIS, December 19, 1977.

5. FBIS, July 10, 1979.

6. FBIS, July 12, 1979.

7. Royal Scientific Society, 'Alaqat al-Mamlakah al-Urdunniyyah al-Hashimiyyah bi-Dawlat al-Kuwayt, 1978–1988 (Amman, 1990) (hereafter 'Alaqat al-Mamlakah, p. 2.

8. FBIS, May 13, 1980.

9. MEED, May 16, 1980.

10. Royal Scientific Society, 'Alaqat al-Mamlakah, p. 6.

11. MECS, 1981–82, pp. 68–89.

12. FBIS, April 12, 1978.

13. FBIS, December 22, 1977.

14. Anthony Cordesman, Jordanian Arms and the Middle East Balance (Washington, D.C.: Middle East Institute, 1983) Table 3, p. 22.

15. Ibid., p. 184.

16. Abdul-Reda Assiri, Kuwait's Foreign Policy: A City State in World Politics, (Boulder: Westview, 1990), p. 10.

17. Ibid., p. 38.

18. MEES, April 8, 1975.

19. MEED, February 14, 1975.

20. Badran interview.

21. MEED, February 4, 1977.

22. See chapter 3.

23. MEED, May 25, 1979.

24. MEED, June 8, 1979.

25. MEED, June 6, 1975.

26. Statistical Yearbook, selected years.

27. Ibid.

28. "Cooperation Agreement in the Fields of Building and Development, October 29, 1975," in Hashemite Kingdom of Jordan, Ministry of Industry and Trade, Majmu'at al-Ittifaqiyyat al-Iqtisadiyyah w-al-Tujariyyah bayna al-Mamlakah al-Urdunniyyah al-Hashimiyyah w-al-Duwal al-'Arabiyyah [Compendium of Economic

and Trade Agreements between the Hashemite Kingdom of Jordan and the Arab States] Part 2 (Amman: 1985), pp. 245–248. (Hereafter, *Majmu'at* 2).

29. Ibid.
30. MEED. March 12, 1976.
31. MEED, May 6, 1977.
32. MEED, April 1, and May 20, 1977.
33. MEED. October 21, 1977.
34. FBIS, May 31, and June 6, 1977.
35. MEED, July 29, 1977.
36. See Assiri, chapter 4.
37. FBIS, June 5, 1984.
38. *MECS*, 1983–84, p. 139.
39. Assiri, p. 106.
40. FBIS, September 8, 1987.
41. FBIS, October 1, 1987.
42. FBIS, December 11, 1987.
43. FBIS, December 14, 1987.
44. FBIS, December 8, 1988.
45. FBIS, April 24, 1989.
46. FBIS, January 30, 1990.
47. Assiri, p. 79.
48. MEED, June 10, 1983.
49. Royal Scientific Society, *'Alaqat al-Mamlakah*, p. 3.
50. Interview with Sa'd al-Tall, Director-General of the Jordan Petroleum Company, July 13, 1992.
51. Royal Scientific Society, *'Alaqat al-Mamlakah*, p 4.
52. FBIS, October 20, 1986.
53. FBIS, October 29, 1986.
54. Royal Scientific Society, *'Alaqat al-Mamlakah*, p. 4.
55. FBIS, August 11, 1989.
56. MEED, August 25, 1989.
57. Royal Scientific Society, *'Alaqat al-Mamlakah* (1989 supplement) p. 15.
58. MEED. December 15, 1989.
59. FBIS, June 20, 1990.
60. MEED, July 28, 1989.
61. MEED, May 11, 90.
62. *Statistical Yearbook*, 1990.
63. MEED, October 25, 1986.
64. MEED, September 12, 1987.
65. *Statistical Yearbook*, 1990.
66. MEED, February 15, 1985.
67. MEED, June 28, 1986.
68. FBIS, April 28, 1987; MEED, May 2, 1987.
69. MEED, May 16, 1987.
70. MEED, May 6, 1988.

71. MEED, March 31, 1989.

72. MEED, June 22, 1985.

73. MEED, May 31, 1986.

74. MEED, September 1986.

75. Interview with the late Khalil al-Salim, former head of the Jordanian Senate Finance Committee and former Governor of the Central Bank, October 15, 1991.

76. Assiri, p. 47.

77. Ibid., p. 33.

78. Bilal al-Hasan, *Al-Filastiniyyun f-il-Kuwayt*, (Beirut: PLO Research Center, 1974), p. 11, note.

5. Jordanian-Syrian Relations

1. Alan R. Taylor, *The Arab Balance of Power* (Syracuse: Syracuse University Press, 1982), p. 66.

2. Stephen M. Walt, *The Origins of Alliances* (Ithaca: Cornell University Press, 1987), pp. 132 and 151.

3. This section is taken largely from *Masirat al-Takamul bayna Suriya w-al-Urdunn: 'ala Darb al-Wahdah* [The March of Integration between Syria and Jordan: On the Path of Unity], a publication of the Syrian and Jordanian News Agencies, Damascus, 1977. Hereafter, *Masirat.*

4. Interview with former prime minister Zayd al-Rifa'i, July 11, 1992; interview with Muhammad Saqqaf, former adviser on economic unity affairs and Director of the Social Security Corporation, October 23, 1991.

5. Rifa'i interview.

6. *Masirat*, pp. 48–49.

7. See chapter 7.

8. QER: Syria and Jordan, no. 4 (1975): 12.

9. *Masirat*, pp. 106 amd 108.

10. *MECS*, 1976–77, p. 155.

11. MEED, June 11, 1976.

12. Interview with former Chief of the Royal court and Prime Minister Mudar Badran, July 19, 1992; interview with Rifa'i. See also Patrick Seale, *Asad of Syria: The Struggle for the Middle East* (Berkeley: University of California Press, 1988), pp. 275 and 295.

13. *Masirat*, p. 150.

14. FBIS, March 4, 1977.

15. FBIS, March 25, 1977.

16. FBIS, February 10, 1978; FBIS February 15, 1978.

17. FBIS, March 2, 1978.

18. Rifa'i and Badran interviews.

19. "Agreement on Agenda, March 4, 1975," in *Majmu'at* , Part 1, pp. 200–202.

20. Alistair Drysdale, "Political Conflict and Jordanian Access to the Sea," *The Geographical Review* 77 (1): 97.

21. "Agreement on Economic Cooperation and Organization of Trade Exchange, April 6, 1975," in *Majmu'at*, 1: 203–208.

22. "Commmunique of the Joint Jordanian-Syrian Higher Committee, July 30, 1975," in *Majmu'at*, 1: 212–218.

23. "Communique of the Joint Jordanian-Syrian Higher Committee, October 27, 1975," in *Majmu'at*, 1: 221–226.

24. "Communique of the Joint Jordanian-Syrian Higher Committee, August 26, 1976," in *Majmu'at*, 1: 238–241.

25. FBIS, January 3, 1977.

26. "Agreement on Agenda, March 4, 1975," pp. 200–202.

27. "Communique of the Joint Jordanian-Syrian Higher Committee, August 26, 1975," in *Majmu'at*, 1:238–241.

28. The shares in the company were owned in equal numbers by the two governments. The company's capital exceeded 60 million Syrian Lira from the two sides and the council running the company was composed of six people. The general assembly of the company was composed of the board of directors and the ministers of economy and foreign trade of the two countries.

29. *Masirat*, pp. 50–51.

30. "Communique of the Joint Jordanian-Syrian Higher Committee, May 15, 1976," pp. 234–237 and Communique of the Joint Jordanian-Syrian Higher Committee, August 26, 1976," pp. 238–241; and "Communiqe of the Joint Jordanian-Syrian Higher Committee," November 22, 1976, pp. 242–248; in *Majmu'at*, 1.

31. FBIS, January 18, 1977.

32. FBIS, May 31, 1977.

33. Ewan Anderson,"Water: The Next Strategic Resource," in Joyce R. Starr and Daniel C. Stoll eds., *The Politics of Scarcity: Water in the Middle East* (Boulder: Westview with the Center for Strategic and International Studies, 1988), p. 7.

34. Selig A. Taubenblatt, "Jordan River Basin Water: A Challenge in the 1990s," in Ibid., p. 47.

35. "Agreement on Agenda, March 4, 1975,"

36. "Communique of the Joint Jordanian-Syrian Higher Committee, August 26, 1975," in *Majmu'at*, 1: 238–241.

37. MEED, June 10, 1977.

38. QER: Syria and Jordan, no. 3 (1980): 15.

39. FBIS, March 9, 1978.

40. FBIS, September 21, 1978.

41. Comprising Libya, Algeria, Syria, the PLO and the PDRY, this grouping gathered in Damascus on September 20, 1978, in the wake of Camp David, to determine ways of confronting the results of the September meetings and to explore the possibility of setting up a unified military command.

42. FBIS, November 3, 1978.

43. Badran interview.

44. Interview with former Chief of Jordanian Intelligence and Former Prime Minister Ahmad 'Ubaydat, July 14, 1992.

45. Badran interview.

46. 'Ubaydat interview.

47. MEED, December 7, 1979.

48. Badran interview.

49. FBIS, May 19, 1980.

50. Rifa'i interview.

51. Rifa'i interview.

52. FBIS, May 22, 1980.

53. *Jordan Times* September 16, 1980.

54. FBIS, November 19, 1980.

55. FBIS, November 21, 1980.

56. The numbers of troops deployed vary from account to account. These figures are from *The New York Times* of November 26, 1980.

57. FBIS, December 4, 1980.

58. "Syria, Taking a Hard, Long Look at the Economy," MEED, May 22, 1981.

59. Interviews with Rifa'i and Badran.

60. QER: Syria and Jordan, no. 4 (1980): 14.

61. Badran interview. Interview with former Foreign Minister and former Prime Minister Tahir al-Masri, July 14, 1992.

62. See chapter 6.

63. Amatzia Baram, "Baathi Iraq and Hashemite Jordan: From Hostility to Alignment," *Middle East Journal*, 45 (1): 55.

64. MEED, March 11, 1983.

65. QER: Syria and Jordan, no. 3 (1983): 17.

66. Department of Statistics, Hashemite Kingdom of Jordan, *Statistical Yearbook, 1983.*

67. MEED, May 16, 1980.

68. MEED, December 5, 1980.

69. "Jordanian-Syrian Trade Survives War of Words," MEED, February 20, 1981.

70. "Syria, Taking a Hard Long Look at the Economy," MEED, May 22, 1981.

71. Hashemite Kingdom of Jordan, Department of General Statistics, *Annual Statistical Report, 1983.*

72. MEED, November 12, 1982.

73. MEED, July 21, 1978.

74. MEED, January 6, 1978.

75. MEED, November 3, 1978.

76. MEED, June 30, 1979.

77. MEED, May 14, 1982.

78. MEED, September 3, 1982.

79. Patrick Seale uses this phrase in *Asad of Syria* (p.465), but attributes it to Gerard Chaliand, note 3, p. 519.

80. For a study of the economic effects of the border closure in 1970 see Bassam al-Sakit, "Tahlil al-Athar al-Iqtisadiyyah li-Ighlaq al-Hudud al-Suriyyah ma'a al-Urdunn," unpublished study of the Central Bank of Jordan, no date.

81. FBIS, June 6 and 15, 1984.
82. FBIS, July 24, 1984.
83. FBIS, July 31, 1984.
84. FBIS, November 7, 1984.
85. MEED, November 25, 1984.
86. MEED, September 21, 1985.
87. "The Asad Factor," *The Middle East,* January 1986.
88. MEED, July 27, 1985.
89. FBIS, October 22, 1985.
90. FBIS, November 12, 1985.
91. FBIS, May 24, 1984.
92. FBIS, April 27, 1984.
93. FBIS, May 1, 1985.
94. FBIS, May 1, 1985.
95. FBIS, September 24, 1985.
96. FBIS, December 13, 1985.
97. MEED, December 14, 1985.
98. FBIS, December 11, 1985.
99. MEED, July 20, 1984.
100. *Middle East International,* May 16, 1986.
101. FBIS, August 19, 1987.
102. FBIS, November 27, 1987.
103. *Al-Dustur,* August 16, 1988.
104. MEED, December 2, 1988.
105. FBIS, February 17, 1989.
106. FBIS, March 25, 1986.
107. MEED, June 28, 1986.
108. MEED, August 12, 1988; and FBIS, July 28, 1988.
109. *Statistical Yearbook, 1990;* FBIS, August 2, 1989.
110. Federation of Jordanian Chambers of Commerce, "Annual Report for 1989," (in Arabic) (Amman: April 1990), p. 75
111. FBIS, February 25, 1986.
112. MEED, June 27, 1987.
113. MEED, January 23, 1988.
114. *MECS,* 1987, p. 647.
115. FBIS, August 19, 1987.
116. FBIS, September 4 and 8, 1987.
117. *Middle East International,* September 12, 1987.
118. MEED, October 21, 1988.
119. FBIS, September 5, 1989.
120. MEED, July 27, 1990.
121. Saqqaf interview.
122. Saqqaf interview.
123. Interview with Bassam al-Saket, former economic adviser to the Crown Prince, October 8, 1991.

124. Saqqaf interview.

125. Saket interview.

126. Interviews with Rifa'i and Badran.

6. Jordanian-Iraqi Relations

1. Amatzia Baram, "Baathi Iraq and Hashemite Jordan: From Hostility to Alignment," *Middle East Journal* 45 (1): 52. Peter and Marian Sluglett argue that Iraq's failure to support the PLO in 1970 was the foundation of the close relationship between Saddam Husayn and King Husayn. See their *Iraq since 1958: From Reevolution to Dictatorship* (New York: KPI, 1987), pp. 132–134.

2. QER: Iraq, no. 1 (1975): 5.

3. MEED, May 28, 1976.

4. MEED, November 5, 1976.

5. QER: Iraq, no. 4, 1976, p. 5.

6. QER: Iraq, no. 1, 1975, p. 6.

7. *MECS*, 1976–77, p. 487.

8. Even in the 1950s Jordan had looked to Iraq for financial support, and there had been discussions of unity between the two well before the 1958 Syrian-Egyptian union triggered the announcement of the Hashemite Union in February 1958.)

9. QER: Iraq, no. 4, 1977, p. 7.

10. FBIS, October 11, 1977.

11. MEED, December 15, 1978.

12. FBIS, October 2, 1978.

13. Interview with former Foreign Minister and Prime Minister Tahir al-Masri, July 14, 1992.

14. Interview with former head of Jordanian Intelligence and former Prime Minister Mudar Badran, July 19, 1992.

15. Badran interview.

16. MEED, July 4, 1975.

17. "Protocol Adjusting the Economic and Technical Agreement between the Republic of Iraq and the Hashemite Kingdom of Jordan, June 26, 1975," p. 68 in Hashemite Kingdom of Jordan, Ministry of Industry and Trade, *Majmu'at*, 2.

18. MEED, February 27, 1976.

19. MEES, March 24, 1976.

20. MEED, August 19, 1977.

21. QER: Iraq, no. 4, 1978, p. 11.

22. It is not always clear in documents or journalistic reports whether the dinar in question is Jordanian or Iraqi. At the time, the Jordanian dinar was worth about US $2.80 to $3.00 and the Iraqi dinar about US $3.30.

23. FBIS, December 26, 1978.

24. Department of General Statistics, Hashemite Kingdom of Jordan, *Statistical Yearbook, 1980*.

25. MEES, May 21, 1975.

26. "Minutes of the Meeting of the Joint Jordanian-Iraqi Committee, June 27, 1975," in *Majmu'at*, 2: 69–71.

27. *Statistical Yearbook, 1980*.

28. "Minutes of the Meeting of the Joint Jordanian-Iraqi Committee, March 21, 1976," in *Majmu'at*, 2: 72–75.

29. FBIS, April 21, 1978.

30. MEED, July 4, 1975.

31. *Ibid.*

32. "Minutes of the Meeting of the Joint Jordanian-Iraqi Committee, June 27, 1975," in *Majmu'at*, 2: 70.

33. "Minutes of the Meeting of the Joint Jordanian-Iraqi Committee, 7–May 12, 1977," in *Majmu'at*, 2: 84–88.

34. MEES, March 31, 1975.

35. MEED, June 13, 1975.

36. "Agreement on Economic and Technical Cooperation between the Republic of Iraq and the Hashemite Kingdom of Jordan, June 26, 1975," in *Majmu'at*, 2:65–67.

37. H-5 is a small town that developed around one of the pumping stations on the old Iraq Petroleum Company pipeline in eastern Jordan near the Iraqi border.

38. MEED, November 21, 1975.

39. MEED, August 19, 1977.

40. FBIS, February 16, 1978.

41. "Minutes of the Meeting of the Joint Jordanian-Iraqi Committee, April 1978," in *Majmu'at*, 2: 97–113.

42. MEED, February 29, 1980.

43. QER: Iraq, no. 3 (1980): 8.

44. Alan Taylor, *The Arab Balance of Power*, (Syracuse: Syracuse University Press, 1982), p. 87.

45. *Ibid.*, p. 88.

46. Royal Scientific Society, *Al-'Alaqat al-Urdunniyyah li-Duwal Majlis al-Ta'awun al-'Arabi, 1974–1989* [Jordan's Relations with the States of the Arab Cooperation Council], (Amman: n.d.), p. 5. (Hereafter *Al-'Alaqat al-Urdunniyyah.*

47. MEED, February 29, 1980.

48. MEED, May 9, 1980.

49. Royal Scientific Society, *Al-'Alaqat al-Urdunniyyah*, p. 5.

50. QER: Iraq, no. 4 (1980): 12.

51. Royal Scientific Society, *Al-'Alaqat al-Urdunniyah*, p. 5.

52. *Ibid.*, p. 5; MEED, September 19, 1980.

53. MEED, September 26, 1980.

54. MEED, March 30, 1979.

55. MEED, April 13, 1979.

56. MEED, May 2, 1980.

57. MEED, October 3, 1980.

58. "Minutes of the Meeting of the Joint Jordanian-Iraqi Committee, March 14, 1979,"

in *Majmu'at*, 2: 120.

59. MEED, November 21, 1980.

60. "Developments in the Meeting of the Joint Jordanian-Iraqi Industrial Committee,

September 14, 1980," in *Majmu'at*, 2: 168–170.

61. MEED, February 1, 1980.

62. MEED, February 29, 1980.

63. MEED, April 25, 1980.

64. FBIS, February 20, 1980.

65. "Agreement on Economic and Technical Cooperation Between the Hashemite Kingdom of Jordan and the Republic of Iraq, May 2, 1980," in *Majmu'at*, 2: 155–161.

66. MEED, November 14, 1980.

67. MEED, August 29, 1980.

68. W. Andrew Terrill, "Saddam's Closet Ally: Jordan and the Gulf War," *Journal of South Asian and Middle Eastern Studies* 9 (2): 46–47.

69. See chapter 5.

70. FBIS, February 9, 1982.

71. *MECS*, 1982–83, p. 644.

72. QER: Iraq, no. 3, 1982, p. 13.

73. *Ibid.*, no. 1, 1983, p. 11.

74. FBIS, November 25, 1983.

75. FBIS, March 22, 1984.

76. FBIS, October 9, 1984.

77. FBIS, October 8, 1984.

78. FBIS, January 6, 1981.

79. FBIS, February 23, 1981.

80. Royal Scientific Society, *Al-'Alaqat al-Urdunniyyah*, p. 6.

81. "Minutes of the Meeting of the Joint Jordanian-Iraqi Committee, October 24–26, 1981," in *Majmu'at*, 2: 197.

82. MEED, November 13, 1981.

83. MEED, September 11, 1981.

84. MEED, May 22, 1981.

85. MEED July 10, 1981.

86. MEED, September 24, 1982.

87. *Statistical Yearbook, 1983.*

88. Phoebe Marr, *The Modern History of Iraq* (Boulder: Westview, 1985), p. 301.

89. *Statistical Yearbook, 1990.*

90. MEED, September 9, 1983. The drop in Arab aid to Iraq resulted from the decline in liquidity experienced by the Gulf states as a result in the drop in oil prices during this period.

91. MEED, August 10, 1983.

92. MEED, September 30, 1983.

93. MEED, January 6, 1984.

94. MEED, February 3, 1984.

95. MEED, May 18, 1984.

96. "Minutes of the Meeting of the Joint Jordanian-Iraqi Committee, April 12, 1981," in *Majmu'at*, 2: 176–187.

97. MEED, October 1, 1982.

98. QER: Iraq, no. 1. 1981, p. 7.

99. MEED, January 2, 1981.

100. MEED, March 13, 1981.

101. "Minutes of the Meeting of the Joint Jordanian-Iraqi Committee, October 26, 1981," in *Majmu'at*, 2:191.

102. MEED, June 4, 1982.

103. MEED, August 13, 1982.

104. MEED, March 25, 1983.

105. MEED, November 28, 1980.

106. MEED, August 12, 1981.

107. Marr, p. 292.

108. FBIS February 23, 1983.

109. FBIS, May 21, 1984.

110. FBIS, August 13, 1984.

111. FBIS, May 24, 1984.

112. MEED, March 30, 1984.

113. FBIS, June 13, 1984.

114. MEED, June 15, 1984.

115. MEED, June 22, 1984.

116. FBIS, August 13, 1984.

117. FBIS, August 14, 1984.

118. FBIS, September 27, 1984.

119. "Minutes of the meeting of the Joint Jordanian-Iraqi Committee, October 24–26, 1981," in *Majmu'at*, 2: 196.

120. MEED, March 12, 1982.

121. MEED, October 12, 1984.

122. FBIS, March 19, 1985.

123. FBIS, December 22, 1985.

124. FBIS, December 23, 1985.

125. Ibid., p. 10.

126. MEED, November 9, 1984.

127. *The Middle East*, October 1985, p. 46.

128. FBIS, January 24, 1985.

129. "Minutes of Meetings of the Fifth Round of the Joint Jordanian-Iraqi Ministerial Committee, January 21, 1985," in *Majmu'at*, 2: 226.

130. *Statistical Yearbook, 1990.*

131. FBIS, December 17, 1986.

132. FBIS, December 15, 1987.

133. *Statistical Yearbook, 1990.*

134. FBIS, May 12, 1988.

135. MEED, May 13, 1988.

136. MEED, May 13, 1988.

137. MEED, May 27, 1988.

138. MEED, June 17, 1988.

139. MEED, November 4, 1988.

140. FBIS, September 21, 1988.

141. MEED, August 23, 1986.

142. MEED, February 27, 1988.

143. MEED, January 18, 1985.

144. FBIS, April 3, 1986.

145. FBIS September 27, 1988.

146. FBIS, January 24, 1985.

147. MEED, August 17, 1985.

148. Interview with Sa'd al-Tall, Director-General of the Jordan Petroleum Refineries Company, July 13, 1992.

149. MEED, January 18, 1986.

150. MEED, May 10, 1986.

151. FBIS, August 31, 1988.

152. FBIS, 12 and December 15, 1988.

153. *MECS, 1989,* p. 470.

154. Ibid.

155. FBIS, January 16, 1990.

156. FBIS, January 24, 1990.

157. FBIS, January 29, 1990.

158. FBIS, February 20, 1990.

159. FBIS, February 20, 1990.

160. MEED, June 15, 1990.

161. FBIS, June 1, 1990.

162. FBIS, December 19, 1988.

163. MEED, January 12, 1990.

164. FBIS, January 4, 1989.

165. FBIS, January 24, 1989.

166. FBIS, April 25, 1990.

167. FBIS, June 25, 1989.

168. FBIS, August 18, 1989.

169. FBIS, August 11, 1989.

170. Interview with Bassam al-Sakit, former economic advisor to the Crown Prince and Director-General of the Jordan Cement Company, October 8, 1991.

171. Christine Moss Helms, *Iraq: Eastern Flank of the Arab World* (Washington, D.C.: Brookings, 1984), p. 12.

172. Stephen M. Walt, *The Origins of Alliances* (Ithaca: Cornell University Press, 1987), p. 145.

7. Jordanian-Egyptian Relations

1. See Alan Taylor, *The Arab Balance of Power* (Syracuse: Syracuse University Press, 1982), chapter 5.

2. QER: Egypt, no. 1, 1975, p. 5.

3. FBIS, January 17, 1977.

4. *MECS*, 1976–77, p. 158.

5. FBIS, November 29, 1977.

6. FBIS, December 9, 1977.

7. FBIS, January 9, 1978.

8. FBIS, September 20, 1978.

9. *Statistical Yearbook*, 1979.

10. "Protocol number 4, November 21, 1975," pp. 337–38 and "Protocol number 3, October 31, 1974, pp. 325–26, in Ministry of Trade and Industry, Hashemite Kingdom of Jordan, *Majmu'at*, 1.

11. FBIS, February 17, 1977.

12. FBIS, September 26, 1978.

13. *Statistical Yearbook*, 1983.

14. "Protocol number 4, November 21, 1975," p. 352, in *Majmu'at.*

15. Royal Scientific Society, *Al'Alaqat al-Urdunniyyah li-Duwal Majlis al-Ta'awun al-'Arabi, 1974–1989* [Jordan's Relations with the States of the Arab Cooperation Council] (Amman, 1990), p.36.

16. Interview with former Chief of Jordanian Intelligence and former Prime Minister Mudar Badran, July 19, 1992; interview with former Chief of Jordanian Intelligence and former Prime Minister Ahmad 'Ubaydat, July 14, 1992.

17. FBIS, January 7, 1982.

18. FBIS, January 19, 1982.

19. Royal Scientific Society, *Al-'Alaqat al-Urdunniyyah*, p.32.

20. FBIS, November 2, 1982.

21. FBIS, October 12, 1983.

22. FBIS, October 21, 1983.

23. FBIS, November 23, 1983.

24. *Middle East International,* January 27, 1984,

25. 'Ubaydat interview.

26. FBIS, September 26, 1984.

27. 'Ubaydat interview.

28. FBIS, September 28, 1984.

29. Interview with former Foreign Minister and former Prime Minister Tahir al-Masri, July 14, 1992.

30. MEED, August 17, 1979.

31. MEED, May 25, 1979.

32. MEED, May 25, 1979.

33. *Statistical Yearbook*, 1983.

34. Royal Scientific Society, *Al-Alaqat al-Urdunniyyah*, p. 27.

35. FBIS, January 7, 1982.

36. Royal Scientific Society, *Al-'Alaqat al-Urdunniyyah,* p. 27.

37. FBIS, April 9, 1983.

38. MEED, March 11, 1983.

39. QER: Egypt, no. 2, 1983, p. 21.

40. MEED, April 15, 1983.

41. MEED, December 2, 1983.

42. "Letter Number 2, December 25, 1983" and "Letter Number 3, December 25, 1983," in *Majmu'at,* 1: 403 and 405.

43. FBIS, December 23, 1983.

44. FBIS, August 3, 1984.

45. *Statistical Yearbook,* 1990.

46. FBIS, September 25, 1984.

47. FBIS, October 15, 1984.

48. FBIS, October 26, 1984.

49. FBIS, October 16, 1984.

50. "Chronology," *Middle East Journal,* January 30, 1985.

51. FBIS, May 6, 1985.

52. FBIS, November 25, 1985.

53. *MECS,* 1986, p. 457.

54. Royal Scientific Society, *Al-'Alaqat al-Urdunniyyah,* p. 40.

55. See Chapter on Iraq.

56. FBIS, October 30, 1984.

57. FBIS, October 22, 1984.

58. *Statistical Yearbook,* selected years. Jordan exported $4.5 million of goods to Egypt, while Egypt sold $25.5 million to Jordan.

59. "Minutes of the Meeting of October 22–25, 1984," in *Majmu'at,* 1: 407–409.

60. FBIS, October 30, 1984.

61. MEED, December 14, 1984.

62. FBIS, April 4, 1985.

63. *Statistical Yerabook,* 1990.

64. MEED, April 26, 1985.

65. "Qararat al-Lajnah al-'Uliya al-Misriyyah al-Urdunniyyah al-Mushtarikah fi-Dawratiha al-Thaminah, Amman, 29–July 31, 1988" [Decisions of the Egyptian-Jordanian Higher Joint Committee]." Unpublished paper from the Jordanian Ministry of Industry and Trade.

66. MEED, August 12, 1988.

67. FBIS, January 30, 1989.

68. FBIS, July 15, 1990.

69. *Statistical Yearbook,* 1990.

70. MEED, March 8, 1985.

71. FBIS, April 22, 1985.

72. FBIS, January 31, 1985.

73. MEED, April 12, and July 26, 1986.

74. MEED, September 5, 1987.

75. FBIS, July 26, 1989.

76. MEED, March 22, 1985.

77. MEED, June 15, 1985.

78. MEED, July 13, 1985.

79. FBIS, November 23, 1987.

80. MEED, September 23, 1987 and June 23, 1989.

81. FBIS, February 1, 1985.

82. MEED, January 17, 1987.

83. MEED, July 7, 1989.

84. Interview with Michel Marto, Deputy-governor of the Central Bank of Jordan, October 30, 1991.

85. Interview with Raja'i al-Mu'ashshir, former Minister of Industry and Trade, October 14, 1991.

86. Interview with Mansur Abu Hammud, former commercial attache to the Jordanian Embassy in Cairo, October 16, 1991.

87. Mu'ashshir interview.

88. Abu Hammud interview.

89. See David Baldwin, *Economic Statecraft*, (Princeton: Princeton University Press, 1985), chapter 9.

8. Budget Security and Its Broader Applicability

1. *Middle East Economic Survey* (Hereafter MEES) no. 33, 1989, p. 47.

2. *Washington Post*, January 9, 1990.

3. MEES, no. 33. 1989, p. 47.

4. MEED, August 31, 1990.

5. See Laurie A. Brand, "Liberalization and Changing Political Coalitions: The Bases of Jordan's 1990-91 Gulf Crisis Policy," *Jerusalem Journal of International Relations*, 13 (4): 1–46.

6. See D. Williams, "Arab Truck Drivers Stalled by UN Sanctions," *Los Angeles Times*, September 21, 1990; see also Prince Hasan's news conference on August 15, 1990, in FBIS, August 20, 1990, and Husayn's interview on October 2,, in FBIS, October 3, 1990.

7. Interview with Jordanian official, fall 1991.

8. See, for example, Eberhard Kienle's *Ba'th v. Ba'th: The Conflict between Syria and Iraq 1968-1989* (New York: I.B. Tauris, 1990), chapter 4.

9. Ali E. Dessouki, "The Primacy of Economics: The Foreign Policy of Egypt," in Korany and Dessouki eds., *The Foreign Policy of Arab States* (Boulder: Westview, 1991) second edition, p. 161.

10. Ibid., p. 162.

Bibliography

Periodicals

Annual Report of the Federation of Jordanian Chambers of Commerce (in Arabic)
Al-Dustur
FBIS
Jordan Times
Middle East Contemporary Survey
Middle East Economic Digest
Middle East Economic Survey
Middle East Journal
Middle East International
Middle East Report
Quarterly Economic Report, Economist Intelligence Unit
Al-Ra'i
Statistical Yearbook, Department of Statistics, Hashemite Kingdom of Jordan
Yearly Statistical Series, Central Bank of Jordan

Articles

Altfeld, Michael F. "The Decision to Ally: A Theory and a Test." *Western Political Quarterly*, 37 (4) (December 1984): 523–544.

Armstrong, Adrienne. "The Political Consequences of Economic Dependence." *Journal of Conflict Resolution* 25 (3) (September 1981): 401–428.

Ayoob, Mohammed. "The Security Problematic of the Third World." *World Politics* 43 (2) (January 1991): 258–283.

Baldwin, David A. "Foreign Aid, Intervention, and Influence." *World Politics* 21 (3) (April 1969): 425–447.

Baram, Amatzia. "Baathi Iraq and Hashemite Jordan: From Hostility to Alignment." *Middle East Journal* 45 (1) (Winter 1991): 51–70.

Barnett, Michael N. and Jack S. Levy. "Domestic Sources of Alliances and Alignments: the Case of Egypt, 1962–73." *International Organization* 45 (3) (Summer 1991): 369–395.

Bienen, Henry S. and Mark Gersovitz, "Economic Stabilization, Conditionality, and Political Stability." *International Organization,* 39 (4) (Autumn 1985): 729–754.

Brand, Laurie A. "Liberalization and Changing Political Coalitions: The Bases of Jordan's 1990–91 Gulf Crisis Policy." *Jerusalem Journal of International Relations* 13 (4) 1991: 1- 46.

—. "Economic and Political Development in a Rentier State: The Case of the Hashimite Kingdom of Jordan." in Iliya Harik and Denis Sullivan eds., *Privatization and Liberalization in the Middle East* (Bloomington: Indiana University Press, 1992)

Brecher, Michael, Blema Steinberg and Janice Stein. "A Framework for Research on Foreign Policy Behavior." *Journal of Conflict Resolution* xiii (March 1969): 75–101.

Brecher, Michael. "The Middle East Subordinate system and its impacton Israel's foreign policy." *International Studies Quarterly* 13 (2) (1969): 117–139.

Caporaso, James. "Dependence, Dependency, and Power in the Global System: A Structural and Behavioral Analysis." *International Organization,* 32 (1) (1978): 13–43.

—. "Dependency Theory: Continuities and Discontinuities in Development Studies." *International Organization* 34 (4) (1980): 605–628

Chalala, Elie. "Syrian Policy in Lebanon, 1976–1984: Moderate Goals and Pragmatic Means." *Journal of Arab Affairs,* 4 (1) (spring 1985): 67- 88.

David, Steven R. "Explaining Third World Alignment." *World Politics* 43 (2) (January 1991): 233–256.

—. "Why the Third World Matters." *International Secuerity,* 14 (1): 50–85.

Dawisha, Adeed I. "Internal Values and External Threats: The Making of Saudi Foreign Policy." *Orbis* 23 (1) (Spring 1979): 129–144.

Dolan, Michael B., Brian W. Tomlin, Maureen Appel Molot, and Harald Von-Riekhoff. "Foreign Policies of African States in Asymmetrical Dyads." *International Studies Quarterly* 24 (3) (September 1980): 415–449.

Drysdale, Alistair. "Political Conflict and Jordanian Access to the Sea." *The Geographical Review* 77 (1) (January 1987): 86–102.

East, Maurice. "Size and Foreign Policy Behavior: At Test of Two Models." *World Politics* vol. 25 (1973): 556–576.

—. "Foreign Policy making in Small States: Some Theoretic Observations Based on A Study of the Uganda Ministry of Foreign Affairs." *Policy Sciences* 4 (1973): 491–508.

El-Mallakh, Ragae and Mihssen Kadhim. "Arab Institutionalized Development Aid" *Middle East Journal* 30 (4) (1976): 471–484.

Evron, Yair and Yaacov Bar Simatov. "Coalitions in the Arab World." *Jerusalem Journal of International Relations,* 1 (2) (Winter 1975): 71–107.

Farsoun, Samih K. "Oil, State, and Social Structure in the Middle East."*Arab Studies Quarterly* 10 (2) (Spring 1988): 155–175.

Garnham, David. "Explaining Midle Eastern Alignments During the Gulf War." *Jerusalem Journal of International Relations,* 13 (3) (1991): 63–83.

Garfinckle, Adam M. "Negotiating By Proxy: Jordanian Foreign Policy and U.S. Options in the Middle East." *Orbis* 24 (4) (Winter 1981): 847–880.

Gourevitch, Peter. "International Trade, Domestic Coalitions, and Liberty."*Journal of Interdisciplinary History,* 7 (2) (Autumn 1977): 281–313.

—. "The Second Image Reversed: The International Sources of Domestic Politics." 32 (4) (Autumn 1978): 881–912.

Green, Jerrold D. "Is Arab Politics Still Arab?" *World Politics* 38 (4) (July 1986): 611–625.

Ikenberry, G. John, David A. Lake, and Michael Mastanduno. "Introduction: Approaches to Explaining American Foreign Economic Policy." *International Organization* 42 (1) (Winter 1988): 1–14.

Jreisat, Jamil E. and Hanna Y. Freij, "Jordan, the United States, and the Gulf Crisis." *Arab Studies Quarterly* 13 (1&2) (Winter/Spring 1991): 101–116.

Kaplan, S. "United States Aid and Regime Maintenance in Jordan 1957–1973."*Public Policy* 23 (2) (1975): 189–218.

Keohane, Robert O. "Lilliputians' Dilemmas: Small States in International Politics." *International Organization* 23 (Spring 1969): 291–310.

Kolodziej, Edward A. "Renaissance in Security Studies? Caveat Lector!" *international Studies Quarterly* (1992) 35: 421–438.

Korany, Bahgat. "Dependance financiere et comportement international." *Revue Francaise de science politique* xxviii (December 1978): 1067- 1092.

—. "The Take-Off of Third World Studies?: The Case of Foreign Policy." *World Politics* 35 (3) (April 1983): 465–487.

Krasner, Stephen. "State Power and the Structure of International Trade." *World Politics* vol. 28 (3) (1976): 317–347.

Lawson, Fred H. "Syrian Intervention in Lebanon: A Domestic Politics Explanation." *International Organization* 38 (3) (Summer 1984): 451–480.

Looney, Robert E. "Structural and Economic Change in the Arab Gulf After 1973." *Middle Eastern Studies* 26 (4) (October 1990): 514–535.

Luciani, Giacomo. "The Economic Content of Security." *Journal of Public Policy* 8 (2): 151–173.

Mathews, Jessica Tuchman. "Redefining Security." *Foreign Affairs,* 68 (2): 162–177.

Migdal, Joel. "Internal Structure and External Behavior: Explaining Foreign Policies of Third World States." *International Relations* 4 (May 1974): 510–525.

Mytelka, Lynn K. "The Salience of Gains in Third-World Integrative Systems." *World Politics* 25 (2) (January 1973): 236–250.

Moon, Bruce. "The Foreign Policy of the Dependent State" *International Studies Quarterly,* 27 (3) (September 1983): 315–340.

—. "Consensus or Compliance? Foreign Policy Change andExternal Dependence." *International Organization,* 39 (2) (Spring 1985): 297–329.

Nye, Joseph S. amd Sean M. Lynn-Jones. "International Security Studies: A Report of a Conference on the State of the Field." *International Security* 12 (4): 5–27.

Olson, Mancur and Richard Zeckhauser. "An Economic Theory of Alliances." *Review of Economics and Statistics* 48 no. 3 (1966): 266–279.

Putnam, Robert D. "Diplomacy and Domestic Politics: the Logic of Two-Level Games." *International Organization* 42 (3) (Summer 1988): 427–460.

Richardson, Neil. "Oil and Middle Eastern Politics." 13 (3) (1991): 34–44.

Rothstein, Robert L. "The 'Security Dilemma' and the 'Poverty Trap' in the Third World." *The Jerusalem Journal of International Relations* 8 (4) (1986): 1–38.

Sayigh, Yezid. "The Gulf Crisis: Why the Arab Regional Order Failed." *International Affairs* 76 (3) (July 1991): 487–508.

Skocpol, Theda. "Rentier States and Shi'a Islam in the Iranian Revolution." *Theory and Society* 11 (3) (May 1982): 265–284.

Snyder, Glenn. "The Security Dilemma in Alliance Politics." *World Politics* 36 (4) (July 1984): 461- 495.

—. "Alliances, Balance, and Stability." *International Organization* 45 (1) (Winter 1991): 121–142.

Stein, Janice Gross. "Deterrence and Compellence in the Gulf, 1990–91: A Failed or Impossible Task?" *International Security* 17 (2) (Fall 1992): 147–179.

Terrill, W. Andrew. "Saddam's Closet Ally: Jordan and the Gulf War." *Journal of south Asian and Middle Eastern Studies* 9 (2) (Winter 1985): 43–54.

—. "Jordan and the Defense of the Gulf." *Middle East Insight*, 4 (1) (March/April 1985): 34–41.

Tessler, Mark. "Center and Periphery within Regional International Systems: The Case of the Arab World." *Jerusalem Journal of International Relations*, 11 (3) (1989): 74–89.

Tetreault, Mary Ann. "Autonomy, Necessity, and the Small State: RulingKuwait in the Twentieth Century." *International Organization* 45 (4) (Autumn 1991): 565–591.

Thompson, William R. "Delineating Regional Sub-systems: Visit Networks and the Middle Eastern Case." *International Journal of Middle East Studies*, 13 (1981): 213–235.

Turner, Louis and James Bedore. "The Trade Politics of Middle Eastern Industrialization." *Foreign Affairs*, 57 (2) (Winter 1978/79): 306–22.

Ullman, Richard H. "Redefining Security." *International Security*, 8 (1): 129–153.

Walt, Stephen M. "The Renaissance of Security Studies." *International Studies Quarterly*, 35 (2): 211–239.

Weinstein, Franklin. "The Uses of Foreign Policy in Indonesia." *World Politics* 24 (3) (April 1972): 356–381.

Wilkenfeld, Jonathan, Virginia Lee Lussier, and Dale Tahtinen. " Conflict Interactions in the Middle East." *Conflict Resolution*, 16 (2): 135–154.

Books

Abu Jaber, Kamel, Matthes Buhbe, and Mohammad Smadi. *Income Distribution in Jordan*. Boulder: Westview, 1990.

Al-Ebraheem, Hassan Ali. *Kuwait and the Gulf: Small States and the International System*. Washington, D.C.: Center for Contemporary Arab Studies, Georgetown University, 1984.

Amman Chamber of Industry. *Amman Chamber of Industry: Organization and Functions*. Amman, 1991.

Assiri, Abdul-Reda. *Kuwait's Foreign Policy: City State in World Politics*. Boulder: Westview, 1990.

Badran, Adnan and Bichara Khader. *The Economic Development of Jordan*. London: Croom Helm, 1988.

Baldwin, David. *Economic Statecraft*. Princeton: Princeton University Press, 1985.

Barnett, Michael L. *Confronting the Costs of War: Military Power, State, and Society in Egypt and Israel*. Princeton: Princeton University Press, 1992.

Beblawi, Hazem and Giacomo Luciani. *The Rentier State*. New York: Croom Helm, 1987.

Binder, Leonard. *The Ideological Revolution in the Middle East*. New York: Krieger, 1979

Brand, Laurie A. *Palestinians in the Arab World: Institution Building and the Search for State*. New York: Columbia University Press, 1988

Brown, L. Carl. *International Politics and the Middle East: Old Rules, Dangerous Game*. Princeton: Princeton University Press, 1984.

Buzan, Barry. *People States & Fear: An Agenda For International Security Studies in the Post-Cold War Era*. Boulder: Lynne Reinner, 1991.

Cantori, Louis and Steven Spiegel. *The International Politics of Regions*. New Jersey: Prentice-Hall, 1970.

Cordesman, Anthony. *Jordanian Arms and the Middle East Balance*. Washington, D.C.: Middle East Institute, 1983.

Dawisha, Adeed. *Egypt in the Arab World: The Elements of Foreign Policy*. New York: Wiley, 1976.

Day, Arthur. *East Bank/West Bank: Jordan and the Prospects for Peace*. New York: Council on Foreign Relations, 1986.

Frieden, Jeffry A. *Debt Development, and Democracy: Modern Political Economy and Latin America, 1965–1985*. Princeton: Princeton University Press, 19**.

Garfinckle, Adam M. *Israel and Jordan in the Shadow of War*. New York: St. Martin's, 1991.

Helms, Christine Moss. *Iraq: Eastern Flank of the Arab World*. Washington, D.C.: Brookings, 1984.

Hermann, Charles F., Charles W. Kegley, Jr., and James N.Rosenau. *New Directions in the Study of Foreign Policy*. Boston: Allen & Unwin, 1987.

Hinnebusch, Raymong A., Jr. *Egyptian Politics Under Sadat*. New York: Cambridge, 1985.

Hirschmann, Albert. *National Power and the Structure of Foreign Trade.* University of California Press, 1945.

Holsti, K.J. *Why Nations Realign.* Boston: Allen & Unwin, 1982.

Hudson, Michael. *Arab Politics: The Search for Legitimacy.* New Haven: Yale University Press, 1977.

Job, Brian L., ed. *The Insecurity Dilemma: National Security of Third World States.* Boulder: Lynne Reinner, 1992.

Katzenstein, Peter. *Small States in World Markets.* Ithaca: Cornell University Press, 1985.

Kerr, Malcolm. *The Arab Cold War: Gamal Abd al-Nasir and His Rivals, 1958–1970.* London: Oxford University Press, 1971.

Kienle, Eberhard. *Ba'th vs. Ba'th: The Conflict Between Syria and Iraq 1968–1989.* New York: I. B. Tauris & Co., 1990.

Konikoff, A. *Transjordan: An Economic Survey.* Jerusalem: Economic Research Institute for the Jewish Agency for Palestine, 1946.

Korany, Bahgat and Dessouki, Ali E. Hillal. *The Foreign Policies of Arab States: The Challenge of Change,* Second Edition. Boulder: Westview, 1991.

Korany, Bahgat, Paul Noble and Rex Brynen, eds. *The Many Faces of National Security in the Arab World.* New York: St. Martin's, 1993.

Lawson, Fred H. *The Social Origins of Egyptian Expansionism During the Muhammad 'Ali Period.* New York: Columbia University Press, 1992.

Luciani, Giacomo, ed. *The Arab State.* Berkeley: University of CaliforniaPress, 1990.

Ma'oz, Moshe and Avner Yaniv. *Syria Under Assad: Domestic Constraints andRegional Risks.* New York: St. Martin's, 1986.

Marr, Phoebe. *The Modern History of Iraq.* Boulder: Westview, 1985.

Mutawi, Samir. *Jordan and the 1967 War.* New York: Cambridge, 1987.

Nelson, Joan M., ed. *Economic Crisis and Policy Choice: The Politics of Adjustment in the Third World* (Princeton: Princeton University Press, 1990).

Niblock, Tim, ed. *Iraq: The Contemporary State* (London: Croom Helm, 1982).

Nonneman, Gerd. *Development, Administration and Aid in the Middle East.* New York: Routledge, 1988.

Petran, Tabitha. *The Struggle Over Lebanon.* New York: Monthly ReviewPress, 1987.

Quandt, William B. *Saudi Arabia in the 1980s: Foreign Policy, Security and Oil.* Washington, D.C. Brookings, 1981.

—. *The Middle East Ten Years After Camp David.* Washington, D.C.: Brookings, 1988.

Richardson, Neil. *Foreign Policy and Economic Dependence.* Austin: University of Texas Press, 1978.

Rothstein, Robert. *The Weak in the World of the Strong: Developing countries in the International System.* New York: Columbia University Press, 1977.

Safran, Nadav. *Saudi Arabia: The Ceaseless Quest for Security.* Cambridge: Harvard University Press, 1985.

Satloff, Robert. *Troubles on the East Bank: Challenges to the Domestic Stability of Jordan* (Center for Strategic and International Studies, Georgetown and Praeger, New York, 1986).

Seale, Patrick. *Asad of Syria: The Struggle for the Middle East.* Berkeley: University of California Press, 1988.

Snyder, Jack. *Myths of Empire: Domestic Politics and International Ambition.* Ithaca: Cornell University Press, 1991.

Starr, Joyce R. and Daniel C. Stoll, eds. *The Politics of Scarcity: Water in the Middle East.* Boulder: Westview with the Center for Strategic and International Studies, 1988.

Taylor, Alan. *The Arab Balance of Power.* Syracuse: Syracuse University Press, 1982.

Thomas, Caroline. *In Search of Security: The Third World in International Relations.* Boulder: Lynne Reinner, 1987.

Thomas, Caroline and Paikiasothy Saravanamuttu, eds. *Conflict and Consensus in South/North Security.* New York: Cambridge, 1989

Walt, Stephen M. *The Origins of Alliances.* Ithaca: Cornell University Press, 1987

Waterbury, John. *The Egypt of Nasser and Sadat: The Political Economy of Two Regimes.* Princeton: Princeton University Press, 1983.

Wilson, Mary. *King Abdallah, Britain and the Making of Jordan.* New York: Cambridge University Press, 1987.

Wilson, Rodney, ed. *Politics and the Economy in Jordan.* New York: Routledge, 1991.

Zysman, John. *Governments, Markets, and Growth.* Ithaca: Cornell University Press, 1983.

Arabic Sources

Abu Diyyah, Sa'd. *'Amiliyyat Ittikhadh al-Qarar f-il-Siyasah al-Kharijiyyah al-Urdunniyyah* [The Foreign Policy Decision-Making Process in Jordan]. Beirut: Center for Arab Unity Studies, 1989.

Ahmad, Ahmad Yusuf. *al-Sira'at al-'Arabiyyah al-'Arabiyyah, 1945–1981* [Inter-Arab Conflicts, 1945–1981] Beirut: Center for Arab Unity Studies, 1988.

Al-Nasrawi, 'Abbas et al. *Al-Qita' al-'Amm w-al-Qita' al-Khass f-il-Watan al-'Arabi* [The Public and Private Sectors in the Arab World]. Beirut: Center for Arab Unity Studies, 1990.

Al-Sakit, Bassam. *Tahlil al-Athar al-Iqtisadiyyah li-Ighlaq al-Hudud al-Suriyyah ma'a al-Urdunn.* [Analysis of the Economic Effects of the Closing of the Syrian Border with Jordan]. (Unpublished study of the Central Bank of Jordan, no date.)

Amman Chamber of Commerce, *Munjazat wa-Nashatat Ghurfat Tujarat 'Amman Khilal al-Fatrah 1983–1985* [Accomplishments and Activities of the Amman Chamber of Commerce During the Period 1983–1985]. Amman, 1986.

Arab Company for the Development of Animal Resources, The Consulting Unit for Economic and Technical Studies. *Mu'awwaqat Tabadul wa-Insiyab al-Sila' alati Tantajuha al-Mashari' al-'Arabiyyah al-Mushtarikah bayna al-Duwal al-'Arabiyyah.* [Obstacles to the Exchange and Flow of Commodities Produced by Arab Joint Projects in the Arab World.] (n.p., 1987)

Arab Monetary Fund. *Al-Tujarah al-Kharijiyyah l-il-Duwal al-'Arabiyyah, 1974–84*

[The Foreign Trade of the Arab States, 1974–84]. Abu Dhabi: Bureau of Research and Statistics, 1986.

Arab Monetary Fund. "Tamwil al-Tujarah bayna al-Duwal al-'Arabiyyah w-al-Dawr Sanduq al-Naqd al-'Arabi fi Taqdim al-Tashilat al-I'timaniyyah li-Taysir wa-Tanshit al-Tabadul al-Tujari al-'Arabi." [Financing Inter-Arab Trade and the Role of the Arab Monetary Fund in Providing Credit to Facilitate and Energize Arab Commercial Exchange.]

General Secretariat of the Federation of Arab Chambers of Commerce, "Subul Tatwir al-Tujarah al-'Arabiyyah al-Bayniyyah." [Means of Developing Inter-Arab Trade.] An unpublished study presented to the Conference on Arab Trade, Riyadh, 7–8 February 1987.

General Secretariat, Council on Arab Economic Unity. "Al-Ab'ad al-Takamuliyyah li-Khitat al-Tanmiyah al-'Arabiyyah—al-Manafi' al-Mutabadilah w-al-Mashru'at al-Mushtarikah." [The Integrative Dimensions of the Arab Development Plans—Mutual Benefits and Joint Projects.] (n.p., n.d)

Hawrani, Hani. *Azmat al-Iqtisad al-Urdunni* [The Crisis of the Jordanian Economy]. Cyprus: T.H.O. Publishing Co., 1989.

Mas'ud, Majid. *Ajhizat al-Takhtit f-il-Aqta' al-'Arabiyyah.* [Planning in the Arab Regions]. Dar al-Shabab for the Arab Planning Institute, Kuwait, 1987.

Ministry of Industry and Trade, Hashemite Kingdom of Jordan. *Majmu'at al-Ittifaqiyyat al-Iqtisadiyyah w-al-Tujariyyah bayna al-Mamlakah al-Urdunniyyah al-Hashimiyyah w-al-Duwal al-'Arabiyyah,* [Compendium of Economic and Trade Agreements between the Hashemite Kingdom of Jordan and the Arab States, parts one and two.. Amman, 1985.

"Qanun al-Takhtit, no. 67 of 1971." [The Planning Law.] Photocopy.

Royal Scientific Society. *'Alaqat al-Mamlakah al-Urdunniyyah al-Hashimiyyah bi-Dawlat al-Kuwait, 1978–1989.* [The Hashemite Kingdom of Jordan's Relations with the State of Kuwait] (Amman, 1990).(photocopy)

—. *Al-'Alaqat al-Urdunniyyah li-Duwal Majlis al-Ta'awun al-'Arabi, 1974–89* [Jordan's Relations with the States of the Arab Cooperation Council]. Amman, 1990. (photocopy).

—. *'Alaqat al-Mamlakah al-Urdunniyyah al-Hashimiyyah b-il-Mamlakah al-'Arabiyyah al-Sa'udiyyah, 1978–89* [The Hashemite Kingdom of Jordan's Relations with the Kingdom of Saudi Arabia]. Amman, 1990. (photocopy).

—.*Al-'Alaqat al-Urdunniyyah b-il-Jumhuriyyah al-Suriyyah, 1978–89* [Jordan's Relations with the Syrian Republic]. Amman, 1990. (photocopy).

Syrian Arab News Agency and the Jordanian News Agency. *Masirat al-Takamul bayna Suriya w-al-Urdunn: 'Ala Darb al-Wahdah* [The March of Integration between Syria and Jordan: on the Road to Unity]. Damascus, 1977.

Unpublished Trade, Economic, and Planning Papers

"Al-Dawrah al-Khamisah l-il-Lajnah al-'Uliya al-Urdunniyyah al-Suriyyah al-Mushtarikah, Damascus, 6–7 August 1990." [The Fifth Round of the Joint

Jordanian-Syrian Higher Committee.] From the Ministry of Industry and Trade.

"Al-Dawrah al-Sadisah l-il-Lajnah al-Iqtisadiyyah al-Sa'udiyyah al-Urdunniyyah al-Mushtarikah, Amman, 17–18 December 1986." [The Sixth Round of the Saudi-Jordanian Joint Economic Committee.] From the Ministry of Industry and Trade.

"Al-Dawrah al-Sabi'ah l-il-Lajnah al-Iqtisadiyyah al-Sa'udiyyah al-Urdunniyyah al-Mushtarikah, Riyadh, 7–8 February 1988." [The Seventh Round of the Saudi-Jordanian Joint Economic Committee.] From the Ministry of Industry and Trade.

"Al-Dawrah al-Thaminah l-il-Lajnah al-Iqtisadiyyah al-Sa'udiyyah al-Urdunniyyah al-Mushtarikah, Amman, 8–9 October 1989." [The Eighth Round of the Saudi-Jordanian Joint Economic Committee.] From the Ministry of Industry and Trade.

"Al-Istratijiyyah al-Iqtisadiyyah wa-Khitat al-Tanmiyah f-il-Mamlakah." [Economic Strategy and Development Plans in the Kingdom.] From the Ministry of Planning.

"Ittifaq l-il-Ta'awun al-Iqtisadi w-al-Tujarii w-al-Fanni bayna Hukumat al-Mamlakah al-Urdunniyyah al-Hashimiyyah wa-Hukumat Jumhuriyyat Misr al-'Arabiyyah." Amman, 21 April 1975. [Economic, Commercial, and Technical Cooperation Agreement between the Government of the Hashemite Kingdom of Jordan and the Egyptian Arab Republic.] From the Ministry of Industry and Trade.

"Mahdar Mutabi'at Ijtima' al-Dawrah al-Tasi'ah l-il-Lajnah al-Mushtarikah al-Urdunniyyah-al-'Iraqiyyah, Baghdad, 13–14 November 1989." [Minutes of the Meeting of the Ninth Round of the Joint Jordanian-Iraqi Com mittee.] From the Ministry of Industry and Trade.

"Mahdar Ijtima'at al-Lajnah al-'Uliya al-Misriyyah al-Urdunniyyah al-Mushtarikah, Amman, 5–7 May." [Minutes of the Meetings of the Joint Egyptian-Jordanian Higher Committee.] From the Ministry of Industry and Trade.

"Nabdhah 'an al-Tatawwur al-Tarikhi l-il-Jihaz al-Takhtiti." [A Pamphlet on the Historical Development of the Planning Apparatus.] From the Ministry of Planning.

"Qararat al-Lajnah al-'Uliya al-Misriyyah al-Urdunniyyah al-Mushtarikah fi-Dawratiha al-Thaminah, Amman, 29–31 July 1988." [Decisions of the Egyptian-Jordanian Higher Joint Council, in its Eigth Round.] From the Ministry of Industry and Trade.

"Al-Tajribah al-Takhtitiyyah f-il-Urdunn." [The Experience with Planning in Jordan.] From the Ministry of Planning.

Interviews

All of those interviewed are Jordanians. The government service noted is all with the Jordanian government.

Abu Hammud, Mansur. Commercial attaché to the Jordanian Embassy in Cairo 1984–88. October 16, 1991.

Abu Hassan, Khaldun. President of the Amman Chamber of Industry. November 2, 1991.

Abu Jabir, Fayiz. Political Scientist. October 22, 1991.

Abu Mayzar Musa. Longtime employee at the Ministry of Planning. November 24, 1991.

'Anani, Jawad. Former Minister of Supply (1979–1980), former Minister of Labor (1980–84), and former Minister of Industry and Trade (1984–85). November 4, 1991 and July 20, 1992.

'Ammari, Shabib. Prominent industrialist. November 11, 1991.

'Asfur, Muhammad. President of Jordan Federation of Chambers of Commerce. July 15, 1992.

'Awdah, Hanna. Former Minister of Finance (1984–1989). December 2, 1991.

Ayyubi, Zaki. Prominent businessman. June 23, 1992.

'Azir, Wasif. Former Director of the Phosphate Company. General Manager of the Business Bank. June 22, 1992.

Badran, Mudar. Former Chief of Jordanian Intelligence and former Prime Minister (1976–79, 1980–84, 1989–91). July 19, 1992.

Bataynah, Safwan. Former economic advisor to Prime Minister Zayd al-Rifa'i. October 3, 1991.

Dajani, 'Ali. Long-time official of the Amman Chamber of Industry. November 2 and 12, 1991.

Fanek, Fahd. Economist. June 22, and July 21, 1992.

Ghazawi, Ya'qub. Ministry of Trade and Supply. October 6, 1991.

Hawrani, Hani. Researcher and writer specializing on Jordanian economic and labor affairs. November 23, 1991.

Hamarneh, Munir. Economist at the Council of Arab Economic Unity, Amman. October 7, 1991.

Kan'an, Tahir. Former Minister of Occupied Territories Affairs (1985–86) and of Planning (1986–89) Director of the Industrial Development Bank. June 22, 1992.

Khalaf, Rima. Director of the Jordan Trade Centers Corporation. October 26, 1991.

Marto, Michel. Deputy-governor of the Central Bank of Jordan. October 30, 1991.

Masri, Tahir. Former Foreign Minister (1984–88) and Prime Minister (1991). July 14, 1992.

Mu'ashshir, Raja'i. Former Minister of Trade and Industry (1974–76 and 1985–88). October 14, 1991.

Nusur, Ma'an. Ministry of Planning, November 10, 1991.

Qa'war, Tawfiq. Prominent businessman. July 17, 1992.

Rifa'i, Zayd. Former Prime Minister (1973–76 and 1985–89). July 11, 1992.

Sakit, Bassam. Economic adviser to the Crown Prince in the late 1970s and early 1980s, and Director-General of the Jordan Cement Company. October 8, 1991.

Salim, Khalil. Former Governor of the Central Bank and head of the Senate Finance Committee. October 15, 1991.

Saqqaf, Muhammad. Former adviser on economic unity affairs and Director of the Social Security Corporation. October 23 and 30, 1991.

Suways, 'Awdah. Director of Research, Amman Chamber of Commerce. November 4, 1991.

Tall, Sa'd. Director-General of the Jordan Petroleum Refinery Company. July 13, 1992.

Tarawineh, Fayiz. Former Minister of Supply (1988–89) and economic adviser to the prime minister, 1980–89. October 20, 1991.

Tuqan, Safwan. Deputy Minister of Planning. November 19, 1991.

'Ubaydat, Ahmad. Former Chief of Jordanian Intelligence and former Prime Minister (1984–85). July 14, 1992.

'Umaysh, Samir. Director, Ministry of Industry and Trade. October 5, 1991.

Index

'Abdallah (prince of Saudi Arabia), 91, 94, 95, 177
Abu 'Awdah, 'Adnan, 92, 169, 182, 251–52
Abu Ghazalah, 'Abd al-Halim, 251, 258, 267
Abu Nidal, 198
accommodational strategy, 36
Afghanistan, Soviet invasion of, 95, 127
Agricultural Loan Corporation, Jordanian, 74
Ahmad, Ahmand Iskandir, 158
Algeria: financial aid from, 139;
   and Middle East peace plans, 107
alignment. *See* alliance formation
alliance formation: and budget security, 38, 301;
   description of, 15–16, 28–32
Amal, 195
Amman Chamber of Industry, 56–57, 60, 71–72, 77, 223
Amman Financial Market, 144
Amman Intercontinental Hotel, 198
'Anani, Jawad, 65, 211, 212
Aqaba, Gulf of, 256
Aqaba, port of, 97, 199, 202–3, 204, 207, 208–9, 215–16, 222, 226–27, 234, 236–37
Aqaba Free Zone, 208–9, 226
Arab Bridge Company for Maritime Navigation, proposed, 226–27, 234, 238, 264, 267
Arab Common Market Party, 72

Arab Cooperation Council (ACC), 7, 109, 184, 197, 228–29, 230–31, 235, 238, 240, 259, 265, 270, 273, 283–84
Arab Deterrent Force, 171
Arabia and the Gulf, 91
Arab-Israeli conflict, 2, 5–6, 10–11, 91
Arab-Israeli war (1948), 56
Arab-Israeli war (1967), 43, 242
Arab-Israeli war (1973), 6, 244
Arab League: Egypt in, 7, 183, 184, 247, 254, 258, 269, 282;
   and Jordanian import duties, 101;
   Military Delegation of, 93
—summits: and aid to Jordan, 5, 96–97, 111, 124, 125, 166–67, 178, 200, 232;
   and Arab regional economy, 169;
   and Gulf wars, 136, 183;
   and Middle East peace, 106–7
Arab market zone, proposed, 199
Arab Mining Company, 202
Arab Monetary Fund, 111, 141
Arab National Charter, proposed, 127–28
Arab nationalism, 42–43, 242, 271
Arab Parliamentary Union, 176
Arab Potash Company, 201, 214
'Arafat, Yasir: and Camp David accords, 92;
   and Fahd peace plan, 95;
   Jordanian negotiations with, 107, 258, 259;
   opposition to, 177, 182;
   relations with Egypt, 251, 272

ARAMCO (Arab-American Oil Company), 102, 103, 104
Arab Industrial Investments Company, proposed, 175
'Arar, Sulayman, 90, 199, 211
Asad, Hafiz al-: and Camp David Accords, 92, 166;
and Iraqi-Syrian relations, 168, 170, 221;
and Jordanian-Syrian relations, 154, 159, 176, 177, 182, 183, 185, 195;
pragmatism of, 299;
rise to power, 152;
talks with King Husayn, 90, 154, 156, 183–84
Asad, Rif'at al-, 170
'Asfur, Walid, 59, 217
'Atiqi, 'Abd al-Rahman Salim al-, 131
'Awdah, Hanna, 60, 76, 137, 143
'Awn, Michel, 184, 188
Ayoob, Mohammed, 25
'Aziz, Sultan bin 'Abd al-, 91
'Aziz, Tariq, 211

Badran, Mudar: and Jordanian-Egyptian relations, 246;
and Jordanian financial problems, 200;
and Jordanian-Kuwaiti relations, 125, 130, 138;
and Jordanian-Saudi relations, 90, 93, 98, 112;
and Jordanian-Syrian relations, 156, 157, 158, 167, 170, 185, 192;
and private sector development, 59
Baghdad Pact, 30, 87, 284, 285
Bakr, Hasan al-, 199–200
balance of power theory, 29–31, 294
Baldwin, David, 8, 269
Barnett, Michael, 31–32, 36, 37
Basra, 209
Ba'th party, Iraqi, 7, 198
Ba'th party, Syrian, 7, 156, 299
Baz, Usama al-, 251
Bazoft, Farzad, 232
Bechtel Corporation, 217, 218
Begin, Menachem, 247

bilateral relationships, 4, 8, 89
bin Shakir, Zayd, 90–91, 93, 94, 141, 158
Brown, L. Carl, 29
budget security: and Arab-Israeli peace process, 295–97;
definition of, 2, 277;
and exchange elements, 34–35;
and national security, 15–16;
and regime security, 25–28;
strategies for achieving, 36–38;
suggestions for application of concept, 10;
threats to, 35–36
Butrus-Ghali, Butrus, 251
Buzan, Barry, 22, 24

Camp David Accords, 92, 99, 126, 166, 171, 199–200, 235, 247, 251, 269, 280
Carter, Jimmy, 90
Carter Doctrine, 127–28
Cement Supply Bureau, Egyptian, 261
Central Bank of Jordan, 67, 74, 186, 223–25, 253, 262
Cold War, end of, 1
colonialism, 22–23
Conference of Trade Ministers (1977), 198–99

Dabbas, Muhammad, 131
Dajani, Najm al-Din al-, 162
Damascus Chambers of Industry and Trade, 180
David, Stephen, 31, 34, 302
debt, and budget security, 27
dependent states (countries), 16–17
Dessouki, Ali E. Hillal, 18–19, 299–300
"Development—Between Planning and Implementation in the Arab Homeland" (seminar), 140
domestic economics: and debt, 28;
and financial solvency, 32–34;
role in foreign policy, 16–19.
See also economics
domestic economic structure arguments, 3, 32–34

domestic politics: and interstate
    behavior, 2;
    post-Cold War importance of, 1
Dustur, al-, 138, 176, 231

Eastern Front, proposed, 166, 229, 231
Eastern Question system, 29
economic aid: and foreign policy, 33–34;
    and political dependency, 16
economic integration (*takamul*), 162
economics: role in foreign policy theo-
    ries, 16–19;
    role in Jordan's foreign policy, 3.
    See also domestic economics
economic security, definition of, 20–25
Economic Security Committee (ESC),
    Jordanian, 67–69
Egypt: agricultural sector in, 4;
    bureaucracy in, 268;
    and control of Suez Canal, 26–27;
    currency and foreign exchange in, 4;
    developments between 1975 and 1979
    in, 244–49;
    developments between 1979 and 1984
    in, 3, 250–57;
    developments between 1985 and 1990
    in, 257–66;
    economic liberalization in, 6;
    economic structure of, 18;
    foreign aid to, 97, 98, 99, 200, 253–54;
    foreign aid to Jordan from, 87;
    industrial cooperation with Jordan,
    243, 248–49, 262–64, 267–68;
    military assistance to and from Jor-
    dan, 258;
    protective tariffs in, 4;
    public sector in, 4;
    and regional hegemony, 5;
    relations with Iraq, 7, 184, 211–12,
    221, 228, 240, 273;
    relations with Israel, 5–6, 7, 91, 92, 93,
    97, 99, 126, 136, 244–47;
    relations with Jordan, 5, 64, 69, 107,
    135, 177, 180, 181, 193–94, 226,
    242–74, 279, 282–83, 290, 299–300;
    relations with Syria, 91, 92, 108, 153,
    155–56, 184, 231, 245, 249, 270–71;

trade relations with Jordan, 5, 64, 69,
    243, 248, 254–56, 260–62, 266–67;
    U.S. relations with, 6, 99, 242.
    See also Camp David Accords
EgyptAir, 253
Egyptian-Jordanian Company for Invest-
    ment and Development, 263
Egyptian-Jordanian Joint Holding Com-
    pany, 262–63, 267
Egyptian Ministry of War Production,
    267
Egyptian Shipping Company, 263–64
Egyptian-Syrian Joint Command, pro-
    posed, 90
Euphrates River water projects, 197,
    209, 218–19
European Debt Commission, 26
export credits scandal, 223–25, 233,
    235, 237, 240, 290
Export-Import Bank, 218

Fahd (crown prince of Saudi Arabia):
    and Arab League summit of 1985,
    108; and Middle East peace plans, 95,
    107, 110;
    and Saudi relations with Jordan, 92,
    98, 109, 111–12
Fahd plan (for Middle East peace),
    95–96, 107, 110
Fahmi, Isma'il, 98, 245
Fanek, Fahd al-, 68
Fateh, 198, 289
Faw Island, 135, 209
Fayiz, 'Akif al-, 176
Faysal (king of Saudi Arabia), 97
Faysal, Sa'ud al-, 98
Federation of Charitable Societies, Jor-
    danian, 212
Federation of Jordanian Chambers of
    Commerce, 186.
    See also, Jordanian Chamber of Com-
    merce
financial security. *See* budget security
Foreign Broadcast Information Service, 8
Foreign Policies of Arab States, The
    (Dessouki and Korany), 18
Free Liberals, 72

Free Zone Company, 175, 190, 208
Frieden, Jeffry A., 40, 41

General Establishment for Passenger
    Transport, Iraqi, 208
Geneva Middle East peace conference:
    first (1973), 90;
    second (1977), 90, 125, 245, 249
Glubb Pasha, 42, 43
Great Britain: control of Suez Canal by,
    26–27;
    and control of Transjordan, 42, 196;
    financial support to Jordan, 42
Group of 70, 72
Gulf Cooperation Council (GCC), 95,
    128, 136, 141
Gulf crisis (1990–91), 6, 7, 10, 89, 124,
    284–95

Hammadi, Sa'dun, 167, 199, 204
Hasan (crown prince of Jordan): and
    anti-Syrian activities in Jordan, 169;
    and Arab relations with Egypt, 156;
    and development planning, 76, 133;
    and economic decisionmaking, 65–66;
    and Jordanian-Egyptian relations,
    245, 260;
    and Jordanian- Kuwaiti relations, 127,
    136, 137;
    and private sector development, 57,
    59, 62
Hasan (king of Morocco), 96
Hashem, House of, 87
Hashemite Kingdom of Jordan.
    See Jordan
Hashemite Union, 319n. 8
Hawadith, al-, 177
Higher Economic Advisory Council, Jor-
    danian, 58–59, 60
Hijaz Railway Project, 104, 106
Hirschman, Albert, 16
Housing Bank (*Bank al-Iskan*), 132–33
Husayn (king of Jordan): Arabism of,
    287–88;
    and Arab nationalism, 43, 121;
    and Baghdad Pact, 87, 284, 285;
    balancing by, 294–95;

and British foreign aid, 42;
and economic decisionmaking, 65,
    66;
and Egyptian-Israeli peace, 99–101,
    201, 269;
and internationalization of Lebanese
    conflict, 168–69;
and Iraqi-Kuwaiti relations, 232;
and Jewish settlement of the West
    Bank, 109, 138, 231;
and Jordanian- Egyptian relations,
    242, 245–47, 250, 253, 256–58,
    263–64, 266, 283;
and Jordanian-Iraqi relations, 199,
    204, 205, 210, 211, 219–22, 229–32,
    234;
and Jordanian-Kuwaiti relations,
    125–27, 135–39;
and Jordanian military role in Gulf
    conflicts, 106, 128;
and Jordanian- Saudi relations, 89–95,
    97–98, 99–101, 108, 109, 121;
and Jordanian-Soviet relations, 97;
and Jordanian-Syrian relations,
    152–58, 166–68, 170, 172, 176–79,
    183–85, 190, 278;
and Kuwaiti-Saudi relations, 123;
and Middle East peace plans, 107;
and Palestinian issues, 6, 108–9, 126;
relationship to Sadat, 193;
visit to Oman, 89

Ibn Sa'ud (founder of Saudi Arabia),
    87
Ibrahim, Hasan, 126, 199, 204
Ibrahim, Hikmat, 200
Ibrahimiyyah College, 206
Idris, Lt. Gen. Muhammad, 93
'Imadi, Muhammad al-, 180
image, manipulation of, 30
Industrial Development Bank, Jordan-
    ian, 142
International Contracting and Invest-
    ment Company (ICICO), 213
International Monetary Fund (IMF),
    27–28, 36, 137, 230, 232, 233, 262,
    284, 288, 290, 294, 301

international strategy, 36–37
Intras of East Germany, 174
Iran: and cease-fire, 222;
    relations with Syria, 136, 183
Iran-Iraq war, 94, 106, 108, 128, 134,
    139, 169, 196, 209, 210–12, 213,
    219, 220–22, 269, 290
Iraq: agricultural sector in, 4;
    currency and foreign exchange in, 4;
    developments between 1975 and 1978
        in, 197–204;
    developments between 1979 and 1980
        in, 3, 204–10;
    developments between 1981 and 1984
        in, 210–20;
    developments between 1985 and 1988
        in, 220–29;
    developments between 1989 and 1990
        in, 229–35;
    economic liberalization in, 6;
    foreign aid to Jordan from, 4–5, 97,
        196, 198, 199, 201, 204, 206–7,
        212–13, 232, 235, 239–40;
    industrial cooperation with Jordan,
        202, 207–8, 214–15, 225–26, 238;
    military assistance from Jordan to,
        210, 219, 222;
    oil exports to Jordan from, 5, 118,
        216–18, 227–28, 233, 236, 286;
    protective tariffs in, 4;
    public sector in, 4;
    and regional hegemony, 5;
    relations with Egypt, 7, 107, 184,
        211–12, 221, 228, 240, 273;
    relations with Jordan, 5, 7, 64, 68,
        124, 171, 175–76, 182, 193,
        196–241, 281, 290;
    relations with Saudi Arabia, 94–95,
        205;
    relations with Syria, 7, 108, 109, 167,
        171–72, 175, 182–83, 197, 204, 211;
    Soviet relations with, 6; trade rela-
        tions with Jordan, 5, 7, 64, 68, 124,
        196, 198, 201–3, 207, 208–9,
        213–14, 215–16, 222–25, 226–27,
        232–33, 234, 236–38, 243, 286;
    U.S. relations with, 6;

Revolutionary Command Council
    (RCC), 199–200.
    See also Euphrates River water projects.
    See also Kuwait, Iraqi invasion of
Iraqi Awqaf Ministry, 212
Iraqi Development Fund, 201, 213, 215
Iraqi Fund for External Development,
    207
Iraqi-Jordanian Land Transport
    Company (IJLTC), 209, 216, 238
Iraqi Oil Marketing Establishment, 216
Iraqi State Establishment for Special-
    ized Transport, 208
Iraqi State Organization for Consumer
    Goods, 214
Iraqi State Overland Transport
    Company, 202
Iraqi Women's Union, 206
Iraqi-Jordanian Industrial Company
    (IJIC), 225–26
Iraq Petroleum Company, 320n. 37
Islamic Conference Organization, 136,
    184
Isma'il (khedive of Egypt), 26
Israel: relations with Egypt, 5–6, 7, 91,
    92, 93, 97, 99, 136, 244–47;
    relations with Syria, 7;
    U.S. support for, 43, 93.
    See also Camp David Accords

Jane's Defense Weekly, 135
Jardaneh, Basil, 59
Jazrawi, Taha al- (Taha Yasin
    Ramadan), 202, 220, 221
JETT bus company, 208.
    See also, Jordan Express Transport
    Company
Joint Higher Command, Jordanian-Syri-
    an, 155, 156
Joint Higher Committee, Jordanian-
    Syrian, 154, 161, 163, 186
Joint Higher Council, Jordanian-Syrian,
    155
Joint Iraqi-Jordanian Company for
    Industry, proposed, 214–15
Jordan: agricultural exports from, 5,
    101, 113–14, 178, 180, 207, 223;

Jordan (*continued*)
  agricultural sector in, 42;
  army recruitment in, 52;
  as banking and service center, 293;
  bureaucracy in, 49–52, 59, 62–63, 64,
    72–73, 80, 268;
  civil service system in, 63;
  currency issues in, 68, 109, 137, 225;
  customs tariffs in, 49, 69, 101, 112,
    118, 160–61, 185–86, 191, 207, 255;
  description of, 2;
  development of, 42;
  development of indigenous produc-
    tion in, 48;
  development of West Bank by, 110,
    124, 140, 183, 258, 289;
  development planning in, 74–77, 97,
    110–11;
  economic decisionmaking in, 40–41,
    82–83;
  economic liberalization in, 6, 81,
    293–94;
  economy of, 39–83;
  Egyptian expatriate workers in, 254,
    264–65, 269–70;
  ethnic divisions in, 49–52, 62, 63, 65,
    72;
  exchange rate of dinars in, 303;
  external debt of, 75, 76, 222, 230, 232,
    284, 290;
  foreign aid from Egypt to, 87;
  foreign aid from Iraq to, 4–5, 97, 196,
    198, 199, 201, 204, 206–7, 212–13,
    232, 235, 239–40;
  foreign aid from Kuwait to, 4–5, 9, 43,
    96, 111, 123, 124, 125, 126, 127,
    129–31, 139–42, 145–47, 149,
    150–51, 153, 286;
  foreign aid from Saudi Arabia to, 4–5,
    9, 43, 87–89, 96–102, 103, 110–12,
    116–17, 118–19, 121–22, 145, 170,
    286;
  foreign aid from Syria to, 87;
  foreign aid to, 41–49, 76, 81–82,
    154–55, 165, 178, 200, 277;
  foreign investment in, 115, 132–33,
    143–44, 147;

  and foreign trade, 77–81;
  and foreign trade with Egypt, 5, 64,
    69, 243, 248, 254–56, 260–62,
    266–67;
  and foreign trade with Iraq, 5, 7, 64,
    68, 124, 196, 198, 201–3, 207,
    208–9, 213–14, 215–16, 222–25,
    226–27, 232–33, 234, 236–38, 243,
    286;
  and foreign trade with Kuwait, 124,
    131–32, 142, 147–48, 286;
  and foreign trade with Saudi Arabia,
    100, 101–2, 112–14, 286;
  and foreign trade with Syria, 5, 7, 64,
    69, 154, 159–61, 172, 173–74, 176,
    178, 179–80, 185–86, 191–92;
  free market economy of, 6, 49, 74,
    118;
  government as employer in, 48,
    49–53, 73;
  income taxes in, 49, 52;
  industrial cooperation with Egypt,
    243, 248–49, 262–64, 267–68;
  industrial cooperation with Iraq, 202,
    207–8, 214–15, 225–26, 238;
  industrial cooperation with Syria,
    161–63, 174–75, 181, 186;
  martial law in, 53, 63, 64, 66–67, 82;
  and Middle East peace plans, 107;
  military expenditures in, 8, 65, 213;
  military stability of, 5, 64;
  oil exports from Iraq to, 5, 118,
    216–18, 227–28, 233, 236, 286;
  oil exports from Saudi Arabia to, 5,
    94, 101, 102–4, 114–15, 118,
    286–87;
  Palestinians in, 11, 42, 43, 52, 94,
    295–97;
  parliament of, 71–72;
  phosphate and potash industry in, 48,
    161, 201, 202, 214, 222;
  political liberalization in, 7, 8–9,
    57–58, 71, 72, 81, 109, 138, 289,
    291;
  political parties in, 71, 72;
  private sector in, 52, 53–64, 73;
  professional associations in, 71;

public sector in, 49–53, 72–73, 75;
relations with Egypt, 5, 64, 69, 107,
135, 177, 180, 181, 193–94, 226,
242–74, 279, 282–83, 290, 299–300;
relations with Iraq, 5, 7, 64, 68, 94,
171, 175–76, 182, 193, 196–241,
281, 290;
relations with Kuwait, 123–51;
relations with PLO, 108, 170, 177,
199, 245–46, 258–59, 289;
relations with Saudi Arabia, 87–122;
relations with Syria, 5, 7, 64, 69, 95,
104, 120, 152–95, 196, 206, 239,
278–79, 281–82, 290, 299;
role in Arab-Israeli conflict, 2–3,
10–11;
role of ministers in, 69–71;
role of popular opinion in, 288, 292;
role of the cabinet in, 65–66;
standard of living in, 48, 138;
state services and infrastructure of,
48;
strategic location of, 41–42, 81, 88;
support for Fahd peace plan in, 95,
110;
taxation in, 49;
U.S. relations with, 43;
vulnerability of, 3
Jordan Express Transport Company,
144
Jordan Fertilizer Industries Company,
140, 202, 261
Jordanian Agricultural Marketing Products Corporation (AMPCO), 178,
179, 180
Jordanian Armed Forces Medical Corps,
129
Jordanian Chamber of Commerce, 56,
57, 60, 71–72, 179, 180
Jordanian Cooperative Organization,
179
Jordanian-Kuwaiti Agricultural Company, 144, 147
Jordanian-Kuwaiti Company for Agricultural and Food Products, 143
Jordanian Ministry of Education, 105,
133

Jordanian Ministry of Information, 212
Jordanian Ministry of Labor, 265
Jordanian Ministry of Planning, 75, 77
Jordanian Ministry of Public Works, 215
Jordanian Ministry of Supply, 58
Jordanian Ministry of Supply, Trade,
and Industry, 185
Jordanian Ministry of the National
Economy, 77
Jordanian Ministry of Trade and Indus-
try, 80, 214, 254
Jordanian Ministry of Trade and Sup-
ply, 77
Jordanian Ministry of Transportation,
226
Jordanian-Palestinian Accord (1985),
182
Jordanian Royal Scientific Society, 206
Jordanian-Saudi Industrial Agricultural
Company, 115
Jordanian Social Security Corporation,
212
Jordanian-Syrian Commercial Bank,
163, 174, 175, 190
Jordanian-Syrian Company for Land
Transport, 163, 174, 186
Jordanian-Syrian Industrial Holding
Company, proposed, 174–75
Jordanian-Syrian Joint Industries Com-
pany, 174, 175
Jordanian-Syrian Maritime Transport
Company, 174, 175, 186
Jordanian-Syrian Overland Transport
Company, 174
Jordanian Writers' Assocation, 289
Jordan-Kuwait Bank, 133, 147
Jordan National Shipping Lines, 263–64
Jordan Petroleum Refinery Company
(JPRC), 216, 217, 227–28
Jordan Phosphate Mines Company, 52
Jordan Times, 253
Jordan Trade Centers Corporation,
77–80
Jordan Valley Authority, 76

Kan'an, Tahir, 137, 140, 143
Kasm, 'Abd al-Ra'uf, 177, 178

Khaddam, 'Abd al-Halim, 96, 98, 154, 167, 176, 190
Khalid (king of Saudi Arabia): funeral of, 106;
  and Saudi oil exports, 103, 118;
  and Saudi relations with Jordan, 89, 90, 91, 93, 94, 97, 98, 110
Khammash 'Amir, 91, 93
Kharafi, Jasim al-, 137, 140
Kharg Island, 179
Khomeini, Ayatollah, 200, 239
Khorramshahr, 211
Khulayfawi, 'Abd al-Rahman, 157
Khuzistan, 211
Kissinger, Henry, 278
Korany, Bahgat, 18–19
Kurds, 197, 203
Kuwait: currency of, 4;
  developments between 1975 and 1981 in, 125–34;
  developments between 1982 and 1990 in, 134–45;
  foreign aid to Jordan from, 4–5, 9, 43, 96, 111, 123, 124, 125, 126, 127, 129–31, 139–42, 145–47, 149, 150–51, 153, 286;
  free market economy of, 4, 118;
  independence of, 123;
  investment in Jordan by, 132–33, 143–44, 147;
  Iranian threats to, 135, 136;
  Iraqi invasion of, 6, 88, 139, 141, 146, 234, 259–60, 280;
  Iraqi threats to, 123, 138–39, 197;
  Jordanian expatriate workers in, 5, 119, 123–24, 133–34, 144–45, 148, 149–50, 293;
  military assistance to and from Jordan, 128–29, 148–49;
  neutrality of, 6, 149;
  oil exports from, 4, 228, 286;
  relations with Jordan, 123–51;
  Sunni versis Shi'i population of, 134;
  trade relations with Jordan, 124, 131–32, 142, 147–48, 286
Kuwait Development Fund, 140
Kuwait Fund for Arab Economic Devel-
opment (KFAED), 129, 134, 142, 146
Kuwaiti Armed Forces Medical Corps, 129
Kuwaiti Ministry of Education, 133–34, 144
Kuwait Public Transport Company, 144
Kuwait Real Estate Investment Corporation (KREIC), 132–33

Law 219 (The Companies Law [Temporary]) of 1989, 73
Lawzi, Dr. Salim al-, 185
leadership (regime) security, 23–28, 302, 306n. 18.
  See also security
Lebanon: civil war in, 7, 75, 90, 155, 156, 245;
  internationalization of conflict in, 168–69;
  Israeli invasion of, 7, 92, 106, 166, 171, 210;
  oil exports from Saudi Arabia to, 102, 103;
  Palestinians in, 107, 211;
  relations with Syria, 152, 156, 178, 183–84, 195, 197
legitimacy, of regimes, 30
Levy, Jack, 31–32
Libya: financial aid from, 110, 139, 153;
  oil exports from, 179
Libyan-Syrian Union, 169
Likud party, Israeli, 231
Luciani, Giacomo, 21, 24

Madani, Col. Wajih al-, 128
Madrid Middle East peace conference (1991), 295
Mahfuz, Nagib, 250
Majali, 'Abd al-Salam al-, 105, 133
Majali, Rakan al-, 206
Majallah, al-, 258
Majid, 'Ismat 'Abd al-, 257–58
Mansur, Anis, 250
Masri, Tahir al-, 66, 137, 183, 211
Middle East Economic Digest, 8
Middle East News Agency (MENA), 251

military aid, and political dependency, 16

military security, 21, 26

Moon, Bruce, 8, 17

Morocco: and Middle East peace plans, 107;
support for Fahd peace plan in, 95

Mu'ashshir, Raja'i al-: and Jordanian-Kuwaiti relations, 137, 143, 145;
and Jordanian-Syrian relations, 180, 185;
and private sector development, 59

Mubarak, Husni: and Egyptian-Iraqi relations, 185, 229–30;
and Egyptian-Jordanian relations, 246, 250–52, 257–59, 264, 273;
and Egyptian-Syrian relations, 185;
and Iran-Iraq war, 220;
support for PLO, 272–73

Muhammad (the prophet), 87

Muhammad 'Ali, 26

multilateral Arab meeting (January 9–10, 1977), 90

Muslim Brotherhood (Ikhwan), 167–70, 239

Mu'tah University, 212

Nabulsi, Muhammad Sa'id al-, 262

Nasir, Gamal 'Abd al-, 242, 244, 266

National Consultative Council (NCC), Jordanian, 71, 250, 289

National Planning Council, Jordanian, 74–75

National Power and the Structure of Foreign Trade (Hirshman), 16

national security. *See* security

Natural Resources Authority, Jordanian, 181

Nayif (prince of Saudi Arabia), 91, 92, 108

Noble, Paul, 18

North Yemen, 93, 105, 204, 283

Nusur, 'Ali al-, 173

Official Gazette, 68

oil boom, impact on regional politics, 18, 43

Oman, Sultanate of: domestic unrest in, 105;
foreign aid from, 111;
Jordanian assistance to, 89, 117

omnibalancing, 31, 34, 100–101, 302

OPEC, 18, 233

Origins of Alliances, The (Walt), 29

Osirak nuclear reactor, 237

Oslo agreement (1993), 295

Pahlavi, Mohammad Reza, 93, 95, 200, 204

Palestine Liberation Organization (PLO): Arab League recognition of, 278;
and Fahd peace plan, 96;
foreign aid to, 97, 98, 99;
and Jordanian expatriate workers in Saudi Arabia, 120;
Kuwaiti relations with, 125, 140, 141, 145, 150;
and Middle East peace plans, 107;
relations with Egypt, 272–73;
relations with Iraq, 198;
relations with Jordan, 108, 170, 177, 199, 245–46, 258–59, 289;
relations with Syria, 198;
U.S. and Israeli refusal to recognize, 99

Palestine Liberation Organization (PLO)- Lebanese National Movement, 156, 245

Palestine National Council, 177

Palestine National Fund, 150

Palestinians, 6; autonomy for, 99, 126;
Jordanian relations with, 7, 182, 245–46, 295–97;
Syrian support for, 7

pan-Arabism, 5, 88, 121

patron-client relationships, 16

Persian Gulf, neutrality in, 95

political warfare, 18

Ports Corporation (of Jordan), 76

pragmatism, 244, 299

Qabas, al-, 127, 182

Qabus (sultan of Oman), 264

Qaddafi, Mu'ammar, 179
Qasim, 'Abd al-Karim, 123
Qasim, Marwan al-, 135, 137, 211, 251
Qatar, foreign aid from, 110, 111
Queen Alia Fund, 206, 212

Radio Monte Carlo, 231
Ra'i, al-, 128, 138, 169
Rapid Deployment Force, proposed, 95, 106, 127, 205
Reagan, Ronald, 107, 136, 250
Reagan Plan, 172, 250–51
Reconstruction Council, Jordanian, 74
regime (leadership) security, 23–28, 302, 306n. 18. *See also* security
restructural strategy, 36, 37
Richardson, Neil, 16–17
Rifa'i, Zayd al-: appointment as prime minister, 71, 177, 180, 181;
  and Jordanian-Egyptian relations, 245;
  and Jordanian-Iraqi relations, 220;
  and Jordanian-Kuwaiti relations, 137, 140;
  and Jordanian-Saudi relations, 98, 108, 121;
  and Jordanian-Syrian relations, 154, 157, 158, 159, 168, 170, 177–78, 187, 192;
  and private sector development, 58–59, 60, 293;
  and Syrian-Iraqi relations, 182–83;
  visit to Saudi Arabia, 90
Rothstein, Robert, 20, 21, 22
Royal Jordanian Airlines, 186, 220

Sabah, Sa'd 'Abdallah Salim al-, 128–29
Sabah, Sabah al-Ahmad al-Jabir al-, Shaykh, 125, 127, 133, 136
Sa'd (crown prince of Kuwait), 127, 138, 205
Sadat, Muhammad Anwar: assassination of, 212, 228, 250, 252, 257;
  and Egyptian-Israeli peace process, 7, 91, 92, 99, 125–26, 158, 166, 168, 199, 239, 242, 244–47, 249, 269, 278, 280, 300;

and Egyptian- Jordanian relations, 242, 266;
and Fahd peace plan, 95;
Kuwaiti support for, 125–26;
movement away from Arab consensus, 193;
U.S. relations with, 165
Saddam Husayn: and Arab League summits, 166, 170–71, 209–10, 239;
  and Iran-Iraq conflict, 94, 222;
  and Iraqi invasion of Kuwait, 139, 235;
  and Iraqi-Jordanian relations, 168, 199, 200, 204–6, 210, 212, 229–32, 235, 283, 285;
  and Iraqi-Syrian relations, 168, 221;
  and Middle East peace plans, 107;
  opposition to, 122;
  popularity of, 240, 291;
  and proposed Arab National Charter, 127;
  rise to power of, 259
Safran, Nadav, 94
Salih, 'Ali 'Abdallah, 230
Salim, Dr. Khalil al-, 67
Saqqaf, Muhammad, 267
Sa'ud, House of, 87
Saudi Arabia: agricultural exports from, 113–14;
  currency of, 4;
  dependency on oil, 4;
  developments between 1975 and 1981, 89–106;
  developments between 1982 and 1990, 106–16;
  financial contributions to Arab unity, 92;
  foreign aid to Jordan from, 4–5, 9, 43, 87–89, 96–101, 103, 110–12, 116–17, 118–19, 121–22, 145, 170, 286;
  founding of, 87;
  free market economy of, 4, 118;
  investment in Jordan by, 115;
  Jordanian expatriate workers in, 5, 88, 104–5, 115–16, 119–20, 293;
  and Lebanese civil war, 90;
  and mediations between Egypt and Syria, 91, 92;

and Middle East peace plans, 107;
military assistance to and from Jordan,
    87, 91, 93, 97–98, 129;
oil exports from, 5, 94, 101, 102–4,
    114–15, 118, 228, 286–87;
relations with Iraq, 94–95, 205;
relations with Jordan, 87–122;
Shi'i anti- regime activity in, 94;
support for Fahd peace plan in, 95–96;
trade relations with Jordan, 100,
    101–2, 112–14, 286;
U.S. relations with, 6
Saudi Arabia Monetary Agency (SAMA),
    96
Saudi Development Fund (SDF), 96,
    98–99, 104
Saudi-Jordanian Company for Market-
    ing and Investment, 115
Saudi Ministry of Education and Higher
    Education, 96, 116
Saudi Ministry of Finance, 96
Saudi Press Agency, 95
security: and domestic stability, 20;
    national versus regime, 22–25, 32;
    redefinition of, 1–2, 20–25;
    relative versus absolute, 22;
    and self-reliance, 22, 95, 191;
    threats to, 2, 22–25, 29, 31–33.
    See also budget security; economic
    security; military security
shah of Iran. See Pahlavi, Mohammad
    Reza
Sharaf, 'Abd al-Hamid: and Jordanian-
    Egyptian relations, 246;
    and Jordanian-Saudi relations, 90–91,
    93;
    and Jordanian-Syrian relations, 166,
    169;
    and private sector development, 59
Sharaf, Fawwaz, 199
Shukr, Muhammad Shafiq, 180
Shultz, George, 183, 258
Siyasah, al-, 125
socialism, 5, 121
society-centered approach (to economic
    decisionmaking), 40, 49–64

Somalia, 23
Southern Cement Company (SCC), Jor-
    danian, 215, 261
sovereignty, and budget security, 28
Soviet Union: collapse of, 1, 23;
    invasion of Afghanistan by, 95, 127
state-centered approach (to economic
    decisionmaking), 40, 64–73
Steadfastness and Confrontation Front,
    166, 168, 311n. 24
Suez Canal, 26–27, 103, 159, 242, 249
Suhaymat, 'Ali, 98
Syria: agricultural sector in, 4;
    and Arab-Israeli conflict, 6;
    boycott of 1980 Arab League summit
    by, 170;
    currency and foreign exchange in, 4;
    developments between 1975 and
    1977 in, 3, 152–65;
    developments between 1978 and
    1983 in, 166–76;
    developments between 1984 and
    1985 in, 176–81;
    developments between 1986 and
    1990 in, 182–88;
    economic liberalization in, 6;
    foreign aid from Saudi Arabia to,
    156;
    foreign aid to, 97, 98, 99;
    foreign aid to Jordan from, 87;
    industrial cooperation with Jordan,
    161–63, 174–75, 181, 186;
    internal instability of, 167–68, 171;
    Jordan's attempted rapprochements
    with, 3, 169, 176–79, 244;
    and Middle East peace plans, 107;
    oil supplies from Iran to, 177;
    opposition to Fahd peace plan in, 95,
    96;
    protective tariffs in, 4;
    public sector in, 4;
    and regional hegemony, 5;
    relations with Egypt, 91, 92, 108, 153,
    155–56, 184, 231, 245, 249, 270–71;
    relations with Iran, 136, 183;
    relations with Iraq, 7, 108, 109, 167,

Syria (*continued*)
  171–72, 175, 182–83, 197, 204, 211,
    221;
  relations with Israel, 6, 7, 153;
  relations with Jordan, 5, 7, 64, 69, 95,
    104, 120, 152–95, 196, 206, 239,
    278–79, 281–82, 290, 299;
  Soviet relations with, 6;
  trade relations with Jordan, 5, 7, 64,
    69, 154, 159–61, 172, 173–74, 176,
    178, 179–80, 185–86, 191–92.
  See also Yarmuk River project
Syrian Central Bank, 185
Syrian Chamber of Commerce, 179
Syrian Chamber of Industry, 180
Syrian Federation of Chambers of Com-
    merce, 186
Syrian General Company for Vegetables
    and Fruits, 180
Syrian-Jordanian Committee for Indus-
    trial Integration, 162
Syrian-Jordanian Industrial Company,
    181
Syrian National Petroleum Company,
    181
Syrian Supply Company, 179
systemic-level approach (to economic
    decisionmaking), 40, 41–49

Tabba', Hamdi, 58, 59, 180
Talabani, Dr. Mukarram Jamal, 203
Tall al-Za'tar refugee camp, 156
Tapline (Trans-Arabian Pipeline),
    102–4, 114–15, 118, 216, 217
Tarabulsi, 'Ali al-, 180
Taylor, Alan R., 152
Telecommunications Corporation (of
    Jordan), 77
Thomas, Caroline, 20
trade relations: and foreign policy,
    33–34; and political dependency,
    16
Trans-Arabian Pipeline, *see* Tapline
Transjordan, 42, 196. *See also* Jordan
Trocon (TransOrient Engineering and
    Contracting Company), 213, 217

Tunisia, and Middle East peace plans,
    107
Turkey, oil exports to Jordan from,
    216
'Ubayd, Farhi, 226
'Ubaydat, Ahmad, 71, 135, 177
Ullman, Richard H., 25
Umm al-Qasr, 209
'umra, 107, 312n. 63
United Arab Emirates (UAE): foreign
    aid from, 110, 111;
  military assistance from Jordan to, 129;
  support for Fahd peace plan in, 95
United Arab Republic, 30
United Nations: sanctions against Iraq,
    234, 286;
  voting patterns of client states in,
    16–17
United Nations Relief and Works
    Agency (UNRWA) for Palestine
    Refugees in the Near East, 43
United States: foreign aid from, 96
United States Agency for International
    Development (USAID), 164, 188
United States Department of Com-
    merce, 208
United States Department of State, 218
Usaymi, Sa'ud al-, 136

Wallerstein, Immanuel, 40
Walt, Stephen M., 20–21, 29–31, 153,
    239, 293
War, 1967, 43, 242
  —1973, 6, 244
war mobilization, 36
Weinberger, Caspar, 106
World Bank, 36, 188
world systems theory, 40

Yarmuk Forces, 210
Yarmuk River project, 154, 163–64,
    187–88
Yasin, Dr. Salim, 180
Yemen, People's Democratic Republic
    of (PDRY), 93, 105, 204
Yugoslavia, collapse of, 23

GPSR Authorized Representative: Easy Access System Europe, Mustamäe tee
50, 10621 Tallinn, Estonia, gpsr.requests@easproject.com